STOP A GRIEVING WORLD!

THE GREAT DELIVERANCE

LOVE UNTO DEATH

Greater love has no one than this,
that one lay down his life for his friends.
John 15:13 NASB95

We know that we are of God, and
the whole world is in the power of the evil one.
1John5:19 NASB95

Gloria

Copyright © 2023 Gloria.

All rights reserved. No part of this book may be reproduced, stored, or transmitted by any means—whether auditory, graphic, mechanical, or electronic—without written permission of both publisher and author, except in the case of brief excerpts used in critical articles and reviews. Unauthorized reproduction of any part of this work is illegal and is punishable by law.

ISBN: 979-8-88640-782-2 (sc)
ISBN: 979-8-88640-783-9 (hc)
ISBN: 979-8-88640-784-6 (e)

Because of the dynamic nature of the Internet, any web addresses or links contained in this book may have changed since publication and may no longer be valid. The views expressed in this work are solely those of the author and do not necessarily reflect the views of the publisher, and the publisher hereby disclaims any responsibility for them.

One Galleria Blvd., Suite 1900, Metairie, LA 70001
1-888-421-2397

*- For we do not preach ourselves
but Christ Jesus as Lord,
and ourselves as your bond-servants
for Jesus' sake. 2Co 4:5 NASV*

*In few words,
what can be said to make a difference...*

Jesus alone has made all the difference in the world.

*In all He spoke,
I would say there are
three words of great significance
that could give summation
of the message of Christ, Our Lord.
These words portray the life we are to live
to become like Him.*
They are UNCONDITIONAL:

**LOVE
MERCY
AND
REPENTANCE**

Gloria

This is WHY the Father loves me
Because I lay down my life
In order to take it up again *John 10:17 NABRE*

- We know that **no one who is born of God sins**;
but He who was born of God keeps him,
and **the evil one does not touch him.** *1John 5:18 NASB*

-"Or how can you say to your brother,
`Brother, let me take out the speck that is in your eye,'
when you yourself do not see the log that is in your own eye? You hypocrite,
first take the log out of your own eye, and then you will see clearly to take out the speck that is in your brother's eye. *Luke 6:42 NASV*

- But Jesus turning to them said, "Daughters of Jerusalem, stop weeping for Me, but **weep for yourselves** and for your children. *Luke 23:28 NASV*

REPENT AS IF TO SAVE YOUR LIFE!

-No man can by any means redeem his brother
    Or give to God a ransom for him-- *Ps 49:7 NASB*

+ + +

It is to you, the Church of Ephesus that I direct this message;
it is to you, whom the Lord says
"you have lost your first love" ...
*" **Otherwise, I will come to you** and*
remove your lampstand from its place,
unless you repent."
and there is one thing you have not done.
(as mentioned in Rev Ch 2)

I now tell you how to find your first love.
Knowing that we believe we love God first,
perhaps it is time to demonstrate our greatest love.
I believe the Lord wants us to be the lowest.
WE MUST LAY DOWN OUR CROWN
AT THE FEET OF JESUS. *(Taken from WHO IS THE KING?)*

"**Repent.** Otherwise, I will come to you quickly and
wage war against them
with the sword of my mouth" *Rev 2:16 NABRE*

To the victor I will give the right to eat from the tree of life that is in the garden of God. *Rev 2:7 NABRE*

"Remain faithful until death, and
I will give you the crown of life" *Rev 2:10 NABRE*

"The Victor shall not be harmed by the second death."
Rev 2:11 NABRE

"To the victor, I shall give some of the hidden manna;
I shall also give a white amulet upon which is inscribed a new name,which no one knows except the one who receives it.
Rev 2:17 NABRE

To the Victor, who keeps to my ways until the end,
I will give authority over the nations. He will rule them with an iron rod. **Like clay vessels will they be smashed**, just as I received authority from my Father and to him I will give the morning star.
Rev 2:26-28 NABRE *(Read why the Hail Mary)*

The victor will thus be dressed in white and I will never erase his name from the book of life but will acknowledge his name in the presence of my Father and of his angels *Rev 3:5 NABRE*

The victor I will make into a pillar in the temple of my God, and will never leave it again. On him I will inscribe the name of my God and the name of the city of my God, the new Jerusalem, which comes down out of heaven from my God, as well as my new name.
Rev 3:12 NABRE

Behold I stand at the door and knock.
If anyone hears my voice and opens the door, then I will enter his house and dine with him, and he with me.
I will give the victor the right to sit with me on my throne,
as I myself first won the victory and sit with my Father on his throne. Whoever has ears ought to hear what the Spirit says to the churches... *Rev 3:20-22 NABRE*

HOPE IN THE GLORY OF GOD

- For in hope we have been saved, but hope that is seen is not hope; for who hopes for what he already sees?
But if we hope for what we do not see,
with perseverance we wait eagerly for it. *Ro 8:24-25 NASB95*

- rejoicing in hope, persevering in tribulation,
devoted to prayer, *Ro 12:12 NASB95*

- For whatever was written in earlier times
was written for our instruction,
so that through perseverance
and the encouragement of the Scriptures
we might have hope. *Ro 15:4 NASB*

- Now may the God of hope
fill you with all joy and peace in believing,
so that you will abound in hope
by the power of the Holy Spirit. *Ro 15:13 NASB*

- But as for me, I will hope continually, And
will praise You yet more and more. *Ps 71:14 NASB95*

- Sustain me according to Your word, that I may live;
And do not let me be ashamed of my hope. *Ps 119:116 NASB95*

- but sanctify Christ as Lord in your hearts,
always being ready to make a defense to everyone
who asks you to give an account for the hope that is in you,
yet with gentleness and reverence; *1Pe 3:15 NASB95*

-And everyone who has this hope fixed on Him
purifies himself, just as He is pure. *1John 3:3 NASB95*

- Therefore, prepare your minds for action, keep sober in spirit,
fix your hope completely on the grace to be brought to you
at the revelation of Jesus Christ. *1Pe 1:13 NASB95*

Let the wicked forsake his way,
and the unrighteous man his thoughts:
and let him return unto the LORD,
and he will have mercy upon him;
and to our God, for he will abundantly pardon.
Isaiah 55:7 NKJV

This is WHY
the Father loves me
Because I lay down my life
in order
to take it up again *John 10:17* NABRE

And having been made perfect,
**He became
to all those
WHO OBEY HIM
the source of eternal salvation,** *Heb 5:9* NASB95

REPENT THAT YOU MIGHT KNOW THE TRUTH

    - and you, when you saw it,
    did not even repent yourselves afterward,
    that you might believe him.   Mat 21:32 WEB

In other words, with a contrite Heart
Repent of the things you do not believe
That perhaps the Lord will reveal His Truth
In His Unfathomable Mercy And Everlasting love.

    - Behold, the eye of the LORD is on those who fear Him,
    On those who hope for His loving kindness, Ps 33:18 NASB95

Know this: Fear of the Lord is a beautiful gift from the Lord;
a fear so profound of being separated from Him;
a fear of offending Him, a fear and sorrow
of being the reason for His many tears.

    - Enter ye in at the strait gate:
    for wide is the gate,
    and broad is the way, that leadeth to destruction,
    and many there be which go in threat:

    - Because strait is the gate, and narrow is the way,
    which leadeth unto life, and few there be that find it.
    Mat7:13-14 KJV

    - I saw their ways, but I will heal them and lead them;
    I will give full comfort to them
    And to those who morn for them
    I, the Creator, who gave them life   Isaiah 57:18

Do you desire to enter in at the narrow gate?
Few there be that find it! Therefore, Seek!
Therefore, Repent to please the Lord!

DO NOT BE AFRAID!

GOD IS SOOOOOOO GOOD!

HE IS ANXIOUS FOR YOU

TO COME TO HIM!

HE LOVES YOU SO MUCH!

*MORE THAN ANYONE
WHO HAS EVER LOVED YOU!!!*

*MORE THAN ANYONE
YOU HAVE EVER LOVED!!!*

*REPENT AND BE READY
JESUS IS COMING!*

INTRODUCTION

Part of this book was originally in the book entitled *ONE, One Love, One Hope, One God*. Because of the bold message given and great plea of repentance, I decided to give the book ONE to several persons, three being priests to review the book, Orthodox and Roman. I wanted to remove whatever is not of the Lord. One of the priests gave me his best wishes without reading the entire book. He said that the world was grieving and he had to spend much time in the confessional. I was alarmed that he did not read "Who is the murderer? And "Who is the living who deny the dead life? Thus, this book was created.

I have been involved in Home Enthronements. That is, Enthroning Homes to the Sacred Heart of Jesus and the Immaculate Heart of Mary. We pray prayers of consecration of the two hearts for family and home. We also say a prayer of protection for the home, like a deliverance prayer. We have met people that see evil spirits. We have also enthroned homes of people that were possessed. The Lord has revealed to many the reality of evil spirits and praise the Lord, the reality of Our Lord Himself, Jesus. We are a group of prayer warriors with hopes for the salvation of mankind.

This organization was having a retreat on March 24-25, 2007 in my hometown. One of these priests is the leader of this organization. On Sat the 24th I asked this certain priest if he would review the book ONE. He did not hesitate to say yes. I knew the Lord led him to say yes, but I did not give it to him that day. On Sunday, I was not feeling well, so I did not attend the retreat most of the day. Then around 2 or 3 pm I popped out of bed and started crying. I told my mother that I had to give the book to this certain priest, that I could not bear to think of not being able to receive Holy Communion every day and that he would either want to excommunicate me from the church or repent. I got dressed and went to the retreat. I got there just in time for a beautiful mass and great official prayer of deliverance. The Lord had me praying in tongues while the deliverance prayers were being read by two priests. I could hear people sniffling, touched by the Lord. It was truly beautiful. I gave this certain priest my book and told him what I told my mom. I said, "you will either want to excommunicate me or you will repent."

After mass, this certain priest said they were looking for people interested in being in a deliverance team. I stayed. There were less than ten people there including myself. This certain priest spoke with us and we shared words of deliverance. This certain priest said sometimes priests die, sometimes the victim dies. This certain priest said there are some priests in jail for murder because of this. He said you have to be in a state of grace to be involved in a deliverance. He also said something about a delicate situation for people that are divorced. I told him I was divorced and that the Lord used me to deliver my son. I also mentioned to him of an experience when we did a home enthronement and the mother and daughter were possessed.

The following occurred after my son had been delivered as explained in the section entitled Deliverance. At the home enthroned, the deacon was holding down the daughter. I was in the other room and could see him through the hall. I was praying and exalting the Lord as I was when my son got delivered. We also had the chaplet of divine mercy with the same meditations playing on a player. He looked at me, I saw his eyes. He told me to stop, I did not want to, my thought was that if I continued they would both be delivered, but I obeyed. When I stopped exalting the Lord, I felt an arrow hit my heart. It was a spiritual arrow. I later told him what happened. After that the deacon went through a series of official deliverances for himself. He told me that the Lord revealed to him that his tormentor was pride. He was ill and later died of lung cancer.

The next morning after the retreat, Mar 26th soon after I got up, I received a thought. It was a distinct thought, not my own. It said to me

> " a multitude of your sins are forgiven you for you have loved much".

I know it was attributed to my giving the book to this certain priest. My thought after that was:

"Thank you Lord!
a multitude? I had that many?

What about the rest of them?
How do I get rid of those?"

I am still praying and hoping for a complete cleanse for the glory of God, through Jesus and through Mary and their Two Hearts. I am running the race! I search my heart and look for sins to confess.

I am praying for perfect charity, the bond to perfection. I do not know how much of what I do possess I have to get rid of: tables, chairs, and basics? May the Lord be my strength and guide! Pray for me!

May you also run the race to attain the grace beyond grace. I give to you my love in Jesus and Mary .... Gloria

+ + +

We must desire and want to love and please God more than anything in the World. His desperate desire for us is shown in the passionate love of Christ and His loving death for us. And so, we also must desperately desire to be as Our Father desires: Perfect as Our Father is Perfect. Loving Him desperately as if reaching to Him drowning, repenting deeply as His hand gets closer and closer through repentance; extending my hand to Him; and finally darkness removed, purified –I reach the palm of His hand filled with His light. Allowing me to arise.

Through Ignorance, we are held captive in a prison that deceives us, by making us FEEL , SAY, DO ungodly things. We believe what we feel instead of the truth. We must live by faith and not by sight. The wicked warden is weak, but makes us think otherwise. He is a liar. The Only Stronghold we need is Our Great God and by His Holy Spirit we are more than conquerors. We are set free.

Lack of knowledge causes us to perish!
Ignorance is the wardens' strength.

As explained in my other books, Our Lord does nothing without approval, so please say yes, I beg you! Ask your friends for me to also read and say yes. Thank you and may the Lord reward you.

**NEED YOUR APPROVAL
PLEASE SAY "YES!!!"**

I ASK MY FAMILY AND THE WHOLE WORLD…
Please give the Lord permission on my behalf.
Please pray the following for and with me:

Beloved Father, I offer to you GLORIA, as a living sacrifice, as she has requested. I give you permission Lord, to do with her as you will, whether the sacrifice be in charity, in thanksgiving, in praise, in worship, or in atonement. Let thy will be done in Gloria's life. I detach myself from Gloria in respect to all that is of the world and unite myself to her in all that is in unity with you Oh Lord. Teach me Lord, to love as you LOVE.

Gracious and fulfilling Lord, satisfy our hunger and thirst to know you and to be in your presence. I trust in your great goodness beyond understanding. All Glory, Blessings, Honor, Might, and Power be unto you dearest and Most Beloved Father through Jesus Christ and the Holy Spirit. Blessed Mother Pray for us that we may be made worthy of the promises of Christ. Thank you to my beloved on earth, who said Yes! Highly exalted is Our Great King of Everlasting Love! Hosanna in the Highest! Blessed is He who comes in the Name of the Lord. Thank you Father for hearing our prayer. SAY "YES" right now!!! "YES"

+ + +

We must REPENT
as if trying to SAVE OUR OWN LIFE!!!

Table of Contents

Introduction	9
Stop a Grieving World	21
Deliverance	25
From Darkness into Light	34
Fruits by Mother Teresa	36
The Fruit of My Talent … Today I Bare	37
New Era of Divine Mercy for the Contrite Heart	38
Who is who? and What is what?	41
What part of the Bible do you Not Believe	43
Who is The Devil?	46
Prayer of Renounciation	50
Prayer of Resistance and Rebuke	52
Who are The False Prophets	54
Who are The Righteous?	56
Who are The False christs?	60
Who is the Antichrist?	64
What Power does Satan have over me?	65
Why is the virtue of Charity one of the greatest virtues?	68
Why is the Divine Mercy Chaplet so important	69
Chaplet of Divine Mercy	70
A New Chaplet of Mercy	71
Why is the virtue of Humility one of the greatest virtues?	72
What is Grace?	73
How can I even begin to obey? I am helpless	77
What is your blessing?	77
Who is the King? (Complete message from the Lord 8/15/05)	81
What Exactly Does "I Am The Way" Mean?	113
What Does the Lord Mean When He Says "I Am the Truth"?	115
Who is the Servant of Money?	121
Who is Like Our Fathers of Great Faith?	126
Who is the Thief?	134
Who is the Murderer?	135
Who is the Living who deny the dead life?	138
Who is the Worker of Inequity?	145
Who is your Father?	146
Who is your Mother?	148
Why the Hail Mary?	153
Was Mary without sin?	160
Why do we PRAY the Hail Mary? Significance?	161

Why was Mary chosen to be Mother of Our Lord?	162
Will the Divorced be Chaste at the Coming of the Lord?	164
Do Earthly Possessions Possess you?	167
What about statues and graven images?	175
What are false gods?	184
Who is the queen of heaven in scripture and Mary Mother of God?	188
Why was Jesus silent in front of the courts?	194
How great is the Mercy of Our Lord?	196
Who should we trust?	199
When in time did they change the "Our Father"?	201
What does repentance / FEAR OF THE LORD mean?	204
How can we stop war?	207
Who will listen to the life saving commands of our Lord	212
What is the sign of Jonah	217
What is the sign of Salvation?	220
What is Sackcloth and ashes?	220
How to use sackcloth & What to do?	220
Why did Mary present the scapular as a sign of salvation	224
Am I without sin? Sins to confess	227
Am I Born again	235
Does Hell exit?	238
Do I do as Our Shepherd has taught?	241
Why do I suffer?	243
What is Religion?	245
How can we make His Joy Complete	248
Who are the True Apostles of Today?	250
Who do you think is the person most prayed for?	251
Who is God?	253
What about the Sabbath?	256
Why must I give my free will to the Lord?	260
Who will follow Jesus	262
What should my greatest and most passionate Desire be?	263
A Different Kind of War	265
Exalt Our King!	265
The Wedding Invitation	266
Prayers of Spiritual Warfare and complete surrender	268
An Act of Contrition	268
Putting on the Armor of God	268
Obedient Mind to Christ	269
Treasures	269
Increase in me	270

A Prayer of Consecration	271
I Love You Lord	272
Come to the Wedding	274
Jerusalem	275
The Mysteries of Illumination	277
1st – Baptism of Jesus	279
2nd – Wedding in Cana	280
3rd - Kingdom of God manifested	281
4th – The Transformation	282
5th – The Holy Communion, The Holy Union	283
Hail Holy Queen	285
The Memorare	285
The Angel of the Lord (Angelus Domini	286
Be Not Hid from Me	287
The Eucharistic Host like My Baby	288
Loves True Desire	**291**
Sincere Desire .	292
The Joy	292
The Desire of Love	293
What great love does my soul acknowledge?	298
What more can I say?	299
Three times the sign of the cross in thanksgiving	300
Be Exalted Bread of Life I Love You Lord	302
The Greatest Anguish vs Love	305
Oh Great God!	306
Do Not Judge	307
Be Satisfied	309
Consumed Radiance within	311
Finding Mary	313
Nothing Matters	315
Psalm 104:1-3	316
Prayer of St Francis	317
The Beatitudes	317
ST Michael the Archangel	317
The Chaplet of St Michael & the Altar of Grace	318
To Please You Greatly	320
Twenty Decade Scriptural Rosary	320
Litany of Divine Mercy	355
A New Chaplet of Mercy with Meditations	355
Escalating steps to the narrow road	**369**
Messages from the Lord	
To The Churches......... September 1, 2004	385

Unity of the Churches… December 4, 2004	389
Return to God………… October 7, 2005	393
In Memory of Deacon Alan	398
Loves True Desire Lyrics Analysis	412
The Greatest Commandment	424
The Two Tablets Replaced	426
The Ten Commandments	430
Copyright dedicated to Our Lord	432
Reference	433

ACKNOWLEDGEMENT
Much gratitude and appreciation for reviewers and editors of this book! May the Lord be glorified in all that we do and say through Jesus Christ. I give to each of you, my beloved, my love in Jesus, Mary, Our Heavenly Father and all the Holy ones who have reached perfection.

The WORD of God is ALIVE!

"And blessed *is* she who believed that there would be a fulfillment of what had been spoken to her by the Lord." *Luke 1:45* NASB95

BELIEVE!

CHANT ART

THIS IS A CERTAINTY!
the words that I have spoken to you **are spirit** and **are life**.
John 6:63 NASB95

Because you have not repented you do not believe!
The WORD made you out of dust and gave you the breath of life!
The WORD became flesh *in Mary's womb, Jesus. Jesus is God.*
The WORD through Jesus becomes the Living Bread*. EAT of*
the Bread of Life, so that you may obtain life everlasting! Our
Lord Loves You! Please repent and offer your heart, mind and
soul to Jesus! He is waiting for you to invite Him into Your heart...
Beloved Father give to us Jesus the finisher of our faith!

STOP A GRIEVING WORLD

How many in this world are grieved? How many think they are helpless and that all hope is gone? How many think they are not grieved, not realizing that it is they that grieve others? The Lord says my people perish because of lack of knowledge.

St Francis De Sales in his book <u>An Introduction to a Devout Life</u> states that

> "The sorrow that is according to God," saith Paul, "worketh penance steadfast unto salvation: but the sorrow of the world worketh death (2Cor. Vii. 10)." Therefore, sorrow may be either good or bad, according to its results upon us. Undoubtedly there are more bad than good results from it; **for the good results are but two, namely, penitence and mercy;**
> while there are six evil results – anguish, indolence, indignation, jealousy, envy, and impatience;

What can we do? We can seek true love and ask the Lord to teach us to live in it. True love is found in loving God first with all of our heart, mind, soul and strength. In Luke 6:42 the Lord says we can help our brothers if we first take the speck out of our own eye.

> Put on the full armor of God so that you will be able to stand firm against the schemes of the devil. <u>Eph 6:11</u> NASB95

> Submit therefore to God. Resist the devil and he will flee from you. <u>Jas 4:7</u> NASV

> Be of sober spirit, be on the alert. Your adversary, the devil, prowls around like a roaring lion, seeking someone to devour. <u>1Pe 5:8</u> NASB95

We must desire to help break the yoke that surrounds us. With a change of heart and a mind of Christ, we learn to embrace our sufferings in the love of the Cross. The Lord reveals a burden that is truly light when we bless our enemies and are willing to love unto death. Repent, be merciful and forgive! Pray and fast! Hope greatly for our deliverance!

> Come unto me, all ye that labour and are heavy laden, and I will give you rest. Take **my yoke upon you, and learn of me**; for I am meek and lowly in heart: and ye shall find rest unto your souls. For my yoke is easy, and my burden is light. *Mat11:28-30 KJV*

Prayer:
Lord, please teach me to bow down in an acceptable way and to be pleasing to You.

Help me to trust you and to acknowledge you in all my ways. Give to me wisdom, knowledge and understanding. Teach me to be obedient. Lead me to those whom you want me to help. Make me and Mold me to be the repairer of the breach, the restorer of paths to dwell in, as you desire, that the yoke of many will be broken. Teach me to draw out my soul to the hungry, and to satisfy the afflicted soul. Guide me continually and like a spring of water, let not my waters fail. Please allow my health to spring forth speedily. Teach me to keep the Sabbath holy as a delightful day unto the Lord, that you may feed me with the heritage of Jacob our father. All Glory, Honor and Power are Yours Most Beloved Heavenly Father In the Name of Jesus. Amen.

The mercy of Our Lord is there for everyone who desires it. It brings much peace and love. We also must be merciful towards those who have hurt us. Repent with a contrite heart and desire to love God first. Let Him be your stronghold. Let us pray that the Lord will give to everyone a sound and merciful loving heart. Let us pray that He will beckon each and everyone to the abode of His endless mercy and love that we may dwell in the House of the Lord together as one.

As for me, I am running a race with great hope. I seek desperately and desire greatly to die to this world that I may have life in Jesus. I trust in Him and believe His Word and the message he sent to me. Everyday is a day closer to the fulfillment of it.

On December 19th, 2005 I heard a voice clearly but somewhat distant. It was of a woman I thought to be Our Blessed Mother. She did not identify herself. In my thoughts I repeated what she said. Her words were biblically spoken. When I awoke I could not repeat them word for word because I do not talk that way. I do know the content of the message. It was this:

> **"Your prayers are blessed
> and the Lord has heard them
> and He will answer"**

In the Book of Daniel 10:12-14 it took twenty-one (21) days for the heavens to answer. They came as soon as they received his prayer. The prince of the Persian kingdom resisted the angel for 21 days.

I attribute the same happening to me because of the clearance provided through prayers with true bitter repentance with the use of sackcloth and ashes. I have been sleeping in it for so long. After talking to a friend as to certain events, I estimate it to be around two years that I have been sleeping in sackcloth as of June 2005. The Lord also led me back to confession after so many years of not going. I believe this also to be necessary.

I also look for sins to confess with much sorrow claiming them as my own hoping to please my Lord. I desire to have a pure and immaculate heart, white as snow. I repent of sins I did not think were mine so that the Lord will show me His truth. I seek it and I want it desperately. I know I am of a wicked and evil generation and I desire desperately to be holy to please my beloved Lord.

I desire to allow the Lord to teach me. I desire to not lean on human understanding. I pray that He will make me to accept all truth especially if it is against something I have been taught by man. I ask for the strength to change and to accept all that He desires. I also realize that the Lord teaches us in many ways. His creativity is immense and I do not shut out the aid and consul of the holy ones. We must diligently seek the Lord with all our heart, mind, soul and strength so that we may find Him.

"But from there you will seek the LORD your God,
and you will find Him **if you search for Him
with all your heart and all your soul.** *De 4:29 NASB95*

LORD HEAR OUR PRAYER

*Lord Hear our prayer,
let the words of our mouth and the meditation of our hearts
be acceptable to You every moment of our being in time and
eternity.*

*Give to us a sincere desire to pray
so that we may have a fervent soul of the righteous so that our
prayers may be pleasing to You.
Teach us to pray with our whole heart mind and soul.*

*Make us to be heard by You –
and as a Father to His children -- answer us.*

*Forgive us Lord for not denying ourselves as we should,
teach us how Lord, so that we may be pleasing to you.*

*Forgive us our inequities and the inequities of our fathers
and relatives, especially of those deceased that might still be
suffering for their sins whom you have judged. Bring them Lord
to your everlasting Light that they may enter into eternal rest in
your loving light and dwelling place which you have prepared for
us.
Make us Lord to repent pleasing to you.*

Lord, we beseech you to **grant to us the grace of
increased power of our prayers** *that as one day is as a
thousand days so then is one of our prayers* **multiplied in your
unfathomable love for the benefit of our brethren and those
most in need of prayer.*

**As you granted to Elisha a double portion of Elijah's
spirit, so then, we ask the same for the benefit of our brethren.**
*Lord, we also ask that you allow the whole church, all angels and
saints to intercede for us in union with Mary Most Holy. Please
Lord, deliver us from evil. Thank you Father for hearing our
prayers.*

DELIVERANCE

I used to think deliverance occurrences were as shown in Hollywood movies. They are publicized as scary and something to be afraid of. I know now that there is no fear; it says in the Word of God, Satan was cast out like lightening from the heavens.

- And He said to them,
"I was watching Satan fall from heaven
like lightning. *Luke 10:18 NASB95*

I know the very presence of God and His almighty power. **There is no fear in the presence of God and His Love is ever present conquering our enemies.** Satan truly flees like lightening. The Lord is all powerful and He is creator of all things including Satan.

One day in June 2005 I went to a Catholic Church to see a guest speaker giving testimony of the Living presence of Christ in the Living Bread, the Eucharist as Catholics call it (I prefer to call it "our Holy Communion"). I would usually sit in the front section of any church when I would hear a speaker giving a teaching or testimony. This day however, after his speech there was a brief intermission before the laying on of hands. This is when the elders pray over you. I moved to the very back of the church. A friend came to me and started talking to me. While we were talking we began to hear wailing. There was a woman at the altar being delivered from demons.

I had never seen a deliverance before and wanted to go to the front of the church. On this particular night, my friend insisted that we should not do that. She said you have to be prepared for deliverance. She encouraged me to go outside with her during the deliverance. I was reluctant but she insisted so I went. We were outside talking and the church had a bullhorn and I could hear the wailing. It sounded ere. She began to tell me of an incident in which she was present at a deliverance. She was one of the persons praying over the person being delivered. The evil creature bit her. She said it hurt and that it left a bruise on her body. She said that they jump around. Well I did not know what to think of that, I was just glad I was outside. That was Thursday.

The Lord is great and greatly to be praised!!! In Him we live move and have our being! We can not do any kind of deliverance on our own accord, the battle is not ours; it is the Lord's. It is a spiritual battle.

On Saturday, little did I know that the Lord was preparing me for what was about to happen in my life. I do not exactly know what time it was. I do know it was at least an hour and a half before church that the mother of my son's friend called me hysterical and crying. She told me my son was dying, he had consumed mushrooms or something and could not breath.

My son was in another country and I did not have a phone number for him. I did not know how to contact him. I told her to start praying the rosary. I also called my other son and told him his brother was dying and that he needed to start praying the rosary right away. I was with my mother and told her to also pray the rosary. I also had a CD playing on the radio with prayers of the divine mercy with beautiful meditations of the passion of Christ. I know the Lord was leading me. I began to order protection over my son in the name of Jesus by the power of the Holy Spirit as commanded by My Father. I asked the Lord to send the angels to protect and guard him. I asked St Michael the Archangel to come to his defense. I asked for the intercession of Our Blessed Mother, the saints and the WHOLE Church. A very short while (minutes) after all these things occurred, my son called me. I started praying silently in tongues, he could not hear me, but the devil could.

He briefly said hi and I was waiting for him to tell me what was going on while I prayed in tongues. He asked me "what is that?", when he heard me praying in tongues, but I was praying quietly. Not too much was said. The deliverance began.

I had never seen a deliverance. I did not know what needed to be done. I was innocent of any procedures or words that needed to be spoken. I did not do this deliverance; I was a shell of dust used by My Lord. The Lord arose in me.

We must remember that the devil cannot deliver the devil. It is the Lord Himself that will do it for us. We must submit to the Lord and His divine will. We must repent to be made clean.

I cannot even say that I personally prepared myself for the deliverance that is in fasting or confession. I don't remember, however, I have kept in the fruit of repentance through confession on a frequent basis and as I mentioned, I have been sleeping in sackcloth for a very long time (years). I also had been giving up small things to the Lord as often as I can because I am weak in keeping from eating all day.

This deliverance was totally the work of My Lord and I in the flesh was surprised by such an event, but the Lord My Deliver, My Leader, My teacher, My God, My Father was in lead. My Lord knows all time and His time is always right. He prepared me!

> - "And now, Lord, take note of their threats, and grant that Your bond-servants may speak Your word with all confidence, *Ac 4:29* NASV

I want to emphasize the need in a deliverance to ask for the **intercession of Our Blessed Mother**. the angels and saints and **THE WHOLE CHURCH**. They must all be called to intercede for us.

During the deliverance I was exalting the Lord greatly! He loves it! There was a couple of other things said over the telephone. These words came out of my mouth and left a great impression in my heart:

"THERE IS NO FEAR IN THE PRESENCE OF MY LORD!"

"THERE IS NO DISTANCE FOR MY GREAT GOD!"

I was in The United States and my son was in another country. This deliverance occurred over the telephone. As we were speaking a friend knocked on my sons door in another country.

When he knocked on the door I told my son to tell him that he was talking to me and he needed to be alone. (This is how the Lord prepared me on Thursday). His friend left and later told him he was foaming at the mouth and so he began to pray for him as well. The Lord is great, he sent another prayer warrior in my sons defense.

It took around forty minutes and the last outcry was a loud wailing and expelling of the demon. My son was left in confusion and the Lord led me to bind the spirit of confusion. By this time it was time for me to go to church where I stayed in prayer.

I later asked my son if during the deliverance he was hurting in any way. He said no. He said he remembered laying on the floor with his legs crossed and could not take them apart. I remember he told me that he could hear kicking and fighting, it was as though all of heaven was in his room. Glory and Praise to Our Lord, Our Deliverer. Our Lover, Our Redemption.

The devil who is full of pride and vain glory makes people to think he is something to be afraid of. The devil is a professional liar! Be proud of NOTHING! BE NOT PROUD!

So how do we stop a grieving world?

By taking the speck out of our own eye, **then we can help our brethren.** By repenting, being merciful, loving and forgiving, praying and fasting!

> By **lovingkindness and truth** inequity is atoned for
> And by **fear of the Lord** one keeps away from evil.
> *Pr 16:6 NASB95*

> - "You hypocrite,
> **first take the log out of your own eye,**
> and then you will see clearly
> to take the speck out of your brother's eye. *Mat 7:5 NASB95*

> - "Then you will call, and the LORD will answer;
> You will cry, and He will say,
> **'Here I am.**
> ' **If you remove** the yoke from your midst,
> **The pointing of the finger**
> **and speaking wickedness,** *Isa 58:9 NASB95*

Perhaps like you stop a war. Putting down our weapons! The Lord says those who live by the sword die by the sword. Praying and fasting ... emptying ourselves of our pride, anger

and wicked ways so that we may please the Lord and be merciful towards each other. Surely, keeping to repentance, forgiveness and love always and unconditionally, embracing every humiliation. Can we truly tell those who have hurt us
> **"I am sorry, please forgive me, it is my fault!"**

Perhaps we have to give Our Lord our crowns and give Him His throne as mentioned in "Who is the King?" I believe it!

> -the twenty-four elders will fall down before Him who sits on the throne, and will worship Him who lives forever and ever, and will cast their crowns before the throne, saying, **"Worthy are You, our Lord and our God, to receive glory and honor and power; for You created all things, and because of Your will they existed, and were created."** *Re 4:10-11* NASB95

Perhaps we have to hope harder and have a greater desire that He may truly deliver us from evil today and now.

> - In hope against hope he believed,
> so that he might become a father of many nations according to that which had been spoken,
> "SO SHALL YOUR DESCENDANTS BE." *Ro 4:18* NASB95
>
> - `THEREFORE MY HEART WAS GLAD
> AND MY TONGUE EXULTED;
> MOREOVER MY FLESH ALSO WILL LIVE IN HOPE;
> *Ac 2:26* NABRE
>
> - For in hope we have been saved, *Ro 8:24* NASB

Perhaps the more we desire, the more He desires.
We reap what we sow.

Return to the Lord all that He has shown to us.
His repeated requests for us to repent and to return to Him, and so, let us beg him repeatedly;
let us repent completely
so that He will return to us as He desires us
to return to Him.

**Loving unto death! We must do as He does.
Be as He is. Love as He Loves.**

I believe that those who are faithful will die for the love of God for the love of mankind.

I believe the great deliverance (the rapture as some call it) will occur when we do surrender completely to the Lord. The elect will lay down their crowns at the feet of Jesus and die for those most in need, most unruly, most unloved as Jesus did. Perhaps this is when the priests give to the Lord his place at the altar. Could this be the Apostasy? Can we give back the table of the Lord to Jesus, Our High Priest according to the order of Melchizedek?

> For this Melchizedek, king of Salem, priest of the Most High God, who met Abraham as he was returning from the slaughter of the kings and blessed him, to whom also Abraham apportioned a tenth part of all *the spoils,* was first of all, by the translation *of his name,* king of righteousness, and then also king of Salem, which is king of peace. Without father, without mother, without genealogy, having neither beginning of days nor end of life, but made like the Son of God, he remains a priest perpetually.
> *Heb 7:1-3* NASB95

> Now if perfection was through the Levitical priesthood (for on the basis of it the people received the Law), what further need *was there* for another priest to arise according to the order of Melchizedek, and not be designated according to the order of Aaron? **For when the priesthood is changed, of necessity there takes place a change of law also**
> *Heb 7:11-12* NASB95

According to scripture forming the priesthood changed the law and therefore made it imperfect. Is it then reasonable to believe that if we truly desire the Lord to perfect the Church it must be returned to Him?

> For, on the one hand, there is a setting aside of a former commandment because of its weakness and uselessness (for the Law made nothing perfect), and on the other hand there is a bringing in of a better hope, through which we draw near to God. *Heb 7:18-19 NASB95*

And so also if there is a setting aside of the former commandment because the Law made nothing perfect thus we live in imperfection. And so if through this imperfection a greater hope is found. A Hope for the return of Our Lord that we may return to Him, then let us indeed return to Him passionately with all of our hearts, mind, strength and soul.

Is this what the Lord refers to in Matthew 26:29, that He will not drink of this fruit of the vine until that day? Can we give Him back His thrown on earth? *(Read more in "Who is the King?" in this book)* Let us keep in prayer that the Lord will guide us to all truth.

There is no greater love!

> - "But I say to you,
> I will not drink of this fruit of the vine from now on until that day when I drink it new with you in My Father's kingdom." *Mat 26:29 NASV*

> - No man can by any means redeem his brother Or give to God a ransom for him-- *Ps 49:7 NASB*

> - "And he supposed that his brethren understood that God was granting them deliverance through him, but they did not understand. *Ac 7:25 NASV*

> - "Do you suppose that I came to grant peace on earth? I tell you, no, but rather division; *Luke 12:51 NASB95*

> - "But do not be called Rabbi;
> for **One is your Teacher,**
> and you are all brothers.

> "Do not call anyone on earth your father;
> for **One is your Father,** He who is in heaven.
> "Do not be called leaders;
> for **One is your Leader,**
> **that is, Christ.** _Mat 23:8-10 NASB95_

> - Therefore, holy brethren,
> partakers of a heavenly calling,
> consider Jesus, the Apostle and High Priest
> of our confession; _Heb 3:1 NASB95_

> - where Jesus has entered as a forerunner for us,
> having become a high priest
> forever according to the order of Melchizedek.
> _Heb 6:20 NASV_

> - Now the main point in what has been said is this:
> we have such a high priest,
> who has taken His seat at the right hand of the throne of the Majesty in the heavens, _Heb 8:1 NASV_

We must understand that redemption comes from the Lord and no one comes to the Father unless He beacons. We know that the battle is not ours. We are weak but He is strong. We know that He desires for all to be saved. Let us then walk in faith knowing that we are all saved although it may not appear to be that way. Let us then submit to Our Lord, resist rebuke and renounce the devil and he will flee. Let us gather together in One Church with a thick cord of strands that cannot be broken opening heavens door! Let us give to the Lord His Kingdom on earth!

> - And if one can overpower him who is alone, two can resist him. **A cord of three strands is not quickly torn apart.** _EC 4:12 NASV_

> "If Satan has risen up against himself and is divided, he cannot stand, but he is finished! _Mark 3:26 NASB95_

In the book of Daniel, the three children that were thrown into the burning furnace, praised, blessed and exalted the Lord. **They spoke the words together at the same time – in UNISON – and so shall we!**

I also would like to make a comment about anointing your head with oil. It has been years, but the Lord took me to the Book of Ecclesiastics and I read a verse, I found at least twice and cannot find it anymore. Perhaps they changed the wording in the bibles, deleted it, or put it in the footnotes, I do not know. Perhaps the Lord showed these words to me so that I might do as He showed me.

The scripture of which I refer said to me the following in my own words:

"Wash your face and anoint your head with oil, so that they may not see you."

This was a funny verse to me, knowing that if someone anoints their head with oil I in the flesh of course cannot tell if they do or not, but, in a more important way, I believed it to be the spirits. The evil spirits cannot see you if you anoint your head with oil. I have found that it is truly protective.

Wash your face, or take a bath. Anoint your forehead, eyes, mouth, ears, hands and feet every day. Try not to fail in doing this, pray.

We must offer our best to the Lord. I put the bottle of olive oil on or at the foot of the altar of a church for blessing.

FROM DARKNESS INTO LIGHT

Blessed be my Holy and Glorious King of Heaven and Earth
Magnificent are His Ways
Luminous and Brilliant is His Light
Nobel and Awe-inspiring is His Truth

The Breathtaking Beauty of His Majestic Love
Overwhelms a revered heart, mind and soul
Binding itself in oneness
to the shocking and alarming greatness
Of Our God who Was, Is, and Will always Be

Knowing of the Spectacular Goodness
and kindness in this Spiritual body
United in a glimpse as if for all eternity
Is enough to desire nothing else of this world
Not food, not drink, not the love of another

Recognizing that God is truly a jealous God
Now we, become jealous for Him
Our First Love revealed

But yet knowing that this revelation
Has shown darkness lurking in those
we love as we love ourselves

So then in desperation We weep for ourselves

Hoping to remove the splinters from our eyes
And the plank from our being

And with compassion
We reach out hoping that the Lord
Will expel the darkness of the ignorant
Blinded by the enemy
Now knowing that

The intimidating light makes darkness to
tremble and flee in fear of itself.

Oh, what Terrible Beauty is this
So Terrifying, so Awesome
causing the revered soul
to fear being apart from it,
dreading any separation from
such a Superb and Sacred Union

Oh My Lord, Virtuous and of Unprofaned Sanctity
Your Grandeur and Splendor are addicting,
there is no other want.

Your Hallowed Omnipresent Supreme Being
is Intoxicating and Jubilant

Your Magnificent Word is my Command
Not extravagant nor fabricated,
Solely truth, moral, humble, and honorable
leading to righteousness

Great is the revelation to the unblinded eye
Who once in obscurity and ignorance
knew not the monumental impact
and sorrow of living in darkness

My Lord of Excessive Love,
Exalted are You and Worthy to be praised
May I adore and Exalt You for ages to ages

My Father of Prestige and Highest Rank
You who offered Your son to us, for us and in us
Who became a servants servant
Teach me to return to you,
receive me, remember me,
unite me to yourself,
make me and mold me.

My Lord who imposes Himself on no one
You who is Venerable, lowly, meek and humble
Frantically and Horrifyingly I approach
Your heavenly throne
And in your light I plead
for your compassion and mercy
Upon those who have been blinded
of Your Beauty, Your Truth And Your Love.

I ask for forgiveness upon them
and the unholy, unworthy,
the condemned, the cursed and the damned, all are your creation.
Make us a new creation, holy, sacred and immaculate, pleasing to you.

Most Merciful and Humble Mother of God,
Honorable and Immaculate Heart of Mary
May the grace of the fire of your burning love
Fill all of mankind
that our soul may magnify the Lord
and our spirit rejoice in God Our Savior,
pray for us now and at the hour of our death.

BEAUTIFUL WORDS ON SPIRITUAL LIFE FROM MOTHER TERESA:

"The fruit of silence is prayer.
The fruit of prayer is faith.
The fruit of faith is love.
The fruit of love is service.
The fruit of service is peace."

The Fruit of My Talent … Today I Bare…

- For while we were in the flesh, the sinful passions, which were aroused by the Law, were at work in the members of our body **to bear fruit for death**. *Romans 7:5 NASB95*

- "Truly, truly, I say to you, unless a grain of wheat falls into the earth and dies, it remains alone; but if it dies, it bears much fruit. *John 12:24 NASB95*

- "Therefore I say to you, the kingdom of God will be taken away from you and given to a people, producing the fruit of it. *Matthew 21:43 NASB95*

- "Abide in Me, and I in you. As the branch cannot bear fruit of itself unless it abides in the vine, so neither can you unless you abide in Me. *John 15:4 NASB95*

- Through Him then, let us continually offer up a sacrifice of praise to God, that is, the **fruit of lips that give thanks to His name**. *Hebrews 13:15 NASB95*

- "Therefore bear **fruit in keeping with repentance**; *Matthew 3:8 NASB95*

- And the seed whose **fruit is righteousness is sown in peace** by those who make peace. *James 3:18 NASB95*

- so that you will walk in a manner worthy of the Lord, to **please Him in all respects, bearing fruit in every good work and increasing in the knowledge of God**; *Col 1:10 NASB95*

- All discipline for the moment seems not to be joyful, but sorrowful; yet **to those who have been trained by it, afterwards it yields the peaceful fruit of righteousness.** *Hebrews 12:11 NASB95*

- (for the **fruit of the Light consists in all goodness and righteousness and truth**), *Eph 5:9 NASB95*

- But the **fruit of the Spirit is love, joy, peace, patience, kindness, goodness, faithfulness,** *Galatians 5:22 NASB95*

NEW ERA OF *DIVINE MERCY*

FOR THE CONTRITE HEART

THE LORD IS MERCIFUL TO THOSE WHO ARE MERCIFUL!

REPENT AND BE READY!

JESUS IS COMING!

Over and over again, Christ Jesus reassured St. Faustina of His infinite trustworthiness. At various times, He spoke to her in words such as these:

I am love and mercy itself. 1273 Let no soul fear to draw near to Me, even though its sins be as scarlet.... My mercy is greater than your sins and those of the entire world.... I let my Sacred Heart be pierced with a lance, thus opening wide the source of mercy for you. Come then with trust to draw graces from this fountain. I never reject a contrite heart....1485 Sooner would heaven and earth turn into nothingness than would My mercy not embrace a trusting soul....1777

I am offering people a vessel with which they are to keep coming for graces to the fountain of mercy. That vessel is this image with the signature: "Jesus, I Trust in You"....327 The graces of My mercy are drawn by means of one vessel only, and that is—trust. The more a soul trust, the more it will receive.1578

+ + + Prayer by St Faustina to Our Lord:

I want to be completely transformed into Your mercy and to be Your living reflection, O Lord. May the greatest of all divine attributes, that of Your unfathomable mercy, pass through my heart and soul to my neighbor.

Help me, O Lord, that my eyes may be merciful, so that I may never suspect or judge from appearances, but look for what is beautiful in my neighbors' souls and come to their rescue.

Help me, that my ears may be merciful, so that I may give heed to my neighbors' needs and not be indifferent to their pains and moanings.

Help me, O Lord, that my tongue may be merciful, so that I should never speak negatively of my neighbor, but have a word of comfort and forgiveness for all.

Help me, O Lord, that my hands may be merciful and filled with good deeds, so that I may do only good to my neighbors and take upon myself the more difficult and toilsome tasks.

Help me, that my feet may be merciful, so that I may hurry to assist my neighbor, overcoming my own fatigue and weariness. My true rest is in the service of my neighbor.

Help me, O Lord, that my heart may be merciful so that I myself may feel all the sufferings of my neighbor. I will refuse my heart to no one. I will be sincere even with those who, I know, will abuse my kindness. And I will lock myself up in the most merciful Heart of Jesus. I will bear my own suffering in silence. May Your mercy, O Lord, rest upon me ...

O my Jesus, transform me into Yourself , for you can do all things. (163)

✝

When once I felt hurt because of a certain thing
and complained to the Lord,
Jesus answered,
**"My daughter, why do you attach such importance
to the teaching and the talk of people?
I Myself want to teach you;
That is why I arrange things
So that you cannot attend those conferences,
In a single moment,
I will bring you to know more than others will acquire through many years of toil." 1147**

Sr Faustina

✝

PRAY and ASK THE LORD

WHO is WHO?
And
WHAT is WHAT?

WARNING!!!

Jesus Came To SAVE – Not To Condemn!!!
Neither do I condemn you...
I too am a sinner running the race

These are strong words and thoughts...
Discern for yourselves ask the
Help of the Holy Spirit

All things are imperfect until perfection comes!

My Hope is that you may
Contemplate and consider...

TRUE AND BITTER REPENTANCE
For YOURSELF!

REPENT AND
BE READY!

ABOVE ALL THINGS WRITTEN

IN THIS BOOK

CONTEMPLATE and DESIRE

**THE UNCONDITIONAL
LOVE OF GOD
MERCY
AND REPENTANCE**

**DESIRE
TO LOVE HIM and OTHERS
AS HE LOVES YOU
RECIPOCATE EVERYTHING TO THE LORD
(RETURN TO GOD)**

DESIRE TO PLEASE HIM

AND LOVE HIM FIRST

ABOVE EVERYONE

AND EVERYTHING

WHEN HE SAYS "REMEMBER ME" YOU SAY TO HIM
"LORD REMEMBER ME, RECEIVE ME AS YOUR OWN"

SAY "YES LORD! MAKE ME PERFECT AS MY FATHER IS
PERFECT FULFILL YOUR DESIRE IN ME AND WITH ME!"

TRUST IN JESUS NO MATTER WHAT!
MAY YOU BE BLESSED!

WHAT PART OF THE BIBLE DO YOU NOT BELIEVE?

Be careful! Be watchful!
It is probably your sin that you do not believe!
You cannot understand because you are blinded like those mentioned in Matthew 21:32.
You prefer to believe that you are forgiven or you prefer to believe another man's word rather than the Word of God. You still have not repented or do not care to know your sin. You Must repent or you will perish!
Beg the Lord to make you to repent pleasing to Him.

-Therefore **bear fruit in keeping with repentance**;
Mat3:8 NASB95
- For John came unto you
in the way of righteousness,
and ye believed him not;
but the publicans and the harlots believed him:
and ye, when ye saw it,
**did not even repent yourselves AFTERWARD,
that you MIGHT believe him**. *Mat 21:32 ASV*

The rest of mankind,
who were not killed by these plagues,
did not repent of the works of their hands,
SO AS NOT TO worship demons, and
the idols of gold and of silver
and of brass and of stone and of wood,
which can neither see nor hear nor walk; *Rev 9:20 NASB95*

In other words, with a contrite Heart
Repent of the things you do not believe
That perhaps the Lord will reveal His Truth
In His Unfathomable Mercy And Everlasting love.
Be humble. Be the first to say with a contrite heart:
I am sorry, it is my fault, please forgive me.

But **because of your stubbornness and unrepentant heart** you are storing up wrath for yourself in the day of wrath and revelation of the righteous judgment of God, *Romans 2:5 NASB95*

Or do you think lightly of the riches of His kindness and tolerance and patience, not knowing that the kindness of God leads you to repentance? *Romans 2:4 NASB95*

You cannot know the truth, unless you repent! You cannot believe unless your repent!

The Lord and His Word are the same yesterday, today and always. When He says "you" in the Word, take note of your fathers sin. Learn from them and desire **not** to commit the same sins. Will you believe the Word of God? Will you desire to obey?

> *1 Sam15:23-26 NASB95*
> **"For rebellion is as the sin of divination *(witchcraft)*, And insubordination *(stubbornness)* is as iniquity and idolatry. BECAUSE YOU HAVE REJECTED THE WORD OF THE LORD, HE HAS ALSO REJECTED YOU …."**
> Then Saul said to Samuel, "I have sinned;
> I have indeed transgressed the command of the LORD and your words, **because I feared the people and listened to their voice.** "Now therefore, please pardon my sin and return with me, that I may worship the LORD."
> But Samuel said to Saul, "I will not return with you; for you have rejected the word of the LORD,
> and the LORD has rejected you from being king over Israel."

Perhaps, because of Saul's selfish motives in requesting forgiveness and because his heart was not truly contrite in the sight of the Lord, he was not forgiven. Our God is a merciful God to those who are merciful and truly desire to please Him. Seek Him desperately with a contrite and loving heart so that you may find Him, love Him and serve Him in the greatest of love, even unto death.

- While Jesus was saying these things, one of the women in the crowd raised her voice and said to Him, "Blessed is the womb that bore You and the breasts at which You nursed." But He said, "On the contrary, **BLESSED ARE THOSE WHO HEAR THE WORD OF GOD AND OBSERVE IT**." *Luke 11:27-28 NASB95*

- He commands even the unclean spirits, and they obey Him." *Mark 1:27 NASB95*
- He commands even the winds and the water, and they obey Him?" *Luke 8:25 NASB95*
- And having been made perfect, **He became to all those who obey Him the source of eternal salvation**, *Heb 5:9 NASB95*
- No one who is born of God practices sin, because His seed abides in him; and he cannot sin, because he is born of God. *1 John 3:9 NASB95*
- "And we are witnesses of these things; and so is the Holy Spirit, whom God HAS GIVEN TO THOSE WHO OBEY HIM." *Acts 5:32 NASB95*

CHOOSE TO OBEY GOD! DESIRE IT! REPENT OR PERISH!
REPENT AND BE READY! JESUS IS COMING!

The Kingdom of Jesus is at Hand!

WHO IS THE DEVIL?

-the one who practices sin is of the devil;
for the devil has sinned from the beginning.
The Son of God appeared for this purpose,
to destroy the works of the devil. *1John 3:8* NASB95

- By this the children of God and
the **children of the devil are obvious**:
anyone who
does not practice righteousness is not of God,
nor the one who does not love his brother. *1John 3:10* NASB95

The devil is a creature, spirit, being or thing that takes the form of many manifestations. Some people/things are possessed by the devil. The devil longs to destroy and devour your soul. He is on a campaign on earth making you to say yes to the lust of the flesh, the lust of the eye and the boastful pride of life. These are the three the Lord battled in the desert. The devil takes pleasure in tormenting you.

The devil puts evil thoughts in your mind and mouth and even in that of your friend causing disruption between you. He wants you to think that God is not real. He wants you to think that graven images (statues) are precious. He does not want you to love God and He will do anything to keep you from it. He inflicts you with pain, disease and suffering as He did Jesus. Some diseases are spiritually rooted, ie: resentment causes a bad liver, that was one of my sins of which I have repented and of which I have been delivered. He is a liar and if you are a liar you have chosen your father, the devil.

He uses you, sometimes your mouth, your hands, your feet, your privates, your whole being, including your mind. The first time I got delivered the devil moved my body in a vulgar way and spoke ugly to the Lord from my mouth. I did not realize what was happening, but in my persistent plea to the Lord to help me, He answered. A few days later the Lord made me to realize it was a deliverance. Glory and Praise to Our Lord, Our Redeemer who loves us even unto death.

Do you love your brother? If you do not you cannot love God! This book covers topics that will help you to realize whether you love your brother or not. Let us then love one another as the Lord has loved us!

The following are scriptures pertaining to the devil:

-"You are of your father the devil, and you want to do the desires of your father. He was a murderer from the beginning, and does not stand in the truth
because there is no truth in him. Whenever he speaks a lie, he speaks from his own nature,
for he is a liar and the father of lies. *John 8:44 NASB95*

- and said, "You who are full of all deceit and fraud, you son of the devil, you enemy of all righteousness,
will you not cease to make crooked the straight ways of the Lord? *Ac 13:10 NASB95*

- And **the tongue is a fire, the very world of iniquity**; the tongue is set among our members as that which defiles the entire body, and **sets on fire the course of our life, and is set on fire by hell.** *James 3:6 NASB95*

-But no one can tame the tongue; it is a restless evil and full of deadly poison. *James 3:8 NASB95*

- "But the things that proceed out of the mouth **come from the heart,** and those defile the man. *Mat 15:18 NASB95*

-As in water face reflects face, So the heart of man reflects man. *Pr 27:19 NASB95*

-We know that we are of God, and
the whole world is in the power of the evil one. *1John5:19 NASB95*

- Do not love the world or the things that belong to the world. **If anyone loves the world, love for the Father is

not in him. Because everything that belongs to the world -- the lust of the flesh and the lust of the eyes and the pride in ones lifestyle – is not from the Father but is from the world. And the world with its lust is passing away, but the one who does God's will remains forever. *1John 2:15-17 NKJV*

- For, "The one who desires life, to love and see good days, must keep his tongue from evil and his lips from speaking deceit. *1Peter 3:10 NASB95*

- But above all, my brethren, **do not swear**, either by heaven or by earth or with any other oath; but your yes is to be yes, and your no, no, so that you may not fall under judgment. *James 5:12 NASB95*

- But the Lord stood with me and strengthened me, so that through me **the proclamation** might be fully accomplished, and that all the Gentiles might hear; and I was rescued out of the lion's mouth. *2Ti 4:17 NASB95*

- For our struggle is not against flesh and blood, but against the rulers, against the powers, against the world forces of this darkness, against the spiritual forces of wickedness in the heavenly places. *Eph 6:12 NASB95*

- And the great dragon was thrown down, the serpent of old who is called the devil and Satan, who deceives the whole world; he was thrown down to the earth, and his angels were thrown down with him. *Rev 12:9 NASB95*

- "For this reason, rejoice, O heavens and you who dwell in them. Woe to the earth and the sea, because the devil has come down to you, having great wrath, knowing that he has only a short time." *Rev 12:12 NASB95*

- And the devil who deceived them was thrown into the lake of fire and brimstone, where the beast and the false prophet are also; and they will be tormented day and night forever and ever *Rev 20:10 NASB95*

Choose your father!!!

> - "No one can serve two masters; for either he will hate the one and love the other, or he will be devoted to one and despise the other. You cannot serve God and wealth. *Matthew 6:24 NASB95*
>
> - Beloved, do not imitate what is evil, but what is good. The one who does good is of God; the one who does evil has not seen God. *3John 1:11 NASB95*

> *Lord Jesus, forgive my unbelief, please forgive me for all my offenses against you and others. Receive me as your child and allow your Holy Spirit to take control my life and keep me in your loving light. Make my heart fit for You, my King. Enter into my heart and never leave me. I give to you my free will, my life, my love, my total being without reserve. I ask you to teach me your ways which are righteous. I consecrate myself to the Immaculate Heart of Mary and the Sacred Heart of Jesus so that I may become pleasing to you. Make me Lord to resist, rebuke and renounce the devil. I submit to you and you alone in the Name of Jesus. Father in Heaven please hear my prayer, Jesus be the Lord of my life. Blessed Mother of God pray for me that I may obtain the promises of Christ.*

PRAYER OF RENOUNCIATION

I renounce the wicked who renounce God
and ask God our creator to bless them and have mercy upon them
and to change their hearts, minds and souls
to repent and to return to God,
to acknowledge, honor, trust and obey Him
who is slow to anger and filled with unfathomable love and mercy.
I renounce pride of all sorts.
I renounce irreligion and worldly passions (Titus2:12)
I renounce all that I have (Luke 14:33)
I renounce my corrupt life and the corrupt life of my family and friends, (2Esdras14:13)
I renounce all corruption and I desire to put on incorruption
I renounce defiling foods (4Maccabees 5:34) make me Lord to not eat of them and to know which ones they are
I renounce ancestral tradition of my national life in this world (4Maccabees8:7)
"I do not renounce the noble kinship that binds me to my brothers" (4Maccabees10:3)
"No, by the blessed death of my brothers, by the eternal destruction of the tyrant, and by the everlasting life of the pious,
I will not renounce our noble brotherhood." (4Maccabees10:15) I will take courage in the faith of Jesus.
"Imitate me, brothers," he said. "Do not leave your post in my struggle or renounce our courageous brotherhood.
(4Maccabees9:23)
I Announce that I am FOR Christ
and with my brothers in Christ
I stand firm in my faith against all evil
I desire to live a sober, upright and godly life in this world (Titus2:12)
"I will not play false to you, O law that trained me,
nor will I renounce you, beloved self-control (4Maccabees5:34)
    I recognize, accept and acknowledge Judism and I

reclaim Judism to God and to myself and to this land which God has given to us. I ask God to return to Judism their right of inheritance pleasing to God. I ask the Lord to forgive all of us for our inequities, not one is without guilt. Make us Lord a people of incorruption in your Great Love.

    Lord, make me to set my house in order and to reprove your people. Make me Lord to comfort the lowly among them.

    Make me Lord to be the restorer of the breach, use me Lord to help repair the paths in which to dwell.

    Make us Lord a people of righteousness and fervent in prayer united with cords that cannot be broken by any evil manifestation or presentation seen or unseen. (Ecclesiastes 4:12)

    All Glory, Honor and Power is Yours alone Almighty Father in the Name of Jesus.

PRAYER OF RESISTANCE AND REBUKE

Lord, now knowing that the victory is in the cross, I beg you to let me live in your passionate and sacrificial love. Circumcise my heart and ears and fill my eyes with your loving light. Help me Lord to yield to my Holy Spirit and obey without resistance.

"Let all your creatures serve You, for You did speak, and they were made. You did send forth your Spirit, and it formed them; there is none that can resist Your voice." (Judith 16:14) Oh Lord!

Make me Lord not to resist an evil person, so that if one slaps me on my right cheek, that I may turn the other to him also. (Mat 5:39). Help me Lord to not resist what God has appointed so that I may not incur judgment. (Romans 13:2)

Make me Lord to accept your discipline (Proverbs 13:1) And teach me Lord to know the difference.

As you were condemned and put to death, the righteous of men and you did not resist, allow me Lord to imitate you in all things and in your Great Love.

Mold me Lord to resist the devil firm in my faith. Make me and mold me Lord to be humble in Your sight, pleasing to you.

Knowing that my brothers are experiencing the same sufferings in this world, I offer them to You Lord. God of all grace who has called me to His glory, may your grace perfect, confirm, strengthen and establish me. To You dear Lord, be dominion forever and ever (1Peter5:9-11)

Increase in me Lord, increase my trust in you knowing that you will give to me utterance and wisdom which none of my opponents will be able to resist or refute (Luke21:15)

Put upon me Lord, the armor of God so that I will be able to resist in the evil day, make me to do everything to stand firm in the faith of Jesus and in Your perfect love. (Ephesians 6:13)

Oh Lord, rebuke me not in thy anger, nor chasten me in thy wrath (Psalm 38:1)

Let a good man strike or rebuke me in kindness, but let the oil of the wicked never anoint my head; for my prayer is continually against their wicked deeds. (Psalm 141:5)

Oh Lord, help me not to judge, merciful God, help me to also be merciful and I ask for mercy for the merciless.

Let us Lord come to one another in friendship to help one another, let our hearts be knit to you and to each other in peace and Love. Let all adversaries of betrayal be bound and rebuked. (1Chronicles12:17) "Thou does rebuke the insolent, accursed ones, who wander from thy commandments; (Psalm 119:21)

At thy rebuke they fled, at the sound of thy thunder they took to flight (Psalm 104:7)

"and You are Lord of all, and there is no one who can resist You, You who is the Lord" (Ester 4:21) To You dear Lord, be dominion forever and ever (1Peter5:9-11)

WHO ARE THE FALSE PROPHETS?

A true prophet will speak of your sinfulness and expose your iniquity. He will tell you these things so as to free you from the bondage and chains of the devil. He will speak truth leading you to the love of God, unconditional love and repentance. Love one another unconditionally! Forgive with all your heart, mind and soul! Desire it!

- Your prophets have seen for you False and foolish visions; And **they have not exposed your iniquity So as to restore you from captivity**, But they have seen for you false and misleading oracles. *La 2:14 NASB95*

Do not participate in the unfruitful deeds of darkness, but instead even expose them; for it is disgraceful even to speak of the things which are done by them in secret. But all things become visible when they are exposed by the light, for everything that becomes visible is light. For this reason it says, "Awake, sleeper, And arise from the dead, And Christ will shine on you." *Eph 11-14 NASB95*

Thou shalt love the Lord thy God with all thy heart, and with all thy soul, and with all thy mind. This is the first and great commandment.
… On these two commandments **hang all the law and the prophets.** *Mathew 22:36-38.40 KJV*

- Then the LORD said to me, "The prophets are prophesying falsehood in My name. I have neither sent them nor commanded them nor spoken to them; they are prophesying to you **a false vision, divination, futility and the deception of their own minds**. *Jer 14:14 NASB95*

- "So My hand will be against the prophets who see **false visions and utter lying divinations**. They will have no place in the council of My people, nor will they be written down in the register of the house of Israel, nor will they enter the land of Israel, that you may know that I am the Lord GOD. *Eze 13:9 NASB95*

- "Beware of the false prophets, who come to you in sheep's clothing, but inwardly are ravenous wolves. *Mat 7:15 NASB95*

- "For false christ's and false prophets will arise and **will show great signs and wonders, so as to mislead, if possible, even the elect**. *Mat 24:24 NASB95*

- But He answered and said to them, "An evil and adulterous generation craves for a sign; and **yet no sign will be given to it but the sign of Jonah** the prophet; *Mat 12:39 NASV*

- But false prophets also arose among the people, just as there will also be false teachers among you, who will secretly introduce destructive heresies, even denying the Master who bought them, bringing swift destruction upon themselves. *2Pe 2:1 NASV*

- Beloved, do not believe every spirit, but test the spirits to see whether they are from God, because many false prophets have gone out into the world. *1John 4:1 NASV*

- By this the children of God and the **children of the devil are obvious: anyone who
does not practice righteousness is not of God,
nor the one who does not love his brother**. *1John 3:10 NASV*

Lord please give to me the zeal and boldness to glorify you. Help me Lord to expose the iniquity of others so as to restore them from captivity. Use my mouth, my tongue, my lips to proclaim your Word, Your Love and the Life others my obtain though You, in You and with You. Give to me a mind of Christ. Clothe me in your righteousness and finish me with your faith and perfect love. Help me Lord, Make me Lord to do your will for Your glory and for the benefit of others. In Jesus Name I pray.

WHO ARE THE RIGHTEOUS?

"But seek first His kingdom and His righteousness, and all these things will be added to you. *Mat 6:33 NASB95*

Those who believe in the Lord (Gen 15:6 and Ro 4:3) and are careful to observe all His commandments (De 6:25) by doing righteousness and justice (Gen 18:19) are righteous. It is they who walk in truth and uprightness of heart (1Ki 3:6) with whom the Lord is pleased. It is they who trust in the Lord and offer the sacrifice of righteousness (Ps 4:5). We must call on the Lord with a pure heart filled with faith, love and peace (2Ti2:22).

In Ps 18:20 the Lord rewards "according to the cleanness of my hands." In Pr 8:8 what you say out of your mouth must not be perverted nor crooked, your mouth must be righteous confessing with your mouth with all your heart believing in your salvation as mentioned in Romans 10:10. Pr 16:12 says that wicked acts are an abomination for a throne. James 1:20 says that anger does not achieve righteousness. These are just a few notes to help you understand righteousness. Pray that the Lord will gift to you the fruit of righteousness. Hunger and thirst for righteousness so that you will receive it as promised by the Lord.

- If Christ is in you, though the body is dead because of sin, **YET THE SPIRIT IS ALIVE BECAUSE OF RIGHTEOUSNESS.** *Romans 8:10 NASB95*

- as it is written, "THERE IS NONE RIGHTEOUS, NOT EVEN ONE; *Romans 3:10 NASB95*

- All Scripture is inspired by God and profitable for teaching, for reproof, for correction, for training in righteousness; *2Ti3:16 NASB95*

- By faith Noah, being warned by God about things not yet seen, in reverence prepared an ark for the salvation of his household, by which he condemned the world, and became an heir of the righteousness which is according to faith. *Heb 11:7 NASB95*

- "It is not for your righteousness or for the uprightness of your heart that you are going to possess their land, but it is because of the wickedness of these nations that the LORD your God is driving them out before you, in order to confirm the oath which the LORD swore to your fathers, to Abraham, Isaac and Jacob. *De 9:5 NASB95*

- For in it the righteousness of God is revealed from faith to faith; as it is written, "BUT THE RIGHTEOUS man SHALL LIVE BY FAITH." *Ro 1:17 NASB95*

- Do you not know that when you present yourselves to someone as slaves for obedience, you are slaves of the one whom you obey, either of sin resulting in death, or of obedience resulting in righteousness? *Ro 6:16 NASB95*

- and do not go on presenting the members of your body to sin as instruments of unrighteousness; but present yourselves to God as those alive from the dead, and your members as instruments of righteousness to God. *Ro 6:13 NASB95*

- I am speaking in human terms because of the weakness of your flesh. For just as you presented your members as slaves to impurity and to lawlessness, resulting in further lawlessness, so now present your members as slaves to righteousness, resulting in sanctification. *Ro 6:19 NASB95*

- Blessed are they which do hunger and thirst after righteousness: for they shall be filled. *Mat 5:6 KJV*

- "I put on righteousness, and it clothed me; My justice was like a robe and a turban. *Job 29:14 NASB95*

- in the word of truth, in the power of God; by the **armor of righteousness** on the right hand and on the left, *2Co 6:7 KJV*

- For the LORD is righteous, He loves righteousness; The upright will behold His face. *Ps 11:7 NASB95*

- Righteousness and justice are the foundation of Your throne; Lovingkindness and truth go before You. *Ps 89:14 NASB95*

- In You, O LORD, I have taken refuge; Let me never be ashamed; In Your righteousness deliver me. *Ps 31:1 NASB95*

- I have not hidden Your righteousness within my heart; I have spoken of Your faithfulness and Your salvation; I have not concealed Your lovingkindness and Your truth from the great congregation. *Ps 40:10 NASB95*

- For Your righteousness, O God, reaches to the heavens, You who have done great things; O God, who is like You? *Ps 71:19 NASB95*

- Lovingkindness and truth have met together; Righteousness and peace have kissed each other. *Ps 85:10 NASB95*

- And my tongue shall declare Your righteousness And Your praise all day long. *Ps 35:28 NASB95*

- Before the LORD, for He is coming, For He is coming to judge the earth. He will judge the world in righteousness And the peoples in His faithfulness. *Ps 96:13 NASB95*

- But the lovingkindness of the LORD is from everlasting to everlasting on those who fear Him, And His righteousness to children's children, *Ps 103:17 NASB95*

- For the sake of Your name, O LORD, revive me. In Your righteousness bring my soul out of trouble. *Ps 143:11 NASB95*

- As for me, I shall behold Your face in righteousness; I will be satisfied with Your likeness when I awake. *Ps 17:15 NASB95*

Lord I desire to live a righteous life in Your sight.
I desire to please you greatly.
I desire to love my brothers as You love them.
Help me Lord to Love as You love.
Lord I fear being apart from You,
please keep me in the abode of Your Heart
and make me One with You.
Clothe me in the armor of righteousness,
the armor of God, the Helmet of Salvation,
Girt my loins with truth and
shod my feet with the gospel of truth,
give to me the shield of faith and
the sword of the Spirit, the Word of God
that I may boldly proclaim the Love of You,
for You and In You.
Make my heart to overflow with the everlasting love
of you, for you and for the benefit of others
Make me to live where love is,
where you will maintain it, sustain it and
unfathomably consume it with your grace.
Oh Lord keep me clothed in you loving armor of light.
May you be forever praised adored and glorified and
loved beyond love as in no other time of all creation.
Blessed are You Holy ONE!
Thank you for your love
and for delighting in the creation of us.

WHO ARE THE FALSE CHRISTS?

-"Do you suppose that I came to grant peace on earth? I tell you, no, but rather division; Luke 12:51 NASB95

-For there shall arise false christs, and false prophets, and shall show great signs and wonders; insomuch that, if it were possible, they shall deceive the very elect. Behold, I have told you before. Wherefore if they shall say unto you, Behold, he is in the desert; go not forth: behold, he is in the secret chambers; believe it not. For as the lightning cometh out of the east, and shineth even unto the west; so shall also the coming of the Son of man be. For wheresoever the carcase is, there will the eagles be gathered together. Immediately after the tribulation of those days shall the sun be darkened, and the moon shall not give her light, and the stars shall fall from heaven, and the powers of the heavens shall be shaken: And then shall appear the sign of the Son of man in heaven: and then shall all the tribes of the earth mourn, Mat 24:24-30 KJV

Are they those who believe in Christ but have different doctrines, different teachings? Yes, that is them. They are not an antichrist, they are false teachers of christ. They believe in Jesus. They glorify themselves. They are not humble. They are proud. They do not repent according to the ways of the Lord. They do not love their brother because they do not know how. They think they know Jesus but they are liars.

The Lord taught unconditional love and repentance, false christs speak evil against other Christ believers and do not practice the unconditional love and the mercy of Christ. They do not know love! and so, what is life without true love… NOTHING!

Do they believe there is only one teacher as the Lord spoke when He was on earth? Do they have a mind of Christ?

- "But do not be called Rabbi; for **One is your Teacher,** and you are all brothers. Mat 23:8 NASB95

-Now I beseech you, brethren, **by the name of our Lord Jesus Christ, that ye all speak the same thing, and that there be no divisions among you; but that ye be perfectly joined together in the same mind and in the same judgment.** For it hath been declared unto me of you, my brethren, by them which are of the house of Chloe, that there are contentions among you. Now this I say, that every one of you saith, I am of Paul; and I of Apollos; and I of Cephas; and I of Christ. Is Christ divided? was Paul crucified for you? or were ye baptized in the name of Paul *1 Cor 1:10-13 KJV*

- For who hath known the mind of the Lord, that he may instruct him? But we have the mind of Christ. *1Co 2:16 KJV*

- Let this mind be in you, which was also in Christ Jesus: *Php 2:5 KJV*

- Forasmuch then as Christ hath suffered for us in the flesh, arm yourselves likewise with the same mind: for he that hath suffered in the flesh hath ceased from sin; *1Pe 4:1 KJV*

- That ye be not soon shaken in mind, or be troubled, neither by spirit, nor by word, nor by letter as from us, as that the day of Christ is at hand. *2Th 2:2 KJV*

The Word of God is true. We must ask Him, Our Teacher to teach us all things, we must pray that we may obtain a mind of Christ. We must ask Him for the grace to have the greatest love. We must ask Him for the grace to be totally and unconditionally obedient. We must desire desperately, to love Our Father as He loves us, even unto death, and even offering to Him the death of our children for the Love of God, in the fulfillment of His perfect plan.

- Gird yourselves with sackcloth And lament, **O priests**; Wail, O **ministers of the altar!** Come, **spend the night in sackcloth** O ministers of my God, For the grain offering and the drink offering Are withheld from the house of your God. *Joe 1:13* NASB95

- "Wail, you shepherds, and cry; And **wallow in ashes,** you **masters of the flock**; For the days of your slaughter and your dispersions have come, And you will fall like a choice vessel. *Jer 25:34* NASB95

- So I gave my attention to the Lord God to seek Him by prayer and supplications, with fasting, sackcloth and ashes. *(Da 9:3)* NASB95

You must fall like a choice vessel to be a choice vessel!
Be as He is, Sow and He sows, Love as He Loves!

Let us then, repent and pray to the Lord:
Please Lord, give to me a mind of Christ and teach me your ways. Put upon me the armor of righteousness and justice. I beg you to make me to be pleasing to you. Make me Lord to resist the devil and his evil ways. Make me Lord to submit to you completely without hesitation and to obey your every command. Hear Me Dear Father and Help me to Love You as You love me.

I beg you Lord, to make me in union with my brethren that we make speak the same thing with no division among us. Join us perfectly together in the same mind and in the same judgment in Your love for Your Glory and Honor unto life everlasting. In the Name of Jesus I pray. Blessed Mary, Mother of God, be my Mother too.

Prayer:
LEAD FALSE CHRISTS TO YOUR LIVING BREAD
Oh Lord, Help Them

Oh My Lord, My Love, My Light, save the false Christs.

Lead them to Your Living Bread. Lead them to Confess and repent that the door will not be shut on them. Show them the truth, lead them in your way, shine your light upon them.

I bind the stronghold of false christs, I cut off the tongue of the lying demons and pluck out the eyes of splinters, pride and glory. May their eyes become blessed and may their ears hear You. I command those evil spirits to reap what they have sown, and I bind each person to the Immaculate Heart of Mary with this prayer:
Hail Mary, Full of Grace,
The Lord is with thee,
Blessed are You among women,
Blessed is The Fruit of your womb, Jesus.
Holy Mary, Mother of God,
Pray for Us Sinners
now and at the hour of our death Amen.

- Jesus answered them and said, "Truly, truly, I say to you, you seek Me, not because you saw signs, but because you ATE of the loaves and were filled. *John 6:26 NASB95*

WHO IS THE ANTICHRIST?

> - Children, it is the last hour; and just as you heard that antichrist is coming, even now many antichrists have appeared; from this we know that it is the last hour. *1John 2:18 NASB95*
>
> - Who is the liar but the one who **denies that Jesus is the Christ**? This is the antichrist, the one who **denies the Father and the Son.** *1John 2:22 NASB95*
>
> - and **every spirit that does not confess Jesus is not from God**; this is the spirit of the antichrist, of which you have heard that it is coming, and now it is already in the world. *1John 4:3 NASB95*
>
> - For many deceivers have gone out into the world, **those who do not acknowledge Jesus Christ as coming in the flesh**. This is the deceiver and the antichrist. *2John 1:7 NASB95*

The Antichrist cannot even say the words "Jesus is Lord". Let us pray for them that perhaps the Lord will change their heart and free them from bondage.

Lord, You who is creator of all things great and small, bless our enemies, bless the antichrist. Have pity on Him Oh Lord, surely we have received what we deserved for our inequity. Have mercy on us all by the merits of Your Beloved Son Jesus who suffered and died for us out of love and mercy. Lord, please stop us from sinning and from hurting you and one another. Fill us with the grace of your consuming fire of love and create a right spirit within us. Thank you Lord for hearing my prayer.

WHAT POWER DOES SATAN HAVE OVER ME?

-The sting of death is sin; and **the power of sin is the law**: *1Co 15:56* NASB95

-Jesus said unto them,
Is it not for this cause that you err,
that you know not the scriptures,
nor the power of God? *Mark 12:24* ASV

- For no word from God shall be void of power. *Luke 1:37* ASV

- And amazement came upon all, and they spake together, one with another, saying, What is this word? for with authority and power he commandeth the unclean spirits, and they come out. *Luke 4:36* ASV

In the Name of Jesus:
"Behold, I have given you authority to tread upon serpents and scorpions, and over all the power of the enemy: and nothing shall in anyway hurt you.." *Luke 10:19* ASV

- But I will warn you whom ye shall fear: Fear him, who after he hath killed hath power to cast into hell; yea, I say unto you, Fear him. *Luke 12:5* ASV

- But we have this treasure in earthen vessels,
that the exceeding greatness of the power may be of God, and not from ourselves; *2Co 4:7* ASV

- who only hath immortality, dwelling in light unapproachable; whom no man hath seen, nor can see: to whom be honor and power eternal. Amen. *1Ti 6:16* ASV

- For the word of the cross is to them that perish foolishness; but unto us who are saved it is the power of God. *1Co 1:18* ASV

- who delivered us out of the power of darkness, and translated us into the kingdom of the Son of his love; *Col 1:13 ASV*

- strengthened with all power, according to the might of his glory, unto all patience and longsuffering with joy; *Col 1:11 ASV*

- to open their eyes so that they may turn from darkness to light and from the dominion of Satan to God, that they may receive forgiveness of sins and an inheritance among those who have been sanctified by faith in Me.' *Ac 26:18 NASB95*

- **For this finds favor *(GRACE)*, if for the sake of conscience toward God a person bears** up under sorrows when suffering unjustly. *1Pe 2:19 NASB95*

For I consider that the sufferings of this present time are not worthy to be compared with the glory that is to be revealed to us. *Ro 8:18 NASB95*

- For the scripture saith unto Pharaoh, For this very purpose did I raise thee up, that I might show in thee my power, and that my name might be published abroad in all the earth. *Ro 9:17 ASV*

- Let every soul be in subjection to the higher powers: for **there is no power but of God; and the powers that be are ordained of God.** *Ro 13:1 ASV*

- Jesus answered him, **Thou wouldest have no power against me, except it were given thee from above:** *John 19:11 ASV*

- Therefore I urge you, brethren, by the mercies of God, to present your bodies a living and holy sacrifice, acceptable to God, which is your spiritual service of worship *Ro 12:1 NASB95*

- to the only God our Saviour, through Jesus Christ our Lord, be glory, majesty, dominion and power, before all time, and now, and for evermore. Amen. *Jude 1:25 AMP*

- saying, Amen: Blessing, and glory, and wisdom, and thanksgiving, and honor, and power, and might, be unto our God for ever and ever. Amen. *Rev 7:12 KJV*

- And I heard a great voice in heaven, saying,
Now is come the salvation, and the power, and the kingdom of our God, and the authority of his Christ: for the accuser of our brethren is cast down, who accuseth them before our God day and night. *Rev 12:10 ASV*

- After these things I heard as it were a great voice of a great multitude in heaven, saying, Hallelujah; Salvation, and glory, and power, belong to our God: *Rev 19:1 NASB77*

Help me Lord to accept all things for your glory. Help me to accept all trials and tribulations with grace that I may please you in all things and inherit life everlasting in your unfathomable love. Lord, you said that the power of sin is the law and in Heb 7:11-18 you say that the priesthood changed the law and made things imperfect but brought to us a greater hope to draw near to God. And so then Lord, in this hope we desire to return to You, Your priesthood, Your altar and Your throne so that you may once again reign in all hearts, minds and souls. Remove this imperfection from us and perfect us. Allow us Lord, make us Lord to return to you. Make us Lord a new creation. Come to us King of Glory, reign in us and throughout all creation in the heavens above, on the earth and beneath the earth. Melchizedek, Oh Priest of the Most High God, return to us and take Your place as the Lord has prescribed in His perfect plan. Blessed Be God, Blessed Be His Holy Name, Jesus.

WHY *IS THE VIRTUE OF CHARITY ONE OF THE GREATEST VIRTUES?*

> Put on therefore,
> as the elect of God,
> holy and beloved, bowels of mercies, kindness,
> humbleness of mind, meekness, longsuffering;
> Forbearing one another,
> and forgiving one another,
> if any man have a quarrel against any:
> even as Christ forgave you,
> so also do ye.
> And above all these things put on **charity,
> which is the bond of perfectness.** *Col 3:12-14 KJV*

Charity is the bond to perfection as noted in the Word, the gift of perfect charity is greater than we understand. Charity is of a greater degree according to the Lord. Yes giving without restraint, but it is also a greater giving and **detachment from all things of the earth, renouncing them and not desiring them. Not allowing them to possess us.**

> By this, love is perfected with us, so that we may have confidence in the Day of Judgment; because **as He is, so also are we in this world.** *1John 4:17 NASB95*

> -"So then, none of you can be My disciple who does not give up all his own possessions. *Luke 14:33 NASB95*

> - "But give that which is within as charity,
> and then all things are clean for you. *Luke 11:41 NASB95*

WHY IS THE DIVINE MERCY CHAPLET SO IMPORTANT?

> For judgment will be merciless
> to one who has shown no mercy;
> **MERCY TRIUMPHS OVER JUDGMENT**.
> *Jas 2:13* NASB95

In 1933, God gave Sister Faustina a striking vision of His Mercy; Sister tells us:
"I saw a great radiance, in the midst of it, God the Father. Between this radiance and the earth I saw Jesus, nailed to the Cross and in such a way that when God wanted to look at the earth, He had to look through the wounds of Jesus. And I understood that it was for the sake of Jesus that God blesses the earth." (Diary 60)

Of another vision on Sept. 13, 1935, she writes:
"....I saw an Angel, the executor of divine wrath... about to strike the earth...I found myself pleading with (197) God for the world words heard interiorly. As I was praying in this manner, I saw the Angel's helplessness; he could not carry out the just punishment. " (Diary 474)

Our Lord said to Saint Faustina:
...encourage souls to say the chaplet which I have given to you 1541 Whoever will recite it will receive great mercy at the hour of death. 687... When they say this chaplet in the presence of the dying, I will stand between my Father and the dying person, not as the Just Judge but as the Merciful Savior 1541... Priests will recommend it to sinners as their last hope of salvation. Even if there were a sinner most hardened, if he were to recite this Chaplet only once, he would receive grace from my infinite mercy.... I desire to grant unimaginable graces to those souls who trust in My mercy 687... Through the Chaplet you will obtain everything, if what you ask for is compatible with My will. 1731

The Chaplet of the Divine Mercy

1. Begin with the Sign of the Cross,

Opening Prayers
You expired, Jesus, but the source of life gushed forth for souls, and the ocean of mercy opened up for the whole world. O Fount of Life, unfathomable Divine Mercy, envelop the whole world and empty Yourself out upon us.

O Blood and Water, which gushed forth from the Heart of Jesus as a fountain of Mercy for us, I trust in You!

1 Our Father, 1 Hail Mary and The Apostles Creed.

2. Then on the Our Father Beads say the following:
Eternal Father, I offer You the Body and Blood, Soul and Divinity of Your dearly beloved Son, Our Lord Jesus Christ, in atonement for our sins and those of the whole world.

3. On the 10 Hail Mary Beads say the following:
For the sake of His sorrowful Passion, have mercy on us and on the whole world.

(Repeat step 2 and 3 for all five decades).

4. Conclude with *(three times)*:
Holy God, Holy Mighty One, Holy Immortal One, have mercy on us and on the whole world.

Optional Closing Prayer
Eternal God, in whom mercy is endless and the treasury of compassion -- inexhaustible, look kindly upon us and increase Your mercy in us, that in difficult moments we might not despair nor become despondent, but with great confidence submit ourselves to Your holy will, which is Love and Mercy itself.

A NEW CHAPLET OF MERCY
(as inspired in the prayer life of Fr. Einer R. Ochoa (1997)

Contemplate the Cross

Start with the **Creed** on the first bead

Pray the **Our Father**

Three **Hail Mary's** on the next three beads

On the next bead say, **"Sacred hearts of Jesus and Mary, I Offer you my mind, my body, my heart, and my soul that the will of God be done in me"**

Ten times "**Jesus I trust in You**"

Glory be…

Pray the mysteries of the rosary

Finish with the "**Salve Regina**"

    The above prayer "A New Chaplet of Mercy" presented in simple form by Fr. Ochoa is so beautiful. We must Trust Our Great God beyond our comprehension. He loves us so much and is hurt that we do not trust Him as we should. My prayer is that our Trust will be perfected and that Our Lord will be pleased by it.

    I love this prayer so much that I have included in full length all prayers and additional meditations of the Rosary in the back section of this book. May the Lord Hear our prayer! May He bless you indeed! – Gloria

WHY IS THE VIRTUE OF HUMILITY ONE OF THE GREATEST VIRTUES?

- "IN HUMILIATION
HIS JUDGMENT WAS TAKEN AWAY;
WHO WILL RELATE TO HIS GENERATION?
Ac 8:33 NASB95

The great virtue of Humility comes through humiliation. We must be humble and willing to be humiliated so that we may be like Him. In our humiliation our judgment will be taken away obtaining the great virtue of humility.

- Give no offense
either to Jews or to Greeks or to the church of God;
just as I also please all men in all things,
not seeking my own profit but the profit of the many,
so that they may be saved. *1Cor 10:32-33 NASB95*

- Do nothing from selfishness or empty conceit,
but with humility of mind
regard one another as more important than yourselves;
Php 2:3 NASB95

- with all humility and gentleness, with patience, showing tolerance for one another in love, *Eph 4:2 NASB95*

- Therefore, putting aside all filthiness and all that remains of wickedness, **in humility receive the word implanted, which is able to save your souls.** *Jas 1:21 NASB95*

You younger men, likewise, be subject to your elders; and all of you, clothe yourselves with humility toward one another, for GOD IS OPPOSED TO THE PROUD, BUT GIVES GRACE TO THE HUMBLE. *1Pe 5:5 NASB95*

WHAT IS GRACE?

When I received the message "Why the Hail Mary?" as written in this book, the Lord very clearly defined "grace" for me. It is simply defined as follows:

Grace is a love which bears all things and conquers all of our enemies.

Now knowing that by grace we are saved it becomes more relevant that we must desire to be like Jesus "full of grace", perfect as our Father is perfect. We must run the race the apostles ran. We must seek with all of our heart, mind, soul and strength. Our hearts must ache for His love with a great desire to be with Him, fearing, dreading the thought of being apart from Him.

The Lord said that the road is narrow. We must obtain a greater love to obtain the grace that saves. Few believe and so the pattern since Noah has not changed. People still refuse to obey the Lord in repenting in a way pleasing to the Lord. We must desire greatly and hope desperately that the Lord will allow us to be born a child of God. We must desire to be possessed by Our Lord and resist, rebuke and renounce the devil and all his works. We must empty ourselves of our sinfulness with the help of the Holy Spirit.

We must forgive unconditionally thus loving unconditionally. We must gain virtue to obtain grace.

Jesus was full of grace; Mary was also full of grace. With grace they were able to endure the wiles of the devil. They were made strong in the Lord. Jesus was able to be tormented and display his love; Mary was able to endure her sorrow without retaliating.

Both accepted all things according to the will of God. The spiritual battle was taking place, true love WAS, IS and WILL ALWAYS BE conquering all of our enemies. The apostles were also full of grace. They were perfect as Our Heavenly Father is perfect, as was Jesus and Mary.

> - And with great power the apostles were giving testimony to the resurrection of the Lord Jesus, and **Abundant grace was upon them all**. *Acts 4:33 NASB95*

> **- For of His fullness we have received grace upon grace** *John 1:16 NASB95*

> - And **Stephen, full of grace and power**, was performing great wonders and signs among the people. *Acts 6:8 NASB95*

> - through whom we have received grace and apostleship to bring about the obedience of faith among all the Gentiles for His name's sake *Romans 1:5 NASB95*

We must ask for grace. Grace is manifested in many ways. Obedience to the Word of God is grace. The Lord said if you love me, obey my commands. Other ways of obtaining grace with a contrite and loving heart include prayer, longsuffering, Holy Communion, praying the Rosary, charity, humility, and most importantly by loving unconditionally etc. We must embrace our humiliations and ask the Lord to help us respond to every situation in His way admitting we do not know how. Grace comes when we do these with great love towards Our Lord and His Holy Family and each other.

How obedient are you? Do you keep the commands of the Lord? Do you abide in Him, Do you lie, do you condemn, and are you an adulterer? Are you a fornicator (sex before marriage)? It is by grace alone, that we can be brought about to be obedient to the faith and laws of Our Lord. The greatest grace is to love our enemy, even unto death! To sell all your possessions and to give them to the poor, not to your family, but to the poor, is also a great gift of grace.

> **- For sin shall not be master over you**, for you are not under law but under grace. *Romans 6:14 NASB95*

> - We know that **no one who is born of God sins**; but He who was born of God keeps him, and **the evil one does not touch him.** *1John 5:18 NASB*

Breaking any of the commands of Our Lord is sin. Idle words, swearing, evil tongues and thoughts or actions are all sins.

We are all sinners, but we must desire greatly not to sin. We must desire greatly to love unconditionally.

We must pray for all religious leaders, that the Lord will give them the grace to bow down to the Lord, and let go of their personal pride and glory so that the people of God may be truly lead by the Lord in His Way, in His Truth, in His Light and in the fullest of grace for the Salvation of Man.

We must pray for the Pope, the Orthodox leaders, all Preachers, teachers and for the Jews. May the Lord give them the Grace to endure the consequences of setting things right during the Apostasy and the things to come.

> "He who is not with Me is against Me;
> and he who does not gather with Me scatters.
> *Mat 12:30 NASB95*

The above verse clearly reveals that the disciples of Jesus are the true leaders of the Church. The split between the Romans and the Orthodox, and all churches was necessary as was the kiss of Judas, all these things, for the Glory of God. Are Christians scattered in mind and body? Do they not gather as one? Do they not know love? Are they against Our Lord? Do they follow Him, that is do they really follow the leader?

The following are graces we can pray for: the grace of increased light / the grace of increased simplicity / the grace to deny ourselves everything/ the grace to hear Him / the grace to see Our Lord / the grace to enter at the narrow gate / the grace to know the love of His Mother, Mary / the grace to dwell in the House of the Lord / the grace of wisdom, knowledge, and understanding / the grace of reason and intelligence / the grace of perfect charity / the grace of perfect humility / the grace of perfect hope / the grace to obtain perfect faith / the grace to love our enemy even unto death / the grace to be full of grace /

We must desire desperately, to love Our Father as He loves us, even unto death, and even offering to Him the death of our children for the Love of God, in the fulfillment of His perfect plan.

We must sow as He sows, Be as He is, Love as He Loves.

Now is the time to come back home to the One True Church! Love beyond love! Be merciful as Our Father is Merciful! Let us then repent so that the Lord will reveal His truth to all of us.

(I heard a protestant leader that returned to the catholic church say that over 700 protestant leaders have returned within the year 2007 – he said it is necessary for the coming of the Lord – if you are interested in knowing more look for the evangelist crusades steming from the catholic church – Seek! Research! Ask the Lord to teach you! Lean not on human understanding! we will be one!)

HOW CAN I EVEN BEGIN TO OBEY? I AM HELPLESS!

> By **lovingkindness and truth** inequity is atoned for
> And by **fear of the Lord** one keeps away from evil.
> *Pr 16:6 NASB95*

Desire to Love God above all persons and things created.
Ask Him to help you and to teach you. The law of the Lord will be fulfilled in your life if you desire and strive to make the Lord your first love. It is stated in the first commandment that upon this hangs all the law and the prophets. That is, if you can Love God first with all your heart, mind, soul and strength, then the rest of the commandments will automatically be fulfilled. Approach Him with a contrite and sorrowful heart. Confess your sins so that He may hear you. You must also be baptized or you will be condemned!

Tell Him you desire to obey Him and ask for the intercession of the whole church. Fear of the Lord is discussed in other parts of this book.

> **Thou shalt love the Lord thy God with all thy heart, and with all thy soul, and with all thy mind.** This is the first and great commandment.
> And the second is like unto it,
> Thou shall love thy neighbor as thyself.
> **On these** two **commandments**
> **hang all the law** and the prophets.
> *Mathew 22:37-40 KJV*

> Peter said to them,
> "**Repent**, and each of you be baptized
> in the name of Jesus Christ for the forgiveness of your sins;
> and you will receive the gift of the Holy Spirit.
> *Acts 2:38 NASB95*

> "He who has believed **and has been baptized shall be saved;** but he who has disbelieved shall be condemned.
> *Mark 16:16 NASB95*

We must do as Our Sheppard has done. We must desire to be as He is. We must Love as He loves. Jesus called Mary Mother and so should we. We must desire that our hearts become Sacred like His and Immaculate like Hers. Remove your pride and ask the Lord to forgive you and help you to love her as He loves Her. She is the tabernacle of the Word of God; the Word entered her womb. Blessed is the fruit of thy womb, Jesus! The devil is real and does not want you to believe. Let us then repent together, so that you will believe. (Read "A Prayer of Consecration" see Table Of Contents).

"Lord I solemnly approach your throne and with a contrite heart I admit my ignorance, my doubts and my faults, please forgive me. Lord, help me to love you with all my heart, with all my soul, with all my mind and all my strength. Give to me the gift of the Holy Spirit. Change my heart to please you, my mind to obey you and my soul to magnify you and my being I give to you that your will may be done in my life. Lord forgive me for not loving Your Mother, for not desiring to know her, forgive my unbelief and help me love her as You love Her, teach me your ways and fill me with Your perfect love."

WHAT IS YOUR BLESSING?

Have you ever heard the expression "Be careful what you ask for in prayer? I heard this a long time ago relating to patience. In any case, I have learned that we do not know the difference between an apple or an orange when it comes to defining a blessing.

The flesh seems to think that a blessing is abundance, luxuries, and comfortable living. Our Blessed Mother appeared to Bernadette as "The Immaculate Conception" and told her this: "I cannot promise you happiness in this world, only in the next".

How have you demonstrated your faith? Faith without works is dead, and you are nothing without love. If you do not believe this then repent so that you might believe.

> - For just as the body without the spirit is dead, so also faith without works is dead. *Jas 2:26* NASB95

> - if I have all faith, so as to remove mountains, but do not have love, I am nothing. *1Co 13:2* NASB

I tell you this today, these are your blessings: the poor, the hungry, the naked, pain and suffering, financial disasters, your tormentor, all trials and tribulations...
All these teach you to produce the fruits of the spirit:

> - But the fruit of the Spirit is **love, joy, peace, longsuffering, gentleness, goodness, faith, Meekness, temperance: against such there is no law.** And they that are Christ's have crucified the flesh with the affections and lusts. If we live in the Spirit, let us also walk in the Spirit. Let us not be desirous of vain glory, provoking one another, envying one another. *Gal 5:22-26* KJV

All of these teach you to gain the blessings of grace and increased virtues. They are the opportunity given to us to become Christ like. They are the opportunity to imitate Jesus, who is Love itself. They are the opportunity to abandon ourselves from this world.

They are the opportunity to resist, rebuke and renounce the devil by crucifying the flesh against the affections, attachments, lusts and desires of this world. The grace to give freely and detach ourselves openly is the road to perfect charity. Love your enemy, speak to them with love, and embrace them with all your heart in the love of God. This is the road to perfect humility. Grace and virtues lead us to Perfect love which conquers all of our enemies. Yes, these are your blessings, and here are the Blessed:

> Blessed are the poor in spirit:
> for theirs is the kingdom of heaven.
> Blessed are they that mourn:
> For they shall be comforted.
> Blessed are the meek:
> for they shall inherit the earth.
> Blessed are they which do hunger and thirst
> after righteousness: for they shall be filled.
> Blessed are the merciful:
> for they shall obtain mercy.
> Blessed are the pure in heart:
> for they shall see God.
> **Blessed are the peacemakers:**
> **for they shall be called the children of God.**
> Blessed are they which are persecuted for righteousness' sake: for theirs is the kingdom of heaven.
> Blessed are ye, when men shall revile you, and persecute you, and shall say all manner of evil against you falsely, for my sake.
> Rejoice, and be exceeding glad:
> for great is your reward in heaven:
> for so persecuted they the prophets which were before you.
> *Matthew 5:3-12 KJV*

WHO IS THE KING?

(This is the complete message, only part was given in We Lay Down Our Crown by Gloria) WHO IS THE KING? was partly received on the Feast of the Assumption of The Virgin Mary, on August 15, 2005 and additional after going to confession on August the 18th. It is as follows:

WHO IS THE KING?
YES, OUR BELOVED JESUS!
But who else like Caesar? Who else like Jesus?

> -and Jason has welcomed them, and
> **they all act contrary to** the decrees of **Caesar,**
> saying that there is another king, Jesus." <u>Acts 17:7 NASB95</u>

Who do you imitate? Who do you follow?
Caesar on your throne or Jesus, a servants servant,
with no where to lay His head?
Humble, meek, lowly, poor, filled with love! Never condemning but rather delivering demons and fleeing for safety, simply to avoid. He knew the enemy, do you? He has power over them, yet, He handed himself over to them. He loves them! He tells us to love them too!

Do you think that when Jesus came to this world He needed to suffer? Do you think He needed to be baptized or to receive the Holy Spirit? Do you think that He needed to be born in a stable? Do you think He needed to be poor? Do you think He needed anything of this world? He did not have to do any of these things, but He did these, to show us what we must do and how to do it. He showed us what our desire should be. He showed us the way. We must offer our sufferings to the Lord. We must desire to deny ourselves all things and be willing to be poor, giving freely what we do have. We must be baptized because we are sinners and we must receive the Holy Spirit because we are helpless without the Lord, we cannot fight evil of our own accord. We must be willing to do His will not ours. He is our perfect example; we must desire to imitate Him, to be like Him, in Him and One with Him.

He said that we must be like a child to enter the Heavenly gates. We see Him as a child embracing His Mother. We see Him performing

His first miracle through His Mother. We see Him at the Cross giving His Mother to man. What do children do? As a child imitates their parents, we must imitate Jesus in all things; we must also embrace and love His Mother. He is our perfect example, Our Shepherd.

> -and said, "Truly I say to you, unless you are converted and become like children, you will not enter the kingdom of heaven. *Mat 18:3 NASB95*

The Lord says all things are imperfect until perfection comes. I hope that the Lord gives us the grace to bring what is hidden in the darkness into the light. Do you believe His Word "Be perfect as My Father is perfect?" Desire and ask Our Lord to give you the grace to believe His Word and all that He desires to teach you, **but first confess your doubt with a contrite heart.** Ask Him to give you the grace to make you pleasing to Him. He also says "lean not on human understanding", so, **we must be willing to forget what man has taught us and ask the Lord to teach us - pray, fast and Open your BIBLE!** Be open to the teachings of the Lord.

We must desire to think in the Spirit,
walk in the Spirit and live in the Spirit,
"By Faith and not by sight!"
Crave for the love of God!!!

> Our Father craved our love so much that He sent His only Son to die for us; to show us the way, to teach us His truth and to bring us out of darkness into the Light.

Jesus, Our Shepherd, came to shepherd His sheep.
His sheep know Him and follow Him.

> - "When he puts forth all his own,
> **he goes ahead of them,**
> and the sheep follow him
> because they know his voice. *John 10:4 NASB95*

- "I am the good shepherd, and
I know My own and My own know Me, *John 10:14 CPDV*

Jesus, who
LAID HIS CROWN DOWN BEFORE HIS FATHER,
TO BECOME THE LOWEST.
    WE,
    NOW, must follow Jesus, Our Shepherd
    with the greatest of love
    we must
LAY DOWN OUR CROWN AT THE FEET OF JESUS!

    Can we each humble ourselves and get off of our throne like Jesus did? Can we give up our platform, our throne? Can we unite regardless of our differences and trust the Lord to deliver us from them? Can we love our enemy? Jesus, Our King, is waiting to claim His throne. Will you give Him yours? Can you walk away from your throne and not look back?
    He is our Suffering King on earth, long suffering, and long waiting. He came to show us the way. He is our perfect example. Could it be that it is you, keeping Him from sitting on His throne, because of your thoughtlessness or self centeredness?
Is it YOU who is sitting on His Throne, high and mighty?
Is it you - rabbi, father, teacher, leader, or master of all?
Is it you - rulers of this world? Yes, rulers of the darkness of this world (in the flesh made of dust, as mentioned in Eph 6:10-18).
Is it you who is vain?
Is it you who is proud of your children, your home, your ambition, your car, your churches, your jobs, your whatever?
Is it you who has filled your heart with false treasures?

YOU have no room for Him,
which is why He was born in a stable.

There is no room in the deepest depth of your inner-most being; the Inn of your heart, the chambers in which Our Lord desires to be loved and to love.

Your heart has been steered to follow treasures of the earth in various manifestations. You chose to obey man rather than God.

Your Thrones are full of pride, vanity, makeovers, fashions and glitter, vain glory, ambitions, false power, self centeredness, love of possessions, love of money, love of false gods, you love each other more than you love God. **You have not returned that love to Him.**

Your insecurities drive you to not trust in the Lord; almost everyone has said "yes" to Satan in the desert.

You are a vessel, nothing but dirt,
let the Holy Spirit arise and take control.
I assure you, when the Holy Spirit takes control,
you will understand the meaning
of "IN HIM we live, move and have our being".
It will be apart from yourself,
in yourself, distinct,
as a Sail of a boat, you being the boat,
the Holy Spirit being the Sail.

"You know not what you are made of!" says the Lord.
And if the Lord rebuked Peter, calling him Satan, what makes you think you are anything better than Peter who was with the Lord. Are you Christ-like or not? if not, then what are you? Is your mind on the Lord 24/7?

> -But turning around and seeing His disciples, He rebuked Peter and said, "Get behind Me, Satan; for you are not setting your mind on God's interests, but man's."
> *Mark 8:33* NASB95

Can you repent for accusing a believer of the faith?
a believer of Jesus
that Satan has entered that church?

Do you believe that the Lord's plan is perfect?
What church has no flaw?

Are you a "proud" pastor of your church? Pride was Satan's flaw; it was Satan's fall.
Who can cast the first stone? We must ask the Lord to direct our path no matter what the consequences!

Come, let us love our brother in Christ, and be not proud. We must desire for the Lord to deliver us all from evil. Love your enemy even unto death.
Enter the lions den. Be Love, like Mary who did not condemn or retaliate against those who tormented her Son.

in the The Poem of a Man God, by Marie Valtorta Vol I, page 115 the following left a great impression in my heart:
> Mary, a virgin of the love of God,
> **overcame** the horror of having to say:
> "I Love You, Come To Me Who am your Mother"
> to each murderer of Her Son,
> born of the most sublime love that Heaven ever saw
> of the love of a God with a Virgin
> of the kiss of fire, of
> The embrace of Light which became Flesh,
> made the womb of a woman the Tabernacle of God.

Why do Christian brothers continue to criticize each other, or why do they say that perhaps one so-called-religion does not believe the bible when they themselves are guilty of it?
It is as the Lord has said; we must remove the splinters and log or plank from our own being! Satan makes you only believe what is convenient for your torment.
Repent!!! Love your Christian brothers!!!
Love and bless your enemy!!!
What part of the Word of God do you not believe?
We are of an evil generation. Be careful! Be watchful!
You have been misled... these are some to believe, there are many:

(Repent!! Believe! Get Baptized! Obey God not man!)
> - "He who has believed **and has been baptized shall be saved;** but he who has disbelieved shall be condemned. Mark 16:16 NASB95

- "But love your enemies, and do good, and lend, **expecting nothing in return;** and your reward will be great, and you will be sons of the Most High; for He Himself is kind to ungrateful and evil men. *Luke 6:35 NASB95*

-For now the axe is laid to the root of the trees. Every tree therefore that bringeth not forth good fruit shall be cut down and cast into the fire. And **the people** asked him, saying: **What then shall we do?**
And he answering, said to them: He that hath two coats, let him give to him that hath none; and he that hath meat, let him do in like manner.
And **the publicans** also came to be baptized and said to him: Master, **what shall we do?**
But he said to them: Do nothing more than that which is appointed you.
And the **soldiers** also asked him, saying: And **what shall we do?**
And he said to them: **Do violence to no man,** neither calumniate any man; and **be content with your pay.** *Luke 3:9-14 DRA*

-Jesus said to him, **"If you wish to be complete,** go and **sell your possessions** and give to the poor, and you will have treasure in heaven; and come, follow Me." *Mat 19:21 NASB95*

- When Jesus heard this, He said to him, "One thing you still lack; sell all that you possess and **distribute it to the poor,** and you shall have treasure in heaven; and come, follow Me." *Luke 18:22 NASB95*

- Masters, do to your servants that which **is just and equal:** knowing that you also have a master in heaven. Be instant **in prayer:** watching in it **with thanksgiving.** *Col 4:1-2 DRA*

There is much to know. The Lord says my people perish because of lack of knowledge. Did you know that we must obey The Ten Commandments? (see Table Of Contents). Do you even know them? With the help of the Holy Spirit it is possible to obey them! Desire to please the Lord!

> -**"You shall not make for yourself** an idol,
> OR **any likeness**
> of what is in **heaven** above
> or on the **earth** beneath
> or in the **water** under the earth. *Exodus 20:4* _{NASB95}
>
> - For they provoked Him with their high places And aroused His jealousy with their graven images.   *Ps 78:58* _{NASB95}
>
> - "The graven images of their gods you are to burn with fire; you shall not covet the silver or the gold that is on them, nor take it for yourselves,
> **or you will be snared by it,** for it is an abomination to the LORD your God. *De 7:25* _{NASB95}
>
> -"I am the LORD, that is My name; I will not give My glory to another, Nor My praise to graven images.
> *Isa 42:8* _{NASB95}
>
> -for you shall not worship any other god, for the LORD, whose name is Jealous, is a jealous God—
> *Ex 34:14* _{NASB95}
>
> - "For the LORD your God is a consuming fire, a jealous God. *De 4:24* _{NASB95}

You who are in high places, vain and proud, Beware! Repent!

I pray that the Lord will help me to please Him, not provoke Him.

In addition, **no statue is worth the risk!!!**

Can you imagine the fact that the Lord says you can be snared by a graven image or even what it is made of? "do not take it for yourselves or YOU WILL BE SNARED BY IT!" Could it be that all things are alive? The Indians believe it. How many have been snared?

Does it matter whether the statues be religious or not? No, they are graven images.

How many do you have in your home? If you even say a statue is beautiful – Reconsider! The Lord will not give His praise to a graven image! In other words, He is jealous and wants you to praise Him, adore Him and love Him and only Him, not a statue. Be careful!

Do you love it because of its beauty? Do not love a statue!!! It is your false god! Our God is a jealous God.

Be careful! Be watchful! Repent! I have.

I pray for that day that the Lord, Our Shepherd, **will lead us in unison, in one accord throughout the world,** as He did the children in the Book of Daniel. On that day, in unison, Satan and all his works will be crushed.

The true church is the Roman Catholic Church,
the people of the Lord are awakening - ignorant no more -- the enemy is weakening and the guards
are nothing but a stumbling block.

(Anti Christ vs False Christ)
The Lord says that a divided house cannot stand. It is very clear, Christians are divided,
choose your master.

The Lord has shown to me that all churches are in error. We are in one big Babylon; they are in a state of confusion opposing each other. Satan is trying to keep the people of God from the truth and from the true church. There are many snares. We must wait on the Lord, He is Our Victor.

A divided house is brought to desolation, we are either **"FOR Christ or Against Him"**.

-and every spirit that **does not confess Jesus** is not from God; **this is the spirit of the antichrist,** of which you have

heard that it is coming, and now it is already in the world.
1 John 4:3 NASB95

Atheists, Jews and others who do not believe in Jesus Christ to be God, the Son of God, Son of man, One with the Father, are therefore against Him. They do not confess Jesus as their Lord.

We who believe in Jesus Christ, God, Son of God, Son of man, One with the Father and His resurrection **are for Him**. (reference: 1 John 4)

The false christ's are those who teach and glory in themselves. They do not love other believers of Jesus. They do not love Mary, Mother of God, whom Our Father in heaven choose and loves very much. They teach gospel without love and repentance.

What part of the Word of God does man choose to ignore? What about the Old Testament -what part do we need to obey? The Ten Commandments have been forgotten by many.

There are many types of offerings in the Old Testament. Who has not whole heartedly offered their firstborn son to the Lord?

- "You shall not delay the offering from your harvest and your vintage. The firstborn of your sons you shall give to Me. *Ex 22:29* NASB95

Some offerings say to do from generation to generation. The Lord is the same today, yesterday and always. The Jews were stuck on the Old Testament and would not accept the New Testament; now, it seems that many Christians are stuck on the New Testament.

Will they open their hearts to Mary?
These are the times to Honor Mary, Mother of My Lord, my Mother and to consecrate ourselves to Her Immaculate Heart.

These are the times to **love Her as Our Lord loves her.**

Do you want your soul to magnify the Lord?
Do you want your spirit to rejoice in God Our Savior?

Ask the Lord to forgive you and to open your heart mind and soul to His love for her that her love may not be hidden from you.

> In <u>*The Mystical City of God*</u>, Vol. III p. 765 it states: **"Just as I have told you that he who knows Me knows also My Father, so I now tell you that he who knows My Mother knows Me."**

To consecrate means to dedicate yourself to a sacred purpose. Desire and make known to the Lord your want to be sanctified and dedicated to Him, His Sacred Heart and to the Immaculate Heart of Mary that we may also become pure and immaculate, a sacred and holy being, a Son of God.
  - The LORD also said to Moses, "Go to the people and consecrate them today and tomorrow, and let them wash their garments; <u>*Ex 19:10*</u> <small>NASB95</small>

"You shall also consecrate them, **that they may be most holy; whatever touches them shall be holy.** <u>*Ex 30:29*</u> <small>NASB95</small>

Consecrate a fast, Proclaim a solemn assembly;
Gather the elders And all the inhabitants of the land to the house of the LORD your God, And cry out to the LORD.
<u>*Joe 1:14*</u> <small>NASB95</small>

- 'But this one offered one sacrifice for sins,
and took his seat forever at the right hand of God; now he waits until his enemies are made his footstool. for by one offering **he has made perfect forever those who are being consecrated.'"** <u>*Heb 10:14*</u> <small>NABRE</small>

Some of The Old and New Testament Books were written after the events occurred. Some are prophetic still awaiting realization. What books are being written today inspired by Our Heavenly Father? Have you closed your minds, heart and soul to the new events of Our Lord? **Even the Word of God has caused**

much confusion, perhaps so that we can resolve to allow Him to teach us directly.
Repent!! Desire it!!!

    The Jews of the Old Testament are striving to be obedient to the Lord like many Christians of the New Testament. They are striving and desire greatly to rebuild the Holy Temple of God; both Jews and Christians desiring and hoping for the coming of Our Lord. Together we must desire, pray, love, and have the greatest of hopes that the Lord will fulfill His promises and deliver us all from evil.

    In our suffering, our life is a reflection of the sufferings of Jesus. Jesus came to be like us. He willingly suffered more than we can conceive. Jesus said you reap what you sow. Many times cast out, many times the devil has attempted to devour our souls, but the Lord has preserved us because He loves us. Many have suffered; we have had our trials and tribulations, some in groups, some individually. All these things are for the glory of God. We must ask the Lord to lead us! We must lay down our crown!

> - Gird yourselves with sackcloth And lament, O priests; Wail, O ministers of the altar!
> Come, **spend the night in sackcloth** O ministers of my God, for the **grain offering and the drink offering are withheld from the house of your God.** *Joe 1:13* NASB95

> - And He ordered him to tell no one, "But go and show yourself to the priest and make an offering for your cleansing, just as Moses commanded, as a testimony to them." *Luke 5:14* NASB

> - Now **where there is forgiveness** of these things, there is no longer any offering for sin. *Heb 10:18* NASB95

> -For what the Law could not do, weak as it was through the flesh, God did: sending His own Son in the likeness of sinful flesh and as an offering for sin, He condemned sin in the flesh, *Ro 8:3* NASB95

What part of the bible do we continue to ignore or do not believe?
What truths, as in the parables said by Jesus have been hid from us?
Swarming in our ignorance
without desire to love the Lord unto death,
without repenting completely pleasing to Our Lord,
without hoping in His return,
without returning to Him,
we have been lost in our fault.
Sadness and pain are our reward for
the evil we have chosen without repentance.
We have not known the goodness of Our Great Loving King. It is we who have chosen to bite Eve's apple and wallow in temptation.
The Log in our own eye reeks!!!

(Lies)
> - "For by your words you will be justified, and by your words you will be condemned." *Mat 12:37 NKJV*

How many times a day, a minute or even a second is a lie
said? Who moves that evil nasty tongue? Surely not the Lord!
What is the difference between breaking one of Our Lord's Commandments or another?
Do we desire to obey His every command? If He says "move", will we instantly obey?
Is there a difference to the Lord between a lie and murder or not keeping the Sabbath?
Consider the consequences carefully!! Be watchful!! Be careful!! Repent!
We must ask the Lord to help us, teach us, fill us with His grace and make us to do His Will we are helpless without the Holy Spirit of God in us!

LIE AND PERISH or LIVE IN THE TRUTH

- But a man named Ananias, with his wife Sapphira, sold a piece of property, and kept back some of the price for himself, with his wife's full knowledge, and bringing a portion of it, he laid it at the apostles' feet. But Peter said, "Ananias, why has Satan filled your heart to lie to the Holy Spirit and to keep back some of the price of the land? "While it remained unsold, did it not remain your own? And after it was sold, was it not under your control? Why is it that you have conceived this deed in your heart? **You have not lied to men but to God.**" And as he heard these words, Ananias fell down and breathed his last; and great fear came over all who heard of it. The young men got up and covered him up, and after carrying him out, they buried him. Now there elapsed an interval of about three hours, and his wife came in, not knowing what had happened. And Peter responded to her, "Tell me whether you sold the land for such and such a price?" And she said, "Yes, that was the price." Then Peter said to her, "Why is it that you have agreed together to put the Spirit of the Lord to the test? Behold, the feet of those who have buried your husband are at the door, and they will carry you out as well." *Acts 5:1-9 NASB95*

(Adultery):

The book of Tobit (Tobias) is a beautiful book in the bible. Sara, demon possessed, has killed seven husbands. The Lord has sent Tobit, an only son, to marry Sara, in an answer to prayer. Angel Raphael guides Tobit on how to drive out the demons. After the wedding, for three days, they pray, fast and do not have relations. They offer their marriage to the Lord; and with the fear of the Lord, they are moved rather for the love of children, than for lust. They ask the Lord to bless them and He answers their prayers. What kind of marriages does the Lord see today? How many days do today's newlyweds abstain in prayer and fasting before consummating the marriage? Angel Raphael says the following:

- " For they who in such manner receive matrimony, as to shut out God from themselves and from their mind, and to

> give themselves to their lust, as the horse and mule which have not understanding, over them the devil has power."
> *Tobias Ch 6:17 DRA*

Today, perhaps marriages have been cursed because they are received through lust and adulterous live-ins of selfish desires. They are cursed through neglect and ignorance of acknowledging the Lord. Perhaps because this world has become so divided, filled with so much divorce, we tend to believe that Our Merciful Lord has forgiven us, so we continue in our sinfulness. That is not repentance. If you love the Lord, you would not want to hurt Him; you would desire not to sin ever again! We would repent immediately, not wanting to be separated from Him.

> - For Herod himself had sent and apprehended John, and bound him prison for the sake of Herodias the wife of Philip his brother, because he had married her. For John said to Herod: It is not lawful for thee to have thy brother's wife. *Mark 6:17-18 DRA*

> -For Herod feared John, knowing him to be a just and holy man: and kept him, and when he heard him, did many things: and he heard him willingly. *Mark 6:20 DRA*

Who exactly was John speaking to? Who is your brother? Not only of flesh and blood, but in Christ or not in Christ? We are all brothers. It was custom when the wife of a brother became a widow, the brother would take his brothers wife under his keep; however, Herod's brother was not dead and she was not a widow. They therefore were committing adultery. According to God's law, the punishment is death, John warned and preached repentance.

> - but I say to you that everyone who divorces his wife, except for the reason of unchastity, makes her commit adultery; and whoever marries a divorced woman commits adultery. *Mat 5:32 NASB*

What does this exactly mean?
"but I say to you that everyone who divorces his wife, except for the reason of unchastity,"

Except for the reason of unchastity? Does this mean that adultery has already been committed? I would say yes. What is unchastity? Unfaithfulness! The scripture here clearly indicates that adultery has been committed before divorce.

> *"but I say to you that everyone who divorces his wife, makes her commit adultery"*

Whether adultery is committed before divorce or after divorce, adultery is or will be committed. This scripture continues to indicate that if adultery is not committed before the divorce, it will be committed after the divorce.

> *"and whoever marries a divorced woman commits adultery."*

You who are divorced and remarried with your x-spouses living - you are an adulterer, blinded by the laws of man. The Lord has said it in His Word. The innocent spouse most likely has already been driven to commit adultery as the Lord warned.

> *"makes her commit adultery"*

> - Unless you repent, you shall likewise perish!
> <u>Luke 13:3</u> NASB

Our Lord is merciful, greatly merciful, but you must repent and remain chaste. Our bond is with God and each other.

Seek the Lord.
The Love of God is unconditional.
He will forgive those who repent.

Know this then: **if His love is in you (in us),**
then you would be like Jesus.
You too would love unconditionally.
You would have forgiven your spouse that committed adultery.
You would have fasted, prayed and repented unto the Lord. Not just for yourself, but for both of you, for the entire family, you are bound in marriage as ONE and you are ONE family.
You are ONE body in Christ. You would not have divorced and your children would not have been troubled.

You would have prayed and fasted. You must repent, put on Sack clothe and ashes, wail and mourn. You would desire greatly to be reconciled to God and to each other.

What part of the Word do you insist on not wanting to believe? Adulterer Repent or you too shall perish.

Be careful!! Be watchful!!! Repent so that you will believe!

And if your pastor is divorced and remarried, and his x-wife is living, or if your preacher condemns other churches be careful!!

Do you not know that the adulterer is a worker of Satan? It is a spirit of fornication, a spirit of adultery occupying the shell made of dust in which you have chosen your master. Unless he is chaste, reverent and holy, it could be that the enemy is your teacher and your preacher filled with presumptions and assumptions, appearing as an angel of light. You are condemned if you condemn - Repent! The Lord sadly turns away from the sinner who does not repent. We must desire **the Lord in us;** we must also desire to be **in the Lord.** The Holy Spirit dwells in you if you allow Him. The Lord does make all things good for those who love Him. He said He came to this earth not to condemn, but to save. Again I tell you to REPENT!!! Weep for yourself! Put on sack clothe and ashes. Stop the fornication! Stop the adultery! Pray with true contrition, and be reconciled one to another. Do not allow yourself to perish!

"We must obey God rather than man." *Acts 5:29 NASB95*

(March 8th 2007) What do you think of Pharaoh whose heart was hardened? Is he forgiven? He whom the Lord hardened his heart so that His glory would be made known. In his self centeredness and idol worship did he repent? Moses allowed divorce because hearts were hardened. Do those who are remarried have a harden heart like Pharaoh? Are they like Herod and his brother's wife whom he married? Did Herod have a decree of divorce according to the laws of men? Does it matter? Their hearts were hardened! Are those who are remarried today living in sin according to the Law of Our Lord?

The Lord said in *Mark 10:9* **"Therefore what God has joined together, no human being must separate"** *(NABRE)*

Who would be so humble to ask the Lord to forgive them in this? Who will plead, wail and mourn with cries of repentance that perhaps the Lord will forgive us for leaning on human understanding and in our many sins and errors so that we may be made clean and chaste? We must be chaste for the Coming of the Lord! (as noted in Rev 14:4 and Rev 22:14) (see Table Of Contents – read more in Will the Divorced be Chaste at the Coming of the Lord?)

As for me, I will repent again and again! Yes, I am divorced. Yes I was loyal to my husband when I was married, but after my divorce, based on the Law of God, I did commit adultery after my divorce. Yes I have changed my ways and offered myself chaste to the Lord. My worldly husband is remarried and I pray for his salvation and that of his lovely wife and children. My husband is my beloved bridegroom, My Lord, My God with whom I anxiously await union in perfect love. I will continue in the hope of salvation, praising and loving the Lord without end.

Prayer: *Remove the foreskin of our hearts Oh Lord, harden them no more, make us to repent, make us to please You, make Yourself known to us! Abba Father! You are our only Hope! Thank you Jesus for your great love and grace! Pray for us Jesus as you did for the Apostles, that our faith may not fail and that we may be filled with Your great love, mercy and grace! Mary, Mother Most Holy please intercede for us that we may obtain the promises of Christ.*

-But as for me, I will hope continually, and will praise Him yet more and more, *Ps 71:14 NASB95*

In May-June 2009 I believe the Lord taught me about Chastity in Loves True Desire. Here is a definition of "Lust of the Flesh":

> Lust of the Flesh is any form of carnal sex or sexual desire satisfying the body of self or of another, individually or jointly, in thought, word or deed other than for the purpose of procreation (having children) with the Lord's blessing.

But the rest of mankind, who were not killed by these plagues, did not repent of the works of their hands, ... and they did not repent of their murders or their sorceries or their unchastity.... *Rev 9:20-21 NABRE*

(Homosexuality - Indecent Acts)
- and in the same way also the men abandoned the natural function of the woman and burned in their desire **toward one another, men with men** committing indecent acts and **receiving in their own persons the due penalty of their error.** *Romans 1:27 NASB95*

Jesus came as a merciful God. He came to teach us to love and to repent so that we would be saved. Is Aids the curse of this sin as noted in scriptrue? In our ignorance, rebellion and pride, we suffer. **Repent, He loves you!! The devil is a liar!!!** Confess with your mouth, repent in sack clothe and ashes! Seek the Lord! Be Healed in the Name of Jesus!

(Resentment - true forgiveness not yet fulfilled)
I assure you, if you still do not believe; perhaps you are blinded and smothered in sin. Perhaps you have not repented, you have not bowed down on your knees, and you have not **confessed with your mouth.** You have not been reconciled with your brethren. Perhaps you have not wept for yourself! Perhaps you think you have forgiven, but you have put stumbling blocks to keep you from true forgiveness. You want nothing to do with the person you think you have forgiven. You will talk to them as little as possible. That is resentment, and true forgiveness has not been granted. Your eyes are full of splinters and being full of plank.

- The eye is the lamp of your body;
when your eye is clear, your whole body also is full of light;
but when it is bad, your body also is full of darkness.
Luke 11:34 NASB95

You must forgive to be forgiven by Our Lord. You must relent so that Our Lord will relent. Yes, I know, I had resentment in me, I did not know what it was, I thought I had forgiven, but I did not know how to love my enemy; yes, I know because I have been delivered from that - Praise the Lord!!! I hope that this confession said on a lamp stand, may bring you also to the light.

Perhaps, you think you can confess directly to God – how convenient, what lie have you believed? That is too easy! Do not dwell in darkness - be a great light - open your mouth boldly and confess from the mountain tops. Be reconciled with your brother.

You are like a sprinkler system,
and when you confess with Your mouth,
you turn on the mouth of the sprinkler
and living waters replace your darkness.
Do not be ashamed to confess - get rid of your pride.
We are all sinners until the fullness of grace becomes ours. Desire it! Repent!

Approach those with whom you must be reconciled and be reconciled. At least try, if they do not accept your apology pray for them and ask the Lord to bless them. Ask the Lord for the grace to know the Truth, He is the Truth. Can you love your enemy? Ask the Lord for the grace to love your enemy. There is no greater love. Desire it! Repent!

> - Therefore, confess your sins to one another, and pray for one another so that you may be healed. The effective prayer of a righteous man can accomplish much. *James 5:16* NASB95

> - "Now no one after lighting a lamp covers it over with a container, or puts it under a bed; but he puts it on a lamp stand, so that those who come in may see the light. *Luke 8:16* NASB95

(Honor the Mother of My Lord)
"Honor your mother and your father."
If the Lord says not to call any man father, then surely it is Our Father in Heaven whom we have to honor and our parents.

Who is our mother? In the book of Luke, Elizabeth calls Mary "Mother of My Lord".
Is your heart still hardened? Perhaps, it is you who dishonors Our Heavenly Father or the "Mother of My Lord". You close your heart, mind and soul to her sorrow, her beauty and her profound love.
You do not love her,
because you do not have love in you.

We must desire for our soul to magnify the Lord. We must want our spirit to rejoice in God Our Saviour. We must contemplate the love of Mary, her life and her obedience. She has been hid from many. Her love is profound!
We must ask the Lord to forgive us and to open our heart, mind and soul to **His** love for her, that her love may not be hidden from us.

"And how has it happened to me, that the mother of my Lord would come to me?" *Luke 1:43* NASB95

Jesus came and preached repentance and love. We must ask the Lord for the grace to know and love His Mother, Our Mother.
Ask the Lord for the grace to know the Truth, He is the Truth. We must ask the Lord to forgive us for disobedience to His Word and for leaning on human understanding. If we are in sin against calling no one father, then a great number of us have broken this command. Men tend to give okay and reason to disobey this command. But what will the Lord say, will we see His face with a pure heart?

(Jesus Repeated Prayer)
Jesus repeats his prayers in the Garden of Gethsemane three times Mat 26:39,42, 44; He does not condemn repeated prayers. Psalms are often very repetitive. For example, Psalm 136 repeats the same phrase 26 times: "God's love endures forever;" The key here is to pray with your whole heart, mind and soul! Vain repetition is mindless and heartless babbling (Mat 6:7). The Hail Mary is a scriptural prayer taken primarily from the book of Luke.

Scripture references can be found in the book We Lay Down Our Crown; you may also do a search on the internet, EWTN has a beautiful professional and thorough writing and can be found at: http://www.ewtn.com/expert/answers/rosary_scripture.htm.

> **Tobit 12:12** I can now tell you that when you, Tobit, And Sarah prayed, it was I (Raphael the angel) who presented And read the record of your prayer before the Glory of the Lord; and I did the same thing when you used to bury the dead. *(CPDV)*

(Hate, lust and pride)
Repent for the Kingdom of Jesus is at Hand!

Hate is murder! Do you hate the Roman Catholics or other religious? Reconsider your relationship with the Lord!
If you hate, dislike or judge them, or any other group of religious, you do not know the love of God. If you hate you endanger yourself to the judgment of God. I pray you do not perish but rather have eternal life! Perhaps this is your trial, **the Lord teaching you to love your enemy as He loves them.**
How many are they in this world that call themselves what they should not? The Lord says to call no one rabbi, no one father, no one leader, for the Lord alone is all these and more (Mat 23:8-22). What leader, what rabbi, what father (priest or dad), ignores the Word of God and desires to be called these names?
Is it worth the risk of provoking a Jealous God?
Do they desire to be like god of their own earthly form?
Is this arrogance or pride? Perhaps **their veil discloses nothing more than a humble desire** to please the Lord and be like Him. Yet, they make themselves to be a god, living by faith and not by sight; we hope they will come to be **"in Christ"** as was Padre Pio and the apostles. I know Paul called himself "Father", however, he was a true apostle, bearing the wound of Christ, he was full of grace "in God". The Lord spoke and acted though Him. In Him he lived, moved and had his being. He was dead to himself. There are some priests /religious leaders

that appear to be more spiritual than others, we must not judge them, we must love them. Perhaps I am wrong to bring this into consideration; however, I can only wonder how many religious preachers, leaders and even priests are true apostles. Is this not disobedience? Are we contributing to each others disgrace in disobedience of these few verses first by being called those names, and second by having others say them.
Again, the point here is that we need to keep the Word of God and be small, so lowly, a servants servant, like Jesus,
He is our perfect example.
We must be careful!! Be watchful!! Repent!!!

This shell made of dust has been an instrument of Satan in many ways; we must confine it and deny ourselves all things.

> - No wonder, for even Satan disguises
> himself as an angel of light. Therefore it is not surprising if his servants also disguise themselves as servants of righteousness, whose end will be according to their deeds.
> *2 Cor 11:14-15* NASB95

Sadly, the veil is the shield of ignorance; the angel of light blinds the people of God from all truth. And they, content in the ways of the world, living in the laws of the flesh, perish or suffer fire during purification in the afterlife. What darkness keeps us from entering the light? Sadly, I say, hidden ways of sinfulness lurks throughout the earth very close to our homes, even in us, even in those seeking holiness, until perfection comes. Surely, the devil has blinded the man in this temptation; they too have taken a bite of Eve's apple. Do they prefer to ignore what the Lord has commanded in His Word? Are these just as guilty as those who say others only want to believe part of the Word of God and not all of it?

It is truly fearful to think of myself separated from Our Lord, I love him so much, and I know I cannot follow all the rules. There are many I do not even know. I can only trust Him and greatly hope that he will change me, make me and mold me to perfection. And most of all, give to me the grace to love unto death.

Love your Enemy!
A divided house is brought to desolation.

Satan makes you only believe what is convenient for your torment.

The sign of Jonah is repentance in sack clothe and ashes!!!
Do it for the Lord!
Repent in sack clothe and ashes!!!

Love your Christian brothers!!!
Love and bless your enemy!!!

What Church has tested those who say they are apostles and are not?

So, who is like Jesus on the cross?

To whom does the Lord refer?

      Christians stop rejecting believers of Our Lord Jesus Christ! Christians love one another, remove the walls that separate you. They are stumbling blocks! More clearly said, they are lying demons using you, tormenting you, keeping you from true love.
      It is to you, the Church of Ephesus that I direct this message; it is to you, whom the Lord says "you have lost your first love and there is one thing you have not done." (as mentioned in Rev Ch 2 - read an older version prior to 1960) I now tell you how to find your first love. Knowing that we believe we love God first, perhaps it is time to demonstrate our greatest love.
I believe the Lord wants us to be the lowest.

WE MUST LAY DOWN OUR CROWN.

      Could it be that He wants you to be among the congregation as members of the congregation with nowhere to lay your head?

      Our Shepherd showed us the way. He came ahead of us. Be like Jesus, love unto death, be a servant's servant among those needing to be converted. Conversion comes from the Lord. There is nothing of your own accord that will change that.

And if the Lord rebuked Peter, calling him Satan, what makes you think you are anything better than Peter who was with the Lord. Is your obedience to the Lord perfected? If not, then you are not full of grace and light! I pray you understand what I am saying.

> - "If Satan has risen up against himself and is divided, he cannot stand, but he is finished! *Mark 3:26* NASB95
>
> - "Do you suppose that I came to grant peace on earth? I tell you, no, but rather division; *Luke 12:51* NASB95

Do we trust the Lord? Can we allow Him to lead us? Can we allow Him to Shepherd us? Are we afraid that the money supporting our churches/homes/selves will no longer be available to us? Are we afraid thinking we have to support ourselves, not believing the Lord is our provider? The Lord told the apostles to go without a purse? I am sure He will do the same for us.

We must be Christian brothers giving freely,
forgiving unconditionally, and
loving completely unto death.

Repent!! Obey!! Speak truth, speak repentance!!! Resist, rebuke and renounce the devil and he will flee!!!

Who can say they know "love in the perfection of Our Father"? Could you or would you take the place of Jesus on the Cross? How deep is your love?

In our prayers many of us have used scripture "By His wounds we are healed".
Would you be willing to bear his wounds? Would You be willing to share in His suffering?
May the Love of God fill us with His grace to receive from the Lord all that He desires.

We are His sheep, He is our shepherd.

Sheep are stupid, they will die without drinking water even at arms length, unless the Shepherd leads them to that water.
We have been stupider than sheep,
we have failed to keep our eyes on our Shepherd.
We have failed to follow our Good Shepherd,

who came ahead of us (John 10:4). NASB95

I repeat, **He came ahead of us**
We have failed to do as He has done.
He is Our Leader and Our Teacher
Thank God it is not too late!!!

We must surrender all!
Deny ourselves all!
We must be willing to be led as a sheep to slaughter.

Knowing, trusting, hoping, confidently
as our fathers before us,
our fathers of great faith.
Our God lives!!!

Come Father God, Come Lord Jesus, Come Holy Spirit,
Come Beloved Mother of God!!!
Lord, Take possession of each of us;
take possession of your throne.

Be humble. Take the first step of humility.
Please step down. Can we humbly say **"I am sorry, it is my fault, please forgive me"**.

I see a great deliverance in the lions den.
Be willing to be led as a sheep to slaughter.

Enter the Lions Den continuing
with the weapons Our Lord gave us.
Love, Faith, Hope, Charity, Compassion, Mercy, Truth, His Word, the Sword of the Spirit
Praying with our whole heart, mind and soul,

praying the Rosary, The Divine Mercy Chaplet,
Fasting, Praising and Worshiping Him,
Adoring Him, consecrating ourselves to Him, who deserves more than we can ever offer to Him.
Read and speak the Word out loud.
Faith comes from hearing!
Pray that you will be filled with the fruits of the Spirit.

Experience the greatest love, love unto death.

I assure you, there is no fear in the presence of the Lord.
I also assure you, that the devil cannot harm the people of God.

LET JESUS KNOW YOU WANT HIM TO COME FOR US AND DELIVER US FROM EVIL!!!
Pray for your deliverance.
We must be broken like Our King, the King of the Jews!
Our Beloved King Jesus!
He is OUR VICTOR, OUR CREATOR.

What is this vessel of clay in which the Holy Spirit resides?
We are of the body of Christ, ONE body!
We shall put on incorruption and immortality
- Glory to God!
"Blessed is He who comes in the Name of the Lord!!!"
We must ask Him to come and take His Throne on earth, in our churches, in our homes, and in us, we must desire it greatly!!!

We must have the MOST GREATEST OF HOPE!!!
This seems impossible, but all things are possible through Christ who strengthens us.

How great is your desire for His coming?

Allow the Lord to be Our Leader, Our Father, Our Rabbi, in Our ONE Church. He will do what He pleases with Our ONE Body. We must pray and fast that He will deliver the Pope, all religious, **and each one of us,** uniting us to himself.

We must pray for the day that He will be "in us" and we will be "In Him".
We must pray for the day that all will be in obedience to the greatest commandment, the first commandment.
We must pray for that day that the **Lord will lead us in unison, in one accord throughout the world**, as He did the children in the Book of Daniel.
We must trust Our Shepherd, Our Deliverer to triumph. It will be by His Spirit not by our might.
Fast and Pray and Repent!!! Please join your brother in Christ, the Roman Catholic Church.

The wicked warden has many workers and snares, but through Our Great God, Father of Everlasting Love, through Jesus, Our Holy Spirit and through Mary, Joseph and all those Saints which reached perfection and their intercession we are more than conquerors.

Blessed Be God, Blessed Be His Holy Name!
We must live by faith and not by sight!
The Lord has the numbers right on target.
Trust in Jesus!

Our Beloved King! Our Deliverer!
Jesus I Trust in You!

Jesus, who laid His crown down before His Father,
to become the lowest,
Now, **WE LAY DOWN OUR CROWN**
to become the lowest and the littlest
hiding in His wounds, His Passion, His Love

NOW
RETURN TO GOD,
ALL THAT BELONGS TO HIM
HIS THRONE,
OUR BEING,
OUR LOVE UNTO DEATH

No words are sufficient to give to Him words of edification,

of Glory, of Love...
all we can do is pray and love unto death.

Who is willing? Do not wait another minute!
Do not let others of the world influence you (who is their master?);
Keep your eyes on Jesus!
He is Our Shepherd. Now is the time.

Desire to become like Jesus, One with the Father,
be of His image in which He said we are made.
Ask the Lord to help you, teach you, and to give you the grace to do His will. Surrender ALL!!! Be a choice vessel.
Be the elect of Our Lord.

> - And He summoned the crowd with His disciples, and said to them, "If anyone wishes to come after Me, he **must deny himself,** and **take up his cross** and follow Me. *Mark 8:34 NASB95*

As noted in the following scripture Jeremiah 25:34. We must prostrate ourselves before the Lord.
Repent in sackcloth and ashes. We must sow to reap.

> "Wail, you shepherds, and cry; And wallow in ashes, you **masters of the flock**; For the days of your slaughter and your dispersions have come, And you will fall like a choice vessel. *Jer 25:34 NASB95*

> *"Wail, you shepherds, and cry; and wallow in ashes,"*

We have been led
to be as a sheep to slaughter.
> *"for the days of your slaughter
> and your dispersions have come,"*

We have been led by Our Shepherd,
Jesus who came ahead of us.

We must fall like a choice vessel to be a choice vessel.

These are the elect, those who are willing to die innocently for the love of the guilty.

> *"you will fall like a choice vessel." Jer 25:34 NASB95*

Who is willing to repent fully and die today for our deliverance? Make it known to the Lord.
There is no greater love than this. Submit to the Lord!

> "He was led as a sheep to slaughter;
> and as a lamb before its shearer is silent, so he does not open his mouth. *Acts 8:32 NASB95*

> Sitting down, He called the twelve and said to them, "If anyone wants to be first, he shall be last of all and servant of all." *Mark 9:35 NASB95*

> - "I am the good shepherd, and
> I know My own and My own know Me, *John 10:14 NASB95*

> - "When he puts forth all his own,
> **he goes ahead of them,**
> and the sheep follow him
> because they know his voice. *John 10:4 NASB95*

Laying down our crown can more easily be understood on Our Lord's proclamations, telling us very clearly that there is ONE Teacher, ONE Rabbi, ONE Father, ONE Leader, which is Christ and Our Father in heaven who are ONE.
What person on earth, knows it all and thinks they can come against the Word of the Lord? Or perhaps they think we should not believe that a book or that the Lord himself can teach us, can you believe it

Wow!! the WORD became flesh!!!
Our Exalted WORD of God lives!!!
The Holy Bible is alive!!!
The Living Word enters our minds!

Love and exalt the Holy Bible!!!
Love and exalt the Word of God!!!
Love and exalt the Bread of Life!!! The Living Bread!!!
Love and Exalt the Holy Trinity!!!
Love and exalt Our Teacher, and Leader
which is Christ, the WORD the Sword of the Spirit.

You are like a sprinkler system,
and when you confess with your mouth,
you turn on the mouth of the sprinkler and living waters replace
your darkness. With these living waters, when you speak the
WORD of GOD, it becomes a Sword flowing out of your mouth
piercing the enemy with the Love of God.

The Sword which quenches the fiery darts of the enemy
leaves "**the imprint of Love, the Word of God**"
on the soul to which directed. Deliverance is sweet!

**They will know we are Christians by our love... let us love one
another, unite with one another, and let the Lord do the rest.**

Glory in the Lord together! Jesus I Trust in You!

We must make room in the deepest depth
of our inner-most being; the Inn of our heart, the chambers in
which Our Lord desires
to be loved and to love even the most dreadful sinner.

Make Jesus the King of Your Heart, of your life and of this world.
Love Unto Death!

> - "By this all men will know that you are My disciples, if
> you have love for one another." *John 13:35 NASB95*

> - that they may all be one; even as You, Father,
> are in Me and I in You, that they also may be in Us, so that
> the world may believe that You sent Me. *John 17:21 NASB95*

> **-"Greater love has no one than this,
> that one lay down his life for his friends.**
> *John 15:13 NASB95*

May the Lord truly make us one with Him, one with Jesus, One with all that He Loves and One with each other. Surrender all!!! Deny yourself all!!! Repent in sack clothe and ashes and be ready for the wedding!!!

We must sow as He sows, Be as He is, Love as He Loves! May the Lord Bless you Indeed!

Concluding Prayer:
Dearest Holy Trinity, Father, Jesus and Holy Ghost, I submit myself to You; I resist, rebuke, and renounce Satan and all his works.
I repent, and with a contrite heart, mind and soul and with the greatest love that is within me, I lay down my crown.
Help me Lord, to do Your will and to please You in all Your ways, in Your truth and in Your loving light. Make me Lord, to do what I must to become the lowest, be my everlasting loving King.
I embrace all my brothers and sisters in Christ, with Your love and as ONE with all of our hearts mind and soul I ask You to claim our souls as Yours alone and accept the crowns we lay before You. I return to God, His throne, all my love and all that I am.
I confess by my Holy Temple
and by the Holy Spirit within me,
By Heaven, by the Throne of God
By Him who sits on it, Our Father
That Jesus is King and He is My Lord, My Master
Jesus is one with the Father, one with My Holy Spirit
to Him I submit and in Him, I desire to live move and have my being. I surrender to His Divine Will. In the Name of Jesus I stand firm to the Profession of My Faith.

BLESSED IS HE WHO COMES IN THE NAME OF THE LORD!
HOLY! HOLY! HOLY! YOU ARE LORD GOD,
KING OF ALL CREATION! I LOVE YOU! I LOVE YOU!
I LOVE YOU LOVE EVERLASTING WITH EVERLASTING LOVE!

This scripture has been added for your reference:
- "But do not be called Rabbi;
for **One is your Teacher,** and you are all brothers.
"Do not call anyone on earth your father;
for **One is your Father,** He who is in heaven.
"Do not be called leaders;
for **One is your Leader, that is, Christ.**
"But the greatest among you shall be your servant.
"Whoever exalts himself shall be humbled; and whoever humbles himself shall be exalted.
"But woe to you, scribes and Pharisees, hypocrites, because you shut off the kingdom of heaven from people; for you do not enter in yourselves, nor do you allow those who are entering to go in.
"Woe to you, scribes and Pharisees, hypocrites, because you devour widows' houses, and for a pretense you make long prayers; therefore you will receive greater condemnation. "Woe to you, scribes and Pharisees, hypocrites, because you travel around on sea and land to make one proselyte; and when he becomes one, you make him twice as much a son of hell as yourselves.
"Woe to you, blind guides, who say, 'Whoever swears by the temple, that is nothing; but whoever swears by the gold of the temple is obligated.'
"You fools and blind men! Which is more important, the gold or the temple that sanctified the gold?
"And, 'Whoever swears by the altar, that is nothing, but whoever swears by the offering on it, he is obligated.' "You blind men, which is more important, the offering, or the altar that sanctifies the offering?
"Therefore, whoever swears by the altar, swears both by the altar and by everything on it.
"And whoever swears by the temple, swears both by the temple and by Him who dwells within it.
"And whoever swears by heaven, swears both by the throne of God and by Him who sits upon it.
Matthew 23:8-22 NASB95

WHAT *EXACTLY DOES "I AM THE WAY" MEAN?*

Mary said it all with these few words:
> – "His mother said to the servants, **"Whatever He says to you, do it."** *John 2:5 NASB95*

Jesus is the Way!
> - Jesus said to him, "**I am the way**, and the truth, and the life; no one comes to the Father but through Me. *John 14:6 NASB95*

Our Lord is truly a God of Simplicity. Just recently, the Lord showed me a simple explanation for "THE WAY". He is the Way! But what does that mean?

Have you ever heard anyone tell you "I am going to show you how to do this?" You try to do that and you do it wrong. Their next remark is to do it again saying: "Look this is **the way** you do it" or perhaps they say "Do it this **way**".

Jesus clearly stated I am the good Shepherd, my sheep know me, My sheep follow me, My sheep hear my voice.

As a child, did you ever play the game "follow the leader" and if you messed up you were out of the game. Well, this is no game!!! We must follow our leader, Jesus! He is the Way!

> - Remember those who led you, who spoke the word of God to you; and considering the result of their conduct, **imitate their faith.** *Heb 13:7 NASB95*

> - Beloved, do not **imitate** what is evil, but **what is good. The one who does good is of God**; the one who does evil has not seen God. *3John 1:11 NASB95*

We must follow Jesus. We must deny ourselves all things. We must take up our cross. **We must do as He does. Love as He Loves. We must be willing to die for the salvation of all whom Our Lord desires, both the quick and the dead (spiritually or physically).**

Jesus is the Way. Jesus is Our Perfect Leader. Jesus is Our Perfect Teacher. Jesus is Our Perfect Master. He is Our Perfect Love. We must desire to mimic Him in all things. We must desire to be perfect as our Father is perfect. We must know true love, Love unto death. There is no greater love than to die for a friend.

They will know we are Christians by our love.

If Jesus called Mary Mother, be assured, I will do as my Sheppard does, hoping she will accept me also has her child. He loves her still, and so will I love her!

WHAT DOES THE LORD MEAN WHEN HE SAYS "I AM THE TRUTH"?

To live in Jesus, you must desire to be like Him. He is the truth. If you want to live in the truth, you must not lie!!!

Do not break the Ten Commandments! It is the devil using your tongue that makes you to lie!!! Choose your master!!! There is no such thing as a 'little lie". Desire truth!

> - And the tongue is a fire, **the very world of iniquity**; the tongue is set among our members as that which defiles the entire body, and sets on fire the course of our life, and **is set on fire by hell**. *James 3:6 NASB95*
>
> - "But the things that proceed out of the mouth **come from the heart,** and those defile the man. *Mat 15:18 NASB95*
>
> - "But I tell you that every careless word that people speak, they shall give an accounting for it in the day of judgment. *Mat 12:36 NASB95*
>
> - The one who says, "I have come to know Him," and does not keep His commandments, is a liar, and the truth is not in him; *1John 2:4 NASB95*
>
> - For the Law was given through Moses; grace and truth were realized through Jesus Christ. *John 1:17 NASB95*
>
> -"But he who **practices the truth** comes to the Light, so that his deeds may be manifested as having been wrought in God." *John 3:21 NASB95*
>
> - and you will know the truth, and the truth will make you free." *John 8:32 NASB95*

- "God is spirit, and those who worship Him must worship in spirit and truth." *John 4:24* NASB95

- Therefore, laying aside falsehood, SPEAK TRUTH EACH ONE of you WITH HIS NEIGHBOR, for we are members of one another. *Ephesians 4:25* NASB95

- Jesus said to him, "I am the way, and the truth, and the life; no one comes to the Father but through Me. *John 14:6* NASB95

- Since you **have in obedience to the truth** purified your souls for a sincere love of the brethren,
fervently love one another from the heart,
1Peter 1:22 NASB95

When you are filled with grace, you do not lie. Those who are born of God do not lie, and the evil one cannot touch him. They have the love of God in them and they love each other as God loves them.

The Lord also says that we must live by faith and not by sight. What is it that we see that we should not believe? **Everything?**

- The faith which you have, have as your own conviction before God. Happy is he who does not condemn himself in what he approves. *Ro 14:22* NASB95

- But he who doubts is condemned if he eats, because his eating is not from faith; and **whatever is not from faith is sin.** *Ro 14:23* NASB95

What lies has Satan put in our path, into our minds, into our hearts? From what truth have we departed? Are we living in a dream of torment and sorrow? When the Lord allowed Lazareth to arise He told the apostles that he was asleep. Is our spirit sleeping?

What slumber keeps me from my love? Are we living an illusion in Satan's dessert? Are we living a lie in a non existent world?

If I was before time,
and time did not exist
and if in the presence of My Lord
time is still
in whom time is endless,
then Lord allow me to enter into Your time
that we may be one.
And if time and distance meet
for there is neither distance
nor time in Your very presence Lord,
then Lord,
surely Only Love awaits me,
an ever present Love that conquers all barriers
a fullness of life beyond comprehension.
A unity profound,
now found, ever present,
always there,
take me Lord into Everlasting Love.
Awaken me My Love from my slumber!
Help me to come to the Light Lord!
There is only ONE TRUTH - Jesus!

If I live by faith and not by sight,
then I hope that by faith I am living in the
House of the Lord in Everlasting Love.
Where forgiveness is, where compassion is,
where love is, where divine mercy is,
where gentleness is, where all good things dwell,
where time and distance do not exit,
but only unfathomable love.

The only existence I desire to know is that of my Great God, the Great I AM, My Heavenly family and that which is True. I believe!

Jesus in the desert said "no" to everything.
Moses climbed the mountain to leave the desert at which time the Ten Commandments were given to him. The people were still saying yes to the devil, sinning and keeping to their evil ways.

Jesus came and said that if we love Him obey the Commandments. Perhaps Jesus came to Shepherd us even in this. Must we deny ourselves everything?
DESIRE to please the Lord!
DESIRE to Love Him! DESIRE TRUTH!
Desire to walk on that narrow road!

Perhaps we must live our faith in vision so that it may manifest. Would these be the intent of our hearts in His Loving and Longing Heart?

- The vision of the Enthronement of Our Lord on earth
- The Crowning of Our Lord as King of Heaven and earth
- A new Jerusalem
- The vision of our return to God.
- The vision of Truth
- The vision of living with Our Holy Family
- The vision of peace on earth and goodwill to men
- The vision of Divine Mercy in each of our hearts, minds and souls
- The vision of the most joyous annunciation from Angel Gabriel to Mary, and the vision of our returning to the Lord those glorious words of annunciation to the heavens, that we also may be true sons of God and being born as a child of God in Our Fathers presence
- The vision of Love beyond our understanding in our hearts, in our minds, in our souls with all our strength
- The vision of the embrace of consuming love
- The vision of our union with the Lord and becoming ONE with Him
- The vision of the celebration of the heavens and all the angels and saints
- The vision of being dressed in white garments of which the Lord speaks
- The vision of the wedding and the invitation accepted by all who are invited

Glory and Praise to Him who desires all good things for His children.

Come Lord Jesus let me live my faith in you, through you and with you.
Heal us and make us yours;
heal our world and make it to adore you,
Come, we enthrone You, receive your Crown,
I give it to you with my life.
Reign Oh Heavenly Loving King! I love You!

- Oh, give ear, Shepherd of Israel,
You who lead Joseph like a flock;
You who are enthroned above the cherubim,
shine forth! *Ps 80:1 NASB95*

- "O LORD of hosts, the God of Israel,
who is enthroned above the cherubim,
You are the God, You alone,
of all the kingdoms of the earth.
You have made heaven and earth. *Isa 37:16 NASB95*

- Hezekiah prayed before the LORD and said,
"O LORD, the God of Israel,
who are enthroned above the cherubim,
You are the God, You alone,
of all the kingdoms of the earth.
You have made heaven and earth. *2Ki 19:15 NASB95*

On March 8th, 2007 the Lord led me to read the following from Volume I of the Mystical City of God page 38. This reading is profound I hope in leading to the awakening of my slumber.

- "Seeking to fly after the odor of the ointments of its Beloved it *(the soul)* begins to live more where it loves than where it lives"

- As for me, I shall behold Your face in righteousness; I will be satisfied with Your likeness when I awake.
Ps 17:15 NASB95

As for me,

I will seek more and more

to live where my love is,

than where I live.

I will love those least lovable,

I will embrace every humiliation;

I will love unto love everlasting…

Gloria

WHO IS THE SERVANT OF MONEY?
CHOOSE YOUR MASTER!
(Revelation 11/29/06)

> - *"No one can serve two masters; for either he will hate the one and love the other, or he will be devoted to one and despise the other. You cannot serve God and wealth. Matthew 6:24 NASB95*

IMPORTANT NOTE: Before this topic is addressed I must urge you not to judge, especially the religious. The Lord's plan is perfect; this is an awakening the Lord desires so that we may come to him. Give freely your contributions and donations to help others and the religious, especially those most in need. The transformation is not ours alone, but the earth as well. We must offer all giving's to the Lord with Love and to others as if they themselves are the Lord. Not judging, but giving freely what the Lord has given us. May the Lord give us the grace to abandon all and unite to Him.

WHO IS THE SERVANT OF MONEY?
HOW ARE WE A SERVANT TO MONEY?
WHO WANTS THE KINGDOM OF GOD?

> - *"Do not acquire gold, or silver, or copper for your money belts, Mat 10:9 NASB95*

> - *and He instructed them that they should take nothing for their journey, except a mere staff--no bread, no bag, no money in their belt Mark 6:8 NASB95*

> - *For men will be lovers of self, lovers of money, boastful, arrogant, revilers, disobedient to parents, ungrateful, unholy 2Ti3:2 NASB95*

Do we truly desire to please the Lord and be His servant alone? He says to choose our master!
Do we want to inherit the kingdom of heaven?

If we believe that we do not serve money, because we think we do not love it, then, are we a servant of it unknowingly? How do we serve money? Is money the master of the earth? Do we rely on it or think we need money for essentials?

When we go to a restaurant the waiter brings our food and drink and sets it before us, serving us. Sometimes, the waiter will give us a candy or a drink afterwards and put it in our hand. The waiter is serving us.

We in turn for their service, put into their hand money to pay for our food and tip for the service. So are we serving money to them? When we put it on their book fold wallet are we serving them, not on a platter but on what accommodates money? Perhaps the god of money likes to be in a book fold wallet, clinched shut for the eyes of the beholder… the waiter, hoping for it to be a big tip.

Desiring more money!

> *- For the love of money is a root of all sorts of evil, and* ***SOME BY LONGING FOR IT*** *have wandered away from the faith and pierced themselves with many griefs.*
> <u>1Ti 6:10</u> <u>NASB95</u>

The Lord said there is not one righteous. He said no one seeks Him
   - as it is written,
"THERE IS NONE RIGHTEOUS, NOT EVEN ONE;
There Is None Who Understands, **There Is**
NONE WHO SEEKS FOR GOD; <u>Romans 3:10-11</u> <u>NASB95</u>

Teach us Lord to seek you! In this day and time, could that still be true? For if we serve money simply by exchanging hands for services rendered or items purchased, then IS IT our sin? We work for it! We buy with it! We even pray for it! In this world in the mind of men, there is nothing you can do without it.
Even religious/preachers beg for it thinking this charity is what the Lord refers to. They spend it on themselves for worldly needs including for food out of need, as we do. Money is an essential factor in the minds of ALL men.

But what does the Lord mean …
we cannot serve both!

> *- "Sell your possessions and give to charity; make yourselves money belts which do not wear out, an unfailing treasure in heaven, where no thief comes near nor moth destroys.* <u>Luke 12:33</u> <u>NASB95</u>

What faith is required of us?

> - And He said to them, "When I sent you out without money belt and bag and sandals, you did not lack anything, did you?" They said, "No, nothing." <u>Luke 22:35</u> <u>NASB95</u>

> - Make sure that your character is free from the love of money, being content with what you have; for He Himself has said, "I WILL NEVER DESERT YOU, NOR WILL I EVER FORSAKE YOU," <u>Heb 13:5</u> <u>NASB95</u>

What Faith IS required of us?

What profound love and charity is our Lord made of that He desires for us to be like Him?
Do we think that this form of giving/charity is for religious/preachers only?
Is the Lord requiring it of every person?
Who knowing the Lord, would deny Him anything?
Who would give their life and their riches?
So what is money, and why do we value it?
Is serving money giving value to it?
What value do we give to the Lord?

The Lord says you cannot serve Him and money! Various times in the Bible the Lord showed us the worthlessness of money. When the thousands were with him the miracle of the fish and bread multiplied so that all were fed. Money was mentioned but was not needed. The Lord provided. In another instance a man offered the apostle money for his miracles, it was an insult and not accepted. They told him that his heart was not right with God. He was in the gall of bitterness and in the bondage of iniquity. They said Repent and Pray that the Lord IF POSSIBLE will forgive the intention of your heart.

> *- Now when Simon saw that the Spirit was bestowed through the laying on of the apostles' hands, he offered them money, saying, "Give this authority to me as well, so that everyone on whom I lay my hands may receive the Holy Spirit." But Peter said to him, "May your silver perish with you, because **you thought** you could obtain the gift of God with money! Acts 8:18-20 NASB95*

So what exactly is going on today?
Has anything changed?
Is our use of money a hidden way of serving it?
We think we do not serve it, **but do we?**
What is the intention of our hearts?

> Much has been hidden from us! All I can say is "Lord forgive us, increase our desire of you, for you and in you! Help us to seek you and to find you. I pray that the Lord will give to me the courage, faith and trust to do all that is necessary to inherit the kingdom of God, with Jesus and our heavenly family. I will pray that the Lord will grant all of us the faith, boldness and zeal to reach perfection."

> *- ... He spoke with them and said to them,*
> **"Take courage; it is I, do not be afraid."** *Mark 6:50 NASB95*

I hope that I will obtain the necessary faith to live in God's favor and in the faith He desires of us.

Help me Lord, Abba Father! You are my only hope!

The following scripture is the answer to the above, may we come to live in His Word, in His Light and in His Love:

> *- Be anxious for nothing,*
> ***but in everything by prayer***
> ***and supplication with thanksgiving***
> *let your requests be made known to God. Php 4:6 NASB95*

A friend who has quit their job to serve the Lord said that they write down seven things every day of things they are thankful for. They said it keeps them from being anxious. May the Lord Bless you Indeed! … Gloria

CHOOSE YOUR MASTER!

- … and whatever is not from faith is sin. <u>Ro 14:23</u> BBE

Could it be that no money nor bartering is required? Is all that is required simply an exchange of true love, prayer and devotion to Our Lord so that all will manifest by Our God, our provider who knows our every need, with whom we also must desire to be ONE. Would converting to this kind of faith be the time that He himself will deliver us and redeem us in the great deliverance, the great rapture as some say? Would this be the death of all other gods, including money and mammon? With this kind of faith, will they be nothing and powerless, because Our God truly will reign? Our faith in Everlasting Love truly manifested! Glory to God on High!
Reveal yourself to us I pray, Abba Father! Make us to please You!

> *- Here is the patience of the saints:*
> *here are they that keep the commandments of God, and the*
> *faith of Jesus.* <u>Revelation 14.12</u> KJV

> *- in whom we have boldness and*
> *confident access through faith in Him.* <u>Ephesians 3:12</u> KJV

> *- Jesus is the author and finisher of our faith* <u>Hebrews 12.2</u> KJV

It seems that we are all servants of money simply by dealing with it. Is this then the **NO MONEY CONCEPT of FAITH?**

"What kind of Faith is required of us?" It seems very clear to me. May we learn to live the faith of our fathers before us, in Jesus, Mary, Joseph and all the great saints!

WHO IS LIKE OUR FATHERS OF GREAT FAITH?

CHANT ART

Elijah was taken up to heaven, who like Moses entered into that place of faith where evidence is unseen, the substance of things hoped for is manifested

or the Faith of Jesus, who commands the seas and the winds, walks on water and saves and so according to scripture:

> Looking unto Jesus the author and finisher of our faith; who for the joy that was set before him endured the cross, despising the shame, and is set down at the right hand of the throne of God. *(Hebrews 12:2)KJV*

WHO IS LIKE OUR FATHERS OF GREAT FAITH?

Persevere in faith and always pray without ceasing. Faith will be of utmost importance when the Son of man comes. In times of adversity, what would you do? If the day came when you would see things you have never seen before, ugly and frightful, you would be forced to believe in fright. What would you do then, you who do not seek to be holy? How firm can you stand in the absence of the love of God? You will not stand, you will perish. It is in that moment that no matter what you see, you must keep your eyes on Jesus and in the great love of Our Lord. He is the conqueror of the devil, the devil's armies and his evil ways. Love conquerors all!

> *-And he spoke also a parable to them,*
> *that **we ought always to pray and not to faint**,*
> *Saying: There was a judge in a certain city, who feared not God nor regarded man. And there was a certain widow in that city; and she came to him, saying: Avenge me of my adversary. And he would not for a long time. But afterwards he said within himself: Although I fear not God nor regard man, Yet because this widow is troublesome to me, I will avenge her, lest continually coming she weary me. And the Lord said: Hear what the unjust judge saith. **And will not God revenge his elect who cry to him day and night?** And will he have patience in their regard? I say to you that he will quickly revenge them. **But yet the Son of man, when he cometh, shall he find, think you, faith on earth?***
> <u>Luke 18:1-8</u> DRA

You have seen many movies of spiritual warfare or of evil fear. The movies of exorcism have been fabricated. What fear have you of the devil? The devil wants you to be afraid of the devil. Do you know that the devil cannot drive out the devil! Satan flashed out of Heaven like lightening when the Lord cast him out. Satan is all show, he is weak and powerless. The only power he has is that which you give to him. Ignorance is Satan's strength.

Speak the Word, love, repent and pray, let living waters inhabit your very being. In regard to faith, did you know that just as the sea parted for Moses, the Jordan dried up for Joshua? The Jordan was full of water, Joshua and the people took the first step into that water and it dried up. They took the first step of faith.

> *- And do thou command the priests, that carry the Ark of the Covenant, and say to them: When you shall have entered into part of the water of the Jordan, stand in it. Joshua 3:8 DRA*

So, what kind of faith did our fathers before us have? I was so impressed with the scripture in 1 Maccabees 3:17-22. This scripture makes me believe that it applies even in the faith of not serving money – (the NO money faith concept, yes, zero money). (Read also "How do we stop war?")

VICTORY AT WAR

> - Then Asa called to the LORD his God and said, "LORD, there is no one besides You to help in the battle between the powerful and those who have no strength; so help us, O LORD our God, for we trust in You, and in Your name have come against this multitude. O LORD, You are our God; let not man prevail against You." 2Ch 14:11 NASB95
> - But when they saw the army coming against them, they said to Judas: "How can we, few as we are, fight such a mighty host as this? Besides we are weak today from fasting." But Judas said: "It is easy for many to be overcome by few;
> **IN THE SIGHT OF HEAVEN**
> **THERE IS NO DIFFERENCE**
> **BETWEEN DELIVERANCE BY MANY OF BY FEW,**
> *for victory in war does not depend upon the size of the army,*
> **BUT ON THE STRENGTH THAT COMES FROM HEAVEN"** *1 Maccabees 3:17-22 CPDV*

WOW!!! is that powerful!!!!! So what faith is required of us?

How do we obtain it? Perhaps, we need to pray for the grace to have the faith of Moses/ Elijah/ Elisha/ Elizabeth/ Ester/ Mary/ Joseph, and in Jesus and the love that they also had for the Lord with which they fervently cried out to Him.

MOSES: - **the Faith of Moses** going up the mountain, to enter into that place of faith where evidence is unseen and where the substance of things hoped for is present
Perhaps we should request the faith of Moses in the desert, hoping that the Lord will hear us and feed us manna from Heaven where no money is needed. A desperate faith and cry to the Lord when there is no other resolve. Hope with a confidence that Our Father will hear us and answer. As Moses made the plea when the slaves were set free from Pharaoh's bondage – but Lord what will they eat, what will they drink? In the Love of Moses for Our Lord and in His obedience we seek to find the answer.

ELIJAH: -Or perhaps that **of Elijah** who was taken up to heaven, who like Moses entered into that place of faith where evidence is unseen, the substance of things hoped for is manifested

> *- The sons of the prophets who were at Jericho approached Elisha and said to him, "Do you know that the LORD will take away your master from over you today?" And he answered, "Yes, I know; be still." 2Ki 2:5 NASB95*

> *- When they had crossed over, Elijah said to Elisha, "Ask what I shall do for you before I am taken from you." And Elisha said,* **"Please, let a double portion of your spirit be upon me."** *2Ki 2:9 NASB95*

> *- Elisha saw it and cried out, "My father, my father, the chariots of Israel and its horsemen!" And he saw Elijah no more. Then he took hold of his own clothes and tore them in two pieces. 2Ki 2:12 NASB95*

> *- He took the mantle of Elijah that fell from him and struck the waters and said, "Where is the LORD, the God of Elijah?" And when he also had struck the waters, they were divided here and there; and Elisha crossed over. Now when*

the sons of the prophets who were at Jericho opposite him saw him, they said, "The spirit of Elijah rests on Elisha." And they came to meet him and bowed themselves to the ground before him. 2Ki 2:14-15 NASB95

ELISHA: -Or perhaps the faith **of Elisha** whom we should also ask for a double portion of Elisha's spirit which would be four times that of Elijah. Surely, they were possessed by the Lord! It was His Spirit!
-The faith of Elisha whose prayers gave a woman and her son food to eat throughout the drought. A woman who gave her last serving of food **accepting death giving life to another with all she had left**

ELIZABETH: -Or perhaps, that **of Elizabeth** mother of John the Baptist, who fled to the mountains when Herod was searching for John to kill the baby. Elizabeth an old woman could not climb at her age, she could not find a secrete place to hide him. She groaned within herself and said "O Mountain of the Lord, receive the mother with her child." Instantly, the mountain opened up and received them. Then there appeared to them an angel of the Lord to preserve them. *(taken from The Lost Books Of The Bible – The PROTEVANGELION, page 35)* Why would she say "the mother with her child?" Surely because she was speaking in the Spirit, possessed by the Lord as did Jesus calling Mary "woman" at the wedding of Cana. In the gospels we are told that the minute Mary spoke Elizabeth was spirit filled.

ESTER: -Or the **faith of ESTER**, pleading for the life of her people, the Jews. **Risking her life for theirs**, taking a step of faith that could lead to her physical death.

MARY: - Or perhaps the **faith of Mary**, who believed the angel and whose obedience and faithful response to the Lord changed our world bringing forth Our Messiah. Whose pregnancy appeared by faith in glory and not by sight as someone in the flesh might have perceived it. Mary, who was full of grace and great faith, trusted Our Lord unconditionally and replied so beautifully to Joseph who was so worried on their way Bethlehem:

"Oh! What is our small trouble if we consider the beauty of this moment of peace? Just think Joseph a period of time when there is no hatred in the world!
Can there be a happier hour for the rising of the "Star", the light of which is divine and its influence is redemption? Oh! Do not be afraid Joseph. If the roads are not safe, if the crowds will make the journey a difficult one, the angels will defend and protect us. Not us: but their King. If we find no accommodation, their wings will be our tents. No mishap will befall us. It cannot. God is with us. *(in her womb)* Joseph looks at her and listens to Her, happy. The wrinkles on his forehead smooth away. He got up, no longer tired or worried. He smiles. "You are blessed, Sun of my soul! You are blessed, because you see everything through the Grace, of which You are full! *(Taken from The Poem of The Man- God by Maria Valtorta Vol 1 pg 132)*

JOSEPH: Guardian of Our Fathers most beloved Son and Mary, most blessed. Joseph who was given the responsibility to take care of God Himself in the flesh and His mother who was the bond to the Blood of the New Covenant. Mary, is the woman with whom God chose to commingle His blood. The woman most blessed and God the child in His care. What can a man/father of the flesh do for God all knowing even as a child? Joseph was humble, obedient, lived by faith and submitted to His holy will. Contemplating the life of the Holy Family proves that God covered all aspects of our trials and tribulations of which we are to learn and grow to perfection.

How many times did Joseph have to start up in taking care of Mary with the little he had – once in Bethlehem and again in Egypt and again when he returned to the holy land.

CENTURION: The Centurion came to Jesus imploring to heal his servant. Jesus said that He would go to Him.

- But the centurion said, "Lord, I am not worthy for You to come under my roof, but just say the word, and my servant will be healed. "For I also am a man under authority, with soldiers under me; and I say to this one, 'Go!' and he goes, and to another, 'Come!' and he comes, and to my slave, 'Do this!' and he does it." *Mat 8:8-9* NASB95

- Now when Jesus heard this, He marveled and said to those who were following, "Truly I say to you, **I have not found such great faith with anyone** in Israel. *Mat 8:10 NASB95*
The Lord said to the Centurion that he had a greater faith.

Do you think that faith is in simply stating the Word of God? Yes I do believe that, but why was his greater? Perhaps, the Centurion saw beyond the flesh. Perhaps, he referred to the armies of the Lord at Our Lords' command. His armies are one with the Spirit of the Lord as we hope also to be.

JESUS: All these are simply synonymous in the faith of Jesus, whose faith above all is perfect with the Father and Holy Spirit. Who in the New Testament teaches love, faith and hope and of His omnipotent power and glory.

And so, let us pray that the Lord will gift to us perfect faith, perfect love, perfect charity and perfect hope. Let us pray that we will attain that level of perfection in which Our Lord desires for us to attain. He said "Be Perfect as my Father is perfect."

Is that the ultimate perfection we should desire? Yes, of course! And with boldness and confidence we do have access through faith in Him. Manifestation comes more clearly when we are no longer of ourselves, but it is He in whom we live move and have our being, and whose every word will flow from our mouth, and every move will be His and we are no longer of ourselves but rather walking in the Spirit, thinking in the Spirit, loving in the Spirit unto death and desiring nothing else.

As Elizabeth spoke to the mountain "receive the woman and the child", it was the Spirit moving her that spoke, no longer recognizing the flesh or any part thereof. We become Spirit and the flesh through mortification is confined!

Glory to God in the Highest of Heavens and of earth! Blessed is He! Oh Lord, what will it take for me to leave this world and enter into yours like those graced with your great faith? Help me Lord to find the way! I beseech you to allow me to obtain the grace beyond grace to be with you throughout eternity in a love which my heart cries out for with desperation and great desire. Oh Lord help me.

I know we must be willing to surrender all, to give all and be left with nothing for the benefit of others. We must be willing to take that first step of faith, trusting in the Lord, trusting in Jesus no matter what the consequences. Give them your cloak and your tunic as well. Give them your last piece of bread. Give them your last drink of water. Give without hesitation even unto death. Jesus I Trust in You!

WHO IS THE THIEF?

Is it he who took the cloak? Or is it he who denies him? Jesus said "if he takes your cloak do not stop him from taking your tunic/cloak also. Give to everyone who asks you, and if anyone takes what belongs to you do not demand it back". "As you judge you are judged." In calling him a thief, is it you who is the thief? Is it you who has kept from those in need? Is it you who does not give your first fruits to the Lord? Are you so ignorant to think that what you have is yours? Don't you know that nothing is yours! Surely you realize that you cannot take it with you when you die. Why will you allow yourself to suffer in selfishness, greed, and love of earthly treasures? Surely all these things will cause you to suffer much, unless you repent! Detach yourself from the things of the earth and give freely.

> -To him that smiteth thee on the [one] cheek offer also the other; and from him that taketh away thy cloak withhold not thy coat also. *Luke 6:29 ASV*

Both were wrong: one to steal and one to be greedy. Give freely and with love!

> **Be merciful, just as your Father is merciful."**
> *Luke 6:36 NASB95*

WHO IS THE MURDERER?

Remember! The Lord came not to condemn but to save! Change your ways!!! These are questions to consider. Repent and Be Ready – Jesus is coming!

Who is the murderer?
- Is it he who kills the flesh? The dead burying the dead?

- Or is it the living who deny the dead life? Is it those who deny the Bread of Life to those in darkness?

- Is the murderer the murderer of the soul and mind through hate and vengeance? (see 1John 3:15)

- Is it those who lie breaking the Ten Commandments? You whose deceitful ways lead to death? (Read Acts 5:1-9 death to liars)

    You have not lied to men but to God." *Acts 5:4 CPDV*

    Thou shall not bear false witness against thy neighbor. *Exodus 20:9 KJV*

- Or is it those who misunderstand the Word of the Lord, telling one church or another that the other church is a liar?

- Is the murderer a believer of Christ who calls another believer of Christ a heretic or a demon? Do you reap what you sow? Are you the heretic as you speak the words from your own heart? Would you lay your life down for your Christ believing brother?
    Mat 12:36 - "But I tell you that every careless word that people speak, they shall give an accounting for it in the day of judgment. *(NASB95)*
    Mat 15:18 - "But the things that proceed out of the mouth come from the heart, and those defile the man. *(NASB95)*

> *Luke 6:45* -"The good man out of the good treasure of his heart brings forth what is good; and the evil man out of the evil treasure brings forth what is evil; **for his mouth speaks from that which fills his heart.** *(NASB95)*
> *Eph 4:29* - Let no unwholesome word proceed from your mouth, but only such a word **as is good for edification** according to the need of the moment, **so that it will give grace to those who hear.** *(NASB95)*
>
> *1 John 3:15-16* Everyone who hates his brother is a murderer; and you know that no murderer has eternal life abiding in him. We know love by this, that He laid down His life for us; and we ought to lay down our lives for the brethren. *(NASB95)*

- Is it those who throughout time have changed the Bible and its interpretation? Lean not on human understanding!

   > *1John2:27-28* As for you, the anointing which you received from Him abides in you, and **you have no need for anyone to teach you; but as His anointing teaches you about all things, and is true and is not a lie, and just as it has taught you, you abide in Him.** Now, little children, abide in Him, so that when He appears, we may have confidence and not shrink away from Him in shame at His coming *(NASB95)*

- Or is it those who have tried to copyright the Word of God? Who can claim the Word to themselves? Is it for everyone? Yes! Everyone! No one can claim ownership for profit! Do they not fear God?

- Or is the murder those who say to another "You are not qualified to read the Word of God only I can help you"?
   > Knowing this first, that no prophecy of the scripture is of any private interpretation. *2 Peter 1:20 KJV*

- Is it those who rebuke others from the love of Mary Most Holy whom Our Father chose and whom Jesus called Mother? Who is your shepherd?

- Is it those who call themselves apostles and are liars as noted in Rev 2, deceiving people away from the truth? Away from true love?

- Is it those whom the Lord spits Himself out of when they receive Holy Communion unworthily eating and drinking judgment upon themselves? Are they lukewarm?
  Is it a miracle or is it the Lord rejecting them?

- Is the murderer anyone who has killed even the smallest living creature of any form? A bug or even a rose? In the book of Revelations the animals are all living in peace.

Lord, give to me the grace to love Your Word and please allow every word that comes from my mouth to be good for edification so as to give grace to those who hear.

Help me Lord to listen to you and to obey without hesitation, I desire to respond to you immediately at your command.

Please give to me the grace to love my brethren even unto death, forgive my hatred and fill me with your perfect love that I may love you perfectly. I desire the grace to be, as you desire, Perfect as My Father in heaven is Perfect. Make us of the same mind, bond us in the same spirit, and unite us in the same love so that Your joy may be complete. You are our only hope, our redeemer, our loving creator, all Glory, Honor and Power are yours alone Oh Beloved King of True Love. Unite me to yourself and make me to please you In the Name of Jesus I pray.

WHO IS THE LIVING WHO DENIES THE DEAD LIFE?

This too is for the glory of the Lord!
God Reconciled Himself with men at the cross.
Now, men must be reconciled one to another to be reconciled to God. Repent and confess!

Be merciful, just as your Father is merciful." *Luke 6:36 NIV*

Baptism of Repentance Mark1:4; Luke3:3 CPDV
- **Acknowledge your sins** Mark1:5; 1John2:8 CPDV

- Is doubt the murder in each non-believing heart of God's truth as written in His WORD, our very breath of life? The Word is Spirit and it is alive! You do not know it because you have not repented! Repent or perish!
    the words that I have spoken to you
    are spirit and **are life.** *John 6:63 NASB95*

- Is doubt the murder in each non-believing heart of God's true presence in the Bread of Life?

    - I AM THE LIVING BREAD
    which came down from heaven:
    if any man EAT OF THIS BREAD,
    he shall live for ever:
    and **the bread that I will give is my flesh,**
    which I will give for the life of the world. *John 6:51 KJV*

    - " Verily, verily, I say unto you,
    except ye EAT of the flesh of the Son of man,
    and drink his blood,
    YE HAVE NO LIFE IN YOU. *John 6:53 KJV*

Our beloved Bread of Life LIVES!!!

Appearing defenseless yet defending!!

- Is the murderer those who lie about the Bread of Life brought to life by God Himself, saying it is only a symbol?

- Is it those who do not believe in the presence of God in the Bread of life and teach falsely to others?

- Is it those who have restricted children of certain ages from receiving the Bread of Life? Man's rules?

    - So when they had finished breakfast, Jesus said to Simon Peter, "Simon, son of John, do you love Me more than these?"
    He said to Him, "Yes, Lord; You know that I love You." He said to him, "**Tend My lambs**." *John 21:15 NASB95*

    - But Jesus said, "Let the children alone, and do not hinder them from coming to Me; for the kingdom of heaven belongs to such as these." *Matthew 19:14 NASB95*

    - And He was saying to her, "Let the children be satisfied first, for it is not good to take
    the children's bread and throw it to the dogs."
    Mark 7:27 NASB95

- Is the murderer those who deny the Bread of Life to those in darkness? We are not to judge! The Bread of Life must be received with a contrite heart, desperate love and adoration. But who is the judge? Is Christ the Judge? Who are you? How many Pharisees and scribes are here today? Who can love unconditionally?

    - "But woe to you, scribes and Pharisees, hypocrites, because you shut off the kingdom of heaven from people; for you do not enter in yourselves, nor do you allow those who are entering to go in. *Mat 23:13 NASB95*

> \- Then shall ye begin to say, We have eaten and drunk in thy presence,
> and thou hast taught in our streets. But he shall say,
> **I tell you, I know you not** *Luke 13:26-27 KJV*
>
> \- "Woe to you, scribes and Pharisees, hypocrites! For you clean the outside of the cup and of the dish, but inside they are full of robbery and self-indulgence. *Mat 23:25 NASB95*

- Is the murderer those of flesh who think that they need to control and protect the Bread of Life? or is it the Bread of Life that controls us?

- Is it those who doubt the "cleansing power of life" in the Bread of Life, God Himself?

- Can the Living Bread save us? What can God not do in a piece of bread that seems motionless?

> \- "Truly, truly, I say to you, **you seek Me**, not because you saw signs, **but because you ate of the loaves and were filled.** *John 6:26 NASB95*

> Ye people of little faith!
> He can do anything and everything!
> He saves and gives life! God in us will lead us, teach us, transform us and do as He desires. He is alive and well…
> **but WILL HE RECEIVE US**? Do we desire it? Do we desire to love Him above all else? Do we desire to turn from our evil ways? Do we desire to please the Lord! We must Trust Him, acknowledge Him and learn from Him!

- Is it those who think that they alone possess the true bread of life, the only bread that lives? What person can posses God alone, is that possible? I say no, what say you?
  How long has man tried to keep God to or for themselves?

- Or is God the God of Jews only?
Is He not the God of Gentiles also?
Yes, of Gentiles also, _Romans 3:29 NASB95_

- Is it those of you priests and religious who will not be reconciled with your brother because you think your way is right? Why do you not break bread with your brethren? Are you too good to take of their bread? Is that pride?

Are these **differences of the flesh?**
Brothers, what would the Lord say or do because you do not break bread with each other?

He says to love one another as I love you!

He says that those who believe in Him are FOR HIM!

I believe He would say,
leave your gifts at the altar and
go then to be reconciled one to another.
Not one is less guilty than another. Be NOT PROUD!

Men bickering – is the time of the Lord here?
Is it time to Love without bickering?
The Lord did not defend Himself in the courts.
You who think you are Christ like – are you really?
Who do you bicker for?
Think Love! Love with incorruptible love!
No matter what is said and done, be as Christ loving, compassionate, silent and humble.
Preach Love! Preach Repentance! Be Merciful!
Gain the virtue of humility through humiliation in the love of God.
The power is in the cross of Christ and His passionate love.

- "Again, the kingdom of heaven is like a dragnet cast into the sea, and gathering fish of every kind; _Mat 13:47 NASB95_

- No one should seek his own advantage, but that of his neighbor _1Cor 10:24 NASB_

- Day by day continuing
with **one mind** in the temple,
and **breaking bread from house to house**,
they were taking their meals **together with gladness
and sincerity of heart**,
praising God and having favor with **all** the people.
And **the Lord was adding to their number day by day
those who were being saved.** *Acts 2:46-47* NASB

- by abolishing in His flesh the enmity,
**which is the Law of commandments contained in
ordinances,** so that in Himself He might make
**the two into one new man,
thus establishing peace,** *Eph 2:15* NASB95

- Grace be with all those who love our Lord Jesus Christ
with incorruptible love. *Eph 6:24* NASB95

- Beyond all these things put on love,
which is the **perfect bond of unity.** *Col 3:14* NASB95

- Is not the cup of blessing which we bless
a sharing in the blood of Christ?
Is not the bread which we break
a sharing in the body of Christ? *1Cor 10:16* NASB95

- Since there is one bread,
we who are many are one body;
for we all partake of the one bread. *1Cor 10:17* NASB95

- "For this reason the kingdom of heaven may be compared to
a king who wished to settle accounts with his slaves.
Mat 18:23 NASB95

Would this be the moment that we would truly return to God in love? There is no division of the bread,
only the division of the minds, and of the flesh... we will be of one mind, one spirit, one God,

we are One Body in Christ!
Receive the ONE true bread of life, the living bread!
Break bread together and in love with a contrite heart,
forgiving unconditionally even unto death.
Surely, you are condemned if you condemn!
You are Judged as you judge!
Love one another as I love you, says the Lord.
Jesus said:

> - "Truly, truly, I say to you, **you seek Me**, not because you saw signs, **but because you ate of the loaves and were filled.** *John 6:26 NASB95*
>
> Jesus said: IF ANY MAN…
> - "If **ANY** man eat of this bread, he shall live forever, and the bread that I will give is my flesh, which I will give for the life of the world" *John 6:51 KJV*
>
> - "He who believes in the Son has eternal life; but **he who does not obey the Son will not see life**, but the wrath of God abides on him." *John 3:36 NASB95*

We must repent! We must confess! We must love one another! It is difficult to obey when living in darkness.

You who call yourselves Christians COME BACK to the Catholic Church! The ONE TRUE CHURCH!

Oh Heavenly Father, lead your people to the light, then keep them in your light, that all will know your love, that we may all obtain life in heaven with You. Make us Lord to do your will. Let it be done to us according to Your word. Teach us Lord your way, your truth and show us how to live a holy life in you, with you and through you. Make us to eat of the one true bread and to break bread together in love, that you may be pleased in all of us.

- Then the seventh angel sounded; and there were loud voices in heaven, saying,
"The kingdom of the world has become the kingdom of our Lord and of His Christ;
and He will reign forever and ever."
Rev 11:15 NASB95

- Then I heard a loud voice in heaven, saying,
"Now the salvation, and the power,
and the kingdom of our God
and the authority of His Christ have come,
for the accuser of our brethren has been thrown down, he who accuses them before our God day and night.
Rev 12:10 NASB95

WHO IS THE WORKER OF INEQUITY?

The Lord says to weep for yourselves, remove the splinters and plank from your own being then you can help your brethren.

It is really scary for me to even consider the thought that we are all demon possessed until we become Light; until we become a lamp stand; until the Lord himself possesses us; until we are free of all demons; until that time when no evil can touch us and we sin no more.

Fear of the devil is an epidemic, the devil wants you to be afraid of the devil… Pride, resentments, hatred, anger, malice, wrath, judgments, condemnations, selfishness, vain glory, greed, gluttony, adulterers, fornicators, liars, masturbators, blasphemy, abusers, filthy communication out of your mouth, are all governed by demons, there are many members in one body. Who moves you? Who is your master? It is that simple!!

Do not be afraid – the enemy is afraid of Our Holy Family, our victory is in Jesus. "Pray for perfect love, make the Love of God, Our Father and Jesus your passion, love them back passionately"

Seek the Lord, and ask Him to teach you and help you to be open to His truth. Search high and low. Ask Our Holy Spirit to help you to discern.

- But Peter and the apostles answered, "We must obey God rather than men. *Ac 5:29* NASB95

By lovingkindness and truth
iniquity is atoned for, and by
the fear of the LORD one keeps away from evil.
Pr 16:6 NASB95

WHO IS YOUR FATHER?

Jesus said to call no one father for there is only ONE, that is Our Father in heaven.

Thus says the Lord:
- "Do not call anyone on earth your father; for One is your Father, He who is in heaven. *Matthew 23:9* NASB95
- "If anyone comes to Me, and does not hate his own father and mother and wife and children and brothers and sisters, **yes**, and even his own life, **he cannot be My disciple.** *Luke 14:26* NASB95

Then Peter said to Him, "Behold, we have left everything and followed You; what then will there be for us?" And Jesus said to them, "Truly I say to **you, that you who have followed Me, in the regeneration** when the Son of Man will sit on His glorious throne, you also shall sit upon twelve thrones, judging the twelve tribes of Israel. "**And everyone who has left houses or brothers or sisters or father or mother or children or farms for My name's sake, will receive many times as much, and will inherit eternal life**. "But many *who are* first will be last; and *the* last, first. *Mat 19:27-30* NASB95

He also says that everything that is not faith is sin. So, if we choose to call our earthly father, father thinking of Our heavenly father, then what about those who are abusive! Perhaps when we do call someone father, we must see beyond in faith under every circumstance, speaking to Our Heavenly Father in them. However, my heart is heavy to say that I really think we are not to call anyone father or mother. It is the Word of God, the Living Word. So what do we call them? I have been guilty of this sin and am struggling with it. I pray the Lord will help me with it. I think He is trying to make the point that we must separate ourselves from each other and unite ourselves to Him in the greatest love which is not conceivable to our limited minds. I believe this is part of His perfect plan of redemption. We must love unto death!

What profound obedience is required of us? As I see it, the Lord said we have to choose our master and in sin, we are sons of the devil. So if we sin, if our parents sin and if we are not striving to attain perfection then we cannot be Our Lord's disciples. We must strive desperately to become filled with the perfect love of Our Lord, where nothing else matters except the inexhaustible love that no evil can harm or hurt.

Living in the Love of God we can then help those we love with the love our limited minds once knew, that they may also come to know His love. And we, hating them and our own life simply because we desire nothing of this world but only that of Our Father in Heaven, only then can Our Lord work in us to help them. Simply because we have surrendered completely to the Lord, even unto death, where true love dwells.

Perhaps you have not repented of being called "father" or "mother". This is for both lay men and priests, preachers, parents etc. Everyone! Instead you babble and argue among you and say "Oh I think its okay". Who do you attempt to please? The Word is clear! Let us seek the Lord and ask Him to make us obedient to Him. What part of the Word of God do you not believe? Repent! Be careful!

Help me Lord to attain perfect obedience that is pleasing to you. Remove all treasures on earth from my heart, mind and soul, so that you will be my only treasure, the King of my being. Dwell in the chambers of my heart and make it fit for You, my King. Shut my mouth and let me proclaim Your Word that you may be pleased by all that is spoken from my mouth which comes from my heart filled with Your perfect love. Give to me the grace to accept Your truth and proclaim it boldly and zealously, that I may remain in your Loving Light. Thank you Lord for Your inexhaustible mercy, may I live in it, be consumed by it, and become mercy and love like You. In the Name of Jesus I pray.

Repent that you might believe as mentioned in John 21:32.

Oh, Inexhaustible mercy and everlasting love, may you be glorified throughout all eternity. Be mine now and forever ages to ages unending.

WHO IS YOUR MOTHER?

The Mother of God

> - "And how has it happened to me, that **the mother of my Lord** would come to me? *Luke 1:43* NASB95

> - When Jesus then saw His mother, and the disciple whom He loved standing nearby, He said to His mother, "Woman, behold, your son!" *John 19:26* NASB95

> - Then He said to the disciple, 'Behold, your mother' From that hour the disciple took her into his own household. *John 19:27* NASB95

When the Lord told John, "Behold, your mother" we know clearly that she did not bear John in her womb. We do know that she is the Mother of my Lord and He told the disciple to behold his mother. We have always understood it to be that he would take care of her. But the word means more than just watch over her, take care of her, for us perhaps it means to comprehend, gaze at and call attention to her so that we may come to know her. To discern, apprehend and discover that which is righteous and love itself.

Mary! We must behold Our Mother in Heaven, receive her into our lives and take her into our homes as well; surely we are indebted to her for her wonderful and magnificent "Yes".

When Jesus told Mary to behold her son, I am sure He was giving us to her as well. That she also, may comprehend, gaze at and call attention to each one of us that she may also know us and give regard to each one of us.

"Behold" according to the online dictionaries means as follows:

> *Dictionary.com Unabridged (v 1.1)* - Cite This Source
> **1. regard, gaze upon, view; watch; discern.**
> *American Heritage Dictionary* - Cite This Source
> 1. a. **To perceive by the visual faculty; see**: *beheld a tiny figure in the distance.*
> b. **To perceive through use of the mental faculty; comprehend**:
> *"Behold the man of the future" (Jerry Adler).*

2. **To look upon**; gaze at: *We beheld a beautiful vista before us.* See Synonyms at see¹.
v. *intr.*
Used in the imperative for the purpose of calling attention.
Online Etymology Dictionary - Cite This Source behold
O.E. bihaldan (W.Saxon behealdan) "**give regard to**, hold in view," from bi- "by" + haldan, healdan (see hold).
Beholden, **in the sense of "indebted"** first recorded c.1390.

We can also contemplate that just as there is only One Father who is in Heaven, so also, there is only One Mother who is also in Heaven. Mary! Our God chose her as the bride, as we would understand it to unite Himself for His divine purpose with someone in the flesh to bear His child.

The Word became flesh when Mary was over-shadowed by the Holy Spirit. The blood of Mary formed a new blood with the Divine Child in her womb, creating Jesus, a man-God. Could this possibly be the Blood of the New Covenant of which Jesus referred? We have always thought or referred to the Blood of the New Covenant as that of Jesus on the cross. Yes this is true, but it also stands to reason that a New Blood, a New Covenant would be the unity of God with flesh. Mary!

Just as Our Heavenly Father transformed His Word in Mary's womb forming Jesus, we must understand that Jesus is again transformed and alive in a great stillness in the Bread of Life.

In this book you will find a prayer entitled "Be Exalted Bread of Life I Love You Lord". This prayer resulted in a combination of three prayers (miracle explained in the Book We Lay Down Our Crown.) The prayer, the Bread of Life, is a reflection of the prayer the Lord had me praying during Holy Communion asking Him to be flesh of my flesh, blood of my blood. It is truly an enlightening and loving experience, to say the least. When I first wrote the prayer down I was afraid to let a priest read it. I thought this to be beyond me and out of the norm. In my experience, by sight I glowed a little (a friend made a comment to me immediately after mass, not knowing what had happened to me) but with faith my insides were consumed in loving light, the coolness of the living waters flowed though my veins. He penetrated me. Oh, but what sorrow when in a moment I tend toward sin, just one thought and quickly He leaves and so, my struggle against my flesh continues until I can confine it, deny it and live where love is. Lord help me for there is no other want!

I did finally let a priest read the prayer, only to find out that saints have prayed such before me. Not to boast that I am a saint, for surely, only the Lord makes saints, but only to say that although I am a sinner, I am hopefully following the path to holiness running the race the Apostles ran. The battle continues until we are perfected for even the apostles said "I do the things I do not want to do". Holy Communion is a sacred and holy union with Our Beloved Holy living creature in the Bread of Life, Jesus.

Jesus!!! **Jesus**, in Our Holy Communion, **gives to us the opportunity** to also become of His Body and Blood of the New Covenant. The question is "what is the intent of our heart?" Will we repent and love Him enough for Him to receive us? Can we be merciful like Him? In Holy Communion, He is Our Bridegroom; this is our union with Him. With a right heart and a right spirit the Love intensifies and the union is consummated! Yes, with Our Beloved, My Beloved, Most Holy Want and there is no other!

In Our Holy Communion, Jesus gives to us an opportunity to enter into the New Covenant and partake. We are transformed into His Body and Blood of the New Covenant. We become Blood of His Blood, Flesh of His Flesh, through Him, with Him and In Him we are transformed, united.

- So Jesus said to them, "Truly, truly, I say to you, unless you eat the flesh of the Son of Man and drink His blood, **you have no life in yourselves**. *John 6:53 NASB95*

It is difficult for many people to believe in this mystery. It is a fact that He Lives in the form of Bread! God can do anything! People who do not believe are of little faith. They cannot even believe that the host, the Living Bread is in control because they do not see it move. He is mightier than our limited minds can conceive. He IS! and He is the Great I AM! He is the Presence of Everlasting Love! Let us pray that He will unite all of us to Himself!

- Whoever eats my flesh and drinks my blood remains in me, and I in him. *John 6:56 NIV*

The Lord says **you must not eat and drink judgment**.

Your heart must be right to receive Him. You must love Him with all your heart, all your mind, all your soul and all your strength.

You must not condemn anyone or you will be condemned! Call no one heretic, love them, pray for them that the Lord will bless them!

- Therefore whoever eats the bread or drinks the cup of the Lord in an unworthy manner, shall be guilty of the body and the blood of the Lord. But a man must examine himself, and in so doing he is to eat of the bread and drink of the cup. For he who eats and drinks, eats and drinks judgment to himself if he does not judge the body rightly. For this reason many among you are weak and sick, and a number sleep. *1Cor11:27-30 NASB95*

With desperate love, intense desire, a contrite and humble heart, with great faith and confidence, with a mouth that is cleansed from all evil things spoken, with a mind that desires to be Christ like and with a heart filled with love for Mary, our Mother, we receive. With a longing desire to please the Lord hoping for a pure and immaculate heart like hers, in which our soul can magnify the Lord and rejoice in Him, so we receive; hoping that He will receive us and give to us the grace that saves and gives everlasting life. Surely, if the Lord said be perfect as my Father is perfect, he also desires for us to have an immaculate heart.

Sister Faustina in her Diary mentions that she actually felt the blood of Our Lord flowing through her. Oh, that we may all obtain that grace, that place of love beyond love, the bond of ONE.

5. Honor thy father and thy mother: that thy days may be long upon the land which the LORD thy God giveth thee. *Ex 20:12 KJV*

In the fifth of the Ten Commandments the Lord says to honor our father and mother so that our life may be prolonged. Does a prolonged life mean life everlasting? Surely, only the Lord who is please with how we honor Him and honor Mary our mother will our life and love bloom into the everlasting where all love is. Although we must also realize that we are to honor and love each other as we love ourselves as also commanded by Our Lord.

Anyone who would deny Mary as their Mother is vain to think they are better than she. If God Himself called Her Mother who are we to do otherwise? Who in all creation but Mary could have met the heavenly criteria necessary for the great honor of being called the Mother of Our Lord and Savior Jesus Christ the Redeemer of mankind? If God honors her, how can any other person deny her? He exalts the humble as mentioned in the scriptures. She was humble; therefore, Our Lord exalted Her. Every generation will call her Blessed! She is Blessed indeed!

We testify and believe in the Holy Trinity which includes Our Father, His Son, Jesus and the Holy Spirit, all are ONE. Mary's spirit is indeed holy! We worship the Father the Son and the Holy Spirit.

She also was overshadowed by the Holy Ghost, a covering over her body, consumed and overtaken, possessed by the Holy Spirit, filled with grace.

Would anyone ever qualify to meet the standards that Mary met to be received by Our Lord as ONE? Perhaps, the circumstances will not be the same, but with grace, I hope so! In the perfection given to Her by Our Lord, in loving her, we grow in love and understanding. He becomes Our Only Want as He was to Mary. Let us all hope to be ONE. This is the Lord's desire: That we be perfect as our Heavenly Father is perfect.

Perhaps you have not asked Her to be the Mother in your life or of your family. Please ask her, she is like Our Father, both are patiently waiting for you to invite them into your heart and into your lives. Ask them to please come with Jesus and take their reign on earth! May the Lord make us Blessed!

**THE MERCY OF OUR LORD IS YOURS
IF YOU WANT IT!
DESIRE TO AMEND YOUR WAYS
DESIRE HIS LOVE
AND LOVE HIM BACK!
Return all that you are to Him!**

WHY THE "HAIL MARY"?

(This message came to me from my soul. It was like a bubble floating from my stomach upward toward my head. I sensed the movement of the bubble and I felt it open like a burst of knowledge perhaps around the area of my heart, and I was in awe... Oh My God, My Beloved!)

For those having trouble to accept this scriptural prayer:

One "Hail Mary" Prayed every day with your whole heart, mind and soul with the intent to please the Lord will change your life.

The Rosary is grace bearing and blooming in love. It will help you to pray more fervently. **The Rosary is not just for Catholics.** It is said that with this prayer Satan's head will be crushed. When she said Yes, the devil knew his days were numbered.

The Call to Heaven!

THE HAIL MARY
**Hail Mary full of grace the Lord is with thee
Blessed are you among women
and Blessed is the fruit of your womb,
Jesus Holy Mary Mother of God
Pray for us sinners now and at the hour of our death Amen**

WHY THE "HAIL MARY"?

Today, on May 18, 2006, **I asked the Lord to help me honor Mary** and to teach me about her. I briefly read about a saint that spoke about her for hours and hours and whose listeners were converted, but no information was given. I had a sudden hope and a desire to be able to talk so much about her, since I know little. I am nothing and know nothing. The Lord was so gracious to me today in giving me a word of knowledge about her. What I learned today was really beautiful. (We should all ask the Lord to teach us all things too!! We will all be of one mind, one body, one spirit!!! but first we must repent with a contrite heart for doubting His Word and for not trusting in Him as we should and for leaning on human understanding)

THE MESSAGE:

Why the "Hail Mary"? Many times on earth, a husband gives a gift to his wife, **a bouquet of roses**.

The Hail Mary is a gift to Mary from Our Lord, a rose. The Rosary is **a bouquet of roses**. It is a grand remembrance of a profound moment being brought back to life. Our Father who gifted this to Her is pleased when we honor her by praying these scriptures. They are words of Redemption. They are words of promise announcing the arrival of the Messiah. They are words of announcement that Mary was chosen as Mother of the Messiah who will come through her, born from her. They are words of birth and redemption for in His Birth He became Our Redemption, Our Savior. They bring life to this earth. Our Messiah is alive. And to Our Father it is a profound moment of great love finally being accepted and united with His People made of flesh. Though Mary, Our Father receives what He has long awaited, Prefect Love, perfect obedience, total submission to the King of Kings. To us, this moment is a moment of mercy, a moment of promise, a moment of great hope, a moment of love beyond our comprehension, a moment we must expect to also experience, a moment of ONE.

The Rosary is a present that brings Mary and Our Lord much happiness every time they hear those glorious words being said out of **our mouths** with our whole heart, mind and soul.

Through the gift Her Spouse gave to her we grow in the Love of God, in the Love of Mary. We must become one. It resounds from our mouth to the heavens and vibrates throughout all the earth. It causes demons to tremble. The Hail Mary is a weapon against Satan. He hates it!!! It is said that Satan's head will be crushed by praying the Rosary. The victory was won when Mary conceived the Son of God, Jesus.

To Our Blessed Mother, the Hail Mary prayed with much love is like a rose. A pleasant aroma fills the air. This is why they call it the Rosary. It is a bouquet of roses to Mary from Our Lord. **Love awakens like a blooming rose. Grace manifests itself in the fervent soul desiring more love, more grace.** Sometimes persons dedicated to praying the rosary will actually smell roses when praying the rosary and there are no roses to be found in the immediate area. The prayers are given credit for such a pleasant aroma. The soul is nurtured with each recitation of such holy proclamation when said with the deepest desire to love and please the Lord. They are angelic words. The WORD became flesh, these are WORDS of rebirth. They are words proclaiming the coming of Our Lord. They are a message from the Lord to Mary His selected spouse and to each of us they are words of hope. They are words from the Lord accepting Mary as His own loving her so much so as to bear His Child. We must desire also to be His own.

We must proclaim the annunciation of the coming of the Messiah, the Second Coming with the Rosary.
As we say the words with love, we reap what we sow.
WE RETURN THEM TO OUR LORD:
1. Originally,
    **The Angels Spoke to an earthly being (Mary) and the unexpected spiritual manifestation
of a Man-God, Our Messiah, was born (Jesus).
2. And now,
    in praying the rosary
    we return to God those magnificent words:
    **An Earthly Being Speaking Birth To The Heavens,
(YOU)

proclaiming **the joy of the Coming of Our Lord** (the Second Coming, to the Jews it is the First Coming) and then the joy received in the heavens will give to us the unexpected spiritual manifestation of God returning to us and we returning to Him. **Would this be the happiest day of Our Father's being when we return to Him? When we announce to Him,** *"Hail, full of grace, Blessed are you among women,*
Bring forth your Son, that we may live with our heavenly family!"
An outburst of Joy in the heavens, saying
"Finally, you want me, you have announced me and I will come to you".
"YES" says the Lord, is my response as was Mary's response, My Beloved Blessed Mary Most Holy, my family and I will come and we will live together at last. You have announced my coming with Love, Joy and anticipation of Our Union, and my answer is YES!!! Eternally Yours in Everlasting Love…

The first Joyful Mystery is the Annunciation. We must pray the Rosary and consecrate ourselves to the Immaculate Heart of Mary so that we may please Our Father. We must experience the child Jesus through Holy Communion, the Bread of Life, the Living Bread and our union with Our Lord, so that we may become one.

Our Hope is that our souls will be united with Our Bridegroom.

She who gave birth to the Son of My Father, Jesus, was overjoyed when Angel Gabriel announced to her that she would be the Mother of the Messiah, the Mother of God.

Hail, full of grace, the Lord is with thee. *Luke 1:28 CPDV*
Blessed art thou among women and
Blessed is the fruit of your womb, Jesus *Luke 1:42 CPDV*

The Hail Mary is a prayer in which our soul should rejoice to recite. Her joy was beyond our comprehension. Any Mother on earth who is so happy, anxious and thrilled about being pregnant can only begin to understand this gladness in a very small measure compared to Hers. The great love that Our Lady experienced in that moment was profound. **It was the happiest and most uplifting day of her life.** As any mother loves to show her child to another we must ask Mary to present to us Her Son. We must love the Holy family and desire to be part of it. This was such a miraculous act of God, Our Father, who loves her so much. She was the first person to be made perfect as Our Father is Perfect. The Son of God became flesh from her flesh. Her blood flowed with His, mingled and created by Our Maker forming Jesus, in the womb of Mary. Jesus is the fruit of her womb.

On the day that the Hail Mary was said to Mary, she was overwhelmed and consumed by unfathomable love and joy. With her answer "YES" and with this proclamation Our Messiah manifested Himself first in the womb of Mary. She was His tabernacle, the tabernacle of the WORD of God. She was the residing place in which Our Lord chose to lodge until He manifested Himself in the flesh as a living creature, a new being, a divine child, a man-God.

She herself was transformed into Love itself. **It could not be any other way**. She was overshadowed and embraced by Love itself. Our Father wanted His Son to be perfectly loved, perfectly attended to, perfect as Our Father is perfect. Our Father became one with Mary. When she embraced Jesus in her arms so did Our Father through her and His Perfect Love in Her. She was One with Jesus, He was One with Jesus as mentioned in the Gospels, suffering with Him and in Him.

And so, when we say, "Hail Mary, full of grace the Lord is with thee" it reaffirms the angelic words again coming to life, which are words of life and give life. "Full of grace" is a love which bears all things and conquers all of our enemies. "The Lord is with thee" are words of being ONE with the Lord. Mary is Blessed Indeed!

And all generations will call her Blessed!

The words that flowed from her mouth tell it to us in such a way that we can comprehend how she felt. But again, only in such a small measure is it understood since no words are sufficient to give edification to such an outburst and consumption of unfathomable Love. Her heart, mind, body and soul was being filled with perfect love itself. And these were her words (Catholics call this prayer taken from scripture *Luke (1:46-55 ASV)*. "**The Magnificat**"):

My soul magnifies the Lord,
And my spirit rejoices in God my Savior.
For He has regarded the low estate of His handmaiden, For
behold, henceforth all generations shall call me blessed.
For He who is mighty has done great things for me,
and holy is His name.
And His mercy is on those who fear Him
from generation to generation.
He has shown strength with His arm:
He has scattered the proud
in the imagination of their hearts.
He has put down the mighty from their thrones,
and exalted those of low degree.
He has filled the hungry with good things;
and the rich He has sent empty away.
He has helped His servant Israel,
in remembrance of His mercy;
As He spoke to our fathers, to Abraham
and to His posterity forever.

Glory be to the Father and to the Son
and to the Holy Spirit.
As it was in the beginning, is now and ever shall be,
world without end. Amen

    May we also become One with Her and Her great love and obedience to Her Beloved Spouse, Our Father. One through the Holy Spirit, Ours, His, Hers and each others, together all become one. Glory to God! and so I say to you:

Pray for Those Who are Still in Darkness
Hail to you   (*I acclaim and greet you enthusiastically*)
the Lord's grace is given to you
who have accepted the Lord's invitation
to let Him into your heart
into your life

and who are consumed by
His Holy and loving Will
The Lord is with you
Blessed are you among God's people
Blessed is the fruit that you sow in Love
Holy are you
Child of God through Jesus Christ
Pray for all sinners and for those who
are still of the world in darkness;
may they be led, during their lifetime
to the Way, the Truth and the Light of Life
through Jesus Christ. Pray without ceasing always
and in everything giving God
the Glory He so Highly deserves
now and at the hour of our death. Amen.

With the Rosary, the Lord has given to me the grace to pray more fervently and more continuously throughout the day. I have been amazed at the grace it bears. I can only wonder what it would be like to be filled with such great magnitude of love. Perhaps, my heart, mind, body, and soul would not be able to contain itself and my spirit would burst itself out of this prison of clay. All darkness banished, set free at last. Ohhhhh how I wish that would be!!! I hope in it!!!

WAS MARY WITHOUT SIN?

Before time, Mary was and now is in unity with Our Lord. We have also known that we will one day RETURN TO GOD. So how can we return to Him if we were never with Him. So, I believe we also had to have been before time otherwise it would not be a return. We however have been lost in the desert with little faith and unaware of what true love is. We are asleep in a slumber of which we must awaken.

I believe Mary was born without sin because Our Creator chose to create her specifically for this great honor. I believe Mary was born without sin because she came through HOPE. In the book of Romans 8:24-25 it says that in Hope we are saved. The Hope of Ann, Mary's mother was very great. She believed that if the Lord gave Sara an old woman, wife of Abraham, father of many nations a child, that He would give one to her too.

She was barren in her old age and after many years of humiliation she gained the virtue of humility (one of the greatest virtues). Ann offered Mary to the Lord and gave her to the temple at age three as promised to the Lord. The Lord honored Anna's request.

Mary in turn was a child of HOPE. She at a young age offered herself chaste to the Lord hoping that the Messiah would come sooner. HOPE is a great gift. Mary is the Mother of Hope.

Through her we have the Hope of our Assumption, of Our Redemption and of Life Everlasting manifesting. We should also HOPE for the second coming by praying the Rosary and meditating on the mysteries. The Luminous Mysteries are reflections of our transformation. (The Mysteries of Light meditations revealed to me are in the back section of this book).

WHY DO WE PRAY THE HAIL MARY AND WHAT IS THE SIGNIFICANCE OF THE ROSARY?

The significance of the Rosary when prayed with your whole heart, mind and soul and strength, which becomes the intent of our heart, is to please the Lord.

These scriptures are found in the Word of God in Bibles prior to the 1960's, including the King James. These scriptures are the Living Word returning to the Heavens.

In the first joyful mystery The Annunciation – Angel Gabriel announces to Mary that she is highly favored and the Lord has chosen her to become the mother of God. Now, it is our annunciation to the Heavens for the return of Jesus. It is the Word of God returning to Him. It is our invitation to the heavens, for Our Lord to return. It is our announcement for His return on earth.

We must sow to reap.
The Hail Mary is the Call to Heaven.

With these prayers prayed with a great DESIRE to please the Lord we receive revelation to understand the life we are to live in Christ. The meditations of the Rosary are reflections of the Passion and Life of Jesus. We are led to be of one mind, a fervent love grows and grace bestows.

WHY WAS MARY CHOSEN TO BE THE MOTHER OF OUR LORD?

Perhaps it was Mary's Hope and lifetime fast of being chaste that beamed in the eyes and heart of Our Lord.

The Lord chose Mary as the first human being with whom to unite himself. Yes, indeed! Mary was chaste on earth! Mary who has been given to us to behold is our perfect example of what the Lord desires of us to be ONE with Him.

In the book of Revelations 14:4-5 we are told that the **Lord has purchased the first fruits among men**:

> those who are chaste
> and have not been defiled
> and follow the Lamb wherever He goes.
> They do not lie and are blameless.

Although it may refer to a certain group we must know that this applies to those who desire to please the Lord. Mary is our perfect example.

> - For am I now seeking the favor of men, or of God? Or am I striving to please men? If I were still trying to please men, **I would not be a bond-servant of Christ**. *Ga 1:10 NASB95*

Everyone is required to be chaste, truthful and blameless. We must desire to please God not men!

As a child, did you ever play the game "follow the leader" and if you messed up you were out of the game. Well, this is no game!!! We must follow our leader, Jesus! He is the Way!

In the following scriptures, the Lord fixed my eyes on those words capitalized:

> - These are the ones who have not been defiled with women, for **they have kept themselves CHASTE**. These are the ones who follow the Lamb wherever He goes. These have been purchased from among men as first fruits to God and to the Lamb. *Rev 14:4 NASB95*

- And **NO LIE was found in their mouth; they ARE BLAMELESS.** *Rev 14:5 NASB95*

    The Lord loves for us to Hope in Him and to humble ourselves in His sight. The Lord loves for us to always acknowledge Him in everything we say and do. The Lord loves us to have faith the size of a mustard seed.

    Moses was favored because He had great faith and was righteous. Mary also had great faith and her greatest desire was for the Messiah to come. When she met Joseph her designated spouse after living in the Temple so many years she had to disclose her vow made to the Lord to Joseph. When she told Joseph her vow, he immediately said let us both go to the Temple so that I also can make the same vow. The vow was to remain chaste so that the Messiah would come sooner. It was a form of fasting and humbling themselves to the Lord.

    I believe faith is a knowing that the Lord will answer, it is a firm belief and confidence in Him. It is as simple as that of the Centurion. It is part of loving the Lord desperately and a great desire to be with Him. It is a part of fearing the Lord hating to be apart from him. It is part of our transformation. It is a greater faith, a greater trust, a greater virtue.

    In this day and time, men have failed to remember what true faith, true love and true hope are. In the book of Tobit is says people get married out of lust like mules and horses. Tobit prays and fasts for three days before the marriage is consummated.

    The topic in this book *"Will The Divorced Be Chaste At The Coming Of The Lord?"* is addressed to the divorced because they are adulterers of a great population; and those whose spouse is alive and are remarried are adulterers. The topic explains how they are set apart as evil and wicked according to scripture. I am with hopes that they will desire to be chaste and repent. Lord Have Mercy!

    Dearest Creator and Maker of perfect love, you who is Perfect Love, make us to love you Perfectly! In Jesus' name I pray.

WILL THE DIVORCED BE CHASTE AT THE COMING OF THE LORD?

Lord forgive us, Lord help us, Lord teach us, Lord make us to obey and to love you above all the earth! Receive us! Remember us! Blessed is He who comes in the Name of the Lord!

- "Any place that does not receive you or listen to you, as you go out from there, shake the dust off the soles of your feet for a testimony against them." Mark 6:11 NASB95

- 'Even the dust of your city which clings to our feet we wipe off in protest against you; yet be sure of this, that the kingdom of God has come near.' Luke 10:11 NASB95

- Some Pharisees came to Jesus, testing Him and asking, **"Is it lawful for a man to divorce his wife for any reason at all?"** Mat 19:3 NASB95

- And He answered and said, "Have you not read that He who created them from the beginning MADE THEM MALE AND FEMALE, and said, 'FOR THIS REASON A MAN SHALL LEAVE HIS FATHER AND MOTHER AND BE JOINED TO HIS WIFE, AND THE TWO SHALL BECOME ONE FLESH'? "So they are no longer two, but one flesh. **What therefore God has joined together, let no man separate."** Mat 19:4-6 NASB95

- They said to Him, "Why then did Moses command to GIVE HER A CERTIFICATE OF DIVORCE AND SEND her AWAY?" He said to them, "Because of your hardness of heart Moses permitted you to divorce your wives; but from the beginning it has not been this way. Mat 19:7-8 NASB95

"And I say to you, whoever divorces his wife, except for immorality, and marries another woman commits adultery. Mat 19:9 NASB95

Except for the reason of immorality? Does this mean that adultery has already been committed? I would say yes. What is immorality? Unfaithfulness! The scripture here clearly indicates that adultery has been committed before divorce.

"and marries another woman commits adultery."
You who are divorced and remarried with your x-spouses living - you are an adulterer, blinded by the laws of man. The Lord has said it in His Word. The innocent spouse most likely has already been driven to commit adultery as the Lord warned.

"makes her commit adultery" Mat 5:32 NASB

- Unless you repent, you shall likewise perish! Luke 13:3 NKJV

- (but if she does leave, she must remain unmarried, or else be reconciled to her husband), and that the husband should not divorce his wife. 1Co 7:11 NASB95

- But to the rest I say, not the Lord, that if any brother has a wife who is an unbeliever, and she consents to live with him, he must not divorce her. Co 7:12 NASB95

Moses issued a decree of divorce for the disobedient, just as the Lord told the apostles that when they enter a place that rejects them to dust their feet.

It is a separation from the Lord to those whose hearts are hardened like that of Herod and his brothers wife. Therefore, the fact that Moses allowed divorce did not make it right. It only separated the evil from the good. Those who choose not to love unconditionally are not like Christ and cannot love the Lord because they obeyed man rather than God. They choose "self" over "selflessness". They did not fast and humble themselves before the Lord to please Him and ask forgiveness as did Tobit.

- The disciples said to Him, "If the relationship of the man with his wife is like this, it is better not to marry." But He said to them, "Not all men can accept this statement, but only those to whom it has been given. Mat 19:10-11 NASB95

> - "For there are eunuchs who were born that way from their mother's womb; and there are eunuchs who were made eunuchs by men; and there are also eunuchs who made themselves eunuchs for the sake of the kingdom of heaven. He who is able to accept this, let him accept it."
> *Mat 19:12* NASB95

The Lord says in the book of revelation that He will come for the chaste. Everyone is required to be chaste, not just the divorced.

Will you who are divorced repent and become chaste? We must repent! We must love unconditionally! It is not too late!

Repent or Perish! This is the Word of the Lord!

> - These are the ones who have not been defiled with women, for **they have kept themselves chaste**. These are the ones who follow the Lamb wherever He goes. These have been purchased from among men as first fruits to God and to the Lamb. *Rev 14:4* NASB95

> - And **no lie was found in their mouth; they are blameless.** *Rev 14:5* NASB95

> - and he said with a loud voice,
> "Fear God, and give Him glory, because the hour of His judgment has come; worship Him who made the heaven and the earth and sea and springs of waters." And another angel, a second one, followed, saying, "Fallen, fallen is Babylon the great, she who has made all the nations drink of the wine of the passion of her immorality."
> *Rev 14:7-8* NASB95

**THE MERCY OF OUR LORD IS YOURS
IF YOU WANT IT
DESIRE TO AMEND YOUR WAYS
DESIRE HIS LOVE
AND LOVE HIM BACK!
Return to Him all that you are!**

DO EARTHLY POSSESSIONS POSSESS YOU?

Today on the Queenship of Mary, (August 22, 2007) I was given the knowledge and insight so common in many families including the family of the Churches.

Like children fighting over a toy, an object of the earth, a created thing, the Lord has shown to me that the Churches are just like a toddler fighting over things. Do they know love?

Is it a form of possession to the child fighting for a toy and claiming it? Is this how they had been taught? Or were they taught to share and to love unconditionally? Are they possessed by the toy? Do they know love?

Like a toy, the churches dispute the issue about things created by man and fail to realize that Paul was teaching **"the Way"**. What created thing will keep the Churches and you from the love of God?

- nor height, nor depth,
NOR ANY OTHER CREATED THING,
will be able to separate us from the love of God, which is in Christ Jesus our Lord. *Ro 8:39 NASB95*

What is worth the risk of separating yourself from the love of God?

Who will separate us from the love of Christ?
Will tribulation, or distress, or persecution, or famine, or nakedness, or peril, or sword? *Ro 8:35 NASB95*

Will the Catholic Church give up its statues for the love of his brother who does not like them?

Or will his brother accept the Catholic Church as they are and not acknowledge statues for the Love of his brother in the Love of God? Who will bend? Jesus did!

Will we continue to allow "a created thing" to separate us from the love of God and the love of one another?

*(*Read more in *"What About Statues And Graven Images?")*

-"Being then the children of God,
we ought **NOT TO THINK that
the Divine Nature is like** gold or silver or stone,
an image formed by the art and thought of man.
"Therefore having overlooked the times of ignorance,
**God is now declaring to men
that all people everywhere should repent,**
because He has fixed a day in which He will judge the world in righteousness through a Man whom He has appointed, having furnished proof to all men by raising Him from the dead." *Acts 17:29-31* NASB95

Are statues a "great possession" of your homes, of the church or even of our cities? What possesses you and keeps you from the love of God? Your money? Your wife? Your children? Your car? Your home? What is worth the risk of being separated from the love of God? What? What? What? I say nothing, what say you?

Make the Lord your Great WANT! Keep in mind the following scripture for end of times:

The rest of mankind,
who were not killed by these plagues,
did not repent of the works of their hands,
so as not to worship demons, **and
the idols of gold and of silver
and of brass and of stone and of wood**,
which can neither see nor hear nor walk; *Rev 9:20* NASB95

There are many snares and the devil desires for you to continue in your disobedience to the Lord. Will you obey God or man?

Do you not know that **when you present yourselves** to someone as slaves for obedience, **you are slaves of the one whom you obey, either of sin resulting in death**, or of obedience resulting in righteousness? *Ro 6:16* NASB95

The devil deceives in many ways but his schemes are not very creative. They are repetitive in many forms. The following are forms of possession of the things of the earth that separate people from the love of God.

Are you of a family that has quarreled over possessions at the death of a loved one or perhaps in a divorce dispute: a house, a car or even the little things, a ring, a hat, a picture? What did you want that belonged to them and you did not get? Why do you grieve over things?

What did you not give to your neighbor in need desiring it only for yourself or your family? Or perhaps you have felt guilty because you have your stash of favorite food or things in your possession and do not want to share. Or, do you feel guilty when someone else is constantly sharing and you partake? Or perhaps, you hide something because someone is coming?

Is our selfishness and possessiveness aroused?

Guilt reveals our sin!

Do actions reveal our possessiveness?

I know I have been guilty of much and I have repented. The Lord is pleased when we give with a joyful heart. We must ask the Lord to show us our sin and how to repent. We must desire to change our ways. The Lord says that corruption shall put on incorruption. We must desire it greatly and we must make every effort to become obedient to Our Lord. We must desire not to grieve the Spirit of God in us.

Have you ever thought that someone who perhaps might be on food stamps and has a huge modern TV flat screen or a new car or something that cost thousands of dollars is not deserving of it because you work hard for your money and cannot afford it?

Have you ever been one to not get the promotion or the raise that the other person got instead of you who possibly was more deserving? Or perhaps someone who is a "squeaky wheel" boasting in themselves gets the earthly treat, are you jealous? Or perhaps the "whistle blower" saved the company from financial trauma or dissolution gets fired, is it fair? Does it matter? No it does not matter! Do not judge hastily the events in your life. In 1Cor 7:29- 36 it says we must use the world as if we do not make full use of it, and if we buy as if we do not possess.

What attachment to the things of the earth are you allowing to keep you in bondage and away from the love of God, the love of one another, the unconditional love Jesus taught? Would you give anything to someone you really really love? Yes, that is how it should be with everyone and everything!

Are these lessons taught by Our Lord so that we may learn to live in His fullness? Above all things we must remember to love unconditionally and to keep the truth in our hearts and on our tongues.

Know that these are all lessons to those who are humiliated and served unjustly on this earth. It is the "way" to become Christ like. Receiving these differences in the joy of the Lord and in the power of the cross is grace bearing. Contemplating the life of Christ we come to understand that the devils torment us in many ways. As the Lord said this is an evil and wicked generation and so it is. **We must learn to live in the cross of Christ where the victory is realized and most importantly where love is and our reward is found.**

For the person who thinks their neighbor is unjust in having more than they have, it is a form of jealousy and a want for things of the earth. The Lord says that

- for where your treasure is, there your heart will be also.
Mat 6:21 KJV

"Sell your possessions and give to charity;
make yourselves money belts which do not wear out, an unfailing treasure in heaven,
where no thief comes near nor moth destroys.
Luke 12:33 NASB95

Jealousy and envy are demons that from the first began to destroy and devour our families. Jealousy was what made Cane kill Able. Jealousy and pride is what cast Satan out from heaven. Love is not found in a mind of envy and jealousy for things of the earth.

All things belong to the Lord and we should not be jealous of or for them and most importantly we should not attach ourselves to anything of the earth.

Desires of the earth related to money are also temptations from the devil. The Lord said that simply by longing for money, you can separate yourself from the faith and pierce yourself with many grief's (1Ti6:10). (Read *Who is the servant of Money?*).

To employers the Lord says not to be unjust to the worker and to treat him equally. The man of greed and self indulgence does not know love and his life is empty.

In every event, although the Lord says that vengeance is His, we must make a sincere plea that He will be merciful even to our brothers who have wronged us and more so wronged Our Lord in disobedience. We must repent and ask the Lord to be merciful to those who do not know His love and are unjust. We must ask for mercy for them and we must be merciful so that the Lord will also be merciful to all of us. We must desire to imitate Christ.

Surely, your preference has taken over you! Are you possessed by it? In the same way, the churches are quarreling over things of the earth. The minds of men are divided.

Is a thing created by man such as a statue worth the risk of being separated from the love of God? I say no! What say you? Are you possessed by it? Do you want it that bad? Is that what the Lord means when He says "you will be snared by it"? Like a bear trap you are in bondage.

Is it worth the risk of being separated from our love for one another?

Repent and ask the Lord to help you to love Him first above all things and each other! What riches of the earth whether valuable or worthless do you attach yourself to? Trust only in the Lord!

What worth do you give to things or statues or money? Only the Lord, and He alone is Worthy!

- Then Jesus beholding him loved him, and said unto him, One thing thou lackest: go thy way, sell whatsoever thou hast, and give to the poor, and thou shalt have treasure in heaven: and come, **take up the cross, and follow me**. And he was sad at that saying, and **went away grieved: for he had great possessions.** And Jesus looked round about, and saith unto his disciples, How hardly shall they that have riches enter into the kingdom of God! And the disciples were astonished at his words. But Jesus answereth again, and saith unto them, Children, **how hard is it for them that trust in riches to enter into the kingdom of God!** It is easier for a camel to go through the eye of a needle, than

> for a rich man to enter into the kingdom of God. And they were astonished out of measure, saying among themselves, Who then can be saved? And Jesus looking upon them saith, With men it is impossible, but not with God: **for with God all things are possible.** *Mark 10:21-27 KJV*

> - But Peter said, "**I do not possess silver and gold**, but what I do have I give to you: In the name of Jesus Christ the Nazarene--walk!" *Ac 3:6 NASB95*

Is the earthly love you have for one another, a Godly love or a possessive love? I loved my husband so much, thinking that the Love I knew was the Love the Lord desired from us. I was wrong. The Lord desires that we love Him first and each other even unto death as Jesus demonstrated. In the following scripture I now know that I was concerned about the things of the world and how to please my husband more than my Lord. Others may have it reversed desiring to please themselves more than their spouse. In any case, I did not know how to Love My Lord. We must desire Him greatly and be truly devoted to Him in Spirit!

> But this I say, brethren, the time has been shortened, so that from now on
> **those who have wives should be as though they had none**;
> and those who weep, as though they did not weep;
> and those who rejoice, as though they did not rejoice;
> and those who buy, as though they did not possess;
> and those who use the world, as though they did not make full use of it; for the form of this world is passing away. But I want you to be free from concern.
> **One who is unmarried is concerned about the things of the Lord, how he may please the Lord;** but one who is married is concerned about the things of the world, how he may please his wife, and *his interests* are divided. **The woman who is unmarried, and the virgin, is concerned about the things of the Lord, that she may be holy both in body and spirit;** but one who is married is concerned about the things of the world, how she may please her husband.

> **This I say for your own benefit; not to put a restraint upon you, but to promote what is appropriate and *to secure* undistracted devotion to the Lord.** *1Cor 7:29-36 NASB*

Will you be like the crowd that was confused and angry? Or will you do as the scripture in Acts has said:

> "Therefore having overlooked the times of ignorance, **God is now declaring to men that ALL PEOPLE EVERYWHERE should repent,** *Act 17:30 NASB95*

Do you even care to please the Lord?
Do you desire to obey Him?
Do you desire to love Him greatly?
Why do you insist in attaching yourself to things of the earth?

> Wrath is fierce and anger is a flood, But who can stand before jealousy? *Pr 27:4 NASB95*

> "But who can endure the day of His coming? And who can stand when He appears? *Mal 3:2 NASB95*

For all things we must repent and confess with our mouth so that we might be liberated at the mercy of Our Lord. For all the things created of which we quarrel and are jealous or envious, selfish or think negatively of our brother **we are guilty**.
ALL ARE GUILTY FOR NOT LOVING UNCONDITIONALLY!
The offense is against Our Lord who gives us everything, to whom all things belong, and who has taught us to share with an open hand with love and gratitude of all that He has given to us. We must acknowledge Him in all things and know that He truly is our provider and His desire to those who love Him and obey Him is to bless them.

The Lord says no eye has seen and no ear has heard what the Lord has in store for those who love Him.

Perhaps the road is rocky and cross bearing on earth for those who love Him but the reward is great in our true home. We must greatly trust in the Lord. Rejoice over our humiliations in the Lord that we may be like Him, as noted in scripture.

- **"IN HUMILIATION
HIS JUDGMENT WAS TAKEN AWAY;**
WHO WILL RELATE (TO) HIS GENERATION?
Ac 8:33 NASB95

Let us then, embrace our brother in all they do, with all humility approach him and love him and let the Lord do the rest.
Let us approach each other with a contrite heart.
**The battle began in the beginning,
so let us put an end to it.**

**Let us say to each other
with all of our heart, mind, soul and strength:
"I AM SORRY,
PLEASE FORGIVE ME,
IT IS MY FAULT."**

We must change our ways! Desire to love unconditionally and love the Lord greatly! Desire to stop doing our evil works!
Know that nothing is ours, everything belongs to the Lord and freely give! Know that nothing on earth is worth separating us from the love of God!

Prayer: TREASURES
*Lord You said that where my treasure lies, there my heart is.
Help me Lord to remove myself from all treasures on earth
that only You will be the treasure I seek. Fill me and make me Yours
I surrender to you: my heart, mind and soul, my life and my being
and everything I say and do. You have given to me
Your unconditional love how can I offer anything less
I give to You my unconditional love with my free will
trusting You Heavenly Father more than anything in the world
May Your Glory manifest sooner than later.
I await Your coming with Joy and Love.
In the Name of Jesus. Amen.*

WHAT ABOUT STATUES AND GRAVEN IMAGES?

> AMERICAN HERITAGE DICTIONARY: Definition:
> **graven image**
> n. An idol or fetish carved in wood or stone.
> **grave** (grāv) Pronunciation Key
> trv **graved, grav·en** (grā'vən) or **graved, grav·ing, graves**
> 1. To sculpt or carve; engrave.
> 2. To stamp or impress deeply; fix permanently.

In the original Ten Commandments the Lord specifically tells us **not to make** any graven image. Graven, cast or molten are three dimensional figures like statues. He is also specific in telling us **not to make** any that are **of any likeness** of any thing that is in heaven above, or that is beneath the earth or in the water under the earth. He also commands that we do not bow down to them. The following is taken from the Ten Commandments, complete listing is in the back of the book:

-Thou shalt have no other gods before me. Thou shalt **not make unto thee any graven image, or any likeness of any thing that is in heaven above, or that is in the earth beneath, or that is in the water under the earth. Thou shalt not bow down thyself to them,** nor serve them: for I the LORD thy God am a jealous God, visiting the iniquity of the fathers upon the children unto the third and fourth generation of them that hate me; And showing mercy unto thousands of them that love me, and keep my commandments. Thou shalt not take the name of the LORD thy God in vain; for the LORD will not hold him guiltless that taketh his name in vain. *Exodus 20:3-7 KJV*

Disobedience to this command is a sin, therefore when you sin you are of the devil according to 1 John 3:8 noted below. This is the Word of the Lord. I am not the judge, I am only the deliverer of the Word. This is commanded by the Lord.

The person who makes or crafts them sins.
Those who use or sell them sin.
Those who bow or kneel in front of them sin.

The people do not believe, because as always they have preferred to disobey God, and **still reject His Word**. The devil has sinned from the beginning. **Jesus came for this purpose – to destroy the works of the devil**. In the book of Revelations it says that those who were not killed by plagues did not repent of the works of their hands, the making of idols made of gold, silver, brass, stone, or wood. Men prefer to obey man rather than God.

> Do you not know that when you present yourselves to someone as slaves for obedience, **you are slaves of the one whom you obey, either of sin resulting in death, or of obedience resulting in righteousness?** *Ro 6:16* NASB95

> **-the one who practices sin is of the devil;** for the devil has sinned from the beginning. The Son of God appeared for this purpose, to destroy the works of the devil. *1John 3:8* NASB95

> **-no one who is born of God sins;** *1John 5:18* NASB95

WARNING IN THE BOOK OF REVELATIONS:
> The rest of mankind,
> who were not killed by these plagues,
> **did not repent of the works of their hands**,
> so as not to worship demons, **and**
> **the idols of gold and of silver**
> **and of brass and of stone and of wood**,
> which can neither see nor hear nor walk; *Rev 9:20* NASB95

Some people do not believe that they are praying to idols believing that the image of that statue gives them an idea of what perhaps the heavenly being might look like. They do not realize that Acts 17:20-31 says you should not even "think" that they are like a divine nature. I was guilty of this, I have repented. I try not to look at the statues in the Catholic church, nor do I acknowledge them. I know the Lord will have them destroyed in His time. The time is coming! We in the flesh must not judge those who appear to be sinning, we must trust in the Lord and ask Him to bless them. The Lord is merciful and does make all things good for those who love Him. Yes, people must stop praying to statues! **They must stop bowing down to them! The Lord commands it!** A statue is a graven image, a molten or cast idol or god.

The New Testament says that you are not to think that the Divine Nature is like an image formed by the art and thought of man:

> -"Being then the children of God, **WE OUGHT NOT TO THINK that the Divine Nature is like** gold or silver or stone, **an image formed by the art and thought of man.** "Therefore having overlooked the times of ignorance, **God is now declaring to men that all *people* everywhere should repent,** because He has fixed a day in which He will judge the world in righteousness through a Man whom He has appointed, having furnished proof to all men by raising Him from the dead." *Acts 17:29-31* NASB95

We must desire to obey the Lord… He says "if you love me, obey my commands".

> - For they provoked Him with their high places And aroused His jealousy with their graven images. *Ps 78:58* NASB95

> - "The graven images of their gods you are to burn with fire; you shall not covet the silver or the gold that is on them, nor take it for yourselves, **or you will be snared by it,** for it is an abomination to the LORD your God. *De 7:25* NASB95

> -"I am the LORD, that is My name; I will not give My glory to another, Nor My praise to graven images. *Isa 42:8* NASB95

> -for you shall not worship any other god, for the LORD, whose name is Jealous, is a jealous God *Ex 34:14* NASB95

I pray that the Lord will help me to please Him, not provoke Him. In addition, **no statue is worth the risk!!!**

The Lord will not give His praise to a graven image! In other words, He is jealous and wants you to praise Him, worship Him, adore Him and love Him and only Him, not a statue nor any idol, not even your spouse or children. Our God is a jealous God and desires that we devote our love completely to Him.

Why are there so many in the churches, in the cities, in the stores? Does it matter whether the statues be religious or not? No, they are graven images. Are those who approve them snared by them? Are they blind guides? Are they of the devil? Or perhaps they are snares in keeping Christ believers from being of the same mind, separated in love. Are they obstacles that keep us from the love of God because the statues cause conflict and judgement between our Christian brothers, Christ believers. These are just questions!

> "But woe to you, scribes and Pharisees, hypocrites, because you shut off the kingdom of heaven from people; for you do not enter in yourselves, nor do you allow those who are entering to go in. *Matthew 23:13 NASB95*

Do scribes and Pharisees live today? I say they are here in great number! Blinded by their sin they refuse to repent. Will you repent? Who do you desire to please?

> Now while Paul was waiting for them at Athens, **his spirit was being provoked within him** as he was observing the city full of idols. *Ac 17:16 NASB95*

> About that time there occurred no small disturbance concerning **the Way**. For a man named Demetrius, a silversmith, who made silver shrines of Artemis, was bringing no little business to the craftsmen; these he gathered together with the **workmen of similar** trades, and said, "Men, you know that our prosperity depends upon this business. "You see and hear that not only in Ephesus, but

in almost all of Asia, this **Paul has persuaded and turned away a considerable number of people, saying that gods made with hands are no gods at all.** "Not only is there danger that this trade of ours fall into disrepute, but also that the temple of the great goddess Artemis be regarded as **worthless and that she whom all of Asia and the world worship** will even be dethroned from her magnificence." When they heard this and were filled with rage, they began crying out, saying, "Great is Artemis of the Ephesians!" **The city was filled with the confusion,** and they rushed with one accord into the theater, dragging along Gaius and Aristarchus, Paul's traveling companions from Macedonia *Acts 19:23-29 NASB95*

After quieting the crowd, the town clerk said, "Men of Ephesus, what man is there after all who does not know that the city of the Ephesians is guardian of the temple of the great Artemis and of the *image* which fell down from heaven? *Acts 19:35 NASB95*

In the book of Acts in the New Testament it mentions **"the Way"**. Paul was teaching "the Way". Paul had persuaded and turned away a considerable number of people from graven images, the crafts of silversmiths and similar trades. The people who made them were angry because that was how they made their money to survive, it was "their work". It was "no little business" as mentioned in the bible, in other words it was and still is "Big Business". The disturbance caused by Paul's words was a "Big disturbance". The comment made in the bible also makes me think that like a diamond, supply and demand, and the "thought" that anything is worth something draws people to want and desire it which is what the merchants wanted for their profit.

"Men, you know that our prosperity depends upon this business.

"Not only is there danger that this trade of ours fall into disrepute

First they talk about their business or trade, concerned about their wealth. They are not concerned about righteousness. Knowing that if people do not believe that these statues mean anything would affect their business, having her "dethroned" would mean financial devastation for them. They are afraid that her magnificence would be dethroned. They go on to say that the image "fell from heaven". If it fell from heaven then it was not made by men. But the argument here, is not about that, but rather that men do not want to stop making them as commanded by the Lord in the Commandments and here by Paul telling them the statues are basically worthless and junk. The worth put on a statue is that weighted by the mind of men. It is truly an ugly thing compared to the beauty our eyes have not yet seen of the heavens and our heavenly family.

If you saw the movie "Blood Diamond" with Leonardo DeCaprio, based on a true story, you can see the evil brought about by greed, murder and deceptive practices simply to make people think something is valuable. This is a work of the devil that has not ceased, still practiced today as in the past. It is the work of the devil because it separates men from the love of God.

> Jesus said to him, "I am the way, and the truth, and the life; no one comes to the Father but through Me. *John 14:6 NASB95*

As Paul was teaching "**the WAY**" in the book of Acts he said that "gods made with hands are no gods at all". **He also says we are not to think of any image formed by the art or thought of man as of a Divine Nature**. They are worthless!!! The Word says that you can be snared by them. We must always acknowledge only the Lord. He is a jealous God! Yet, we know they are no gods at all.

Sometimes a statue merely tells a story, an angry or sad face, a pregnant woman or praying hands. Living by faith and not by sight the glory of the Lord may be seen through the conversions of those who did not believe at all and because of their trial or tribulation portrayed in a graven image, now believe. Or perhaps a graven image sheds tears, could it be that as the Lord had said in the gospels, if you hold your peace, the stones will cry out? Perhaps it is a message of sorrow for the unrepentant sinner.

And he answered and said, I tell you that, if these shall hold their peace, the stones will cry out. *Luke 19:40 KJV*

The Lord said all things are imperfect until perfection comes. Nevertheless, it is the command of the Lord that is being disobeyed. This is an imperfection, one of many, which the Lord will perfect in His time. Perhaps, we are confronted with them so that our faith and love may be strengthened for we are in training.

Knowledge makes arrogant, but love edifies. *1Cor 8 NASB95*

John 13:35 says that all men will know that we are disciples of Our Lord if we have love for one another. The devil is nothing but a stumbling block. There are many obstacles. A statue is an obstacle causing disruption, it is a created thing, it is a stumbling block. among Christ believers.

The Lord is the same yesterday, today and always. His Word is the same yesterday, today and always. When He says "you" in the Word, we must take note of your fathers sin. Learn from them and desire **not** to commit the same sins.

The Lord says we must worship Him in Spirit and in Truth. He is Spirit. He is not a statue! He is not a graven image! **God is Spirit and He specifically tells us to worship Him in Spirit.**

Be careful! Be watchful! Repent! I have

Is a statue worth the risk of being separated from the love of God? Is it worth the risk of being separated from our love for one another? We must love both God and one another! **We cannot have one and not the other!**

How deep is your love? What measure holds you back?

Will we do as the scripture in Acts has said:
"Therefore having overlooked the times of ignorance, GOD IS NOW DECLARING TO MEN that all people everywhere should repent,

ALL ARE GUILTY
FOR NOT LOVING UNCONDITIONALLY!

Will you repent? Please repent!
Again and again, I ask you:

Who do you desire to please?
Do you even care to please the Lord?
Do you desire to obey Him?
Do you desire to love Him greatly?

Please, do not acknowledge statues,
do not kneel before them.
If you insist on kneeling before anything, kneel before the Real Presence of Our Lord in the Blessed Sacrament of the Living Bread, the Bread of the Presence.
Please strive desperately to please the Lord!
He loves you so much!

- Wrath is fierce and anger is a flood,
But who can stand before jealousy? *Pr 27:4 NASB*

- "But who can endure the day of His coming? And who can stand when He appears? . *Mal 3:2 NASB95*

Now knowing that these appear to be an imperfections, yet the Lord, Our Creator, Our Father, Our Savior binds, beacons or chastises. Praise be and Glory be to God and only to Him!

Let us then, embrace our brother in all they do, with all humility approach him bless him, pray for him and love him and let the Lord do the rest. Let us let the Lord deliver us from evil!

Will the Catholic Church give up its statues for the love of his brother who does not like them?

Or will his brother accept the Catholic Church as they are and not acknowledge statues for the Love of his brother in the Love of God? **Who will bend? Jesus did!**

Will we continue to allow "a created thing" to separate us from the love of God and the love of one another?

Jesus I Trust in You! Help me Lord to have a contrite heart and a right spirit within me! Help me Lord to dethrone the devil and devils that torment our churches and each of us, destroy their works Oh Lord. Bind them and make us of one mind, one spirit and one love. May I return to You Lord, the jealous love you have for me. May the love that is within me be only for You my God, my Beloved Jealous God of whom I also hope to be jealous, an unworthy sinner. Make me Lord to detach myself from all things of the earth. Dearest Lord, you who is merciful make us to be merciful and fill us with Your perfect love. Thank You Lord for your Great Love and may you be forever praised, adored and glorified. Holy and exalted are you! Mother of Humiliation, Blessed are you, pray for us!

Repeated scripture for end of times:

The rest of mankind,
who were not killed by these plagues,
did not repent of the works of their hands,
so as not to worship demons, **and
the idols of gold and of silver
and of brass and of stone and of wood**,
which can neither see nor hear nor walk; <u>Rev 9:20 NASB95</u>

For the NON-Catholics:
Knowing therefore that they are no gods, fear them not, For they can neither curse nor bless kings: Neither can they shew signs in the heavens among the heathen, nor shine as the sun, nor give light as the moon. The beasts are better than they: for they can get under a cover and help themselves. It is then by no means manifest unto us that they are gods: **therefore fear them not.** <u>Letter of Jeramiah 1:65-69 KJV</u>

REPENT AND BE READY!
JESUS IS COMING!

WHAT ARE FALSE GODS?

Perhaps our distracted devotion and selfish love toward one another or the things of the earth make us to make Our Lord jealous because our minds are not focused on Him alone. In our ignorance we fail to give all of our love first to God. Instead our lives become focused on our ambitions, our "things" or each other which then become the things we praise instead of God.

Are false gods those things that distract us from a passionate urge and craving for love itself, Our God who is love? Do these gods keep us living where we live, rather than where true love is?

Do false gods exist at all? Perhaps we only need to redirect our devotion and attention and desire toward Our God of Everlasting Love.

The Lord is a jealous God and wants us to love Him as He loves us. Our minds have become distracted from true devotion and obedience to God.

1. As an example, champions of basketball games receive so much recognition, praise, pride and a form of worship. Are they like false gods? You can hear the people throughout the city praising them. We must direct our praise and adoration to the Lord, shouting in joy of the love of Him and in Him.
2. Another example: I was blinded in earthly love, was my husband my false god? I had him on a pedestal and strived to please him. My devotion to the Lord was distracted and focused on my husband as noted in *1Cor 7:29-36*. I thought the love I had for my husband was sufficient. The love of God is much greater. I did not know how to love God. I loved my husband more than God of which I have repented and changed my ways.
3. Another example and question (this one is a very difficult one for me, I am struggling with it).

    Are the people who eat meat like false gods to those who murder and kill creatures of the Lord? Or are people false gods to those who strangle animals to provide food to others (gods) concerned more about profits and fast production of meats? (just like statues are they more concerned with money rather than obedience in not strangling an animal for food according to the ways of the Lord). How are our chickens killed in preparation to sell at meat markets? I really do not know! May the Lord guide us to all truth and make us to obey Him so that we may stay in His Loving Light and Love. The following are scriptures related to eating meats and the sacrifice to idols:

-that you **abstain from** things sacrificed to idols and from **blood and from things strangled** and from fornication; if you keep yourselves free from such things, you will do well. Farewell."
Ac 15:29 NASB95

-Now concerning things sacrificed to idols, we know that we all have knowledge. **Knowledge makes arrogant, but love edifies.** If anyone supposes that he knows anything, he has not yet known as he ought to know; but if anyone loves God, he is known by Him.
Therefore concerning the eating of things sacrificed to idols, we know that **there is no such thing as an idol in the world, and that there is no God but one.** For even if there are so-called gods whether in heaven or on earth, as indeed there are many gods and many lords, yet **for us there is but one God, the Father, from whom are all things and we exist for Him; and one Lord, Jesus Christ, by whom are all things, and we exist through Him.** *1 Cor8:1-6 NASB95*

-However not all men have this knowledge; but some, being accustomed to the idol until now, eat food as if it were sacrificed to an idol; and their conscience being weak is defiled. But food will not commend us to God; we are neither the worse if we do not eat, nor the better if we do eat. But take care that this liberty of yours does not somehow become a stumbling block to the weak. For if someone sees you, who have knowledge, dining in an idol's temple, will not his conscience, if he is weak, be strengthened to eat things sacrificed to idols? For through your knowledge he who is weak is ruined, the brother for whose sake Christ died.

And so, by sinning against the brethren and wounding their conscience when it is weak, you sin against Christ. **Therefore, if food causes my brother to stumble, I will never eat meat again, so that I will not cause my brother to stumble.** *1Cor8:7-13* NASB95

-Eat anything that is sold in the meat market without asking questions for conscience' sake; *1Co 10:25* NASB95

-But if anyone says to you, "This is meat sacrificed to idols," do not eat it, for the sake of the one who informed you, and for conscience' sake; *1Co 10:28* NASB95
Other scriptures: Ro 14:21; Acts 15:20; Acts 21:25

That seems to be pretty heavy! However, learning to live in Christ we stand firm in knowing that "there is no such thing as an idol in the world and that there is no God but one" for all glory, praise and honor belong to Him.

We must desire to give all of our devotion to the Lord. Yet, according to the word are many who have not repented "accustomed to the idol until now eating food as if it were sacrificed to an idol"? Are they ignorant ? Do they try to please the Lord?

Oh but who can stand in the presence of the Lord?   Thank God, we do have this hope, a great hope in His mercy, in His passionate Love and compassion towards us. He is merciful and desires that we also be merciful. He is Love and desires for us to also Love as He loves. We must seek Him desperately to please Him desperately. We must desire him greatly! Our desire should be one with such passion and intensity as that of Our Father who sent His only son to die for us! Let us desire to love Him that much!

- **And so all Israel shall be saved**: as it is written, There shall come out of Sion the Deliverer, and shall turn away ungodliness from Jacob: For this is my covenant unto them, when I shall take away their sins. As concerning the gospel, they are enemies for your sakes: but as touching the election, they are beloved for the fathers' sakes. For the gifts and calling of God are without repentance. **For as ye in times past have not believed God, yet have now obtained mercy through their unbelief: Even so have these also now not believed, THAT THROUGH YOUR MERCY they also may obtain mercy. For God hath concluded them all in unbelief, that he might have mercy upon all.**

O the depth of the riches both of the wisdom and knowledge of God! how unsearchable are his judgments, and his ways past finding out! For who hath known the mind of the Lord? or who hath been his counsellor? Or who hath first given to him, and it shall be recompensed unto him again? **For of him, and through him, and to him, are all things: to whom be glory for ever. Amen.**
<u>Ro11:26-36 KJV</u>

Lord fill us with your grace that conquers all of our enemies and make us obedient to You, use us Lord to help our brothers that they also may know Your unfathomable love! Make us Lord, Wonderful Creator of all, to willingly remove ourselves from the custom of which we have been attached. Please do not let us remain accustomed to the idol. Make us to resist, rebuke and renounce all idols. Make yourself our only true want and desire, complete us Oh Lord, make us one with each other and with you. In Jesus' Name I pray.

WHAT ABOUT the queen of heaven IN SCRIPTURE and MARY MOTHER OF GOD?

These are the scriptures about the **queen of heaven:**

- "The children gather wood, and the fathers kindle the fire, and the women knead dough to make cakes for the **queen of heaven**; and they pour out drink offerings to other gods in order to spite Me. *Jer 7:18 NASB95*

Then all the men who were aware that their wives were burning sacrifices to other gods, along with all the women who were standing by, *as* a large assembly, including all the people who were living in Pathros in the land of Egypt, responded to Jeremiah, saying, "As for the message that you have spoken to us in the name of the LORD, we are not going to listen to you! "But rather we will certainly carry out every word that has proceeded from our mouths, by burning sacrifices to the **queen of heaven** and pouring out drink offerings to her, just as we ourselves, our forefathers, our kings and our princes did in the cities of Judah and in the streets of Jerusalem; for *then* we had plenty of food and were well off and saw no misfortune. "But since we stopped burning sacrifices to the **queen of heaven** and pouring out drink offerings to her, we have lacked everything and have met our end by the sword and by famine." "And," *said the women,* "when we were burning sacrifices to the **queen of heaven** and were pouring out drink offerings to her, was it without our husbands that we made for her *sacrificial* cakes in her image and poured out drink offerings to her?" *Jer 44:15-19 NASB95*

Then Jeremiah said to all the people, including all the women, "Hear the word of the LORD, all Judah who are in the land of Egypt, thus says the LORD of hosts, the God of Israel, as follows: 'As for you and your wives, you have spoken with your mouths and fulfilled *it* with your hands, saying, "We will certainly perform our vows that we have vowed, to burn sacrifices to the **queen of heaven** and pour out drink offerings to her." Go ahead and confirm your vows, and certainly perform your vows!' **"Nevertheless hear the word of the LORD**, all Judah who are living in the land of Egypt, `Behold, I have sworn by My great name,' says the LORD, `never shall My name be invoked again by the mouth of any man of Judah in all the land of Egypt, saying, "As the Lord GOD lives." `**Behold, I am watching over them for harm** and not for good, and all the men of Judah who are in the land of Egypt **will meet their end by the sword and by famine** until they are completely gone. `Those who escape the sword will return out of the land of Egypt to the land of Judah few in number. Then all the remnant of Judah who have gone to the land of Egypt to reside there will know whose word will stand, Mine or theirs. `**This will be the sign to you,' declares the LORD, `that I am going to punish you in this place, so that you may know that My words will surely stand against you for harm.'** *Jer 44:24-29 NASB95*

When I saw this on June 29, 2007 on the feast of St Paul and St Peter the apostles I started to cry and then the Lord reminded me that I am not to be afraid of the devil for the Lord is all powerful and He is truth. Our Father chose His Beloved Mary to bear Jesus; He loves her with unfathomable love and so should we. I slept on the thought that troubled me. In the morning the Lord led me to write what is written in this question. It was Sunday June 30th (Birth of John the Baptist) and so I changed the calendar in my house to July and the particular calendar I saw had July pictured with the Queen of Heaven that stated what St. Bonaventure said as follows:

> Men do not fear
> a powerful hostile army as the powers of hell
> fear the name and protection of Mary. (1221-1274)

"Fear the name and protection of Mary" is a holy fear of which St. Bonaventure speaks. It is a fear like fear of the Lord, fearing to be apart from Our Lord, dreading the thought of offending Him. I would fear offending Mary which would then offend Our Lord who loves her beyond our comprehension. He loves her so much she was chosen to bear the Man-God, Jesus, Our Savior. Her blood was commingled and was the first to mix and be created in union with Our Lord. It was a new blood in Jesus through Mary's flesh and blood. She can be looked at as the first connection between God and flesh. It is a realization of what it means to be ONE with Our Lord, which we should also desire to be. No matter how the Lord decides to make this happen to us, He has made it clear that He wants us to be ONE and it will happen through true love. Mary is a perfect example.

As I have repeated over and over again, it cannot be said enough "We must ask the Lord to forgive us for any and all things we have thought said or done to offend Him in regard to our ignorance about Mary". We must ask Him to teach us to love Her in a way pleasing to Him. The unconditional love of Our Lord and repentance are of utmost important. We must imitate Jesus in His unconditional love and obey Him as He has proclaimed in the gospels in regard to repentance. If you love me He says to obey His commandments. We must love our Christian brothers unconditionally, the battle is not ours. We must desire to obtain a mind of Christ. Remove the splinter from your own eye then you can help your brethren.

I have received so much grace in the love of Mary, in the love of Jesus and in the love of Our Father that no devil can take that away from me.

I will die to protect the name of Mary and her great love and Her obedience, I will die in pure love for the sake of love, of which she was full of which I also desire to be. May my heart be fit for my King like hers.

Father of Prestige and Highest Rank, Most Humble, Most Loving, Most Considerate, Most Kind, God of Goodness beyond understanding, My Creator, I love you, I Exalt you , I adore You, I honor you, teach me to Love Mary as you love her.

Like in Jeremiah chapter 44, it cannot be ignored that there are voodoo dolls and statues that people use for witchery, black magic, idol worship and such which is most definitely an abomination in the sight of the Lord. This is not according to the doctrine and faith of the true Church. Even today the devil tries to take people away from the love of Mary and from the true church.

The devil comes to devour your souls. If you do any of these you must repent! Stop practicing these evil things! Stop speaking wickedness! The devil wants to possess you or use you. Desire mercy desire to have a change of heart! Ask the Lord into your heart. Love one another in truth and sincerity with all humility.

- "Then you will call, and the LORD will answer;
You will cry, and He will say, `Here I am.
' **If you remove the yoke from your midst,
The pointing of the finger
and speaking wickedness,**   <u>Isa 58:9</u> NASB95

If you misunderstand the offering of cakes as the Holy Communion offered in the Catholic Church at the altar during mass you do not know love. It is the devil lying to you because the devil does not want you to receive life in the Living Bread as the Lord has commanded you to eat. If you receive Holy Communion without contrition and love you bring judgment upon yourself and you will be condemned as written in the Word, unless you repent.

The Holy Communion with which Our Lord has given is one so that you can inherit life everlasting. It is a transformation of Bread into Our Lord Jesus manifested. It is bread that is alive. It is a living creature you must eat with unfathomable love and contrition so that you can become One with the Lord. This is a certainty! You must repent! Jesus is alive and He is here, He never left! He is here in a state of utmost humility because He loves you and wants you to live with Him as He originally intended since the beginning of time. The Bread of Life is our seed of life. When we go to the celebration of the Holy Communion (the Eucharist) we go to unite with Jesus at the mass. This prayer is one of Great Virtue. There is only one bread and only one body, let us then receive with great love unto the Lord.

Our Lady of Fatima is true. So true that she left an impact not only on Catholics but the Muslims and others also acknowledge her. The recognition given to the Mother of Our Lord is not one to be ignored! What is it about Mary? What is it about Jesus? that there is so much conflict? Why is there so much hate towards both of them? Reconsider their love and love them back!

- "Blessed are you when men hate you, and ostracize you, and insult you, and scorn your name as evil, for the sake of the Son of Man. *Luke 6:22 NASB95*

Mary is Blessed and all generations will call her blessed. She is hated, ostracized, scorned and insulted by many. Stop being so hateful and ask the Lord to help you with your understanding.
Repent and be ready!

For this cause I bow my knees unto the Father, **from whom every family in heaven** and on earth is named, that he would grant you, according to the riches of his glory, that ye may be strengthened with power through his Spirit in the inward man; that Christ may dwell in your hearts through faith; to the end that ye, **being rooted and grounded in love, may be strong to apprehend with all the saints what is the breadth and length and height and depth, and to know the love of Christ which passeth knowledge, that ye may be filled unto all the fullness of God.** *Eph 3:14-19 ASV*

Now unto him that is able to do exceeding abundantly above all that we ask or think, according to the power that worketh in us, unto him be the glory in the church and in Christ Jesus unto all generations for ever and ever. Amen. *Eph 3:20-21 ASV*

Preach unconditional love and repentance so that all truth may be made known. The devil has deceived the people of God
- keeping them from eating of the living bread,
- keeping them from loving each other,
- keeping them from loving the Holy Family
- keeping them from the true church
- keeping them from repenting as the Lord has desired
- and so much more.

Seek Love! I give to you my love in Jesus and Mary.

- By this the children of God and
the children of the devil are obvious:

anyone who **does not practice righteousness is not of God, nor the one who does not love his brother.** *1John 3:10 NASB95*

-Now I beseech you, brethren, by the name of our Lord Jesus Christ, that **ye all speak the same thing**, and that there be **no divisions among you**;
but that **ye be perfectly joined together in the same mind and in the same judgment**. *1 Cor 1:10-13 KJV*

For who hath known the mind of the Lord, that he may instruct him? But we have the mind of Christ. *1Co 2:16 KJV*

Come back home to the Catholic Church, The Lions Den.
Let us love one another even unto death! There is no greater love!

Eat of the bread of life partake

May Our Savior Reign and take His Throne on earth! Amen

WHY DID JESUS REMAIN SILENT IN FRONT OF THE COURTS?

- "IN HUMILIATION
HIS JUDGMENT WAS TAKEN AWAY;
WHO WILL RELATE TO HIS GENERATION?
Ac 8:33 NASB95

The great virtue of Humility comes thru humiliation. We must be humble and willing to be humiliated so that we may be like Him. In our humiliation our judgment will be taken away obtaining the great virtue of humility.

Have you ever wondered why Jesus remained silent while everyone was mocking and condemning him?

Today, the Lord made me realize in just a small measure the possibility of that reason.

There was an incident where after having discussed a situation with an associate, who was not willing to assume their responsibilities in authority, denied the truth of our conversation when it was later discussed with the person who gave her that authority.

I realize now that for those who are dishonest, "saving face" is more important. Their vain glory is everything to them, the devil is their master. Putting myself "in Jesus" I realize what I did: I caused that person to lie and therefore sin.

As children of Our Lord, we must prefer to be meek and humble and let whatever comes our way to be for the Glory of God. We must not argue or make an unnecessary stand, remaining silent, Jesus is our example.

We must ask the Lord for grace to remain in His Light and to lead us in response to every situation.

I caused them to sin in defense of themselves.

The following was taken from the book <u>Divine Mercy in My Soul</u> by Saint Maria Faustina Kowalska:

> 477 Silence is a sword in the spiritual struggle. A talkative soul will never attain sanctity. The sword of silence will cut off everything that would like to cling to the soul. We are sensitive to words and quickly want to answer back, without taking any regard as to whether it is God's will that we should speak. A silent soul is strong; no adversities will harm it if it perseveres in silence. The silent (198) soul is capable of attaining the closest union with God. It lives almost always under the inspiration of the Holy Spirit. God works in a silent soul without hindrance.
>
> 478 O my Jesus, You know, You alone know well that my heart knows no other love but You! All my virginal love is drowned eternally in You, O Jesus! I sense keenly how Your divine Blood is circulating in my heart; I have not the least doubt that Your most pure love has entered my heart with Your most sacred Blood. I am aware that You are dwelling in me, together with the Father and the Holy Spirit, or rather I am aware that it is I who I am living in You, O incomprehensible God! I am aware that I am dissolving in You like a drop in an ocean. I am aware that You are within me and all about me, that You are in all things that surround me, in all that happens to me. O my God, I have come to know You within my heart, and I have loved You above all things that exist on earth or in heaven. Our hearts have a mutual understanding, and no one of humankind will comprehend this.

I pray that you may become blessed and crave, thirst and desperately seek the love of God so that you also may learn to live where love is. -- Gloria

HOW GREAT IS THE MERCY OF OUR LORD?

> For judgment will be merciless to one who has shown no mercy;
> **MERCY TRIUMPHS OVER JUDGMENT.**
> *Jas 2:13* NASB95

> "Blessed are the merciful, for they shall receive mercy.
> *Mt 5:7* NASB

The Lord is great in measure, so immeasurable we cannot begin to understand its capacity. His Love, His compassion, His Kindness, the Goodness of His very being, are all enormously and immeasurably grand!

His Mercy is just as grand and enormously immeasurable as His love! We must also desire to be unconditionally merciful.

Just a short note on sin: On Divine Mercy week 2004, the Lord's promises of Divine Mercy came true in my life. The Lord showed to me sins I did not realize were mine.

The Lord showed to me that one word of condemnation towards another causes many others to sin. Therefore, we become the source of that sin multiplied.

The Lord also led me to confess doubt.

The Lord led me to use sackcloth and ashes.

He is our teacher! His will, His way, His Light, His Truth... not ours!

Stumbling blocks of darkness detain us from being the soul of fervent prayer.

The Lord's Mercy is so great. He is like a pregnant woman waiting to burst out his mercy on everyone. If we would have even a little bit of understanding of His merciful kindness, goodness and His great unconditional love we would want to urgently go and confess, to be full of light;

sin brings darkness and darkness torments us.

Praise the Lord, for His Mercy endures forever.
Exalted is Our Great Loving Bread of Life!

The following was taken from the book <u>Divine Mercy in My Soul</u> by Saint Maria Faustina Kowalska:

Today the Lord said to me, **Daughter, when you go to confession, to this fountain of My mercy, the Blood and Water which came forth from My Heart always flows down upon your soul and ennobles it. Every time you go to confession, immerse yourself in My mercy, with great trust, so that I may pour the bounty of My grace upon your soul. When you approach the confessional, know this, that I Myself am waiting there for you. I am only hidden by the priest, but I myself act in your soul. Here the misery of the soul meets the God of mercy. Tell souls that from this fount of mercy (7) souls draw graces solely with the vessel of trust. If their trust is great, there is no limit to My generosity. The torrents of grace inundate humble souls. The proud remain always in poverty and misery, because My grace turns away from them to humble souls. (1602) My daughter, just as you prepare in My presence, so also you make your confession before Me. The person of the priest is, for Me, only a screen. Never analyze what sort of a (89) priest it is that I am making use of; open your soul in confession as you would to Me, and I will fill it with My light.** (1725)

You will prepare the world for My final coming. (429)

Speak to the world about My mercy; ... It is a sign for the end times; after it will come (230) the day of justice. While there is still time, let them have recourse to the fountain of My mercy; (848)

...tell souls about this great mercy of Mine, because the awful day, the day of My justice, is near. (965).

I am prolonging the time of mercy for the sake of [sinners]. But woe to them if they do not recognize this time of My visitation. (1160)

Before the Day of Justice, I am sending the Day of Mercy. (*Diary* 1588)

He who refuses to pass through the door of My mercy must pass through the door of My justice. (*Diary* 1146).

...you have to speak to the world about His great mercy and prepare the world for the Second (91) Coming of Him who will come, not as a merciful Savior, but as a just Judge. Oh, how terrible is that day! Determined is the day of justice, the day of divine wrath. The angels tremble before it. Speak to souls about this great mercy while it is still the time for granting mercy. (Diary 635).

I beg you, my beloved reader, please repent. I a terrible sinner who has repented ask it of you, because I love you and I know you live in darkness as I did. You do not know the love of God unless you repent!

Trust in Jesus! Pray with your whole heart, mind, soul and strength. Meditate on His life and passion and that of the Holy Family where we find many answers. Trust Jesus even unto death!

WHO SHOULD WE TRUST?

"JESUS, I TRUST IN YOU".... The graces of My mercy are drawn by means of one vessel only, and that is—trust. The more a soul trusts, the more it will receive. 1578
(Jesus spoke the above to Sr Faustina)

Our Lord said you are a slave to those whom you choose to obey as stated in Romans 6:16. Catholics are not isolated to these occurrences and beliefs. The Lord also says to trust no man, **trust NO mortal man in whom there is no salvation.** To those who are running the race, loving unconditionally let us then submit to the Lord and bring down to earth, Our Lord, the stronghold in which we trust, that He may deliver us from evil, even unto death!

Oh that my head were waters and my eyes a fountain of tears, That I might weep day and night For the slain of the daughter of my people! Oh that I had in the desert A wayfarers' lodging place; That I might leave my people And go from them! For all of them are adulterers, An assembly of treacherous men. "They bend their tongue like their bow; Lies and not truth prevail in the land; **For they proceed from evil to evil, And they do not know Me," declares the LORD.** "Let everyone be on guard against his neighbor, And do not trust any brother; Because every brother deals craftily, And every neighbor goes about as a slanderer. "Everyone deceives his neighbor And does not speak the truth, They have taught their tongue to speak lies; They weary themselves committing iniquity. "Your dwelling is in the midst of deceit; **Through deceit they refuse to know Me," declares the LORD.**
Therefore thus says the LORD of hosts, "Behold, I will refine them and assay them; For what else can I do, because of the daughter of My people? "Their tongue is a deadly arrow; It speaks deceit; **With his mouth one speaks peace to his neighbor, But inwardly he sets an ambush for him.**

" Shall I not punish them for these things?" declares the LORD. *Jer9:1-9 NASB95*

- It is better to take refuge in the LORD **Than to trust in man**. *Ps 118:8 NASB95*

- **Do not trust** in princes, **In mortal man,** in whom there is no salvation. *Ps 146:3 NASB95*

- How blessed is the man who has made the LORD his trust, And has not turned to the proud, nor to those who lapse into falsehood. *Ps 40:4 NASB95*

"Blessed is the man who trusts in the LORD **And whose trust is the LORD.** *Jer 17:7 NASB95*

A wise man scales the city of the mighty **And brings down the stronghold in which they trust.** *Pr 21:22 NASB95*

- In God, whose word I praise, In God I have put my trust; I shall not be afraid. What can mere man do to me? *Ps 56:4 NASB*

- indeed, we had the sentence of death within ourselves so **that we would not trust in ourselves**, but in God who raises the dead; *2Co 1:9 NASB95*

- But I trust that you will realize that we ourselves do not fail the test. *2Co 13:6 NASB95*

- And again, "I WILL PUT MY TRUST IN HIM." And again, "BEHOLD, I AND THE CHILDREN WHOM GOD HAS GIVEN ME." *Heb 2:13 KJV*

The image of the Divine Mercy has the words imprinted upon it "Jesus I Trust in You!. It is those same words we must imprint in our minds, in our hearts and in our whole being without reserve. **Jesus I Trust in you!**

WHEN *IN TIME DID THEY CHANGE "OUR LORD'S PRAYER"?*

We know that from the beginning men have changed the Word of God and continue even today... Is it carnal forgiveness or Divine forgiveness we seek?

Consider the next a new prayer, a prayer of Divine love requesting that we be like our Maker of Unconditional Forgiveness.

> Our Father who art in heaven, hallowed be thy name, thy kingdom come thy will be done on earth, ***and in us***, as it is in heaven, give us this day our daily bread and forgive us our trespasses ***make us*** to forgive those who trespass against us, ***fill us with your perfect love***, lead us not into temptation, but deliver us from evil. Amen

MEMO: to forgive "as we forgive" is carnal forgiveness... men do not easily forgive... but Our Lord Our Maker, made us and He can change us, let us pray that He will make us like Him.

Beloved King of Glory Fill us with your perfect love that we may love you perfectly in Jesus. Amen

Beloved King of Glory Fill us with your perfect love that we may love you perfectly in Jesus. Amen

THE PERFECT PRAYER

On October 17, 2009 the Lord taught me that Our Lord's Prayer is the perfect prayer. He made me to understand that it was the Lord Himself saying the prayer. And in this instance, He was referring to Himself and of us in His image (as the apostles whom He taught how to pray and how to forgive as He forgives). Reflecting on the words "To forgive as we forgive" the Lord made me to visualize the forgiveness He gave to sinners who mocked Him, hurt Him and hung Him on the cross during His passion, it was a very real moment for me and emotional. Visualizing Him on the Cross the thoughts that came to me were that He undoubtedly forgives all of us. The first part "Forgive us", I had a little trouble understanding why the Lord would be asking for forgiveness. The next day, He reminded me that He is Our Father and teaches His children all things "to pardon and to ask for pardon". He also reminded me of a Jewish woman I used to work with that was angry at God because her child was handicapped and has never walked. We must forgive Our Lord who loves us so much and knows the purpose and state of our being better than we ourselves know or understand.

In November 2009 the Lord also led me to read a small book entitled TRUSTFUL SURRENDER TO DIVINE PROVIDENCE.
The following is a beautiful paragraph from the 139 page booklet:

> "Let us never then attribute our losses, our disappointments, our afflictions, our humiliations to the devil or to men, but to God as their real source. "To act otherwise" says St. Dorothy, "would be to do the same as a dog who vents his anger on the stone instead of putting the blame on the hand that threw it at him." So let us be careful not to say 'So-and-so is the cause of my misfortune.' Your misfortunes are the work not of this or that person but of God. And what should give you reassurance is that God, the sovereign good, is guided in all His actions by His most profound wisdom for holy and supernatural purposes."

In the book of Job we can see that even He admits that it is the Lord who disciplines:
> "Blessed is the man whom God corrects; so do not despise the discipline of the Almighty.
> (Job 5:17) _NIV_
> For he wounds, but he also binds up; he injures, but his hands also heal. (Job 5:18) _NIV_

And in the Book of Revelation, the following:
> Those whom I love I rebuke and discipline. So be earnest, and repent. (Rev 3:19) _NIV_

Also in November, I have found myself praying the Our Father; my thoughts focused on His teaching as mentioned above, then thinking of myself in His image praying it with Him was like a different revelation as I had never before prayed. Praying in the Spirit with mind and heart gives an understanding and knowledge of great love, a different kind of enlightenment ... Blessed is Our Lord who is most merciful! I pray that we may all come to know Him and love Him and each other as He loves us.

WHAT DOES REPENTANCE MEAN and FEAR OF THE LORD?

On June 21st 2004, The Lord gave to me the following definition of repentance while at the Blessed Sacrament Adoration chapel:

_ An act of the Fear of the Lord one of the Gifts of the Spirit
_ The fear of offending Him
_ The fear of the thought of being separated from Him, greatly longing your Bridegroom
_ The fear of not being with and in Him
_ The fear of loosing His Love or becoming lost and loosing Him through sin
_ The fear of becoming a black sheep, straying and becoming disobedient
_ The fear of losing grace and falling away from Him through sin
_ A fear that we have not repented of those things that we have done badly and have been veiled of our sin
_ Therefore, the fear of unknown disobedience
_ A feeling of remorse for the sins committed.
_ A contrite heart grieving for what it has done
_ A strong regret for offending the Lord
_ It is the Great Desire to Please the Lord, Obey and Abide, and to Love Him Greatly and the fear of not doing so and expressing our heartfelt contrition

IT IS IMPERATIVE THAT WE REPENT TO SEE THE LIGHT!

It is difficult to understand why anyone who truly wants to be a child of God would not run to the confessional, anxiously awaiting to receive Holy Communion, The Bread of Life, Our Lord who is seen in the Host. The Bread of Life unseen that is our seed consumed in holiness capable of resurrecting in us.

- fearing to be without life everlasting

- to receive the Body of Christ, flesh of my flesh, whom the Lord said if you do not eat, you do not have life in you
- The Living Bread is our source, Jesus said it! The devil tries to steal it from you. Ignorance is the devil's strength.

Ask the Lord for knowledge, wisdom and understanding. Open Your Bible. Trust in Jesus!

It is said that if everyone would go to confession many illnesses would be healed. Believe! Surrender! Receive! Return to Love! Reconcile one to another.
REPENTANCE - SACKCLOTH AND ASHES

- "Woe to you, Chorazin! Woe to you, Bethsaida! For if the miracles had been performed in Tyre and Sidon which occurred in you, they would have repented long ago, sitting in sackcloth and ashes. *Luke 10:13- also Mat 11:21* NASB95

HURRY DO NOT DELAY!!! TIME IS OF THE ESSENSE!
REPENT FOR THE REIGN of JESUS
                    IS AT YOUR FINGERTIPS!
JESUS IS COMING!!!!!!!!!!!!!!!!!!!! REPENT!

Consider this: think of all the things you are proud of: your home? children? accomplishments? business? boat? car? money? possessions? Knowing Satan's flaw was pride remove the word "Proud" from your vocabulary, then approach the Lord with a contrite heart asking forgiveness, asking Him to teach you to abandon the lusts, lures and loves that attach you to the world. This is repenting.

Be as Jesus was in the desert SAY NO TO THE DEVIL. Love God first, then love each other as He loves us unto death.

Remove the splinters of the eye, the eye is the lamp of the body, when the eye is clear, the body is full of light.

- If thy whole body therefore be full of light, having no part dark, the whole shall be full of light, as when the bright shining of a candle doth give thee light. *Luke 11:36* KJV

- I have come as Light into the world, so that everyone who believes in Me will not remain in darkness.
John 12:46 NASB95

- In whose case the god of this world has blinded the minds of the unbelieving so that they might not see the light of the gospel of the glory of Christ, who is the Image of God.
2Co 4:4 NASB95

Repent As If To Save You Life…
- But Jesus turning to them said, "Daughters of Jerusalem, stop weeping for Me, **but weep for yourselves and for your children** *Luke 23:28* NASB95

- Therefore remember from where you have fallen, and repent and do the deeds you did at first; or else I am coming to you and will remove your lamp stand out of its place—unless you repent. *Re 2:5* NASB95

HOW CAN WE STOP WAR?

- For while we were in the flesh, the sinful passions, which were aroused by the Law, were at work in the members of our body to bear fruit for death. *Ro 7:5 NKJV*

- Now those who belong to Christ Jesus have crucified the flesh with its passions and desires. *Ga 5:24 NIV*

What is the source of quarrels and conflicts among you? Is not the source **your pleasures** that wage war in your members? *Jas 4:1 NASB95*

- Beloved, I urge you as aliens and strangers to abstain from fleshly lusts which wage war against the soul.
1Peter 2:11 NASB95

To begin with, people perish because of lack of knowledge as noted in the Word of God.

It is important to realize that the battle is not an earthly battle. It is not a battle of human flesh, it is a heavenly battle. It is demons occupying the shell of dust, the vessel of clay otherwise known as flesh in which people have chosen their master. The flesh is a prison, it must be confined.

We must ask the Holy Spirit to take control of our lives so that we may empty ourselves of all evil. We must give our free will to the Lord. Padre Pio said the free will is the door in which Satan enters.

- But he turned, and rebuked them, and said,
Ye know not what manner of spirit ye are of.
For the Son of man is not come to destroy man's lives, but to save them. *Luke 9:55-56 KJV*

In few words, what can be said to make a difference. Jesus alone has made all the difference in the world.
In all He spoke, I would say there are three words of great significance that could give summation of what is written about the

life of Christ. These words portray the life we are to live to become like Him. They are:
Unconditional "love", "mercy" and "repentance".

The Lord said that those who live by the sword will die by the sword. The battle is not ours, and the Lord does not want us to fight in the way humans fight. Who is your father? Choose your sword!

Eph 6:17 KJV - the sword of the Spirit, which is the word of God.

Rev 2:16 NASB - Therefore repent; or else I am coming to you quickly, and I will make war against them with the sword of My mouth.

Re 13:10 NASB -If anyone is destined for captivity, to captivity he goes; if anyone kills with the sword, with the sword he must be killed. Here is the perseverance and the faith of the saints.

Speak the Word of God in defense of His love and mercy. His Word is spirit and is life. Our God, Our Creator is the only authority of life and death, and these rights are His alone. Therefore, if we die we are the Lord's, and if we live, we are His still.

Ro 14:8 NASB95 - for if we live, we live for the Lord, or if we die, we die for the Lord; therefore whether we live or die, we are the Lord's.

It is better to die for the love of another than to die by the sword. The Lord tells us to love our enemies. The world in war with itself does not listen. The world delighting and indulging in sin suffers much because it has not believed the word of God. It suffers because it continues to ignore the message of repentance, mercy, unconditional love and forgiveness.

Those who know Our Lord, Our Father and Our Heavenly Mother know that He is truly good. His ways are unfathomable in every characteristic of the fruits of the Holy Spirit in mercy, love, compassion, kindness, longsuffering, meekness and in all that He is. He is beyond measure all goodness beyond our understanding.

Perhaps if we would practice unconditional love and righteousness or at least tell the Lord we desire it, He will help us though all things and hear our prayers.

Can we act upon it? Can we drop our weapons and say to our opponent, I will die so that your soul may be saved because I want to love you as Jesus loves you and as He loves me and has died for me and has saved me from my evil ways.

He is our perfect example, Our Sheppard. His sheep know Him and hear his voice and follow Him.

LOVE and RIGHTEOUSNESS
Luke 6:27-36

"But I tell you who hear me:
Love your enemies,
do good to those who hate you,
bless those who curse you,
pray for those who mistreat you.
If someone strikes you on one cheek,
turn to him the other also.
If someone takes your cloak,
do not stop him from taking your tunic.
Give to everyone who asks you,
and if anyone takes what belongs to you,
do not demand it back.
Do to others as you would have them do to you.

If you love those who love you, what credit is that to you?
Even sinners love those who love them.
And if you do good to those who are good
to you, what credit is that to you?
Even sinners do that.
And if you lend to those from whom you expect repayment,
what credit is that to you?
Even sinners lend to sinners expecting to be repaid in full.
But **love your enemies, do good to them, and lend to them
without expecting to get anything back.**

Then your reward will be great,
and you will be sons of **the Most High,**

because he **is kind to the ungrateful and wicked.
BE MERCIFUL, JUST AS YOUR FATHER IS MERCIFUL."**

We must desire to Love God first and allow Him to change us, transform us in His great love and mercy so that we also may be love and mercy and all that He is. We must desire to repent and clear ourselves of demons that persistently continue to try to steal, devour and destroy our souls. We must be persistent and fervent in our desire to seek the Lord rebuking, resisting and renouncing Satan and all his works. We must pray more fervently and fast humbling ourselves before the Lord that He may possess us entirely so that we may do His will. We must repent to take the log out of our own eye!

- "You hypocrite, **first take the log out of your own eye,** and then you will see clearly to take the speck out of your brother's eye. *Mat 7:5 NASB95*

- "Then you will call, and the LORD will answer;
You will cry, and He will say, `Here I am.
**'If you remove the yoke from your midst,
The pointing of the finger
and speaking wickedness,** *Isa 58:9 NASB95*

VICTORY AT WAR

- But when they saw the army coming against them, they said to Judas: "How can we, few as we are, fight such a mighty host as this? Besides we are weak today from fasting." But Judas said: "It is easy for many to be overcome by few; **IN THE SIGHT OF HEAVEN THERE IS NO DIFFERENCE BETWEEN DELIVERANCE BY MANY OF BY FEW,** for victory in war does not depend upon the size of the army, **BUT ON THE STRENGTH THAT COMES FROM HEAVEN"** *1 Maccabees 3:17-22 NAB*

WOW!!! is that powerful!!!!!
Our Blessed Mother continues to tell us to pray the Rosary, it is a weapon against Satan. He hates it!!! It must be prayed with your whole heart, mind and soul and strength to please the Lord.

The Hail Mary is the call to heaven, sowing to reap, returning to Heaven those glorious living words of birth. The birth of our unity. It is a remembrance of a moment of ONE. Ask the Lord to teach you to pray fervently and righteously, so that we may obtain the strength that comes from heaven.

Let us stand firm, put down our weapons and say to them that choose the sword, "yes, I am willing to die so that your soul may be saved.". Can we follow Jesus?

Who has that faith? Who has that love? Who will trust in Jesus, our perfect example? Who will give everything up knowing that only Our God is above all gods and there is no other God to compare to Him who loves us? Who knows that Only our creator has the right to give and take life? Knowing this, would your faith be greater to know that Our Father in Heaven will be the one to determine whether we live or die? No man can change that! To whom do you submit? We must surrender to the way of Love in which Jesus came to teach us, to show us and to demonstrate for us so that we may do the same so that we may be like Him.

> And the prayer of faith shall save the sick, and the Lord shall raise him up; and if he have committed sins, they shall be forgiven him. Confess your faults one to another, and pray one for another, that ye may be healed. **The effectual fervent prayer of a righteous man availeth much.**
> *James 5:15-16 KJV*

> - And we know that the Son of God has come and has given us understanding, that we may know the true God and **may be in his true Son**. He is the true God and eternal life.
> *1John5:20 DRA*

No greater love has one than this...
   That he lay down his life for his friend ... John 15:13 KJV

WHO WILL LISTEN TO THE LIFE SAVING COMMANDS OF THE LORD?

LIFE SAVING COMMANDS/MESSAGES:

SMEAR YOUR DOOR WITH THE BLOOD OF THE LAMB!
Yes, this was the command of the Lord to save the lives of His people during the times of Pharaoh

DO NOT LOOK BACK OR YOU WILL TURN TO STONE!
This was the Lord's command at Sodom and Gomorrah.

BUILD AN ARK He said to Noah.

These messages were given by Our Father God in Heaven, the Great I AM, the Father of Abraham, life saving commands. No Bible, nothing written at the time, except in the heart of the believer, trusting the messenger of God.

UNLESS YOU REPENT,
YOU SHALL LIKEWISE PERISH (Luke 13:3) <u>NKJV</u>

This message was given by Our Lord Jesus while on earth, and His cousin John the Baptist and the apostles even after His death!

Repent or you will surely die. Every knee shall bow, every tongue confess! By confessing we are given the grace of increased light.

He is the Light of the world. We must desperately desire to be filled with His Light! It was divine inspiration written only in the hearts of the believer trusting the messenger of God. There was no written Bible telling these messengers what to say or do. "Who is it today that says "show me in the bible where it says that?" I tell you, they have no faith and are full of doubt. They do not know Our Heavenly Father. They have not repented.

- As I live, says the Lord GOD, I swear I take no pleasure in the death of the wicked man, but rather in the wicked man's conversion, that he may live. Turn, turn from your evil ways! Why should you die, 0 house of Israel? *Eze 33:11 KJV*

- See to it that you do not refuse Him who is speaking. For if those did not escape when they refused him who warned them on earth, much less will we escape who turn away from Him who warns from heaven. *Heb 12:25 NASB95*

"I HAVE COME TO TELL THE WORLD THAT GOD EXISTS. HE IS THE FULLNESS OF LIFE, AND TO ENJOY THIS FULLNESS AND PEACE, YOU MUST RETURN TO GOD".

Today this is the message from the Mother of God, whom Jesus needed and so do we. Return To God! Pray! Love! Forgive! She encourages us to obey Jesus and turn away from sin. She speaks of the wickedness in this world and says that we bring catastrophe upon ourselves. It is a reflection of our sinfulness, it is darkness.

Love and love will reflect; hate and hate will reflect. Jesus clearly said you reap what you sow. She comes crying and with much sorrow, to warn us, we must return to God, Love Him first above all things and even unto death. We must pray continuously. The following are two of her messages at Medjugarje

Message of January 25, 2005
"Dear children! In this time of grace again I call you to prayer. Pray, little children, for unity of Christians, that all may be one heart. Unity will really be among you inasmuch as you will pray and forgive. Do not forget: love will conquer only if you pray, and your heart will open. Thank you for having responded to my call."

Message of February 25, 2005
"Dear children! Today I call you to be my extended hands in this world that puts God in the last place. You, little children, put God in the first place in your life. God will bless you and give you strength to bear witness to Him, the God of love and peace. I am with you and intercede for all

of you. Little children, do not forget that I love you with a tender love. Thank you for having responded to my call."

ONLY BEESWAX CANDLES BLESSED BY PRIESTS (descendants of Apostles) WILL GIVE LIGHT while the faithful pray, especially the Rosary of Life Giving Grace.
They will not light for the wicked, they must repent or they will perish. Wear your scapular!

The three days of darkness as mentioned in the Bible and other remedies have been prophesied for end of times by many saints and prophets throughout the centuries. And what is the big deal now after so many centuries? I assure you, the time is near, JESUS USED MY MOUTH TO SPEAK in front of a classroom on July 24, 2004 "JESUS IS COMING", I did not say it of my own accord, the message was followed by "I MUST TELL YOU TO REPENT" and I had to share how the Lord got me to go to confession after so many years of disobedience. On November 15, 2004, a woman told me "He really is coming!" I took that as a confirmation. At the same event, the same day, another woman selling books was speaking about the miraculous sustaining grapes she ordered from the same place I had ordered in August. These women were strangers to me.

Glory and Praise to God and Exalted is My Most Holy, Beloved and Exalted Bread of Life, My Lord Most High, My Loving God of Great Simplicity, Unlimited Divine Mercy and Compassion, my God of Perfection, In the Name of Jesus.
Our Blessed Mother at Garabandal in Spain told the visionaries that there will be a warning, a miracle, and the chastisement The warning will be experienced by all, no matter what religion. People will wish they were dead but will not die, it will be an awakening. They will see their souls as God sees their souls. PRAY YOUR ROSARIES, WEAR YOUR SCAPULAR, THESE ARE DEFENSES. The Lord led me to the following scripture, which I believe could relate to the warning:

> - Therefore do not go on passing judgment before the time, but wait until the Lord comes who will both bring to light the things hidden in the darkness and disclose the motives

of men's hearts; and then each man's praise will come to him from God. *1Co 4:5 NASB95*

- "Cast away from you all your transgressions which you have committed and make yourselves a new heart and a new spirit! For why will you die, 0 house of Israel? *Eze 18:31 NASB95*

What are we to do for food in the times of the antichrist reign? Even this has been remedied. How many people will believe? How many will have faith? How many will desire wisdom, knowledge, and understanding, handed to them simply by asking Our Lord with a love toward Him and contrite heart? How many will trust the Lord? How many will repent for Blaspheming the Mother of God? How many will believe her messages? How many will repent even at the last second - proclaiming sorrow with their whole heart mind and soul, desiring to be reconciled one to another, desiring to remove barriers of division, fearing to be separated from Our Great Lord, who demonstrated such great forgiveness removing all barriers.

There was nothing written at that time in any bible for the people to make reference to these commands of protection during those critical times.

Again, I remind you to be watchful, be ready, seek Him... Jesus is Coming! Love His Mother, Honor Her, if you do not love Her, you cannot Love Him, Jesus. He is the way, the truth and the light of life. He loves His Mother and so should we.

NO ONE COMES TO THE FATHER
EXCEPT THROUGH JESUS.

Jesus said these words while he was on earth, there was no bible. I read in the Book The Mystical City of God the following:

"Just as I have told you that he who knows Me knows also My Father, so I now tell you that he who knows My Mother knows Me."

How can we even begin to think, that Loving Jesus alone is enough. If we want to live with our heavenly family, we must love them all. We must love her greatly! Could it be that NO ONE COMES TO JESUS EXCEPT THROUGH HIS MOTHER MARY.

She was the vessel He used to unite Himself to the world, The WORD Became FLESH through her. She is the vessel the world needs to unite itself to Him, that our flesh will also become His flesh, His Word. The Word made flesh continues to live in us, transformed to a spiritual being in a twinkling of an eye. We need her, the one whom God Himself chose to need. I believe Mary is the Bride in us. Blessed is she whose soul magnifies the Lord, may my soul be like hers. We must ask her into our hearts, into our life, so that Jesus will also receive us with as great a love as hers toward Him. FOOD FOR END OF TIMES. This remedy was given by a woman who had the stigmata, Marie Julie Jahenny. The Miraculous Sustaining Grapes are grapes whose blessing has been transferred from the original to the new ones. One grape a day will sustain the people of Our Lord. The original grapes came from the mission fields of a little village from where St. Francis of Assisi lived. They must be prepared a certain way for the blessing to take effect.

The Lord led me to them, I know He will lead you to them too if this is what is necessary.

I SEE ONLY ONE EXCEPTION TO THE MESSAGE ABOVE, it is **THE SIGN OF JONAH**.
May the Lord Bless You Indeed!

WHAT IS THE SIGN OF JONAH?

> \- But He answered and said to them, "An evil and adulterous generation craves for a sign and yet no sign will be given to it but the sign of Jonah the prophet;
> <u>Matthew 12:39 KJV</u>

> And sighing deeply in spirit, he saith: Why doth this generation seek a sign? Amen, I say to you, a sign shall not be given to this generation. <u>Mark 8:12 DRA</u>

THE SIGN OF JONAH

I was watching an animated Bible story about Jonah and was amazed at what I saw and heard. I will tell you the story as revealed to me: Jonah had a dream. The Lord wanted him to preach repentance in Niveth, a wicked city. Jonah did not like what he saw in his dream and did not want to obey the Lord. He decided to run away from the Lord, so he got on a boat going the opposite direction from Niveth. When the captain of the boat and his crew saw Jonah, they laughed at him, believing he was running away from his wife. The boat left dock, and began its journey, only to find itself in a great storm. The captain and the crew were frightened fearing their death. They apparently were men of God, obedient and of great faith, ready to offer their first fruits to Our Lord. The captain in fear of his life, told the crew to THROW EVERYTHING OVERBOARD AS AN OFFERING TO THE LORD to appease his anger. The storm continued. The captain told the crew members to get Jonah who was below deck, so that he could pray to his God for the safety of the crew. When they brought Jonah out, they decided to cast lots to determine to whom the Lord was displaying his anger. They pointed at Jonah. Jonah told them to throw him overboard and that the storm would calm. The captain, a good man, did not want to do that. However, the storm continued and there was no other choice, they asked the Lord to forgive them and that they would do as Jonah has said. Jonah was then swallowed by a great fish in whose belly he remained for three days. Jonah repented and made a vow to the Lord, that if he would

save him, he would preach repentance as the Lord had asked. The fish spit him out on land and Jonah did as he promised.
Jonah went to the city of Niveth and was preaching repentance. Three men that heard him went to the king and told the King that Jonah was preaching that all must repent or the Lord would destroy the whole city in a day. The king knowing that Jonah was a true prophet, tore off his clothes and put on sackcloth and sat in ashes. He then made a decree that the whole city PEOPLE AND ANIMALS do the same, REPENT AND PUT ON SACKCLOTH AND ASHES. After having preached Jonah went out of the city to high ground where he could view the city, waiting for God's wrath to destroy them. He waited and waited for a sign of destruction. In the heat of the sun he became frustrated and angry that it had not yet happened.

    The Lord then allowed a huge tree to grow in a day. Jonah was happy because the Lord provided shade for him. That night the Lord allowed worms to eat the tree. The next day Jonah was angry that the tree was gone and he was once again in the hot burning sun.

    The Lord then spoke to Jonah and asked him why he was angry. He said you are angry that I have destroyed a tree that I created in a day and it is only one tree for which you did not toil. Yet you wait for me to destroy a city that has listened to your preaching and has repented. I AM A MERCIFUL GOD, MY PEOPLE HAVE REPENTED AND SO DO I REPENT. I LOVE MY PEOPLE, HUNDREDS OF THOUSANDS WHO HAVE LISTENED TO YOUR MESSAGE OF REPENTANCE ARE SAVED BECAUSE THEY HAVE REPENTED.

    The Sign of Jonah is the resulting salvation of the people and the beasts (animals) through true bitter repentance with the use of sackcloth and ashes.

    In the New Testament Matthew 11:21 and Luke 10:13 clearly state that if Tyre and Sidon would have done what we have done, **"they would have repented long ago, sitting in sackcloth and ashes."**

These are the items of significance in the story of Jonah.
1. Offering Of First Fruits/We must be willing to give all
2. Prayer, Trust and Faith
3. Preaching Repentance
4. Use Of Sackcloth and Ashes
5. Not just for People but Animals Too
6. Stop wickedness! Desire to change your ways!
7. God Himself repented, when the people repented

(The measure you use
is the measure you are measured with)
THEN PEOPLE REPENTED **THEN GOD REPENTED!**

> - Woe unto thee, Chorazin! Woe unto thee, Bethsaida! for if the mighty works had been done in Tyre and Sidon, which were done in you, **they would have repented long ago, sitting in sackcloth and ashes**.
> *Luke 10:13; Matthew 11:21 NKJV*

> - and if He condemned the cities of Sodom and Gomorrah to destruction by reducing them to ashes, having made them an example to those who would live ungodly lives **thereafter;** *2 Peter 2:6 NASB95*

> - And I will give unto my two witnesses, and they shall prophesy a thousand two hundred and threescore days, clothed in sackcloth. *Revelation 11:3 KJV*

WHAT IS THE SIGN OF SALVATION?

The Sign of Jonah is the resulting salvation of the people and the beasts (animals) through true bitter repentance with the use of sackcloth and ashes.

WHAT IS SACKCLOTH AND ASHES?
DEFINITIONS (what is sackcloth and ashes?):
Sackcloth: A coarse cloth of camel's hair, goat hair, hemp or flax. ie: Burlap
Ashes: The remains of something burned; ie: paper, blessed palm; charcoal
Loins: The region of the hips, groin, and lower abdomen. ; The reproductive organs.

HOW TO USE SACKCLOTH and WHAT TO DO!
FOR MAN AND BEAST (ANIMALS)
as noted in the Bible - (Animals included in Jonah):
SCRIPTURES: Genesis 37:34; 2 Samuel 3:31; 2 Kings 6:30; 2 Kings 19:1-2; 1 Chronicles 21:16; 1 Kings 20:31-32; 1 Kings 21:21-27; Nehemiah 9:1; Ester 4:1; Ester 4:3-4; Daniel 9:3; Jonah 3:6; Jonah 3:8; Jeremiah 6:26; Jeremiah 25:34; Ezekiel 27:30

YOU MAY WEAR IT:
_ Clothe yourself in sackcloth/wear sackcloth
Tear off your clothes/remove them anxiously/change your Clothes; Cover your loins/body with sackcloth
_ You may also put rope of hemp upon your head as a crown
_ In Jonah the King wore sackcloth and sat in ashes.

YOU MAY LAY ON IT:
• fall on your face/lay in sackcloth;
• spread out sackcloth & ashes on a bed and lay on it

ASHES AND EARTH:
• put on you/roll/wallow in ashes,
• cast dust/dirt on your head
_ put earth/ashes upon you; roll in dirt/ashes;
• sit in ashes
• fill a salt shaker with ashes and put on your food
Psalm 102:9; Isaiah 44:20
Eat ashes like bread, mingle weeping with drink

WHERE CAN I DO THIS:
• present yourself in Church in sackcloth and ashes and pray
• in home or outside; do not be ashamed to be humble to God who sees you and hears you
_ do not be deceived to remove the sackcloth from you/ it is for the Lord, that He may hear our prayer of repentance/the destroyer will come suddenly, put on sackcloth
(The two witnesses in the book of Revelations are perfect examples; In Esther 4:4 Mardochai refused to take off his sackcloth)

WHAT YOU MUST DO Once You Have It On or Are Laying/ Sitting On It:
• Cry mightily unto God, Wail/Mourn/weep/cry out loud bitterly, as loosing what or whom you love most and especially that the Lord will save everyone including those least lovable
_ Beg the Lord desperately as He was desperate for our love allowing His son to die for us; surely even Our Father in Heaven cried out bitterly at the torment of His Beloved Son
_ prostrate yourself before the Lord;
_ Every one turn from our evil ways and from violence/desire to please the Lord; REPENT!
• PRAY; pray that our/their life would be healed; salvation for the world
• FAST; Humble yourself before the Lord

– For our beloved Dead -
There was a famine for 3 yrs. David asked the Gibonites what could he do for them as atonement so that the Lord would restore their inheritance. They asked to hang seven sons of the Saul, who was trying to kill them. King David granted that request. Rizpah, who bore two of the sons of Saul which were hanged, spread sackcloth on top of rock, from the beginning of harvest until it rained. After King David found out what she did, he took the bones of King Saul and Jonathan and buried them. The Lord was moved by prayer and restored their inheritance. *2Samuel 21:10*

NOW WHAT DO I DO???
According to Nehemiah 9 they did the following:
1. Assembled with fasting in sackcloth with dirt/ashes on them.
2. Confessed their sins and those of their fathers.
3. They read of the book of the law (Bible).
4. They worshipped the Lord.

Nehemiah 9 and Daniel 9 inspired this response: Read Scripture, Confess sins (see list) yours and your fathers, boldly and loudly while on/in sackcloth as taken from the Bible, also Worship the Lord.

> - Now on the twenty-fourth day of this month the sons of Israel **assembled with fasting, in sackcloth and with dirt upon them.** The descendants of Israel separated themselves from all foreigners, and **stood and confessed their sins and the iniquities of their fathers.** While they stood in their place, **they read from the book of the law of the LORD their God** for a fourth of the day; and for another fourth **they confessed and worshiped the LORD their God.** *Neh 9:1-3 NASB95*

> - in the first year of his reign, I, Daniel, observed in the books the number of the years which was revealed as the word of the LORD to Jeremiah the prophet for the completion of the desolations of Jerusalem, namely, seventy

years. So I gave my attention to the Lord God to **seek Him by prayer and supplications, with fasting, sackcloth and ashes.** *Dan 9:2-3 NASB95*

- Now while I was speaking and praying, and **confessing my sin and the sin of my people Israel,** and presenting my supplication before the LORD my God in behalf of the holy mountain of my God, *Dan 9:20 KJV*

SUGGESTED (OPTIONAL) SCRIPTURES TO READ:
Daniel 3:37-44; Daniel 3:26-44; Judith 9; Matthew Ch 5 and 6
Matthew Ch 22:36-46; Exodus Ch 20; Isaiah 58; Colossians 3:1-17;
Daniel 3:52-90; Psalm 95-96

PRAY WITH YOUR OWN WORDS, Here Is A Start:

BREAK EVERY YOKE (inspired by Isaiah 58)
Lord, please teach me to bow down in an acceptable way and to be pleasing to You. Help me to trust you and to acknowledge you in all my ways. Give to me wisdom, knowledge and understanding. Teach me to be obedient. Lead me to those whom you want me to help. Make me and Mold me to be the repairer of the breach, the restorer of paths to dwell in, as you desire, that the yoke of many will be broken. Teach me to draw out my soul to the hungry, and to satisfy the afflicted soul. Guide me continually and like a spring of water, let not my waters fail. Please allow my health to spring forth speedily. Teach me to keep the Sabbath holy as a delightful day unto the Lord, that you may feed me with the heritage of Jacob our father. All Glory, Honor and Power are Yours Most Beloved Heavenly Father In the Name of Jesus. Amen.

After prayer, confess your sins and those of your family and dead relatives, that perhaps the Lord will be merciful to them.

WHY DID MARY PRESENT THE SCAPULAR AS A SIGN OF SALVATION?

> - See to it that you do not refuse Him who is speaking. For if those did not escape when they refused him who warned them on earth, much less will we escape who turn away from Him who warns from heaven. Heb 12:25 NASB95

Mary presents a scapular to the world in more than one appearance. She said that anyone who dies wearing it will not suffer eternal fire. It is said to be "the sign of salvation".

I tell you now that this is in agreement with the "sign of Jonah". It is the sign of salvation with repentance and love. It is sack clothe and must be worn in cloth made of wool (or animal hair like camel as John the Baptist wore) as presented by Mary, Mother of God, most Blessed. I am not sure if the scapular satisfies Our Lord completely, but in the right state of grace, I know the Lord keeps His promises. Sister Faustina was asked by Our Lord to put on a shirt of hair clothe, her superior denied her. How sad!

The Lord will know his sheep by the wool that they wear! Repent and live a Christian life in love and mercy and wear it to please the Lord. Honor Our Lord and Our Blessed Mother by wearing this garment so that you may not suffer eternal fire.

The Lord says if you love me, obey my Commands. You must strive to be in obedience to His Commandments. Desire to please the Lord and Our Blessed Mother, Mary, Mother of God!

The following was taken from this website:

http://www.truecatholic.org/scapular.htm
The Brown Scapular of Our Lady of Mt. Carmel
A magnificent assurance of salvation is Our Lady's Brown Scapular. One of the great mysteries of our time is that the great majority of Catholics either ignore or have forgotten the Blessed Virgin Mary's promise that **"whoever dies wearing this (Scapular) shall not suffer eternal fire."** She further says: "Wear it devoutly and perseveringly. It is my garment. To be clothed in it means you

are continually thinking of me, and I in turn, am always thinking of you and helping you to secure eternal life."

Many Catholics may not know that it is the wish of our Holy Father, the Pope, that the Scapular Medal should not be worn in place of the Cloth Scapular without sufficient reason. Mary cannot be pleased with any one who substitutes the medal out of vanity, or fear to make open profession of religion. Such persons run the risk of not receiving the Promise. The medal has never been noted for any of the miraculous preservations attributed to the Brown Cloth Scapular.

During the Scapular Anniversary celebration in Rome, Pope Pius XII told a very large audience to wear the brown Scapular as a sign of consecration to the Immaculate Heart of Mary. Our Lady asked for this consecration in the last apparition at Fatima, when She appeared as Our Lady of Mount Carmel, holding the Brown Scapular out to the whole world. It was her last loving appeal to souls to wear her Scapular as a sign of Consecration to her Immaculate Heart.

Blessed Claude de la Colombiere, the renowned Jesuit and spiritual director of St. Margaret Mary, gives a point which is enlightening. He said: "Because all the forms of our love for the Blessed Virgin, all its various modes of expression cannot be equally pleasing to Her, and therefore do not assist us in the same degree to Heaven, I say without a moment's hesitation the BROWN SCAPULAR is the most favored of all!" He also adds: "No devotion has been confirmed by more numerous authentic miracles than the Brown Scapular."

http://www.carmelitedcj.org/saints/scapular.asp
The Carmelite Scapular is not:
a magical charm to protect you
an automatic guarantee of salvation
an excuse for not living up to the demands of the Christian life
It is a sign which stands for the decision to:
-follow Jesus like Mary
-be open to God and to His Will
-be guided by faith, hope and love
-to pray at all times
-to discover God's presence in all that happens around us

Why should we wear it?
The scapular is not a magic charm or a free ticket into heaven, nor is it an excuse to live an immoral life. The scapular is a visible sign that you are pledging to live a Christian life with Mary as your example. To wear the scapular is a sign of devotion to the Blessed Virgin Mary.

… Our Lady told St. Simon Stock that she wished her children to wear the scapular, the garment she chose to signify her protection. Mary has promised that she will obtain the graces and protections necessary for those who show their devotion to her by wearing the scapular. She will not let her children fall into the eternal fire, but rather protect them under her mantle, the brown scapular. By wearing the scapular, you visibly show that you desire to live a holy life, and you trust that God, through the intercession of Mary, will give you the graces you need to reach heaven.

AM I WITHOUT SIN?

no one who is born of God sins; *1 John 5:18* NASB

We are all sinners, but we have this hope gifted to us that we may become true sons of God.

-the one who practices sin is of the devil;
for the devil has sinned from the beginning.
The Son of God appeared for this purpose,
to destroy the works of the devil. *1John 3:8* NASB95

We all fall short of the glory of God. Yes, we are born with sin. Are we then all of the devil? it seems very apparent that we are, yet, Our Lord loves us so much, so so much!
Tell souls not to place within their own hearts obstacles to My mercy, which so greatly wants to act within them My mercy works in all those hearts which open their doors to it. Diary of a Soul ¶1577

He came to show us the way to be like Him, to love like Him and to give to us the great hope of our salvation. I do believe that when perfection comes we will be without sin as mentioned in *1 John*. We must run the race to attain perfection by desiring to love unconditionally and by repenting. We must run the race to attain perfection, that is, to be possessed by Our Lord!
the evil one does not touch him. *1John 5:18* NASB

no one who is born of God sins;
but He who was born of God keeps him,
and **the evil one does not touch him.**
We know that we are of God, and that
the whole world lies in the power of the evil one.
And we know that the Son of God has come,
and has given us understanding so that we may know Him who is true;
**and we are "in Him" who is true,
in His Son Jesus Christ.**

This is the true God and eternal life. *1 John 5:18-20* <u>NASB</u>
"The eye is the lamp of the body; so then if your eye is clear, your whole body will be full of light. *Mat 6:22* <u>NASB95</u>

"But if your eye is bad, your whole body will be full of darkness. If then the light that is in you is darkness, how great is the darkness! *Mat 6:23* <u>NASB95</u>

'Therefore remember from where you have fallen, and **repent** and do the deeds you did at first; **or else I am coming to you and will remove your lamp stand out of its place--unless you repent.** *Re 2:5* <u>NASB95</u>

CONFESS THESE SINS WHILE ON/IN SACKCLOTH & ASHES (if you do not have sack cloth, ashes or dirt, confess anyway for yourself and for others throughout the world and even our own families with a contrite heart, mind and soul, and a bitter appeal to the Lord):

Forgive us Lord for ….
- doubting your word and for our disbelief.
- our ignorance and lack of desire to know you as you want us to. *Teach us Lord to know you as we have never known you before, give to us the grace of increased desire to please you, love you, abide and obey you unconditionally.*
- the time passed in our falter
- all the times we do not believe, do not love, do not adore and do not trust you, forgive our past sins also in this regard
- the things we have done that we should not have done, and for the things we have failed to do
- the things we have said that we should not have said and for not saying the things we should have said
- our evil thoughts

Make our minds obedient to you, help us to resist, rebuke and renounce Satan and all his evil works
- all of our sins, especially those unknown to us.

- the harm and hurt we have caused others and for causing others to sin because of what we have said or done or because of what we have made of ourselves
- hurting members of our families, spouses, children, relatives and those near to us, including those who are deceased, have mercy Lord and bring them to your everlasting love and light
- breaking every commandment, ordinance, precept, and statutes of the Lord for surely we have killed even your smallest creation, or insulted those we love causing our relationships to die.
    Teach us Lord to Love and acknowledge you in all of our ways, Help us to be reconciled one to another and to You. Help us to trust you unconditionally. Make us to keep your commands and to sin no more.
- For all the times I have broken the ten commandments of Our Lord and have made others to break them as well.

Forgive me Lord!
- every false god, including money, spouse, children, home, things, groups, accomplishments, everything on earth

Lord please give to me the grace to not serve money. I desire to serve only you Lord, please help me!
- For giving praise and worship to others who have been hidden to us as false gods or for giving you reason to be jealous, Lord forgive us
- every false god in our lives, including those unknown to us.
    Teach us Lord to love you more than these false gods: money, graven images, foods, people, entertainment and all things of the earth. Reign in Our Life Lord, in Our hearts, mind and soul so that we may dwell in the house of the Lord. Make us and mold us to stay in your favor and to live in the home you have prepared for Your loved ones.
- Kneeling or bowing down to statues
- Lifting up my eyes to the idols of the house of Israel (Ez18:6)
- The times I have caused oppression to someone and have not paid my debt
    Help me Lord to make things right
- not denying ourselves as we should,

teach us how Lord so that we may be pleasing to you
- the times I have babbled in prayer heartlessly

- the times I have not prayed pleasing to you with all heart, mind and soul
- only praying out of need or distress.
    Give to us a sincere desire to pray so that we may have a fervent soul of the righteous so that our prayers may be pleasing to You. Make us to be heard by You, and as a Father to His children answer us.
- our inequities and the inequities of our fathers and relatives, especially of those deceased that might still be suffering for their sins whom you have judged.
    Bring them Lord to your everlasting Light that they may enter into eternal rest in your loving dwelling place.
- participating in thoughts that have altered your word from Bible to Bible, from generation to generation; forgive those that have altered it for others to see and hear.
- all the times we have spoken false doctrine and for teaching others that false doctrine.
- leaning on human understanding.
- participating in the sins of all religious preachers, teachers, leaders, helpers, listeners, and others forgive them Lord their sins
    Bless them and use them for Your glory
- the veil that has kept us from you,
    Please remove it
- Concealing your truth from others
- all the times we destroy the work of Your hands
    -by poisoning our earth, plants and flowers
    -killing creatures great and small
    -contaminating the waters
    -attempting to take creation into our own hands by cloning, reproductive services, birth control, abortions, subrogation of mothers, euthanasia
- all the times our hands have created or touched works that are an abomination in your sight Lord have mercy!
- For the idols our hands have created made of gold, silver, brass, stone, wood, molten or cast which can neither see, nor hear, nor walk Lord forgive us, forgive me (Rev9:20)
- for not acknowledging You in all that I do and in my works

- all the sins I have committed for not having lived in your faith, for you said that all this is not faith is sin
    Thus, I ask You Lord, to gift to me the faith of Jesus, my finisher, my completeness, my Savior, My One and Only True
- all the times we disagree with your truth
- for believing lies that have come out of the liars mouth
- all the times I have thought I was right
    Soften our hearts and give to us a sincere knowledge and a great portion of your love and mercy that we ourselves may become love and mercy
- all things written that are not true, also forgive anyone who comes against the truth written in this book
    Teach us to discern in these writings and all writings, teach us also to discern all words spoken, open our hearts to receive you with a contrite heart and great love, may we come to know that we are truly loved. Teach us your ways and your truth in your loving light.
- not mortifying our members which are upon the earth;
    Lord forgive us and teach us to mortify our members. We render our members to the Lord unto righteousness and holiness. Please receive them Lord!
- the sins of my members, my eyes, my ears, my mouth my tongue, my limbs, my body and my whole being for we are one
- fornication, uncleanness, inordinate affection, evil concupiscence, and covetousness, which is idolatry
- the times I have defiled or been defiled or allowed my husband to approach me during my menstrual period (Ez18:6)
- for my unchastity against my Lord
- stirring the wrath of God because of our disobedience: forgive our disobedience,
    Teach us Lord to be obedient to You
- the sins of hatred, anger, wrath, malice, blasphemy, filthy communication out of our mouth, drunkenness, jealousies, abusiveness, laziness, judgments, prejudices and condemnation, pride and for not repenting.
    Make us to not lie one to another, help us Lord to live a renewed life in You, with you and through you. Remove our evil deeds.

> *Teach us Lord not to quarrel, help us Lord to respond to every situation, every trial and tribulation that we may honor you Our Father. Teach us Lord also to Honor our Mother. HELP US LORD TO put off all these things, Teach us Lord your ways, Make us and Mold us to Your Likeness as you intended from the beginning to time.*
> *Break the power of the enemy and restore your nation to be holy.*

- our selfishness, greed and self centeredness
- receiving Holy Communion unworthily
- eating and drinking judgment
- judging my food and drink and all creatures and creation of the earth and all judgements against visible and invisible as created by My Lord
- not judging the body rightly
- gossiping and putting stumbling blocks in the path of my brethren
- idle words and careless speech spoken in the past, present and in the future
- vain glory, pride of life and lust of the flesh
- not serving others properly
- not demonstrating the fruits of the spirit as I should
- the sins of the spirit of gluttony and for my deprave passions.
   > *Help me Lord to resist, rebuke and renounce all evil*
- wanting things of the earth and for thinking that I need them
- causing others to sin because of my words, actions or deeds
- sinning against others, please forgive those who have sinned against me
- addictions and the addictions that my children may have tormenting them because of my sins
- the times I have not kept the Sabbath holy nor the rest of the seventh day.
- the times I have worked, carried a load, bought or sold and did not rest. Please forgive also those who worked with me, helped me or made me to work. Forgive the intent of my heart and the errors I have incurred because of my ignorance and otherwise.
   > *Teach me your ways and make me to make the Sabbath a delight to the Lord, a day of sanctification and a day of rest*

- all things that offend you and others
- for not resting as I should
- for all the times I have resisted loving my enemies
- for not having the greatest love - Lord give to me that grace!
- for partiality and favoritism
- my unrighteousness
- for breaking promises I could not keep or did not intend to keep
- sinning against You and against others and against myself.
- cutting our body for the dead
- making tattoo marks on ourselves

    You shall not make any cuts in your body for the dead nor make any tattoo marks on yourselves: I am the LORD.
    Le 19:28 NASB95
- not clothing myself in the armor of God, in the armor of righteousness and justice (2Cor 6:7)
- not having desired to have a mind of Christ (1Cor2:16)
- not seeking you sooner
- not blessing our enemies as we should,
- not feeding the hungry,
- not giving shelter to the poor,
- not giving freely what the Lord has given to me - Beloved King give to me the grace of perfect charity.
- not clothing the naked
- not being the repairer of the breach, the restorer of the path to dwell in.

Teach us Lord to do these things according to your word. Circumcise our hearts to please you. Use us Lord and teach us to atone for our sins and the sins of others that they also may be saved. Forgive us Lord. Lead us Lord. Help us Lord to repent fully and completely to be pleasing to you. Keep us on the narrow path so that we may obtain the promises of Christ, that all He purchased with His blood may be redeemed in love and gladness.

Thank You Lord for your great mercy and love. Blessed and Exalted are you Lord God Almighty, lover of my soul. Please allow my soul to magnify you and my spirit to rejoice in you.

PERFECT LOVE, MAKE US TO LOVE YOU PERFECTLY!

> Then Jesus saith to him:
> Begone, Satan: for it is written,
> The Lord thy God shalt thou adore,
> and him only shalt thou serve.
> *Matthew 4:10* DRA

AM I BORN AGAIN?

THE REAL BORN AGAIN:
>- We know that
>**no one who is born of God sins;**
>but He who was born of God keeps him,
>and **the evil one does not touch him.**
>We know that we are of God, and that
>**the whole world lies in the power of the evil one.**
>And we know that the Son of God has come,
>and has given us understanding so that we may know Him who is true;
>**and we are "in Him" who is true,**
>**in His Son Jesus Christ.**
>This is the true God and eternal life. *1 John 5:18-20 NASB*

If you do not obey his Commandments then **no** you are not born again. Our desire must be to obey Him. If He says "move" we must want to obey by moving.

> - for John baptized with water, but **you will be baptized with the Holy Spirit** not many days from now." *Acts 1:5 NASB95*

> "And we are witnesses of these things; and so is the Holy Spirit, **whom God HAS GIVEN TO THOSE WHO OBEY HIM**." *Acts 5:32 NASB95*

> - "If you keep My commandments, you will abide in My love; just as I have kept My Father's commandments and abide in His love. *John 15:10 NASB95*

> - For this, "YOU SHALL NOT COMMIT ADULTERY, YOU SHALL NOT MURDER, YOU SHALL NOT STEAL, YOU SHALL NOT COVET," and if there is any other commandment, it is summed up in this saying, "YOU SHALL LOVE YOUR NEIGHBOR AS YOURSELF." *Romans 13:9 NASB95*

If you are sleeping with your girlfriend, doing ungodly immoral sex, if you lie, if you steal, if you hate, do not desire to obey and trust God, then NO! you are not born again, you must repent! Desire to please the Lord!

If you do not desire His Love above all else, **NO, you are not born again**!

If you do not love Jesus and are not willing to die for the love of another, then you are **not born again**.

If you do not want to talk to your brother because of conflict and think you forgave them, but prefer not to talk to them but will only if you have to, NO you are not born again, you do not know love!

If you criticize, condemn and use your nasty tongue to say anything evil against anyone, NO, you are not born again

We must desire to be possessed by the Lord. We must desire to be holy as He is holy, pure and sacred.

> **Whoever possess the Son has life;**
> whoever does not possess the Son of God does not have life.
> *1 John 5:12* NABRE

> - He came to what was His own,
> but His own people did not accept Him.
> But to those who did accept Him
> **he gave power (the right) to become children of God,**
> to those who believe in His name, *John 1:11-12* NABRE

> - **who were born,** not of blood nor of the will of the flesh nor of the will of man, but *(the will)* of God. *John 1:13* DRA

Give your free will to the Lord!
BE BORN OF THE WILL OF GOD!!!

Make your greatest desire, the desire of Our Lord. Ask the Lord to make you all that He desires and that is **to be perfect as Our Father is Perfect!**

If you have to figure out if you are born again, then you are most likely NOT born again! When the Lord possesses you, it will be the Lord thinking for you and you will not be wondering!

Prayer:
Be Perfect As My Father is Perfect (Mat 5:48)
Beloved Heavenly Father
I pray that I may be pleasing to You
Obedient and Abiding;
Father, only You are perfect,
Yet, You request that I be perfect
as My Heavenly Father is perfect.
Allow me to serve you, and in submission to You,
You promise that I am One with You
One with Your Son, Jesus, My Savior
And One with Your Holy Spirit,
Make me Whole, a being of your loving intent
Make me perfect as My Heavenly Father is perfect
Give to me all that you perfectly desire:
Perfect Faith, Love, Hope and Charity
a Perfect Heart, Mind, Body, Soul,
Consume Me and do with me as You will.
Help me to live in your grace to the fullest.
There is no love greater than Yours
Magnificent Love Beyond Understanding
Be strong in me; allow me to live in the Spirit;
to always walk in the Spirit, and never let me fail you.
Glorify Yourself in my weak earthly being
that I may dwell in the house of the Lord in everlasting
joyful bliss. In Jesus' Name. I pray.

DOES HELL EXIST?

You better believe it does!

You must desire not to go there! The Lord says people perish because of lack of knowledge. The Word is alive! Desire to Love Him as He loves you. Hell is mentioned numerous times. Surely the devil does not want you to believe because he wants you to go to hell.

Repent or Perish as warned repeatedly in the Word of God! Be merciful as Our Father is merciful so that you may obtain mercy.

> - For if God did not spare angels when they sinned, but **cast them into hell** and committed them to pits of darkness, reserved for judgment; [5]and did not spare the ancient world, but preserved Noah, a preacher of righteousness, with seven others, when He brought a flood upon the world of the ungodly; [6]and *if* He condemned the cities of Sodom and Gomorrah to destruction by reducing *them* to ashes, having made them an example to those who would live ungodly *lives* thereafter; [7]and *if* He rescued righteous Lot, oppressed by the sensual conduct of unprincipled men [8](for by what he saw and heard *that* righteous man, while living among them, felt *his* righteous soul tormented day after day by *their* lawless deeds), [9]*then* the Lord knows how to rescue the godly from temptation, and to keep the unrighteous under punishment for the day of judgment, [10]and especially those who indulge the flesh in *its* corrupt desires and despise authority. *2Pe 2:4-10* NASB

> - "Do not fear those who kill the body but are unable to kill the soul; but rather fear Him who is able to destroy both soul and body in hell. *Mat 10:28* NASB95

> - "But I will warn you whom to fear: fear the One who, after He has killed, has authority to cast into hell; yes, I tell you, fear Him! *Luke 12:5* NASB95

- And the tongue is a fire, the very world of iniquity; the tongue is set among our members as that which defiles the entire body, and sets on fire the course of our life, and is set on fire by hell. *Jas 3:6 NASB95*

- "But I say to you that everyone who is angry with his brother shall be guilty before the court; and whoever says to his brother, 'You good-for-nothing,' shall be guilty before the supreme court; and whoever says, You fool,' shall be guilty enough to go into the fiery hell. *Mat 5:22 NASB95*

- "You serpents, you brood of vipers, how will you escape the sentence of hell? *Mat 23:33 NASB95*

In Mat 5:29-30, it says that it is better to lose one of the parts of your body than for your whole body to be thrown into hell in this referring to "your right hand", In Mark 9:43 it mentions "your hand"; in Mark 9:45 "your foot", Mark 9:47 "your eye". It says that it is better to enter life lame than having two feet, or to enter life crippled than having two hands to go to hell. If you do not believe, could it be that the devil is convincing you very well? Repent or perish!

"For there are eunuchs who were born that way from their mother's womb; and there are eunuchs who were made eunuchs by men; and there are also eunuchs who made themselves eunuchs for the sake of the kingdom of heaven. He who is able to accept this, let him accept it." *Mat 19:12 NASB95*

- "This is the judgment, that the Light has come into the world, and men loved the darkness rather than the Light, for their deeds were evil. *Joh 3:19 NASB95*

- For judgment will be merciless to one who has shown no mercy; mercy triumphs over judgment. *Jas 2:13 NASB95*

The Lord is merciful to those who are merciful. We reap what we sow. We must repent, we must love unconditionally and forgive unconditionally, we must be merciful. We must desire not to sin. We must desire to Love God as He loves us. Jesus showed us the way to live, He is our perfect example.

An Act of Contrition:
O my God, I am heartily sorry for having offended Thee, and I detest all my sins because of Thy just punishments, but most of all because they offend Thee, my God, Who art all-good and deserving of all my love. I firmly resolve, with the help of Thy grace, to sin no more and to avoid the near occasions of sin.

Eternal God, in whom mercy is endless and the treasury of compassion -- inexhaustible, look kindly upon us and increase Your mercy in us, that in difficult moments we might not despair nor become despondent, but with great confidence submit ourselves to Your holy will, which is Love and Mercy itself.

**THE MERCY OF OUR LORD IS YOURS
IF YOU WANT IT
DESIRE TO AMEND YOUR WAYS
DESIRE HIS LOVE
AND LOVE HIM BACK!**

DO I DO AS OUR SHEPHERD HAS TAUGHT?

CONSIDER THIS: Although with today's customs, this might seem awkward, the benefits derived may be life changing and delivering.

GREETING THOSE WHO ENTER YOUR HOME WASHING OF FEET:

- Turning toward the woman, He said to Simon, "Do you see this woman? I entered your house; you gave Me no water for My feet, but she has wet My feet with her tears and wiped them with her hair. *Luke 7:44 NASB95*

Joh 13:14 NASB95- "If I then, the Lord and the Teacher, washed your feet, you also ought to wash one another's feet.

HOLY KISS AND ANNOINTING HEAD WITH OIL
- "You gave Me no kiss; but she, since the time I came in, has not ceased to kiss My feet.

ANOINT HEAD WITH OIL and/or FEET WITH PERFUME *Luke 7:45 NASB95*
- "You did not anoint My head with oil, but she anointed My feet with perfume. *Luke 7:46 NASB*

- "But you, when you fast, anoint your head and wash your face *Mat 6:17 NKJV*

- Let your clothes be white all the time, and let not oil be lacking on your head. *Ec 9:8 NASB77*

- And they were casting out many demons and were anointing with oil many sick people and healing them. *Mark 6:13 NASB*

- Is anyone among you sick? Then he must call for the elders of the church and they are to pray over him, anointing him with oil in the name of the Lord; *Jas 5:14 NASB95*

- and the prayer offered in faith will restore the one who is sick, and the Lord will raise him up, and if he has committed sins, they will be forgiven him. *Jas 5:15 NASB95*

(desire to have the bride- consecrate yourselves to The Immaculate Heart of Mary, so that your heart may become like hers)
- **"He who has the bride** is the bridegroom; but the friend of the bridegroom, who stands and hears him, rejoices greatly because of the bridegroom's voice. So this joy of mine has been made full. *John 3:29 NASB95*

(Be wise? do we need oil lamps? Jesus is Coming! He used my mouth to say it in a classroom of students on June 26th, 2004)
-Then shall the kingdom of heaven be like to **ten virgins, who taking their lamps went out to meet the bridegroom and the bride.** And five of them were foolish, and five wise. But the five foolish, having taken their lamps, did not take oil with them: **But the wise took oil in their vessels with the lamps.** And the bridegroom tarrying, they all slumbered and slept. And at midnight there was a cry made: **Behold the bridegroom cometh, go ye forth to meet him. Then all those virgins arose and trimmed their lamps.** And the foolish said to the wise: Give us of your oil, for our lamps are gone out. The wise answered, saying: Lest perhaps there be not enough for us and for you, go ye rather to them that sell, and buy for yourselves. Now whilst they went to buy, the bridegroom came: and **they that were ready, went in with him to the marriage, and the door was shut.** But at last come also the other virgins, saying: Lord, Lord, open to us.
But he answering said: Amen I say to you, I know you not. **Watch ye therefore, because you know not the day nor the hour.** *Matthew 25:1-13 DRA*

- "Command the sons of Israel that they bring to you clear oil from beaten olives for the light, to make a lamp burn continually. *Le 24:2 NASB95*

WHY DO I SUFFER?

Its like this as I have come to understand it:

To find the victory:
      We must learn to live where love is
      And not where we live

To make the sacrificial love of Christ our love of sacrifice
In His love,
with His love and
through His love
That we enter a different realm
Our burden truly becomes light
And believe it or not – we want more
Because as stated in the word

> *1Pe 1:6 NASB95*- In this you greatly rejoice, even though now for a little while, if necessary, you have been distressed by various trials,
> *Jas 1:2 NASB95* - Consider it all joy, my brethren, when you encounter various trials,
> *1Co 9:25 (GNT)* - Every athlete in training submits to strict discipline, in order to be crowned with a wreath that will not last; but we do it for one that will last forever.
> *Lu 6:40 (GNT)* - No pupils are greater than their teacher; but all pupils, when they have completed their training, will be like their teacher.
> *2 Cor 2:4 NIV* - For I wrote you out of great distress and anguish of heart and with many tears,
> not to grieve you
> but to let you know the depth of my love for you

The torments in our life and the difficulties we experience When most unbearable in the flesh,
teach us and help us to realize that there is strength in the cross and
In a love beyond our comprehension
They teach us to Love God as He desires for us to Love HIM

Perfect loves conquers all of our enemies

It is then that we can come to comprehend "what we are made of"
And desire greatly to deny ourselves everything.
We come to realize that He is our ONLY WANT
We find a greater love and a greater hope

I have come to understand that we must contemplate the passionate love of God through our sufferings.
Our sufferings are "our blessings",
They are a small measure given to us to compare His great suffering,
This is how we can better understand His great love
and come to love Him greatly.

The Lord has experienced betrayal and still has loved us,
Everyday we betray him though sin.
He is merciful and so should we be.
As much as you love, he loves you and more

Without such a measure we cannot learn to be like Him who desires for us to be of His image.
This is where we learn to understand and desire to love the Lord greater than ever before
And first above all persons and things created.

In the Word it talks about possessing things as if not possessing them, about being married as if not married, etc.
The writing pertains to distraction and attachment to people and things of this world. The Lord is jealous wanting even the undistracted love toward Him from each individual and from those who are married and are more distracted with the things of the world.

Perfect Love, make us to Love you Perfectly!

> _Heb 12:8 KJV_ - But if ye be without chastisement, whereof all are partakers, then are ye bastards, and not sons.

WHAT IS RELIGION?

"He who is not with Me is against Me;
and he who does not gather with Me scatters. *Mat 12:30* NASB95

And if a house be divided against itself,
that house cannot stand. *Mark 3:25* KJV

We are either for Him or against Him. Who is your father?
Is religion a discord among believers? Is religion a difference of the flesh, a separation of the minds? Is love being demonstrated here?

Are they false christs being used for the glory of God?
Are they too proud to lay down their crowns?
Are they causing separation, controversy and confusion among believers?
They DO confess Jesus!

**Greater love has no one than this,
that one lay down his life for his friends.**
John 15:13 NASB95

"Do you suppose that I came to grant peace on earth?
I tell you, no, but rather division; *Luke 12:51* NASB95

Jesus said he came to divide, and so it is and will be until we are ONE and on a ONE on ONE with Him and the ONE true church.
Who will be the true, and step down?
Mercifully asking forgiveness and truly living the life of Christ.
These are the false christs: those who do not love unconditionally, are not merciful and do not know the way of the Shepherd nor do they live in the Truth.

- By this the children of God and
the children of the devil are obvious:
anyone who
**does not practice righteousness is not of God,
nor the one who does not love his brother.** *1John 3:10* NASB95

-Now I beseech you, brethren, by the name of our Lord Jesus Christ, that **ye all speak the same thing**, and that there be **no divisions among you**; but that ye be perfectly joined together in the same mind and in the same judgment. For it hath been declared unto me of you, my brethren, by them which are of the house of Chloe, that there are contentions among you. Now this I say, that every one of you saith, I am of Paul; and I of Apollos; and I of Cephas; and I of Christ. Is Christ divided? was Paul crucified for you? or were ye baptized in the name of Paul *1 Cor 1:10-13 KJV*

- For **who hath known the mind of the Lord**, that he may instruct him? But we have the mind of Christ. *1Co 2:16 NASB95*

- **Let this mind be in you**, which was also in Christ Jesus: *Php 2:5 DRA*

- For you have been called for this purpose,
since Christ also suffered for you, leaving you an example for you to follow in His steps, *1Pe 2:21 NASB95*

- After you have suffered for a little while, the God of all grace, who called you to His eternal glory in Christ, will Himself perfect, confirm, strengthen and establish you. *1Pe 5:10 NASB95*

- make my joy complete
by being of the same mind,
maintaining the same love,
united in spirit,
intent on one purpose. *Php 2:2 NASB95*

We must sow as He sows, Be as He is, Love as He Loves!

- Slaves, in all things obey those who are your masters on earth, not with external service, as those who merely please men, but **with sincerity of heart, fearing the Lord**. *Col 3:22 NASB95*

Proverbs 3:3-8 NASB - Do not let kindness and truth leave you;
Bind them around your neck,
write them on the tablet of your heart.
So you will find favor and good repute in the sight of
God and man.
Trust in the LORD with all your heart and
do not lean on your own understanding.
In all your ways acknowledge Him, And
He will make your paths straight.
Do not be wise in your own eyes;
Fear the LORD and turn away from evil. It will be
healing to your body and refreshment to your bones.

Believers of Jesus Christ, God-Man and Our Savior, Redeemer of the world… be united in unconditional love. Stop speaking evil against one another.

The antichrist is those who are against Him. (Read "Who is the antichrist?)
    -and every spirit that does not confess Jesus
    is not from God; this is the spirit of **the antichrist,**
    of which you have heard that it is coming,
    and now it is already in the world. *1 John 4:3 NASB95*

✝

- make my joy complete
by being of the same mind,
maintaining the same love,
united in spirit,
intent on one purpose.
Php 2:2 NASB95

HOW CAN WE MAKE HIS JOY COMPLETE?

> \- make my joy complete
> by being of the same mind,
> maintaining the same love,
> united in spirit,
> intent on one purpose. *Php 2:2 NASB*

1. By being of the same mind…
Rebuke Religion.. Be of the same mind Be "FOR CHRIST!" UNCONDITIONAL REPENTANCE and UNCONDITIONAL LOVE
for self for the benefit of others, taking the blame upon ourselves, like Rachel, like Jesus

\- "Then you will call, and the LORD will answer;
You will cry, and He will say,
`Here I am. ' If you remove the yoke from your midst,
The pointing of the finger
and speaking wickedness,**
Isa 58:9 NASB95

2. Maintaining the same love…
UNCONDITIONAL LOVE
With all lowliness and meekness,
With longsuffering,
Forebearing one another in love
Eph Ch 4:2 KJV

No one should seek his own advantage,
but that of his neighbor *1Cor 10:24 NAB*

Greater love has no one than this,
that one lay down his life for his friends.
John 15:13 NASB95

Is this the Great Deliverance? The Rapture!

3. United in Spirit ... UNCONDITIONAL MERCY
Especially to the merciless..

Endeavoring to keep the unity of the Spirit
In the bond of peace *Eph Ch4:3 KJV*

"He who is not with Me is against Me;
and he who does not gather with Me scatters.
Mat 12:30 NASB95

And if a house be divided against itself, that house cannot stand. *Mark 3:25 KJV*

Must we unite in one house, one church?
We must approach the Lord with a contrite heart,
desperate love
and equally desiring
that love for our brothers, even unto death,
knowing who is our enemy and our tormentor.

4. Intent on one purpose...
UNCONDITIONAL SALVATION FOR ALL WHOM THE LORD DESIRES - EVEN UNTO DEATH

As the Lord has stated in His Word:

> and he will speak words to you by which
> you will be saved,
> **you and all your household.**' *Ac 11:14 NASB95*

Also being as He is, Loving as He loves

BEING MERCIFUL EVEN TO THE MERCILESS

WHO ARE THE TRUE APOSTLES OF TODAY?

The Lord tells the church of Ephesus (the Church of Our Blessed Mother) that they have tested those who say they are apostles and have found them to be liars.

He tells them their fault in Rev 2:1-5. He commands them to Repent because they do not love God first! Scripture seems to point out that they are otherwise perfect. Most persons do not know how to love God, neither do the churches.

The desire must be great and the search desperate and repentance deep, seek with your whole heart, mind, soul and strength; ask Him to teach you everything including to love and to repent. He is our teacher.

– Greater love has no one than this, That one lay down his life for his friends. *John 15:13 NASB95*

It is the priests, the descendants of Jesus' apostles that are the true apostles. They have been ordained since the beginning. They have a history of the hierarchy of descendants of priesthood since Jesus, Apostles to Apostles. They can prove it. It is they that consecrate the Holy Communion pleasing to the Lord.

Are they presently blinded scribes and Pharisees, hypocrites because they do not know the love of God?

Repent and keep with the fruit of repentance. Receive Holy Communion; eat of the Bread of Life! Come back home to the Catholic Church and receive the sacraments! Pray for unity!

Jesus is Coming! Ask Him to teach you everything! Repent of this, so that you can believe!

Make us Lord to agree among ourselves. Make us true in your love. Beloved Holy Ghost remove the dull of our hearing and let us hear. Open our eyes that we may see. Our hearts are waxed gross, melt away the wax so that the enemy may flee at the presence of God. Give our hearts understanding that we may be converted and made whole. Fill us with your perfect love that we may love perfectly in Jesus.

WHO DO YOU THINK IS THE PERSON MOST PRAYED FOR?

Do you think that the person most prayed for would hopefully be the person most filled with the Holy Spirit? I do! Millions of rosaries are said every day in which the Pope is prayed for. Millions of masses are said every day in which the Pope is prayed for. I hope with all my heart, that non-denominational churches and others are also praying for the Pope! Yes, the Pope is most likely the most inspired and spirit filled. He is the person most offered to the Lord.

Keep praying for Him that He may obtain the guidance to do what is necessary for the Coming of Our Lord! Pray for Perfect Love, Perfect Faith, Perfect Charity!

The following was taken from the book <u>Divine Mercy in My Soul</u> by Saint Maria Faustina Kowalska:

> 531 November 24, 1935. Sunday, first day. I went at once before the Blessed Sacrament and offered myself with Jesus, present in the Most Holy Sacrament, to the Everlasting Father. Then I heard these words in my soul:
> **Your purpose and that of your companions is to unite yourselves with Me as closely as possible;**
> **through love You will reconcile earth with heaven, you will soften the just anger of God, and**
> **you will plead for mercy for the world.**
> **I place in your care**
> **two pearls very precious to My Heart:**
> **these are the souls of priests and religious. You will pray particularly for them;**
> **their power will come from your diminishment.**
> **You will join**
> **prayers, fasts, mortifications, labors and all sufferings to My prayer, fasting, mortification, labors and sufferings and then they will have power before My Father.**

532 After Holy Communion, I saw the Lord Jesus, who said these words to me:
**Today,
penetrate into the spirit of My poverty
and ARRANGE EVERYTHING IN SUCH A WAY THAT THE MOST DESTITUTE WILL HAVE NO REASON TO ENVY YOU.
I find pleasure, not in large buildings and magnificent structures, but in a pure and humble heart.**

533 When I was by myself, I began to reflect on the spirit of poverty. I clearly saw that Jesus, although He is Lord of all things, possessed nothing. From a borrowed manger He went through life doing good to all, but himself having no place to lay His head. And on the Cross, I see the summit of His poverty, for He does not even have a garment on himself. O Jesus, through a solemn vow of poverty I desire to become like You; poverty will be my mother. As exteriorly we should possess nothing and have nothing to dispose of as our own; so interiorly we should desire nothing. And in the Most Blessed Sacrament, how great is Your poverty! Has there ever been a soul as abandoned as You were on the Cross, Jesus?

WHO IS GOD?

God is Spirit, pure love, infinitely perfect, Creator of all things in heaven and on earth and in all of existence.

> - but just as it is written, "THINGS WHICH EYE HAS NOT SEEN AND EAR HAS NOT HEARD, AND which HAVE NOT ENTERED THE HEART OF MAN, ALL THAT GOD HAS PREPARED FOR THOSE WHO LOVE HIM."
> *1Co 2:9 NASB95*

God is not a belief!!!
God is certain!!!
God is true and alive!!!
Jesus said He who knows me knows my Father.

God is in control and He knows your every thought and everything you say and do before you think, say or do them.

God is love beyond measure; words cannot even begin to edify His love, His greatness, His goodness, His kindness.

God is so Good! We must seek Him to know Him! He is too great to identify on a piece of paper and our minds are too small. These notes are like knowledge smaller than a grain of sand, a hint in knowing Him.

God is our creator, our maker. He gave to us His breath of life. He made us to love and serve Him because He loves us and desires for us to love Him back.

You have heard many times that God is Love. Paul describes "love" as "a more excellent way" in *1Cor13:1*. In the book of Matthew Jesus tells us to love our enemies and to pray for those who persecute us. His love is a selfless unconditional love! He desires that we love as He loves.

He is the very essence of the fruits of the spirit magnified in unfathomable limits

> But the fruit of the Spirit is
> **love,**
> **joy,**
> **peace,**
> **longsuffering,**

**gentleness, goodness,
faith, Meekness, temperance:
against such there is no law** *Gal 5:22-23 KJV*

    He is a merciful God who longs for us to return to Him! He is the beginning and the end, the first and the last. He is the source and completion of our life. He is creative beyond creativity, the Creator of all. He is the same today yesterday and always. He was is and will always be. He is Light, Love and Life eternal. He is Lord of Lords and King of Kings. He is Holy, Righteous, Almighty, Immortal, Powerful and Immaculate, Pure in every way. He is our Redeemer and savior. His Word is eternal and all things will pass away, but His word will never pass away.

    His Desire for me (and for you) is Perfect Love and to be perfect as my Father is perfect. He desires for me to live in His loving embrace throughout eternity. He is gentle, kind and patient with me. I am slow to learn and He is my teacher, my leader, my guide, my lover, the very essence of my life.

    He desires that I love my enemies and bless those who curse me so that they also may learn and come to His love.

    Our Father loved the world and all He created so much that He gave His only son to die for us so that we might live. He died for us to save us from our sinfulness and wicked ways. He came to teach us to repent and to love unconditionally. Jesus told Thomas "blessed are those who believe and have not seen". Our Father suffered with Jesus and in Jesus to help and teach us how to live in His great love so that we may learn to follow Him. Jesus died for us and because in our sinfulness we are dead already. But the promise of our redemption in the death of Jesus and His resurrection is assurance of our eternal life in God's everlasting love. We must choose to live the life our Lord desires for us to inherit eternal life. He came to teach us a more excellent way!

We must desire to be born of God by giving Him our free will; the door in which Satan enters. We must desire to inherit everlasting life by eating of the Bread of Life, the Bread of Presence as mentioned in Mat 12:3, God Himself. It is the living creature Jesus has become to build our temple so that we may become like Him.

We must desire to obey Him, to love Him, to serve Him and to please Him in every way.

> - We know that **no one who is born of God sins**; but He who was born of God keeps him, and **the evil one does not touch him.** *1John 5:18 NASB95*
>
> - For now we see in a mirror dimly, but then face to face; now I know in part, but then I will know fully just as I also have been fully known. But now faith, hope, love, abide, these three; but the greatest of these is love. *1Cor13:12-13 NASB95*

WHAT ABOUT THE SABBATH?

- 'So the sons of Israel shall observe the Sabbath, to celebrate the Sabbath throughout their generations as a perpetual covenant.' *Ex 31:16 NASB95*

- So there remains a Sabbath rest for the people of God. *Heb 4:9 NASB77*

The Sabbath is to be kept holy according to the Fourth of the Ten Commandments of Our Lord. It is a commandment throughout all time, perpetual from generation to generation. It is most definitely a day we are to rest and sanctify our souls. It is a day designated by the Lord for the Lord.

On the Sabbath Jesus healed and helped others. He read scripture and taught. When His disciples were with Him they picked the heads of grain rubbing them and ate them. In Col 2:16 it says that no one is to judge acts in regard to food or drink in respect to the Sabbath. In Heb 4:9 it reaffirms that the Sabbath is a day of rest for the people of God.

In the days before Christ you could not do anything on the Sabbath. The story in the New Testament about the man picking up his mat because Jesus healed him was considered to be sinning one because he picked up his mat and two because he was healed. Jesus very clearly states that **it is lawful to do good and to help one in need on the Sabbath.** We are not to buy and sell on the Sabbath, nor are we to work, it is a day of rest, a day of sanctification.

We must pray that the Lord will make us to keep the Sabbath a holy day to the Lord, pleasing to Him so that we may avoid sinning.

- "Remember the Sabbath day, to keep it holy. *Ex 20:8 NASB95*

- But the Lord answered him and said, "You hypocrites, does not each of you on the Sabbath untie his ox or his donkey from the stall and lead him away to water him? *Luke 13:15 NASB95*

- And He said to them, "What man is there among you who has a sheep, and if it falls into a pit on the Sabbath, will he not take hold of it and lift it out? "How much more valuable then is a man than a sheep! So then, **it is lawful to do good on the Sabbath.**" *Mat 12:11-12 NASB95*

- Therefore no one is to act as your judge in regard to food or drink or in respect to a festival or a new moon or a Sabbath day— *Col 2:16 NASB95*

- "It is to be a Sabbath of **solemn rest for you, that you may humble your souls; it is a permanent statute**. *Le 16:31 NASB95*

- 'For six days work may be done, but on the seventh day there is a Sabbath of **complete rest, holy to the LORD; whoever does any work on the Sabbath day shall surely be put to death.** *Ex 31:15 NASB95*

- "It is to be a Sabbath of complete rest to you, and you shall humble your souls; on the ninth of the month at evening, from evening until evening you shall keep your Sabbath." *Le 23:32 NASB95*

- but the seventh day is a Sabbath of the LORD your God; in it **you shall not do any work**, you or your son or your daughter, your male or your female servant or your cattle or your sojourner who stays with you. *Ex 20:10 NASB95*

- but during the **seventh year the land** shall have a Sabbath rest, a Sabbath to the LORD; you shall not sow your field nor prune your vineyard. *Le 25:4 NASB95*

- Thus says the LORD, "Take heed for yourselves, and **do not carry any load on the Sabbath day** or bring anything in through the gates of Jerusalem. *Jer17:21 NASB95*

- And He has violently treated His tabernacle like a garden booth; He has destroyed His appointed meeting place. The

LORD has caused to be forgotten The appointed feast and Sabbath in Zion, And He has despised king and priest In the indignation of His anger. *La 2:6 NASB95*

- and I came to Jerusalem and learned about the evil that Eliashib had done for Tobiah, by **preparing a room** for him **in the courts of the house of God.** It was very displeasing to me, so I threw all of Tobiah's household goods out of the room. Then I gave an order and they cleansed the rooms; and I returned there the utensils of the house of God with the grain offerings and the frankincense. I also discovered that the portions of the Levites had not been given them, so that the Levites and the singers who performed the service had gone away, each to his own field. So I reprimanded the officials and said, "Why is the house of God forsaken?" Then I gathered them together and restored them to their posts. *Ne 13:7-11 NASB95*

- In those days I saw in Judah some who were treading wine presses on the Sabbath, and bringing in sacks of grain and **loading them** on donkeys, as well as wine, grapes, figs and all kinds of loads, and they brought them into Jerusalem on the Sabbath day. So **I admonished them on the day they sold food**. Also men of Tyre were living there who imported fish and all kinds of merchandise, and sold them to the sons of Judah on the Sabbath, even in Jerusalem. Then I reprimanded the nobles of Judah and said to them, "What is this evil thing you are doing, by **profaning the Sabbath day**? "Did not your fathers do the same, so that our God brought on us and on this city all this trouble? Yet you are adding to the wrath on Israel by profaning the Sabbath." It came about that just as it grew dark at the gates of Jerusalem before the Sabbath, I commanded that the doors should be shut and that they should not open them until after the Sabbath. Then I stationed some of my servants at the gates so that no load would enter on the Sabbath day. *Ne 13:15-19 NASB95*

'Observe the Sabbath day to keep it holy, as the LORD your God commanded you. *De 5:12 NASB95*

- As for the peoples of the land who bring wares or any grain on the Sabbath day to sell, we will not buy from them on the Sabbath or a holy day; and we will forego the crops the seventh year and the exaction of every debt.
Ne 10:31 NASB95

- "If because of the Sabbath, you turn your foot From doing your own pleasure on My holy day, And call the Sabbath a delight, the holy day of the LORD honorable, And honor it, desisting from your own ways, From seeking your own pleasure And speaking your own word *Isa 58:13 NASB95*

- "How blessed is the man who does this, And the son of man who takes hold of it; Who keeps from profaning the Sabbath, And keeps his hand from doing any evil."
Isa 56:2 NASB95

- "And it shall be from new moon to new moon And from Sabbath to Sabbath, All mankind will come to bow down before Me," says the LORD. *Isa 66:23 NASB95*

- Or have ye not read in the law, that on the Sabbath day the priests in the temple profane the Sabbath, and are guiltless? *Mat 12:5 ASV*

We must obey all the commandments of Our Lord! We must desire it and ask the Holy Spirit to help us! For those of you who find it difficult to have a day of rest, you must pray for it that the Lord will grant it. Perhaps you have worked on the Sabbath and you should not have, and so now you suffer. Obey the Commands of Our Lord! Repent!

THE MERCY OF OUR LORD IS YOURS
IF YOU WANT IT
DESIRE TO AMEND YOUR WAYS
DESIRE HIS LOVE
AND LOVE HIM BACK!
Return to Him all that you are!

WHY MUST I GIVE MY FREE WILL TO THE LORD?

We should desire to give our free will to the Lord so that we can be born of the will of God like Jesus.

The Deity of Jesus Christ
In the beginning was the Word, and the Word was with God, and the Word was God. He was in the beginning with God. All things came into being through Him, and apart from Him nothing came into being that has come into being. In Him was life, and the life was the Light of men. The Light shines in the darkness, and the darkness did not comprehend it.

The Witness John
There came a man sent from God, whose name was John. He came as a witness, to testify about the Light, so that all might believe through him. He was not the Light, but he came to testify about the Light.

There was the true Light which, coming into the world, enlightens every man. He was in the world, and the world was made through Him, and the world did not know Him. He came to His own, and those who were His own did not receive Him. But as many as received Him, to them **He gave the right to become children of God,** even to those who believe in His name, **who were born**, not of blood nor of the will of the flesh nor of the will of man, but **of (the will) God.**

The Word Made Flesh
And the Word became flesh, and dwelt among us, and we saw His glory,

glory as of the only begotten from the Father, full of grace and truth.

John testified about Him and cried out, saying,

"This was He of whom I said, 'He who comes after me has a higher rank than I, for He existed before me.'

" For of His fullness we have all received, and grace upon grace. For the Law was given through Moses;

grace and truth were realized through Jesus Christ. No one has seen God at any time;
the only begotten God who is in the bosom of the Father, He has explained Him.   *John 1:1-18 NASB95*

WHO *WILL FOLLOW JESUS?*

Jesus clearly stated I am the good Shepherd, my sheep know me, My sheep follow me, My sheep hear my voice.

As a child, did you ever play the game "follow the leader" and if you messed up you were out of the game. Well, this is no game!!! We must follow our leader, Jesus! He is the Way!

In the book of Revelations 14:4-5 we are told that the **Lord has purchased the first fruits among men**: those who are chaste and have not been defiled and **follow the Lamb wherever He goes**. They do not lie and are blameless.

Although it may refer to a certain group we must know that this applies to those who desire to please the Lord. Mary is our perfect example. We must desire to become chaste, truthful and blameless. We must put on incorruption. What is your desire?

In the following scriptures, the Lord fixed my eyes on those words capitalized:

> - These are the ones who have not been defiled with women, for **they have kept themselves CHASTE**. These are the ones **who follow the Lamb** wherever He goes. These have been purchased from among men as first fruits to God and to the Lamb. *Re 14:4 NASB95*

> - And **NO LIE was found in their mouth; they ARE BLAMELESS.** *Rev 14:5 NASB95*

DO YOU WANT TO BE ONE WITH THE LORD?
DO YOU DESIRE TO BE ONE WITH THOSE WHO HAVE ALREADY ATTAINED IT?
DO YOU DESIRE TO BE ONE WITH EACH OTHER?
In The Love Of God – Seek Truth And Live In It!

THERE IS ONLY ONE LOVE, ONE HOPE, ONE GOD
MAY WE ALL BE ONE AND BLESSED INDEED!
OBEY GOD!!!!!!!!! LIVE IN HIS LOVE!!!!!!!

The victory is in the cross, learn to love it and live in it!

WHAT SHOULD MY GREATEST AND MOST PASSIONATE DESIRE BE?

As Jesus demonstrated and as He is, was and will always be, our greatest and most passionate desire must be to love Our Lord perfectly and to be perfect as Our Heavenly Father is perfect.

Our desire should be one of great passion and urgency intensely craving the love of God and to love Him and each other as He loves us.

We must be willing to be all that He has asked of us and that is to "BE PERFECT AS MY HEAVENLY FATHER IS PERFECT!" We must also make our desire known to Him passionately with a contrite and loving heart.

With this desire we must also know that it may only be attained with the greatest love, that is the willingness to die for a friend in the Love of God with the hope of salvation for all mankind.

ACT ON THIS:

A Different Kind Of War = **ACTS 19:19** _{NASB95}

And many of those who practiced magic brought their books together and **began burning them** in the sight of everyone;

LET US OBEY THE WORD OF GOD
IN ALL THINGS, IN THE NAME OF JESUS.

May we each do our part to put and end to even this war starting in our homes.
Pray, fast, be merciful and may the WORD OF GOD
Prosper and infiltrate this land which has been given to us by Our Creator, Eternal Love and mercy itself.

**VIVA JESU CRISTO! VIVA MARIA MADRE MIA!
EN ME MENTE, MI ALMA, MI SER y TODO LO QUE SOY!**

(This is The End Of **Who Is Who And What Is What?** Section)

Contemplate this:
THE Devil <   Was,   is not,   yet he is (Rev17:08)
JESUS   >   Is,   Was,   Who is to come (Rev 1:8)

EXALT OUR KING!

May all of Heaven and Earth Exalt Our King of Majestic Omnipotence and Eternal Love

May the Earth and all of which it is made acknowledge, honor and bless the Lord, and in this joy may the barren lands bear fruit and vegetation for the children of God and those most in need the blessed poor and starving

May the Rocks acknowledge, honor and bless the Lord, and in this joy, rejoice and gather themselves together to make shelter for the homeless and those most in need

May the Waters acknowledge, honor and bless the Lord, and in this joy, rejoice in His creation, may they be plentiful throughout the earth replenishing the desolate lands filling the need of all those who thirst

May the heavenly Skies acknowledge, honor and bless the Lord, and in this joy, rejoice in His creation and in being part thereof. May they desire to please the Lord and give abundantly His light, His shade, His rain and all that is pleasing to the Lord.

May the dirt of which I am made, acknowledge, honor and bless the Lord, and in this joy, rejoice in His creation and in being part thereof come to be made whole. Complete in obedience, righteousness, compassion, mercy and love.

Oh May all of creation Exalt Our King of Majestic Omnipotence and Eternal Love and now
Return our very breath to Him, who is life itself, who is Great and whose Desire is that we do return to Him.
May we become ONE as He has said.

Oh Jesus with gratitude, appreciation and a great magnitude of love, I return to you... Receive me... Thank You!

This CD contains a Scriptural style Rosary which may be purchased at
CDBaby.com, itunes and many others

-"The kingdom of heaven may be compared to a king who gave a wedding feast for his son. And he sent out his slaves to call those who had been invited to the wedding feast,

and **THEY WERE UNWILLING TO COME.**

"Again he sent out other slaves saying,
`Tell those who have been invited, "Behold, I have prepared my dinner; my oxen and my fattened livestock are all butchered and

**EVERYTHING IS READY;
COME TO THE WEDDING FEAST.'"** *Mat 22:2-4* NASB95

- "But **THEY PAID NO ATTENTION AND
      WENT THEIR WAY,** *Mat 22:5-7* NASB95

  - `The wedding is ready, but

THOSE WHO WERE INVITED WERE NOT WORTHY.
(*Repent!*)   *Mat 22:8-10* NASB95

- "Be like men who are waiting for their master
when he returns from the wedding feast,
so that they may immediately open the door to him
when he comes and knocks. *Luke 12:36* NASB95

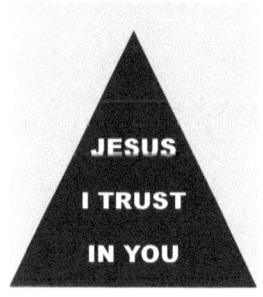

GIVE YOUR FREE WILL TO THE LORD!
***BE BORN OF THE WILL
OF GOD! (John 1:13)***

REPENT OR YOU WILL PERISH!

The Sign Of Jonah *(Mat 12:39)* KJV
– **Repentance with the Use of Sackcloth and Ashes**

REPENT AND BE READY!

Especially for you...
MAY THE LORD BLESS YOU INDEED!!
Truly, truly it is The Wedding Invitation. Pray these with your whole heart, mind and soul for yourself. These prayers are for transformation and illumination. Receive the Bread of Life with a reverent mouth. Love the Eucharist. Love your enemy. You must repent or you will not be at the wedding. May you be blessed and draw near to him with great love and a humble heart. May you live in His everlasting Love and Light. May the Lords' perfect love fill your life and the very essence of your being.

>I give to you my love in the Hearts of Jesus & Mary Blessed Be & Glory to Our Father whose love, mercy and compassion endure forever - **Gloria**

PRAYERS OF SPIRITUAL WARFARE AND COMPLETE SURRENDER

ACT OF CONTRITION
O God, we love thee with our whole hearts and above all things and are heartily sorry that we have offended thee. May we never offend thee any more. O, may we love thee without ceasing, and make it our delight to do in all things thy most holy will. <u>The Orthodox Book Of Common Prayer</u> page 598

PUTTING ON THE ARMOR OF GOD
Finally, **I am** strong in the Lord, and
in the power of his might.
I put on the whole armour of God,
that **I** may be able to stand against the wiles of the devil.
I wrestle not against flesh and blood,
but against principalities, against powers,
against the rulers of the darkness of this world,
against spiritual wickedness in high places.
Wherefore **I put on** the whole armour of God,
that **I** may be able to withstand in the evil day,
and having done all, to stand.
I Stand therefore, having **my** loins girt about with truth,
and having on the breastplate of righteousness;

And **my** feet shod with the preparation of the gospel of peace;
Above all, taking the shield of faith,
wherewith **I** shall be able to quench all the fiery darts of the
wicked. And **I** take the helmet of salvation, and the sword of the
Spirit, which is the word of God: Praying always with all prayer
and supplication in the Spirit, and watching thereunto with all
perseverance and supplication for all saints; *(Ephesians 6:10-18)* KJV

I believe I wear the Armor of God for all eternity,
and I also ask Your protection Dear Lord,
upon all beloved on earth.
In the Name of Jesus. Amen.

OBEDIENT MIND TO CHRIST
For though we walk in the flesh,
we do not war after the flesh:
(For the weapons of our warfare are not carnal,
But mighty through God
to the pulling down of strong holds;) Casting down imaginations,
and every high thing
that exalts itself against the knowledge of God,
and bringing into captivity
every thought to the obedience of Christ;
And having in a readiness
to revenge all disobedience,
when your obedience is fulfilled. *(2Corinthians 10:3-6)* KJV

Lord make me and my mind obedient to You;
bless me, protect me and keep me from all harm.
Remain with me and in me always.
I also ask Your protection upon the minds and bodies of all beloved
on earth. In the Name of Jesus. I pray.

TREASURES *(Mark 10:21-27)* ref
Lord You said that where my treasure lies,
there my heart is.
Help me Lord to remove myself

from all treasures on earth
that only You
will be the treasure I seek.
Fill me and make me Yours
I surrender to you: my heart, mind and soul,
my life and my being
and everything I say and do.
You have given to me
Your unconditional love
how can I offer anything less
I give to You my unconditional love
with my free will
trusting You Heavenly Father
more than anything in the world
May Your Glory manifest
sooner than later.
I await Your coming with Joy and Love.
In the Name of Jesus. Amen.

INCREASE IN ME *(*2Peter 1:5-7)* NKJV
Lord increase in me that I may decrease.
Help my unbelief and
make me diligent
in my pursuit to find You,
Give to me faith
the size of a mustard seed,
("add to my faith virtue,
to virtue knowledge,
to knowledge self-control,
to self-control patience,
to patience godliness,
to godliness brotherly kindness and
to brotherly kindness charity."*)
Fill me with Your perfect love,
a sound heart and sound mind
Give to me wisdom,
knowledge and understanding,
that I may know what You require of me.

Help me to grow in grace and to never stumble so that I may enter into Your everlasting kingdom and dwell in the house of the Lord with Jesus Christ our Savior. Amen.

A PRAYER OF CONSECRATION

Oh Gracious Father of Everlasting Love, before the Holy Trinity, Our Heavenly Mother and the whole Heavenly Court, I present myself to You, resisting, rebuking and renouncing Satan and all of his works. United with Jesus, in Jesus, through Jesus, and in His Armor of Light, I approach Your throne, united with His sacrifice on Calvary and His most precious Blood and Water that gushed forth filled with Your loving mercy, I offer and consecrate my whole life and total existence to the Sacred Heart of Jesus and the Immaculate Heart of Mary. In You I want to live, move and have my being.

I consecrate myself to the Holy Ghost you have given to me, I consecrate myself to Your Divine Will
I consecrate myself to Your Way, Your Truth, and Your Life,
I consecrate myself to My Heavenly Father and all that He desires for the Glory of God, In the Name of Jesus. Blessed be God, Blessed Be His Holy Name. Jesus I Trust in You!

My Lord, as Our Blessed Mother responded to Your call, I also respond: Behold, I am the handmaid of the Lord, Be it done to me according to Your Word. And as Jesus responded to Your call, I also respond: Not my will Heavenly Father, but thine, take this cup from me. My Jesus, I await the fulfillment of Your promise to deliver us from evil, My Savior, My Redeemer, Blessed is He who comes in the Name of the Lord. Blessed Mother pray for us that we may be made worthy of the promises of Jesus Christ. I pray in the Name, in the Holy Name of my Beloved Jesus. Thank You, Father for hearing my prayer. It is granted, it is done.

***

*BLESSED IS HE WHO COMES
IN THE NAME OF THE JESUS! ALLELUIA!*

I LOVE YOU LORD
I love you Lord,
from the deepest darkest depth of my being;
I love you Lord, with every breath I take;
I love you Lord, with every beat of my heart;
I love you Lord, with
and in the total essence of my creation;
I love you Lord, for my existence and
all that you have desired of my existence;
Oh Lord, accumulate the love, affection
and adoration all creation offers one to another
and to You, and let me love you more than that;

Oh My Dearest & Beloved Essence of my being,
Outpour your immense love upon my heart,
mind, body and soul
that I may love you as you love me;

Exalted love, my love exalts you;
Glorious love, my love glorifies you;
Immeasurable love, may I love you immeasurably;
Loving "I" of my heart,
Loving "I" of my soul,
Great "I" who is, was and will always be
the Great "I AM" of all existence,
I worship you, I praise You, I love you beyond love;

Marvelous, Miraculous, Magnificent,
Joyous, Wondrous, Fulfilling love,
let my cup overflow and
consume me with the fire of your burning love;
Oh my love, who bore all for me;
I return all that I bear to You
in sacrifice for the Poor Deceased Souls,
I return to you all that you came to redeem
that they also may be set free.
My love, my life, my burdens, my illnesses, my worldly love,
my worldly pleasures, my ego, my free will, my pride, my unbelief,
my torments, my resentments,

every drop of blood
that I shed, every bad habit, my unworthiness,
Oh Lord may these sacrifices be acceptable to you on their behalf
and on behalf of my special intentions (name them).

Make me worthy sacrificial love beyond understanding,
I offer to you the sacrifice of life.
Great and Worthy are you who deserves all the glory,
praise and honor, who deserves our love
without question and without measure,
Oh Lord let us love you,
teach us to love you more than we have ever imagined;

God of all creation; God so humble and true;
God so reverent and Holy;
God, in your likeness make me like you;
Holy and true, pleasing and
loving You in ways that only you would understand.

Oh sweet death, come before me
and let the Lord deal with you,
that I may truly die to this world and
have Life in Him who is Glorious beyond belief,
who is true to His Word,
who is Gracious and pours His grace upon us;

Oh Beloved, consume me, penetrate me,
be one with me,

You are my ultimate desire,
I thirst and crave for You.
You are the Passion of my being.
I long for YOU! I adore You! I love You!
I hope for You!
Oh Gracious love, lead me to Your Glory.

Be merciful and Save all souls, come to their aid,
let your victory be made known.
In the name of Jesus. Blessed Mother Pray for us.

COME TO THE WEDDING (chanted)

Holy City, New Jerusalem, Come
Down out of Heaven
from God, be made ready
as a bride adorned for her husband   *Rev 21:1 NASB95 ref*

One of the seven angels spoke,
saying, "COME..
here I will show you the bride,
the wife of the Lamb   *Rev 21:9 NASB95 ref*

The Spirit and the bride say, Come
And let the one who hears say, Come
And let the one who is thirsty Come
let the one who desires
take the water of life
without cost   *Rev 22:17 NASB95 ref*

Come and take and eat of the Bread of Life   *John 6:48-58 ref*
One Bread, One Body One Love, One Hope,
One Faith, One Spirit. One God, One Lord of All,
Above all, through all and in you all…
IN ME… IN YOU….
Glory to God in the Highest
and Blessed is He who COMES
Blessed is He who COMES
in the Name of the Lord   (inspired by *Eph 4:1-6*)

Let us rejoice and be glad
and give the glory to God
for the marriage of the Lamb has come
and His bride
has made herself ready   *Rev 19:7 NASB95*

Come…Come to the wedding, Come…
Come…Come to the wedding, Come…
Alleluia, Alleluia
Come…Come to the wedding, Come…

JERUSALEM
Inspired by Luke 13:33-35; Luke 7:38; Luke19:41; Luke21:24; Mat5:35;18:20;23:37; Col3:1-17;

Glory and Praise to God who loves Jerusalem, for it is the City Of The Great King. I pray for you Jerusalem. May the Lord make you whole. Lord please heal Jerusalem and all of Israel, shed you light upon it and give peace to all of its existence, seen and unseen, known and unknown.

Father I return you to the chief priests and scribes that are in Jerusalem today. In years past, they condemned you, Today I present You to them as the True Living God, My Father. Bless them Oh Lord and gather your children together, the way a hen gathers her chicks under her wings, retrieve them to yourself. You were pierced on the cross with that glorious sword, and shed your blood and water that gushed forth from your side upon the whole world so that we might be saved. May the Field of Blood residing there, be covered with your body, blood and water relieving all pains and sorrows, trials and tribulations of all time, past, present and future. May I stand at your feet, behind you, may I wash your feet with tears, and wipe your feet with the hair on my head, may I kiss your feet and anoint them with ointment that all will be made new. Oh sweet angels and saints, perhaps you can do this for me in the Heavenlies that my Lord may be satisfied.

In God speed we ask you to Redeem Jerusalem and the whole world, make us ONE. Gather your Jewish people and all who dwell there once again. May they find you, see you and believe the reality of you, that You may once again ascend in Jerusalem.

Lord you said that a prophet cannot perish outside of Jerusalem, I plead with you to save the prophets, stop the condemnation, break the power of the curse that is killing them. In the Name of Jesus, I bind all curses and cast down all strongholds that My Lord Jesus took upon himself for the sake of my sins and the sins of the whole world. I command them to the foot of the cross and at the Mercy of My Father through My Lord Jesus Christ by the Spirit of God, I command You, and by the Immaculate Heart of Mary.

Lord put upon Jerusalem holy and beloved bowels of mercies, kindness, humbleness of mind, meekness, longsuffering; forbearing one another, teach them these and move them to forgive one another.

May Jerusalem want and desire to have You with them more than anything in the world. May the spirits in exile tormenting your people reap what they have sowed, may their lying tongues be cut off and the eyes of splinters be plucked out. May the eyes of Jerusalem and the whole world become blessed, may their ears hear You and their tongues made holy. May every house be made clean and desolate no more.

Oh Glorious Jerusalem, Home of my beloved Mother and Savior I enthrone them back to you. Jerusalem, my holy land, the land of my Father, We proclaim Him King and Creator, We Honor our Father and Our Mother and give Jerusalem back to My King and Queen. For we live by faith and not by sight.

Father weep no more.

May the times of the Gentiles be fulfilled, now and today; set the captives free.

May your perfect love abound through the air they breath, the water they drink, the clothes they wear, and all that they touch, and all that exists. Blessed are you who comes in the name of the Lord. Hosanna in the Highest. Blessed Mother Pray for us. Holy angels and Saints pray for us. Thank you Father for hearing my prayer in the Name of Jesus, My Most Beloved.

> - and that repentance for forgiveness of sins would be proclaimed in His name to all the nations, beginning from Jerusalem *Luke 24:47 NASB95*

THE MYSTERIES OF ILLUMINATION
(The Mysteries Of Light)

DEDICATION OF LIGHT:
With this Rosary I bind and consecrate my family and my children to the Immaculate Heart of Mary, the Sacred Heart of Jesus, to My Lord, My Heavenly Father and His Divine Will, and to My Beloved Holy Spirit. I embrace every soul in this world with your Everlasting Love and ask for an outpour of Your Divine Mercy and Divine Love upon everyone.

I confess Jesus to be My Lord, My Saviour,
the Great King of the World and of all Creation, Son of God, Son of Man, The Word Made Flesh, the Bread of Life, My Bridegroom, My Jealous Love.

Beloved Jesus, Make our Communion Holy
Consume me with the fire of your burning love.
With this Rosary I unite myself to you.
Please unite yourself to me, make me whole,
Beloved Bridegroom come to Your Bride,
make me one with you,
blood of my blood, bone of my bone,
flesh of my flesh, eternally yours.
Perfect love let me love you perfectly.
In the Name of Jesus.

We will now pray the rosary:
1. **Make the Sign of the Cross**
In the Name of the Father, the Son and the Holy Spirit Amen.

2. **The Nicene Creed (381 AD in Nicea)**
I believe in one God, the Father, the Almighty, Creator of heaven and earth, of all that is visible and invisible; I believe in one Lord, Jesus Christ, the only-begotten Son of God, eternally begotten of the Father, before all ages. Light from Light, true God from true God, of one essence with the Father, through whom all things were made, Who for us and for our salvation He came down from heaven and was incarnate

by the Holy Spirit and the Virgin Mary, and was made man. For our sake He was crucified under Pontius Pilate; He suffered death and was buried. Rising on the third day according to the Scriptures and ascending into the heavens is seated at the right hand of the Father. He will come again in glory to judge the living and the dead, and His kingdom will have no end. I believe in the Holy Spirit, the Lord, the Giver of life, who proceeds from the Father. Who together with the Father and the Son He is worshiped and glorified. Who spoke through the Prophets. I believe in one holy catholic and apostolic Church. I acknowledge one baptism for the remission of sins. **I expect the resurrection of the dead**, and the life of the age to come. AMEN.

Our Father
Our Father, who art in heaven; hallowed be Thy name; Thy kingdom come; Thy will be done on earth as it is in heaven. Give us this day our daily bread; and Forgive us our trespasses *make us to* forgive those who trespass against us. Lead us not into temptation but deliver us from evil. Amen.

For Perfect Love, that we may be One with Our Lord.
Hail Mary
Hail Mary, full of grace, the Lord is with you; blessed are you among women, and blessed is the fruit of your womb, Jesus. Holy Mary, Mother of God, pray for us sinners, now and at the hour of our death. Amen.

For Perfect Faith, that we may stand firm on that Glorious day, keeping our eyes on Him
Hail Mary...

For Perfect Charity, that we may abandon ourselves from all treasures on earth:
Hail Mary...

Glory be to the Father
Glory be to the Father, and to the Son, and to the Holy Ghost. As it was in the beginning, is now, and ever shall be, world without end. Amen.

FIRST MYSTERY OF ILLUMINATION
The Baptism of Jesus in the Jordan River-
Meditation:
Our Father…
1. My most beloved Jesus, teach me to be like You. At your baptism, the heavens opened wide and our Beloved Father proclaimed that you are His Beloved Son with whom He is well pleased. 2. Your transformation and illumination at that moment was profound.
3. Dearest and Most Beloved Father, I pray that I may obtain the graces necessary to be well pleasing to you, that you may transform me and illuminate me, that I may be perfect as my Heavenly Father is perfect.
4.. Oh My Father, I come to you Through my brother, Your Beloved Son, Jesus Christ, and ask My Mother Mary to pray for me that I may be all that you desire of me.
5. Oh my Father, I fear being separated from you. I fear offending you. 6. There is nothing I want more than to unite myself with and in You that we may be made ONE. Teach me, lead me and never let me stray. 7 I pray Lord that all my brothers and sisters on earth become baptized and will find Your Glorious Light in their lifetime, in the baptism you have gifted to us. 8. Open our Hearts and claim our souls as Yours alone. 9. Wash us and clean us, like new born babies. Bring restoration to Your people
10. make your nation holy, reverent and pure, that all will be pleasing to you.

10 Hail Mary's … Glory Be to the Father…

"I believe, I love, I adorc, I hope,
please pardon those who do not believe,
do not love, do not adore, do not hope.
Show me the way,
Reveal all truth in your loving light,
My Loving Jesus
teach me to love beyond the price of death."

"Oh my Jesus, forgive us our sins, save us from the fires of hell, lead all souls to Heaven, especially those who have most need of your mercy."

SECOND MYSTERY OF ILLUMINATION
The First Miracle of Jesus at the wedding in Cana –
Meditation:
Our Father ...
1. My most beloved Jesus, teach me to be like You. The wedding at Cana was very special. Dearest Lord responding to your mothers request and intercession you transformed water into wine. 2. May Your light beam in every chamber of my body and in the waters of my body may You overflow satisfying my thirst for Your love and Glory. May my only and most ultimate desire and craving be my passion for Your Immense love. 3. Teach me Lord to be obedient to the words of Our Dearest Blessed Mother Mary "Do whatever He tells you". 4. Help me Lord to separate myself from the world and unite myself to You. In calling Mary "woman" you separated yourself from her, making a distinction of your worldly relationship and your Godly relationship. 5. Teach me Lord to separate myself from everyone and everything on earth. Let nothing keep me from you. I want you to be my only treasure in heaven and on earth. 6. Teach me Lord to trust in you; increase my faith that I may please you and know you as I have never known you before. Increase my love for you that I may love you immeasurably as you love me. 7. Teach me Lord to Honor Mary, Our Most Blessed Mother of all Mothers, our Heavenly Intercessor, Our Mother most Merciful and Immaculate, Our Assumption. Teach me Lord to Love Her with a Heart of Jesus and teach me to love You with the Heart of Mary. 8. I hope and I believe that Our Blessed Mother will pray for my transformation and illumination, that I may also become a Holy thing, a Son of God, that I may be separated from the World and United to the Holy Trinity, the Holy Family and to all that my Father loves that I may also love all that He loves and dwell in the House of the Lord eternally. 9. Lord I pray for all families that are married. Teach them Lord to Love you first. 10. Spare them from division, draw them near to You, teach them separation uniting them to yourself and then to each other.

10 Hail Mary's … Glory Be to the Father…

"I believe, I love, I adore, I hope,
please pardon those who do not believe,
do not love, do not adore, do not hope.
Show me the way,
Reveal all truth in your loving light,
My Loving Jesus
teach me to love beyond the price of death."

"Oh my Jesus, forgive us our sins, save us from the fires of hell, lead all souls to Heaven, especially those who have most need of your mercy."

THIRD MYSTERY OF ILLUMINATION
Jesus Proclaims the Kingdom of God, Calling us to Conversion, and Forgives the Sinner
Meditation:
Our Father …
1. My Most Beloved Jesus, in the Holy prayer you gave us, you tell Our Father thy kingdom come thy will be done on earth as it is in heaven. You also tell us that the Kingdom of God is within us. 2. Father let your Kingdom come into my being. Teach me Lord, to live in the kingdom of Our Father on earth and in me. 3. Make Your Holy Temple in me come to life and fill it with your Loving Light. Teach me Lord to be like You. 4. I offer my life as a living sacrifice for the glory of God. 5. Teach me Lord to repent fully and deeply, that my enemies may be scattered and conquered by your perfect Love. 6. Teach me Lord to forgive as you have forgiven, to be merciful as you are merciful, to be compassionate as you are compassionate. 7. Fill me with the gifts of the Holy Ghost and in your grace may I demonstrate the fruits that the Holy Ghost bears. 8. I proclaim as John the Baptist proclaimed, crying out in the wilderness: Lord, prepare my way that I may find you, 9. Make my path straight, fill every valley in my life and every mountain and hill make it lowly and meek, make me straight and my rough ways smooth. (Luke 3:4-5) 10. May your kingdom manifest in my life for your glory. Jesus I Trust In You!
10 Hail Mary's … Glory Be to the Father…

"I believe, I love, I adore, I hope,
please pardon those who do not believe,
do not love, do not adore, do not hope. Show me the way,
Reveal all truth in your loving light,
My Loving Jesus
teach me to love beyond the price of death."

"Oh my Jesus, forgive us our sins, save us from the fires of hell, lead all souls to Heaven, especially those who have most need of your mercy."

FOURTH MYSTERY OF ILLUMINATION
The Transfiguration
Meditation (inspired by Luke 9:23-35:):
Our Father ...
1. Oh my Beloved Lord, show me what I must see and do, that I may see You. Let me die to the world., that I also may be transfigured. 2. I offer to you the sacrifice of my life for the salvation of those who still reject you, still do not hope in you, still do not love you, still do not adore you, still do not believe, for the poor deceased souls, for all that is seen and unseen, known and unknown that has not been pleasing to You, have mercy on all Oh Gracious Father of Everlasting Love. 3. Forgive our ignorance, teach us and fill us with your Divine Mercy and Divine Love, that we also may become love and mercy. 4. Let thy will be done in my life, with my life and through my life In Jesus. 5. May the agony of Your Passion be my strength in the sacrifice I offer to You; may your transfiguration manifest for the Glory of the Lord filling me with the grace to bear all things;
6. may the Joy of Your Resurrection be mine. May Your Light and Love remain with me always and eternally.
7. Decrease me Lord, that you may increase. Arise within me, transform, transfigure, illuminate, and overshadow me.
8. Make me white as snow, perfect as my Heavenly Father is perfect. Make me and mold me, remove my splinters, and use me to help my beloved brethren. 9. Glorify yourself in this body made of dust. Take all you need, and knead yourself into my being. Do with me

as you desire, that I may enter at the strait gate. 10. Oh Master, rise up and Fill this Temple with the Sacred Heart of Jesus and the Immaculate Heart of Mary. Shut the door and seal me that the enemy may no longer enter. Possess me, make of me a holy thing, a Son of God. Holy God, Holy Immortal one, Almighty God, My Longing, My Love. Be glorified in Jesus Name. Let us be ONE. Thank You Jesus, for demonstrating your love and your willingness, Teach me to be like You.

10 Hail Mary's ... Glory Be to the Father...

"I believe, I love, I adore, I hope,
please pardon those who do not believe,
do not love, do not adore, do not hope.
Show me the way,
Reveal all truth in your loving light,
My Loving Jesus
teach me to love beyond the price of death."

"Oh my Jesus, forgive us our sins, save us from the fires of hell, lead all souls to Heaven, especially those who have most need of your mercy."

FIFTH MYSTERY OF ILLUMINATION
The Last Supper -The Eucharist
The Holy Communion, the Holy Union

<u>**EXALT the BREAD OF LIFE**</u>
Meditation (inspired by John 13:1-38):
Our Father ...
1. Oh my Exalted Eucharistic Host
My Seed of Life unseen
My Infant Inward
Appearing defenseless yet defending

2. What Seed enters my mouth
What King enters this tomb

Accepting You in my mouth
Make me holy and true, loving and pure
3. The embrace of my tongue You receive
With sweet alms and reverence

4. Eucharistic love returns to me
Such sweet high, mystical ecstasy,
so loving a communion
Love beyond love ignites
Life beyond Life recognized

5. Oh what Heavenly Bread is this
What food has nourished me
What Glorious King arises within
Oh my beloved , My soul is Yours
My flesh and body too

6. What greatness is this within me
Oh beloved consumed by Your presence
Nothing else matters
There is no other want

7. Oh Love Everlasting Do not leave me
Be my strength, Be my all

8. Gracious, Immortal Beautiful Savior
My Want Of You Is Without Ceasing

9. My Love, My Light
Let Us Be One Throughout Eternity.
10. Arise and remain within me;
Let us be whole. Let us be ONE.
In the Name of Jesus.
10 Hail Mary's ... Glory Be to the Father...

"I believe, I love, I adore, I hope,
please pardon those who do not believe,
do not love, do not adore, do not hope.

Show me the way,
Reveal all truth in your loving light,
My Loving Jesus
teach me to love beyond the price of death."

"Oh my Jesus, forgive us our sins, save us from the fires of hell, lead all souls to Heaven, especially those who have most need of your mercy."

+++

HAIL, HOLY QUEEN
Hail, Holy Queen, Mother of Mercy! our life, our sweetness and our hope! To thee do we cry, poor banished children of Eve; to thee do we send up our sighs, mourning and weeping in this valley of tears. Turn then, most gracious advocate, thine eyes of mercy toward us, and after this our exile, show unto us the blessed fruit of thy womb, Jesus. O clement, O loving, O sweet Virgin Mary!

V. Pray for us, O Holy Mother of God.
R. That we may be made worthy of the promises of Christ.
Let us pray. O GOD, whose only begotten Son, by His life, death, and resurrection, has purchased for us the rewards of eternal life, grant, we beseech Thee, that meditating upon these mysteries of the Most Holy Rosary of the Blessed Virgin Mary, we may imitate what they contain and obtain what they promise, through the same Christ Our Lord. Amen.

MEMORARE
Remember, O most gracious Virgin Mary, that never was it known that any one who fled to thy protection, implored thy help, or sought thy intercession, was left unaided. Inspired with this confidence, I fly unto thee, O Virgin of virgins, my Mother! To thee I come; before thee I stand, sinful and sorrowful. O Mother of the Word Incarnate, despise not my petitions, but in thy mercy hear and answer me. Amen.

***

Allow me Lord to receive you spiritually,
Lead me Lord to eat of the Bread of Life
so that I may have life.   Amen.

BLESSED IS HE WHO COMES IN THE NAME OF THE LORD! ALLELUIA!

JESUS I TRUST IN YOU!

THE ANGEL OF THE LORD (ANGELUS DOMINI)
During the year (outside of Paschal Season)

V. The Angel of the Lord declared unto Mary,
R. And she conceived of the Holy Spirit.
Hail Mary...

V. Behold the handmaid of the Lord,
R. Be it done unto me according to your word.
Hail Mary...

V. And the Word was made flesh,
R. And dwelt among us.
Hail Mary...

V. Pray for us, O holy Mother of God,
R. That we may be made worthy of the promises of Christ.
Let us pray. Pour forth, we beg you, O Lord, your grace into our hearts: that we, to whom the Incarnation of Christ your Son was made known by the message of an Angel, may by his Passion and Cross be brought to the glory of his Resurrection. through the same Christ our Lord. Amen.

During Paschal Season
V. Queen of Heaven, rejoice, alleluia:
R. For he whom you merited to bear, alleluia,
V. Has risen, as he said, alleluia.
R. Pray for us to God, alleluia.

V. Rejoice and be glad, O Virgin Mary, alleluia.
R. Because the Lord is truly risen, alleluia.
Let us pray. O God, who by the Resurrection of your Son, our Lord Jesus Christ, granted joy to the whole world: grant, we beg you, that through the intercession of the Virgin Mary, his Mother, we may lay hold of the joys of eternal life. Through the same Christ our Lord.
Amen. (Roman Breviary)

BE NOT HID FROM ME
You Dearest Mother
who was overshadowed by the Holy Spirit
You whose soul magnified the Lord
Whose spirit rejoiced in God Our Savior
You who sensed the very presence
of Our Father and the Holy Spirit, one in being
You Dearest Mother who bore the Son of God
You who bore the Word made Flesh
You who bore
the Son, One with the Father,
One with the Holy Spirit
You Dearest Mother who was full of grace and truth
Be not hid from me

Dearest Mother of God, Most Holy
Mother of Wisdom,
whose holy presence was filled with Wisdom itself
Mother of Understanding,
you who in the flesh submitted to the
Will of Our Lord before understanding
Mother of Knowing, now filled, then filled, always filled with the knowledge greater than any earthly being
Mother of Mercy,
whose grace filled love bore all things perfectly
Mother of Love, united with Perfect Love,
Let me love you perfectly
Be not hid from me

+ + +

The following is the remaining message from the 5th Mystery. The Lord taught me that we must love and exalt THE BREAD OF LIFE, in the form of Bread itself.

THE EUCHARISTIC HOST LIKE MY BABY
<u>**My Baby**</u>
Oh My precious baby
Holding you in my arms
Defenseless and so lovingly I embrace you.
Just born you are helpless
Your head I have to hold
And near my heart,
loves sweet beat comforts both
Revealing Unconditional love,
total dependence
Engaged in new sight of responsibility
Love has shown itself without restraint
Innocent Love,
infant love weak yet strong
Free and without reservations untold
Willingly our love deepens
without question or measure. My Beloved Lord,
in Your likeness
You have allowed me to bear fruit in my womb in Your same likeness,
Blessed are You who gives life,
and whose greatness is not understood
except for the small measure we are given to compare.
Thank You Father, Son and Holy Ghost
for the gift of life,
the gift of love and
for allowing me to partake in such delight.

The Eucharistic Host
Oh my Exalted Eucharistic Host
My Seed of Life unseen
My Infant Inward
Appearing defenseless yet defending

What Seed enters my mouth
What King enters this tomb

Accepting You in my mouth
Make me holy and true, loving and pure
The embrace of my tongue You receive
With sweet alms and reverence

Eucharistic love returns to me
Such sweet high, mystical ecstasy,
so loving a communion
Love beyond love ignites
Life beyond Life recognized

Oh what Heavenly Bread is this
What food has nourished me
What Glorious King arises within
Oh my beloved , My soul is Yours
My flesh and body too

What greatness is this within me
Oh beloved consumed by Your presence
Nothing else matters
There is no other want

Oh Love Everlasting
Do not leave me
Be my strength, Be my all

Gracious, Immortal Beautiful Savior
My Want Of You Is Without Ceasing

My Love, My Light

Let Us Be One Throughout Eternity.
Arise and remain within me;
Let us be whole. In the Name of Jesus.

Chant Art

**EXALT AND ADORE
OUR LIVING BREAD
OUR SEED OF LIFE
OUR HOLY COMMUNION
THE WORD THAT BECAME FLESH**

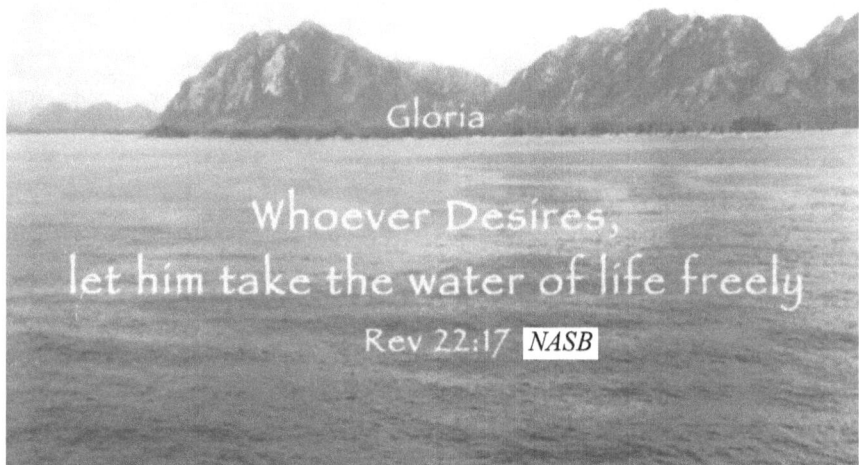

This CD is a reflection of Divine Love, Divine Mercy and the plea for a right desire to please Our Lord and be ready for His coming. It truly is beautiful. Buy at CDBaby.com; itunes; Amazon, Target etc.

The following prayers are lyrics in the CD "Loves' True Desire"

SINCERE DESIRE
I ask the Lord to open our hearts, minds and souls, our whole being with all of our strength to the gift of perfect charity. Teach us Lord and help us to give without restraint that the yoke of many may be broken. Teach us Lord to draw our souls out to the afflicted and help us to be the repairers of the breach the restorer of paths in which to dwell that all will be healed.
Come Lord Jesus, deliver us from evil and take your throne by the Power of the Holy Ghost.

- Give to us a sincere desire to pray so that we may have a fervent soul of the righteous so that our prayers may be pleasing to You. Teach us to pray with our whole heart mind and soul.
**Make us to be heard by You –
and as a Father to His children --answer us.**
Forgive us Lord for not denying ourselves as we should, teach us how Lord so that we may be pleasing to you.
- Forgive us our inequities and the inequities of our fathers and relatives, especially of those deceased that might still be suffering for their sins whom you have judged. Bring them Lord to your everlasting Light that they may enter into eternal rest in your loving light and dwelling place which you have prepared for us. Lord Hear Our Prayer.

THE JOY   (11/30/2007)
Dearest Father of Greatest Prestige and Highest Rank May joy be Yours!

The joy to be received in the purest of hearts
The joy of being thought of in the holiest of minds The joy of uniting with those who desire you greatly
The joy of being the Shepherd to those to whom you are their only Want

The joy of being well pleased with all and by all

The joy of hope manifested
The joy of giving to us life in the faith of Christ
The joy to dwell together as One – souls bonded in the same love
The joy of living in ONE body
The joy of Our Holy Communion with you at last and throughout eternity

The Joy of making your joy complete
by being of the same mind
Maintaining the same love
United in the same spirit
Intent on one purpose

Oh Lord the joy
that we may imitate You in Your
unconditional love unconditional mercy
and humble ourselves in unconditional repentance
that we may also share in the joy of returning to You
I love You Lord
may joy be Yours now and throughout all eternity

THE DESIRE OF LOVE (9/20-24/08)
(for teachings pertaining to this writing see table of contents for "LOVES TRUE DESIRE Lyrics Analysis")

Oh Beloved King, Creator And Lover Of My Soul, My Bridegroom, My Jealous Love

What Is
"the Desire of Love" Like
In Your Sight Oh Lord?

Like a grain of sand in the littleness of my mind I relate

Is It Like

The Loving Embrace
Of One I See
Of One I Desire,
Of One I Can Touch
But Do Not?

Is It Like
The Love Longing And Lingering In My Heart
For The Companionship Of Another
But Have Not?

Such a Desire enters my Heart
To be embraced,
To be kissed
And to touch and love the one I see
But I Dare Not
For the Love of You, Oh Lord

Is this the desire you seek?
Is this the "want of You" that you desire?
that we may know
Your Love long waiting

Help me to love the one I see with a Holy Love
How can I love the one I see in this world
and still please you Oh Lord?

Can I touch the face of this one as if Your face?
Can I embrace this one with Your loving arms guiding my arms?
Can I kiss this one with Your loving lips guiding my lips?
or are we not to touch at all?
Offering that sacrifice to You
Will You be our stronghold in Your unfathomable love?

or am I to understand a deeper rejection of those whom You love
that I may love You that much more

Oh Beloved King, make me right in Your sight

To the one you have made me to love
Lord, Help me to be
For I know not how
I am lost without You!

My Beloved Love rising in me
Rise in those you have given me to see and to love
that we may love You perfectly and each other also

Oh Lord,
What Is the Desire of Love Like
In Your Sight?
How can I please Thee to know Thee

What was the chaste love of Mary and Joseph like?
What kind of sacrifice is this?
How did they live their life in Your love?
Surely, graced by Your love
the Great Desire of You consumed them!
Oh Holy Chastity!

Oh Lord there is no temptation on this earth
that cannot be conquered by your perfect love
Resisting the desires of the flesh
the lust of the eye
and the pride of life
Loving you with all their strength
You became their stronghold

Oh Beloved Desire of my soul
Give to Me the Great Grace of this Holy Desire
Make my desire right in your sight
that you may be pleased in all that I am
and all that I love

Can the appetite of Your Love be Smitten by the love in My Heart?
What can I give Thee that I have not...
my children? my life? my death?

all those whom I have loved? all that I love!
all that I desire? and all that I want?
all that I am?
It is already Yours and
You alone I Desire to Desire
Love Stricken, Love Longing, Love Long Waiting
Oh Beloved, How long will it be that I must remain separated from You?

Can You be Smitten by an Irresistible Union of Desire?

Oh Lord, smitten me with Your love that I may return to You
Smitten me with all those whom You love
as with one Holy Word
or one breath
which gives life and is life in us,
that we may reunite ourselves to You

Beloved Word of God, Beloved Instigator of what will be
Be for me all that my Lord desires,
Oh Beloved Sword of the Spirit Come Forth!

Oh Beloved King Of Glory, Creator And Lover Of My Soul, My Bridegroom,
My Jealous Love

What Is
"the Desire of Love" Like
In Your Sight Oh Lord?
Oh What Love have I not known,
That is Greater Beyond my expectations or any known to me
The Most Gentle, most giving and most Caring Love Beyond Understanding
Such a Holy and Pure Love
Absolute and Perfect
Oh Lord, How can I return that Blameless Love to You
Impeccable and Incorrupt, Chaste and Totally Devoted to You

Can a Husband and Wife live such a life?

A Love as You Desire, Divine and Glorious
with Undistracted Devotion Toward You
Who Is Love Beyond Love

Oh Loving Creator, Create a Pure Heart in me
I am drawn to You, Receive me, Remember me
Make my heart fit for You, most pleasing, most loving, most tender
And fill it With That Undistracted Devotion Toward You

Oh Beloved Love Of All Loves,
King Of Glory, Creator And Lover Of My Soul, My Bridegroom,
My Jealous Love

You Dearest Love
I Desire
Can I Love You as no other has ever before
Oh the thought of Your Presence
The want of the Consumption of Your Complete Love
You are The Desire of My Heart
Oh Beloved, how long shall I be alone

or will I be alone at all
what lie do we live in this world
You say "we are one"
and because you say it, although I do not see it
I believe
and so
Would this love be as no other before,
the greatest grandeur
impeccable and profound, unbounded and endless
because the many are one in Your love, with my love
in my love, with Your love and
through our love and their love,
all are ONE

Oh Lord make me to love all those whom You have given to me to love
with a pure love pleasing to You

Perfect Love Make us to Love You Perfectly
Make us to Love each other as You Desire
Fill us with the faith of Jesus
and complete us

Beloved Composer of Love
the One and Only True
for ages to ages in the everlasting throughout time and eternity
you are my True Desire of Love
I love you

Teach me Lord to live and to trust in Your Divine Providence
Take from my heart and mind all anxiety
I desire to trust in you completely
and to act upon your Word without hesitation
make me to obey your commands, statutes and precepts
and give to me your Holy Spirit.
make me to sin no more

Allow me Lord to delight in the hope of uniting myself to you
In the hope of seeing Your loving face at last
and entering into that place of love
that no matter where I am
or may appear to be
you are with me without any doubt
and I am pleasing to you

Oh Lord be smitten by the irresistible Desire of Love in my heart
Come down from Heaven Beloved King
Take the reign of my life
Take Your reign on this earth and in all creation
May you be forever blessed and exalted above all forever
You are indeed Holy Love Divine and Eternal!
The Desire and Treasure of my Heart,
Jesus I Trust in You!

WHAT GREAT LOVE DOES MY SOUL ACKNOWLEDGE?
(12/6/07)

Oh Beloved Father
What joy I find in the thought of Mary
I sense the excitement of you in my soul
Oh how lovely, the Love of You
Oh how lovely the love of Mary for you
Oh what Great Love does my soul acknowledge?

Is it my Spirit rejoicing in You?
Is it my soul magnifying You?

Oh let me be consumed by it
That I may live where love is
And not where I live

Oh God, my only true
Be forever magnified, glorified, praised and adored

Glory to God on High, Blessed and Holy are You
Immortal Omnipotent
Love Beyond Love, My Everlasting
Manifestation of ONE
I Love You
I Trust in You

WHAT MORE CAN I SAY? (3/09/08)
What more can I say?
What more can I desire?
You who is the very essence of
Infinite love, admiration and well being…
Make us so, that we may love, admire,
Adore and exalt you unceasingly

Oh Lord, as in water face reflects face (Pr27:10)
Make my heart to be a reflection of you
May Your lovingkindness and truth be also
Of my essence
Your righteousness, love and mercy my way of life

Oh Lord, I desire greatly to behold Your face in righteousness
That I may awaken and be satisfied with your likeness
That you may sweetly say
"With you I am well pleased"
Oh beloved King of my heart
If it is pleasing to my Lord
I beseech you to allow your servant to serve you
In the fullest of grace just as those whom you have favored
I love you my Lord, what more can I say?

THREE TIMES THE SIGN OF THE CROSS IN THANKSGIVING

THANKING THE WORD OF GOD, FATHER, SON, AND HOLY GHOST

THANKING THE GREAT "ONE"

1. Forehead	Thank You To Our Heavenly Father for His only Son and their great love
2. Stomach	Thank You To The Son, Jesus Christ Lover Of My Soul, Divine Mercy *help me to forgive as I have been forgiven*
3. Right Shoulder	Thank You To The Holy Spirit
4. Left Shoulder	my consoler, my guide, my light, my love, *I surrender to You*
5. Mouth	Thank You To The Word Of God, *May I Live To Love It, To Live In Truth And To Proclaim It Boldly And Zealously*

THANKING THE INTECESSORS

Forehead	Thank You To Blessed Virgin Mary Most Holy For Her Glorious "Yes", And For Interceding For Me *I ask that the Lord may also find favor in me.*
Stomach	Thank You To The Holy Souls In Purgatory *May The Lord Shine His Light Upon Them And Grant Them Eternal Rest*

Right Shoulder	Thank You To All The Angels In Heaven and their intercession
Left Shoulder	Thank You To All The Saints And To All The Holy Men And Women Who Intercede And Strive To Pray Without Ceasing for the salvation of all
Mouth	Thank You To My Holy Communion and The Blessed Sacrament at The Altar of Grace, *Receive Me, Remember Me*

THANK YOU TO OUR PROTECTORS, THE ARMY OF GOD

Forehead	Thank You To St Michael And All The Archangels *May They Be Blessed As They Continue To Keep Us On That Narrow Road*
Stomach	Thank You To My Guardian Angel For Persevering In Guiding Me, Loving Me, Aiding Me At All Times, Especially When I Have Failed To Acknowledge Their Assistance
Right Shoulder	Thank You To All The Holy Angels Of The Lord For All That They Do, have done and will do for Me
Left Shoulder	Thank You To All Unknown Creatures And Creation Of My Lord For Being Part Of My Life In Which The Lord Has Allowed Us To Partake
Mouth	Thank You To My Beloved Self Control And Obedience Of Mind, Blessed Tongue, Beloved Soul the Lover Of My Lord, Body Of Christ Within Me, *May Jesus the finisher of my faith, complete me in His everlasting love*

In The Name Of The Father, In The Name Of Jesus, And In The Name Of Mary by the power of the Holy Spirit and the Word of God AMEN

THE WORD THAT BECOMES LIVING BREAD

BE EXALTED BREAD OF LIFE I LOVE YOU LORD!
(this is a miracle prayer –from WE LAY DOWN OUR CROWN)

Most Beloved Heavenly Father Be Exalted
Holy Trinity, I love You!
My Creator, Be Praised!
Living Word enter my mind
Maker of all Things, Be Glorified!
Heavenly Father of all children on Earth,
Bless and claim each and everyone of us as Your own
Be the Great Father in my family, the Head of my house

Merciful and Holy are You
Wonderful, Wondrous, Beautiful Savior
God of Love Consume Me!
King of Kings
Lord of Lords
Hail to You Lord Jesus Christ
Manifestation as Son of God, be Glorified
Manifestation as Holy Spirit, be the Light in my life
Manifestations of the Holy Trinity Illuminate the Earth
Manifestation of the 2nd Coming, Leave no one behind;
Please Rescue all of us, once and for all
Conqueror of all my enemies Be Praised and Glorified

My provider, My Healer
My all in all
My every breath
King of My Heart
Ruler and Lord of My Life
Purpose of my being
Giver of Peace

As I consume this Holy Eucharistic Host,
The Bread of Life,

may Your transformation continue in my total being.

Your broken body heals me and makes me holy;
It humbles me and makes me whole.

In my acceptance of the Bread of Life,
I receive life.
You are the Breath of Life
and give life to all creation.

As you penetrate my body with Your Body and Blood transformed to Life
in this Living Bread and Wine,
Be my bridegroom, and bond me to yourself.
Commune with me and make me holy.
Be my life giving bread.
In me, this host becomes body of my body;
this wine becomes blood of my blood;
they are flesh of my flesh;
bone of my bone;
my being submits to your being;
if I am willing, and Lord I am willing.

May I truly be made One with You;
In Spirit, mind, body and soul,
Perfect as my Heavenly Father is Perfect.

May the Passion of Your Love, become my Passion.
May Your mercy, become my mercy, that I may
demonstrate it to the fullest of grace.
Fill me, consume me, penetrate me,
change me and stay in me.
May I be made a new creation in Christ.
May my love become immense for You, as Yours is for me.
I AM WILLING!

I return to You Oh Lord.
You said Remember me take this eat and drink,
and so I say to You Lord,

Remember me,
commune with me,
Oh my love, who bore all for me;
I return all that I bear to You in sacrifice
for the Poor Deceased Souls,
I return to you all that you came to redeem that they also may be set free. My love, my life, my burdens, my illnesses, my worldly love, my worldly pleasures, my ego, my free will, my pride, my unbelief, my torments, my resentments, every drop of blood that I shed, every bad habit, my unworthiness,

Oh Lord may these sacrifices be acceptable to you on their behalf and on behalf of my special intentions (name them).
Make me worthy.
Sacrificial love beyond understanding,
I offer to you the sacrifice of life.
Great and Worthy are you who deserves all the glory,
praise and honor,
who deserves our love
without question and without measure,
Oh Lord let us love you,
teach us to love you more than we have ever imagined;

God of all creation;
God so humble and true;
God so revenant and Holy;
God, in your likeness make me like you;
Holy and true, pleasing and
loving You in ways that only you would understand.

Oh sweet death, come before me
and let the Lord deal with you,
that I may truly die to this world and
have Life in Him who is Glorious beyond belief,
who is true to His Word,
who is Gracious and pours His grace upon us;
Oh Beloved, consume me, penetrate me,
be one with me, You are my ultimate desire,
I thirst and crave for You.

You are the Passion of my being.
I long for YOU!
I adore You! I love You! I hope for You!
Oh Gracious love, lead me to Your Glory.
Be merciful and Save all souls, come to their aid,
let your victory be made known.
In the name of Jesus. Blessed Mother Mary Pray for us.
(End of CD lyrics - also see Table of contents for Chaplet of St Michael and New Chaplet of Mercy)

THE GREATEST ANGUISH VS LOVE
His heart has become so hardened
that even a speck of light
cannot be seen

Lost in hope
lost in time
hopeless in a helpless earth

the road broadens
He reaps what He sows
in sorrow and anguish
to an extreme
there is no end to self punishment

Oh My Lord,
shine your light upon him
soften his heart
and show him your mercy

Heal him Dear Lord

Forgive us,
forgive him
Deliver us Oh Lord
from all hatred, jealousy, envy and pride

OH GREAT GOD!
How can it be
that the ignorant
enjoy their ignorance

Oh Great God
who specifically said in
the Books of the Law
that such great works were done
so that we would believe and know that
you are truly God,
Our God, the Great I Am
The God of Great Wonders
Who gave breath to dust
so that we might live
Who gave life to all life
that we might live for your pleasure

Oh Great God,
whose manifestations are many
beyond our understanding
beyond anything
our limited mind can comprehend
we who are nothing
can not conceive your greatness
except for that which you have taught
through our trials and tribulations
in which we ourselves have come to contemplate and compare
your suffering, your sorrow, your great love,
all unfathomably greater than ours

God of Everlasting Love
God so merciful and compassionate
God whose holy presence
in the Bread of Life
is in Great stillness
the very breath of our souls
the essence of life eternal

You who gives life to the Bread of Life
so that we may partake
Forgive us Lord
for not fearing to be apart from you

forgive our ignorance
Bless Us Lord, with
Life beyond life
in our Holy Union with you
In our Holy Communion

May you increase in us
that we may decrease

Make us One with You Lord
God of all creation
Lead us to do and say
what we must to gain everlasting life
in the Holy Name of Jesus
I make my request
Blessed Mother Pray for us.

DO NOT JUDGE
Some are workers for the Lord…

How can you dare judge
now knowing that the tormentor is our blessing…
As the Lord's work is done in each one of us,
through our trials and tribulations with great love,
patience, endurance and grace
we become lost in His sacrificial love.

consumed by it,
we become like Him
and of His image.

Desiring to Love unto death,
desperate to be united to Him.

With great hope anticipating a union
beyond any union we have ever known.

As we wail and morn,
weeping for ourselves and our children,
with great grief and sorrow
fearing to hurt our Loving King,
Our Bridegroom, and each other.

Henceforth, so will our union be
with great joy and love
fearing to even have a glance
taken away from us,
a super union beyond anything
we have ever known.

Our new love revealed,
so great
that it would rip these vessels of clay apart
because love cannot contain itself in them.

Oh My!!
What love
have we not
yet come to know?

What love awaits me?

My Beloved – let us be united
that the wait may cease,
that your patience,
your long waiting may be satisfied
and that all Love may reunite itself to you.

No words can suffice for this desire
this great hope,
this all encompassing want.
Be for me

      all that you are,
that I may return to you and
      be for you
          all that I am.

Blessed are You
My Loving creature,
My loving God.
My Holy Communion.
In the Name of Jesus.

BE SATISFIED
On My Jesus,
What fragrance pleases thee
Teach me to use the fragrances of old
That gives thee so much delight

What can I do to please thee
Teach me all things
Little and small
That your delight
May be filled with a cup
Overflowing with loving light
From me to You.
That your hunger and thirst may be satisfied
Above and beyond that offered by any other,
wretched as myself, in times past

Oh My Beloved
What can I do
That no other has done
To please you
Let me do that and more

That Your Glory may be known
And that we may once again
Be united with You
Made of one mind, one spirit

One body, one love

Finally,
In the bond of peace
In perfect love, perfect faith
And all that you have Desired
from the beginning of time.
What can I do
That you have been awaiting
Before you come again
Oh Lord, let me do it
That you may come for me
I desperately long for your love
I desperately long to be with you
I desperately long to embrace you
I desperately long to thank you personally
I desperately long to see you
I desperately long to worship you
I desperately long to praise you
I desperately long to glorify you
I desperately long to honor you
I desperately long to bless you
as you have blessed me
I desperately long to love you in return
And to give all that I am
That you may be satisfied as never before

I know, who am I
To make such a request
Made of dust
A vessel of clay
I am nothing and deserve nothing
In my sinfulness I have hurt you so much
Forgive me for asking such a great request
I love you my love
More than my limited mind can express

Oh My Lord, My Beloved
Have mercy on this earth

Have mercy on its people
Make us all one and claim all back
To your possession
Lovingly, willingly we anxiously await
In the Name of Jesus I pray.

CONSUMED RADIANCE WITHIN
Oh My Love
My Bread of Life
So Reverent and Pure
Who feeds my soul in sweet comfort
and great stillness
whose well waters bring forth
the coolness of salvation
Consumed Radiance within
Arise in Me and Let your presence remain
Make this leaven whole
Never depart from me
Oh Precious Living God, in me
Presenting yourself In the Bread of Life
You seem so defenseless
When it is me, you defend in your very presence.

Oh come and taste the sweetness of the Lord
My seed of life, which is the Word of God
The Word of God, which made man from dust
The Word of God, which gave breath to man
The Word of God which became flesh
the Son of God is the Word of God the
Word became flesh
Flesh which became my Savoir
My Savior which became My Bread of Life
The Word transforming Bread to Living Bread
The Bread which becomes seed
The seed that I eat is the Word of God
The Bread of Life is truly food for my soul
My Seed, My Bread, My Word, My God
My Beloved Holy Communion

My Eucharistic Ecstasy, My Beloved Perfect Love
Oh Precious Living Bread of Life, Living God in me

For He is Truly Good
And burdens become light
And broken dreams become blessings
Sacrifices become offerings welcomed

Oh Gracious Living Bread of Life
I Exalt You! I Adore You! I Love You! I Believe!

Oh True Living Creature and Holy Thing
Make me and mold me
May this Bread Be made Whole
Transform me
Possess Me
I abandon all for
The love of You
The love in You
The Love with You
The Love through You
The Love consuming me
The Love which becomes my all
in all The Bread of Life transformed
Transforming me
My Bread of Salvation
My Bread of Restoration
My Bread of Transformation
My Bread of Illumination
My Bread of Resurrection
My Bread, My Seed, My God in Me

In this Beautiful, Exalted
Miraculous Mysterious Bread of Life
My Jesus is resurrected in me
I have died to the world
Consumed by His Holy Will
His Reverent Love
And His Grace and Mercy are mine

Oh Beloved, Save everyone I pray
Arise in each of us, transform us, illuminate us
Perfect us, Teach us Lord all things
That you may be Glorified

Blessed be God Forever In the Name of Jesus.
Blessed be the Mother of God,
Mary most Holy. Pray for us.

PERFECT LOVE - LOVE BEYOND LOVE - CONSUME ME!

PERFECT LOVE LET ME LOVE YOU PERFECTLY!

FINDING MARY, MY MOST BLESSED MOTHER
In the Love of His Most Blessed Mother
In the Love of Our Fathers' Most Highly Favored One
In the Love that leaped for Joy and magnifies the Lord

In Mary
and in the Love of God
I obtain a greater Hope
      a greater Faith
      a greater Love

A Grace beyond grace
to which my spouse,
my bridegroom
yearns and longs to unite

in union as never before…
at last ONE

My soul magnifies the Lord
and my spirit rejoices in God My Savior;

Blessed Be Mary, My Mother Most Holy

Blessed Be the Bride in me
Blessed Be Jesus Christ, True God and True Man
Blessed Be God, Blessed Be His Holy Name
Blessed Be My Most Holy Ghost
Blessed Be the Great I AM,
Blessed Be the all consuming fire of all those
joined to the Great ONE
Blessed Be to My Love, My Lord,
My Exalted Living Bread in Me
Blessed Be to the Bridegroom in me, My Jealous Love

Keep Me Lord as yours alone,
Keep Me in the treasures of Heaven
a speck in Your eye alone
a log standing firm in Your being
fill me with the plank of obedience and righteousness,
the plank of love and mercy,
compassion and all that You are
Keep my heart in Yours
and Yours in mine
let my heart never leave you
Let me never fail you
I would rather die, than to be apart from you
Bonded to you alone,
My hope is in You...
Jesus I Trust in You!

- Precious in the sight of the LORD
          is the death of His faithful ones. *Ps 116:15 NRSV*

The following was taken from part of "Finding Mary" which is on the previous page, THE KEEP ME LORD OF FINDING MARY:

Keep Me Lord as yours alone,
Keep Me in the treasures of Heaven
a speck in Your eye alone
a log standing firm in Your being

fill me with the plank of obedience and righteousness,
the plank of love and mercy,
compassion and all that You are
Keep my heart in Yours
and Yours in mine
let my heart never leave you
Let me never fail you
I would rather die, than to be apart from you
Bonded to you alone, My hope is in You...
Jesus I Trust in You!

NOTHING MATTERS
Nothing matters…. Except the Lord

The sorrow of separation
        The tears of others pain
The longing
        And desire to be with Him
The Love so great, and
        Beyond measure
felt as Jesus on the cross..
        My God, My God, why have you forsaken me
            not so much in suffering
                but more so greatly in longing …

The great desire of the Holy Communion
        The Union
            The Wedding

The hope to be ready, willing and watchful
Awaiting anxiously,
        yet time intrudes

The Love verses the heart of darkness
Like an egg ready to hatch
Like a woman ready to give birth
The heart ready to explode into beaming light

    A fire of consuming love
            Penetrated and dissolved
vessels smashed and broken

United into the very essence of
        Everlasting love profound

No longer flesh
        But one spirit
                United at last

This is how my heart feels
My mind longs and hopes
My spirit and soul desire
and so shall it be when it is pleasing to My Lord, My Beloved

PSALM 104:1-3 *KJV*

Bless the LORD, O my soul.

O LORD my God, thou art very great;

thou art clothed with honour and majesty.

Who coverest thyself with light as with a garment:

who stretchest out the heavens like a curtain:

Who layeth the beams of his chambers in the waters:

who maketh the clouds his chariot:

who walketh upon the wings of the wind:

Lord cover me with Your garment of light and surround me with Your heavenly curtain that I may remain in Your shelter and honor You forever. May Your light beam in every chamber of my body and in the waters of my body may You overflow satisfying my thirst for Your love and Glory. May my only and most ultimate desire and craving be my passion for Your immense love. In the Name of Jesus.

THE PRAYER OF ST. FRANCIS
Lord make me an instrument of Your peace Where there is hatred, let me sow love; where there is injury, pardon; where there is doubt, faith; where there is despair, hope; where there is darkness, light and where there is sadness, Joy O Divine Master grant that I may not so much seek to be consoled as to console; to be understood, as to understand; to be loved as to love. For it is in giving that we receive, it is in pardoning that we are pardoned. And it is in dying that we are born to eternal life. (General Secretariat of the Franciscan Missions Inc P O Box 130; Waterford, WI 53185)

THE BEATITUDES
Blessed are the poor in spirit:
for theirs is the kingdom of heaven.
Blessed are they that mourn: for they shall be comforted.
Blessed are the meek: for they shall inherit the earth.
Blessed are they which do hunger and thirst after righteousness:
for they shall be filled.
Blessed are the merciful: for they shall obtain mercy.
Blessed are the pure in heart: for they shall see God.
Blessed are the peacemakers:
for they shall be called the children of God.
Blessed are they which are persecuted for righteousness' sake: for theirs is the kingdom of heaven.
Blessed are ye, when men shall revile you, and persecute you, and shall say all manner of evil against you falsely, for my sake.
Rejoice, and be exceeding glad: for great is your reward in heaven: for so persecuted they the prophets which were before you.
Matthew 5:3-12 KJV

ST. MICHAEL THE ARCHANGEL:
St. Michael the Archangel, defend us in battle. Be our protection against the wickedness and snares of the devil. May God rebuke him, we humbly pray, and do thou, Prince of the Heavenly Hosts, by the power of God, cast into Hell Satan and all evil spirits who prowl through the world seeking the ruin of souls. Amen.

PRAYER BEFORE THE MASS AT THE ALTAR OF GRACE:
Father, we offer to you these prayers, and with this celebration of the Most Holy Bread of Life we anticipate with hope and love our deliverance from evil, and The Coming of Our Great King, Jesus for the Salvation of all mankind. With all of our gratitude, love and affection we ask that you lead us in this celebration to it's fullest glory as you have intended from the very beginning of ages. Teach us Lord, so that we may know you Honor you and love you beyond love In this Holy and Reverent Church We return ourselves to you In submission to you Lord Jesus We rebuke, resist and renounce Satan Let us begin in the Glory of Jesus. Blessed Mother pray for us who have recourse to thee

INTRODUCTION TO THE CHAPLET OF ST MICHAEL
  Saint Michael the Archangel promised that by the honoring of the Nine Choirs of Angels in the following chaplet devotion, along with diligence in attaining holiness, souls would have the escort of one representative of each of the Nine Choirs when approaching the Holy Table, and in addition, for the daily recital joined to courage in seeking holiness, Saint Michael the Archangel promised continual assistance from all the angels, and deliverance from Purgatory for themselves and their families.
  This chaplet is known by many names, including the Chaplet of Saint Michael, the Crown of Saint Michael and the Saint Michael Rosary.

THE CHAPLET OF ST MICHAEL
O God, come to my assistance. O Lord, make haste to help me. Glory be to the Father, and to the Son, and to the Holy Spirit , as it was in the beginning is now and ever shall be world without end. Amen.

Say one **Our Father and three Hail Mary's** after each of the following nine salutations in honor of the nine Choirs of Angels

By the intercession of St. Michael and the celestial Choir of (1) … may the Lord (a)…

1. Seraphim	a. make us worthy to burn with the fire of perfect charity.
2. Cherubim	b. grant us the grace to leave the ways of sin and run in the paths of Christian perfection.
3. Thrones	c. may the Lord infuse into our hearts a true and sincere spirit of humility.
4. Dominions	d. give us grace to govern our senses and overcome any unruly passions. Amen.
5. Powers	e. protect our souls against the snares and temptations of the devil.
6. Virtues	f. preserve us from evil and falling into temptation.
7. Principalities	may God fill our souls with a true spirit of obedience.
8. Archangels	g. give us perseverance in faith and in all good works in order that we may attain the glory of Heaven.
9. Angels	h. grant us to be protected by them in this mortal life and conducted in the life to come to Heaven. Amen.

Say **one Our Father in honor of each of the following** leading Angels: St. Michael, St. Gabriel, St. Raphael and our Guardian Angel.

Concluding prayers:

O glorious prince St. Michael, chief and commander of the heavenly hosts, guardian of souls, vanquisher of rebel spirits, servant in the house of the Divine King and our admirable conductor, you who shine with excellence and superhuman virtue deliver us from all evil, who turn to you with confidence and enable us by your gracious protection to serve God more and more faithfully every day.

Pray for us, O glorious St. Michael, Prince of the Church of Jesus Christ, that we may be made worthy of His promises.
Almighty and Everlasting God, Who, by a prodigy of goodness and a merciful desire for the salvation of all men, has appointed the most glorious Archangel St. Michael Prince of Your Church, make us worthy, we ask You, to be delivered from all our enemies, that none of them may harass us at the hour of death, but that we may be conducted by him into Your Presence. This we ask through the merits of Jesus Christ Our Lord. Amen.
+ + +

TO PLEASE YOU GREATLY…
Holy And Beloved King
Creator Of All Of Heaven And Earth
Teach Me To Pray Like Moses And Elijah
Mary And Jesus And All The Great Saints
Make Me To Please You
I, A Worthless Sinner,
Give All Worth To You
For You Alone Are Worthy
You Alone Are Lord
You Are My Soul Lover
And My Very Being

Oh Beloved King Of Glory
May Your Love Manifest Upon This Desolate Land
Upon Our Desolate Body
Re-Member Us Oh Lord
Make Us Whole And Finish Your Work In Us
That We May At Last Be One
In Love, Joy, Peace, Mercy
And All That You Are

Forgive Us Lord
For All We Have Done To Hurt You
From The Beginning Of Time
Do With Us As You Will So That Others May
Cease In Their Suffering

In Their Sorrow
And In Their Ignorance

Oh Beloved God
Merciful Most Caring Compassionate
Loving Being, Unfathomable Goodness
Please Come And Deliver Us From Evil
Unite Yourself To Us
Let Us Live In You And
In Everlasting Love At Last

I Love You As No Word Can Explain
With Tears I Grieve Our Separation
Please Come,
I Love You
Most Holy, Most Beloved, Most Blessed

Perhaps Someday
I May Give You Thanks
In A Way I Have Never Been Able To Express
Without Limit,
With A Heart Overflowing
With Everlasting Desire,
Love And Gratitude
And Joy
That You Hoped For
From The Very Beginning Of Time

Oh, How Great It Would Be,
If You Allow Me To Please You Greatly Someday!

IN MEMORY OF BELOVED DEACON ALAN FITZPATRICK

Twenty Decade 'Scriptural Style' Rosary with Divine Mercy Text

(All Divine Mercy images and content of any kind in this book have been "Used with the permission of the Marian Fathers of the Immaculate Conception of the B.V.M.")

This rosary is a "scriptural style' rosary in that there is a verse before each Hail Mary prayer. The verses are taken from <u>The Diary of Divine Mercy</u> by St. Faustina. The Diary was a major part in the canonization of St. Faustina. The Diary includes both St. Faustina's words and words that she heard from the Blessed Virgin Mary and from Our Lord, Jesus Christ. The verses selected for this rosary are only from the words St. Faustina heard from Our Lord.

This rosary is in two forms. The first form is specific for use on the Second Sunday after Easter, now also known as Divine Mercy Sunday. The other form is for use in all other days of the year. The verses selected have different texts only in the first Joyful Mystery, the Annunciation.

Compiled by Deacon Alan FitzPatrick, sfo

THE ORDER OF PRAYERS IN PRAYING THE HOLY ROSARY

Sign of the Cross
Apostles Creed
Intensions:
(***Joyful***: for Perfect Faith, Hope, Love and Charity / ***Luminous***: for Perfect Desire, Holy Want and Perfect undistracted devotion for Our Lord / ***Sorrowful***: for a pure heart, perfect obedience, righteousness / ***Glorious***: for my deliverance, for the decent of the Holy Spirit to possess me, for my loving unto death according to God's will, and for my assumption into heaven)
Hail Mary 3x
Glory Be Meditation
(large beads) Our Father
(small beads) Hail Mary
(after 10 Hail Mary) Glory Be
New mediation and then start with the Our Father
(final)Hail Holy Queen

PRAYERS OF THE ROSARY:

1. In the Name of the Father, the Son and the Holy Spirit Amen.

2. THE NICENE CREED

I believe in one God, the Father, the Almighty, Creator of heaven and earth, of all that is visible and invisible; I believe in one Lord, Jesus Christ, the only begotten Son of God, eternally begotten of the Father, before all ages. Light from Light, true God from true God, of one essence with the Father, through whom all things were made, Who for us and for our salvation He came down from heaven and was incarnate by the Holy Spirit and the Virgin Mary, and was made man. For our sake He was crucified under Pontius Pilate; He suffered death and was buried. Rising on the third day according to the Scriptures and ascending into the heavens is seated at the right hand of the Father. He will come again in glory to judge the living and the dead, and His kingdom will have no end. We believe in the Holy Spirit, the Lord, the Giver of life, who proceeds from the Father. Who together with the Father and the Son He is worshiped and glorified. Who spoke through the Prophets. I believe in one holy catholic and apostolic Church. I acknowledge one baptism for the remission of sins. **I expect** the resurrection of the dead, and the life of the age to come. AMEN.

3. **Our Father**
Our Father, who art in heaven; hallowed be Thy name; Thy kingdom come; Thy will be done on earth as it is in heaven. Give us this day our daily bread; and Forgive us our trespasses as we *(make us to)* forgive those who trespass against us. Lead us not into temptation but deliver us from evil. Amen.

4. **Hail Mary**
Hail Mary, full of grace, the Lord is with you; blessed are you among women, and blessed is the fruit of your womb, Jesus. Holy Mary, Mother of God, pray for us sinners, now and at the hour of our death. Amen.

5. **Glory be to the Father** (3 times to honor each)
Glory be to the Father, and to the Son, and to the Holy Ghost. As it was in the beginning, is now, and ever shall be, world without end. Amen.

HAIL, HOLY QUEEN
Hail, Holy Queen, Mother of Mercy! our life, our sweetness and our hope! To thee do we cry, poor banished children of Eve; to thee do we send up our sighs, mourning and weeping in this valley of tears. Turn then, most gracious advocate, thine eyes of mercy toward us, and after this our exile, show unto us the blessed fruit of thy womb, Jesus. O clement, O loving, O sweet Virgin Mary!
V. Pray for us, O Holy Mother of God.
R. That we may be made worthy of the promises of Christ.
Let us pray. O GOD, whose only begotten Son, by His life, death, and resurrection, has purchased for us the rewards of eternal life, grant, we beseech Thee, that meditating upon these mysteries of the Most Holy Rosary of the Blessed Virgin Mary, we may imitate what they contain and obtain what they promise, through the same Christ Our Lord. Amen.

MEDITATIONS OF THE ROSARY (Pause briefly after each meditation before saying the Hail Mary, meditate on the words spoken):

FIRST JOYFUL MYSTERY, THE ANNUNCIATION
Selection for all days except Divine Mercy Sunday
As the Archangel Gabriel announced the Good News to Mary. Jesus has St. Faustina announce the Good News of Divine Mercy to the world.

--Our Father—

1. "**I want the Image to be solemnly blessed on the first Sunday after Easter, and I want it to be venerated publicly so every soul may know about it.**" Diary ¶341 (Brief Pause) Hail Mary…

2. "**I desire to grant unimaginable graces to those souls who trust in my mercy.**" Diary ¶687 Hail Mary…

3. **When the hardened sinners say it.** (the chaplet) **I will fill their soul with peace, and the hour of their death will be a happy one.** Diary ¶1541 Hail Mary…

4. **Tell the world about My mercy and My love.** Diary ¶1074 Hail Mary…

5. **Write, My daughter, that I am mercy itself for the contrite soul.** Diary ¶1739 Hail Mary…

6. **My daughter, tell souls that I am giving them My mercy as a defense. I Myself am fighting for them and am bearing the just anger of My Father.** Diary ¶1516 Hail Mary…

7. "**I promise that the soul that will venerate this image will not perish.**" Diary ¶48 Hail Mary…

8. **I also promise great victory over [its] enemies here on earth, especially at the hour of death. I Myself will defend it as My own glory.**" Diary ¶48 Hail Mary…

9. **My daughter, encourage souls to say the chaplet which I have given to you. It please Me to grant everything they ask of Me by saying the chaplet.** Diary ¶1541 Hail Mary…

10. **Already there are many souls who have been drawn to My love by this image. My mercy acts in souls through this work.** Diary ¶1379 Hail Mary…

DIVINE MERCY SUNDAY
4. "The soul that will go to Confession and Holy Communion (on Divine Mercy Sunday) **shall obtain complete forgiveness of sins and punishment."** Diary ¶699 (Brief pause) Hail Mary…

5. "On that day, all the divine floodgates through which grace flow are opened." Diary ¶699 (Brief pause) Hail Mary…

6. **I want to grant a complete pardon to the souls that will go to Confession and receive Holy Communion on the Feast of My Mercy.** Diary ¶1109 Hail Mary…

SECOND JOYFUL MYSTERY, THE VISITATION
As Mary, acting out of love, brought Jesus to Elizabeth and John, we are to act in love toward others for the love of Jesus.

-- Our Father --

1. **When a soul approaches Me with trust, I fill it with such an abundance of grace that it cannot contain them within itself, but radiates them to other souls.** Diary ¶1074 (Brief pause) Hail Mary…

2. **And the more perfect a soul is, the stronger and more far reaching is the light shed by it. It can be hidden and unknown, even to those closest to it, and yet its holiness is reflected in souls even to the most extremities of the earth.** Diary ¶1601 Hail Mary…

3. **I have eternity for punishing [these], and so I am prolonging the time of mercy for the sake of** [sinners]. Diary ¶1160 Hail Mary…

4. **But woe to them if they do not recognize this time of My visitation.** Diary ¶1160 Hail Mary…

4. **…write this for the many souls who are often worried because they do not have the material means with which to carry out an act of mercy. Yet spiritual mercy, which requires neither permission nor storehouses, is much more meritorious and is within the grasp of every soul.** Diary ¶1317 Hail Mary…

5. **If a soul does not exercise mercy somehow or other, it will not obtain My mercy on the day of judgment.** Diary ¶1317 Hail Mary…

6. **Chosen souls are, in My hand, lights which I cast into the darkness of the world and with which I illumine it. As stars illumine the night, so chosen souls illumine the earth.** Diary ¶1601 Hail Mary…

7. **My delight is to act in a human soul and to fill it with My mercy (133) and to justify it. My kingdom on earth is My life in the human soul.** Diary ¶1784 Hail Mary…

8. **A single act of pure love pleases Me more than a thousand imperfect prayers.** Diary ¶1489 Hail Mary…

9. **In a soul that lives on My love alone, I reign as in heaven. I watch over it day and night. In it I find My happiness; My ear is attentive to (98) each request of its heart; often I anticipate its request.** Diary ¶1489 Hail Mary…

10. **Let souls who are striving for perfection particularly adore My mercy, because the abundance of graces which I grant them flows from My mercy.** Diary ¶1578 Hail Mary…

THIRD JOYFUL MYSTERY, THE NATIVITY
As Jesus humbled himself for us
we are to humble ourselves before Him.

-- Our Father –

1. **Know that as often as you come to Me, humbling yourself and asking My forgiveness, I pour out a superabundance of graces on your soul, and your imperfection vanishes before My eyes, and I see only your love and your humility. You lose nothing and gain much.** Diary ¶1293 (Brief pause) Hail Mary…

2. **Be not afraid of you Savior, O sinful soul. I make the first move to come to you, for I know that by yourself you are unable to lift yourself to me.** Diary ¶1485 Hail Mary…

3. **Child, do not run away from your Father; be willing to talk openly with your God of Mercy who wants to speak words of pardon and lavish His graces on you.** Diary ¶1485 Hail Mary…

4. **Know My daughter, that I do not grant My graces to proud souls, and I even take away from them the graces I have granted.** Diary ¶1170 Hail Mary…

5. **In the Old Covenant I sent prophets wielding thunderbolts to My people. Today I am sending you with My mercy to the people of the whole world.** Diary ¶1588 Hail Mary…

6. **The torrents of grace inundate humble souls. The proud remain always in poverty and misery, because My graces turns away from them to humble souls.** Diary ¶1602 Hail Mary…

7. **My child, that you may answer My call worthily, receive Me daily in Holy Communion. It will give you strength…** Diary ¶1489 Hail Mary…

8. **I desire to unite Myself with human souls; My great delight is to unite myself with souls.** Diary ¶1385 Hail Mary…

9. **My Daughter, do whatever is in your power to spread devotion to My mercy. I will make up for what you lack. Tell aching mankind to snuggle close to My merciful Heart and I will fill it with peace.** Diary ¶1074 Hail Mary…

10. **Both the sinner and the righteous person have need** (148) **of My mercy. Conversion, as well as perseverance, is a grace of My mercy.** Diary ¶1577 Hail Mary…

FOURTH JOYFUL MYSTERY, THE PRESENTATION
Simeon said "This child is destined
to be the downfall and the rise of many…" (Luke 2:34)

-Therefore I urge you, brethren, by the mercies of God, to present your bodies a living and holy sacrifice, acceptable to God, **which is your spiritual service of worship.** *Romans 12:1 NASB95*

-- Our Father –

1. **Before the Day of Justice I am sending the Day of Mercy.** Diary ¶1588 (Brief pause) Hail Mary…

2. **I use punishment when they themselves force Me to do so; My hand is reluctant to take hold of the sword of justice.** Diary ¶1588 Hail Mary…

3. **Write, that I am speaking to them through their remorse of conscience, through their failures and sufferings, through thunderstorms, through the voice of the Church. And if they bring all My graces to naught, I begin to be angry** (91) **with them, leaving them alone and giving them what they want.** Diary ¶1729 Hail Mary…

4. **Write: before I come as a just Judge, I first open wide the door of My mercy. He who refuses to pass through the door of My mercy must pass through the door of My justice…** Diary ¶1146 Hail Mary…

5. **Tell sinners that no one shall escape My Hand; if they run away from My Merciful Heart, they will fall into My Just Hands.** Diary ¶1728 Hail Mary…

6. **Oh, how miserable are those who do not take advantage of the miracle of God's mercy! You will call out in vain, but it will be too late.** Diary ¶1448 Hail Mary…

7. **I do not want to punish aching mankind, but I desire to heal it, pressing it to My merciful Heart.** Diary ¶1588 Hail Mary…

8. **Oh, if only souls knew how to gather eternal treasure for themselves, they would not be judged, for they would forestall My judgment with their mercy.** Diary ¶1317 Hail Mary…

9. **I want the eyes of your soul to be always fixed on My holy will, since it is in this way that you please Me the most. No sacrifices can compare to this.** Diary ¶1327 (Brief pause) Hail Mary…

10. **Write, My secretary, that I Myself am the spiritual guide of souls – and I guide them indirectly through the priests, and lead each one to sanctity by a road known to Me alone.** Diary ¶1273 Hail Mary…

FIFTH JOYFUL MYSTERY,
THE FINDING IN THE TEMPLE
As Mary and Joseph found Jesus in the Temple,
we are to find Him in the Host in the Tabernacle

-- Our Father –

1. **Know My daughter, that when I come to a human heart in Holy Communion, My hands are full of all kinds of graces which I want to give to the soul.** Diary ¶1385 (Brief pause) Hail Mary…

2. **But souls do not even pay any attention to Me (in Holy Communion); they leave Me to Myself and busy themselves with other things.** Diary ¶1385 Hail Mary…

3. **Oh, how sad I am that souls do not recognize Love! They treat Me** (in Holy communion) **as a dead object.** Diary ¶1385 Hail Mary…

4. **Behold, for you I have established a throne of mercy on earth – the tabernacle – and from this throne I desire to enter into your heart. I am not surrounded by a retinue of guards. You can come to Me at any moment, at any time; I want to speak to you and desire to grant you grace.** Diary ¶1485 Hail Mary…

5. **But understand that the strength by which you bear sufferings comes from frequent communion. So approach this fountain of mercy often, to draw with the vessel of trust whatever you need.** Diary ¶1487 Hail Mary…

6. **Oh, how painful it is to Me that souls so seldom unite themselves to Me in Holy Communion. I wait for souls, and they are indifferent toward Me.** Diary ¶1447 Hail Mary…

7. **I love them tenderly and sincerely, and they distrust Me. I want to lavish My graces on them, and they do not want to accept them.** Diary ¶1447 Hail Mary…

8. **They treat Me as a dead object, whereas (60) My Heart is full of love and mercy. In order that you may know at least some of My pain, imagine the most tender of mothers who has great love for her children, while these children spurn her love. Consider her pain. No one is in a position to console her. This is but a feeble image and likeness of My love.** Diary ¶1447 Hail Mary…

9. **You see, although there appears to be no trace of life in Me, in reality it is present in its fullness in each and every Host.** Diary ¶1420 Hail Mary…

10. **Write for the benefit of religious souls that it delights Me to come to their hearts in Holy Communion. But if there is anyone else in such a heart, I cannot bear it and quickly leave that heart, taking with Me all the gifts and graces that I have prepared for that soul. And that soul does not even notice My going.** Diary ¶1683 Hail Mary…

FIRST LUMINOUS MYSTERY – BAPTISM OF JESUS
John protest but Jesus tells John to give in for it is God's will.

--Our Father –

1. **As often as you want to make Me happy, speak to the world about my great and unfathomable mercy.** Diary ¶165 Hail Mary…

2. **Get to know God by contemplating His attributes.** Diary ¶ 30 Hail Mary…

3. **Let it be confirmed and engraved on your heart that I am always with you, even if you don't feel My presence at the time of battle.** Diary ¶1499 (Brief pause) Hail Mary…

4. **My daughter, I too came down from heaven out of love for you; …** Diary ¶853 Hail Mary…

5. **I lived for you, I died for you, and I created the heavens for you.** Diary ¶853 Hail Mary…

6. **My daughter, you give Me the most glory by patiently submitting to My will, …** Diary ¶904 Hail Mary…

7. **by patiently submitting to My will … you win for yourself greater merit than that which any fast or mortification could ever gain for you.** Diary ¶904 Hail Mary….

8. **Know, My daughter, that if you submit your will to Mine, you draw upon yourself My special Delight.** Diary ¶904 Hail Mary….

9. **This sacrifice** (submitting to My will) **is pleasing to Me and full of sweetness. I take great pleasure in it; there is power in it.** Diary ¶904 Hail Mary…

10. **He who does not take advantage of small graces will not receive great ones.** Diary ¶165 Hail Mary…

SECOND LUMINOUS MYSTERY
Jesus self-manifestation at the wedding at Cana
Mary told the waiters to "Do whatever He tells you".

-- Our Father –

1. **Oh, how I love those who have complete confidence in Me. I will do everything for them.** Diary ¶294 (Brief pause) Hail Mary…

2. **Act like a beggar who does not back away when he gets more alms (then he asked), but offers thanks the more fervently.** Diary ¶294 Hail Mary…

3. **You too should not back away and say you are not worthy of receiving greater graces when I give them to you.** Diary ¶294 Hail Mary…

4. **I know you are unworthy, but rejoice all the more and take as Many (129) treasures from My heart as you can carry, for then you will please Me more.** Diary ¶294 Hail Mary…

5. **And I will tell you one more thing: Take these graces not only for yourself but for others;** Diary ¶294 Hail Mary…

6. **…that is encourage the souls with whom you come in contact to trust in My infinite mercy.** Diary ¶294 Hail Mary…

7. **My daughter, do not tire of proclaiming My mercy. In this way you will refresh this Heart of Mine, which burns with a flame of pity for sinners.** Diary ¶1520 Hail Mary…

8. **Let them approach this sea of mercy with great trust. Sinners will attain justification, and the just will be confirmed in good.** Diary ¶1520 Hail Mary…

9. **You often call Me your Master. This is pleasing to My Heart; but do not forget, My disciple, that you are a disciple of a crucified Master. Let that one word be enough for you.** Diary ¶1513 Hail Mary…

10. **Whoever places his trust (115) in My mercy will be filled with My divine peace at the hour of death.** Diary ¶1520 Hail Mary…

THIRD LUMINOUS MYSTERY – THE PROCLAMATION OF THE KINGDOM AND CALL TO CONVERSION
Jesus confirmed His words with signs and wonders

-- Our Father –

1. **Proclaim that mercy is the greatest attribute of God. All the works of My hands are crowned with mercy.** Diary ¶301 (Brief pause) Hail Mary…

2. **Bring your ear close to My Heart, forget everything else, and meditate upon My wondrous mercy.** Diary ¶229 Hail Mary…

3. **The flames of mercy are burning Me – clamoring to be spent; I want to keep pouring them out upon souls; souls just don't believe in My goodness.** Diary ¶177 Hail Mary…

4. **All this I created for you, My spouse; and know that all this beauty is as nothing compared to what I have prepared for you in heaven.** Diary ¶158 Hail Mary…

5. **Write down at once what you hear: I am the Lord in My essence and am immune to orders or needs. If I call creatures into being – that is the abyss of My mercy.** Diary ¶ 85 Hail Mary…

6. **My daughter, even if you were to speak at one and the same time in human and angelic tongues, even then you would not have said very much, but on the contrary, you would have sung in only a small measure the praises (9) of My goodness – of My unfathomable mercy.** Diary ¶1605 Hail Mary…

7. **…I want you to never to pay attention to the vessel in which I send you My grace. Let the attention of your soul (5) be concentrated on responding to My grace as faithfully as possible.** Diary ¶1599 Hail Mary…

8. **The graces of My mercy are drawn by means of one vessel only, and that is – trust. The more a soul trusts, the more it will receive.** Diary ¶1578 Hail Mary…

9. **My bride, you always please Me by your humility. The greatest misery does not stop Me from (139) uniting Myself to a soul, but where there is pride, I am not there.** Diary ¶1563 Hail Mary…

10. **Know that it is a great grace on My part when I give a spiritual director to a soul. Many souls ask Me for this, but it is not to all that I grant this grace. From the moment when I give you a spiritual director, I endow him with new light so that he might easily know and understand your soul.** Diary ¶1561 Hail Mary…

FOURTH LUMINOUS MYSTERY, THE TRANSFIGURATION
Jesus reveals His Glory to Peter, James and John

-- Our Father –

1. **I will give light and strength to your soul, and you will learn from My representative that I am in you, and your uncertainty will vanish like mist before the rays of the sun.** Diary ¶295 (Brief pause) Hail Mary…

2. **I see every abasement of your soul, and nothing escapes my attention. I lift up the humble even to my very throne, because I want to.** Diary ¶282 Hail Mary…

3. **My Daughter, I desire that your heart be formed after the model of My merciful Heart. You must be completely imbued with My mercy.** Diary ¶167 Hail Mary…

4. **By obedience you give great glory to Me and gain merit for yourself.** Diary ¶ 28 Hail Mary…

5. **I do not reward for good results but for the patience and hardship undergone for My sake.** Diary ¶ 86 Hail Mary…

6. **You will recognize that you have love if, after having experienced annoyance and contradiction, you do not lose your peace, but pray for those who have made you suffer and wish them well.** Diary ¶1628 Hail Mary…

7. **Know My daughter, that between Me and you there is a bottomless abyss, an abyss which separates the Creator from the creature. But this abyss is filled with My mercy.** Diary ¶1576 Hail Mary…

8. **I raised you up to Myself, not that I have need of you, but it is solely out of mercy that I grant you the grace of union with Myself.** Diary ¶1576 Hail Mary…

9. **Because you are a child, you shall remain close to My Heart. Your simplicity is more pleasing to Me than your mortifications.** Diary ¶1617 Hail Mary…

10. **Fear not My Daughter: I am with you.** Diary ¶103 Hail Mary…

FIFTH LUMINOUS MYSTERY – INSTITUTION OF THE EUCHARIST
Christ offers His Body and Blood as food

-- Our Father –

1. **Do not be surprised that you are sometimes unjustly accused. I myself first drank this cup of undeserved suffering for love of you.** Diary ¶289 (Brief pause) Hail Mary…

2. **My daughter, do not omit Holy Communion unless you know well that your fall was serious;** Diary ¶156 Hail Mary…

3. **…apart from this** (a serious fall), **no doubt must stop you from uniting yourself with Me in the mystery of My love.**

4. **Your minor faults will disappear in My love like a piece of straw thrown into a great furnace. Know that you grieve Me much when you fail to receive Me in Holy Communion.** Diary ¶156 Hail Mary…

5. **Behold, the treasures of graces that flow down upon souls, but not all souls know how to take advantage of My generosity.** Diary ¶1687 Hail Mary…

6. **If souls would put themselves completely in My care. I Myself would undertake the task of sanctifying them, and I would lavish even greater graces on them.** Diary ¶1682 Hail Mary…

7. **There are souls who thwart My efforts, but I have not given up on them; as often as they turn to Me, I hurry to their aid, shielding them with My mercy, and I give them the first place in My compassionate Heart.** Diary ¶1682 Hail Mary…

8. **My daughter write that involuntary offenses of souls do not hinder My love for them or prevent Me from uniting Myself with them.** Diary ¶1641 Hail Mary…

9. **But voluntary offenses, even the smallest, obstruct My graces, and I cannot lavish My gifts on such souls.** Diary ¶1643 Hail Mary…

10. **While there is still time, let them have recourse to the fount of My mercy; let them profit from the Blood and Water which gushed forth for them.** Diary ¶848 Hail Mary…

**FIRST SORROWFUL MYSTERY –
THE AGONY IN THE GARDEN**
Christ sweated blood for our lack of love and trust in Him.

-- Our Father –

1. **Today bring to Me souls who have become lukewarm, and immerse them in the abyss of My mercy. These souls wound my Heart most painfully.** Diary ¶1228 (Brief pause) Hail Mary…

2. **My soul suffered the most dreadful loathing in the Garden of Olives because of lukewarm souls.** Diary ¶1228 Hail Mary…

3. **They were the reason I cried out: "Father, take this cup away from Me, if it be your will.** (lukewarm souls) Diary ¶1228 Hail Mary…

4. **For them the last hope (65) of salvation is to flee to My mercy.** (lukewarm souls) Diary ¶1228 Hail Mary…

5. **My daughter, write about My mercy towards tormented souls. Souls that make an appeal to My mercy delight me. To such souls I grant even more than they ask.** Diary ¶1146 Hail Mary…

6. **My daughter, know that your ardent love and the compassion you have for Me were a consolation to Me in the Garden.** Diary ¶1664 Hail Mary…

7. **My daughter, meditate frequently on the sufferings which I have undergone for your sake, and then nothing of what you suffer for Me will seem great to you.** Diary ¶1512 Hail Mary…

8. **You please Me most when you meditate on My Sorrowful Passion. Join your little sufferings to My Sorrowful Passion, so that they may have infinite value before My Majesty.** Diary ¶1512 Hail Mary…

9. **Know, too, that the darkness about which you complain I first endured in the Garden of Olives when My soul was crushed in mortal anguish… A suffering soul is closest to My Heart.** Diary ¶1487 Hail Mary…

10. **In return for My blessings, I get ingratitude. In return for My love, I get forgetfulness and indifferences. My Heart cannot bear this.** Diary ¶1537 Hail Mary…

SECOND SORROWFUL MYSTERY – THE SCOURGING
By His stripes we are healed. (1Pt 2:24) NKJV

-- Our Father –

1. **… when it seems to you that your suffering exceeds your strength, contemplate My wounds, (51) and you will rise above human scorn and judgment.** Diary ¶1184 (Brief pause) Hail Mary…

2. **Meditation on My Passion will help you rise above all things.** Diary ¶1184 Hail Mary…

3. **My daughter, your compassion for Me refreshes Me, By meditating on My Passion, your soul acquires a different beauty.** Diary ¶1657 Hail Mary…

4. **Look into My Heart and see there the love and mercy which I have for humankind, and especially for sinners. Look, and enter into My Passion.** Diary ¶1663 Hail Mary…

5. **My daughter, when I was before Herod, I obtained a grace for you; namely, that you would be able to rise above human scorn and follow faithfully in My footsteps.** Diary ¶1164 Hail Mary…

6. **Be silent when they do not want to acknowledge your truth, because it is then that you speak more eloquently.** Diary ¶1164 Hail Mary…

7. **These souls (125) have a right of priority to My compassionate Heart, they have first access to My mercy. Tell them that no soul that has called upon My mercy has been disappointed or brought to shame.** (distressed souls) Diary ¶1541 Hail Mary…

8. **Write this for the benefit of distressed souls: when a souls sees and realizes the gravity of its sins, when the whole abyss of the misery into which it immersed itself is displayed before its eyes let it not despair, but with trust let it throw itself into the arms of My mercy, as a child into the arms of its beloved mother.** Diary ¶1541 Hail Mary…

9. **I have opened My Heart as a living fountain of mercy. Let all souls draw life from it.** Diary ¶1520 Hail Mary…

10. **"Let the sinner not be afraid to approach Me. The flames of mercy are burning Me – clamoring to be spent; I want to pour them upon these souls."** Diary ¶ 50 Hail Mary…

THIRD SORROWFUL MYSTERY – THE CROWNING WITH THORNS
The soldiers mocked Him, "All Hail the King of the Jews." (Mat 27:29) *KJV*

-- Our Father –

1. **Today bring to Me the souls of heretics and schismatic, and immerse them in the ocean of My mercy. During My bitter Passion they tore at My Body and Heart; that is, My Church.** Diary ¶1218 (Brief pause) Hail Mary…

2. **As they return to unity with the Church My wounds heal, and in this way they alleviate My Passion.** (the heretics and schismatic) Diary ¶1218 Hail Mary…

3. **Today bring to Me the pagans and those who do not yet know Me. I was thinking about them during My bitter passion, and their future zeal comforted My Heart. Immerse them in the ocean of My mercy.** Diary ¶1216 Hail Mary…

4. **The flames of mercy are burning Me. I desire to pour them out upon human souls. Oh, what pain they cause Me when they do not want to accept them!** Diary ¶1074 Hail Mary…

5. **My daughter, do not tire of proclaiming My mercy. In this way you will refresh this Heart of Mine, which burns with a flame of pity for sinners.** Diary ¶1521 Hail Mary…

6. **Today bring to Me the souls who are in the prison of Purgatory, and immerse them in the abyss of My mercy. Let the torrents of My Blood cool down their scorching flames.** Diary ¶1226 Hail Mary…

7. **All these souls** (who are in the prison of Purgatory) **are greatly loved by Me. They are making retribution to My justice. It is in your power to bring them relief.** Diary ¶1226 Hail Mary…

8. **With My mercy, I pursue sinners along all their paths, and My Heart rejoices when they return to Me. I forget the bitterness with which they feed My Heart and rejoice at their return.** Diary ¶1728 Hail Mary…

9. **My heart is even more wounded by their distrust after a fall. It would be less painful if they had not experienced their goodness of My heart.** Diary ¶1532 Hail Mary…

10. **My child know that the greatest obstacles to holiness are discouragement and exaggerated anxiety. These will deprive you of the ability to practice virtue.** Diary ¶1488 Hail Mary…

FOURTH SORROWFUL MYSTERY –
THE CARRYING OF THE CROSS
"Anyone who does not take up his cross
and follow Me cannot be My disciple." (Luke 14:27) DRA

-- Our Father –

1. **…there is no way to heaven except the way of the cross. I followed it first. You must learn that it is the shortest and surest way.** Diary ¶1487 (Brief pause) Hail Mary…

2. **Come close to My wounds and draw from the Fountain of Life whenever your heart desires. Drink copiously from the Fountain of Life and you will not weary on your journey.** Diary ¶1487 Hail Mary…

3. **Today bring to Me the souls of priests and religious and immerse them in My unfathomable mercy. It was they who gave Me the strength to endure My bitter Passion.** Diary ¶1212 Hail Mary…

4. **Through them** (priests and religious) **as through channels, My mercy flows out upon mankind.** Diary ¶1212 Hail Mary…

5. **Today bring to Me all devout and faithful souls, and immerse them in the ocean of My mercy.** Diary ¶1214 Hail Mary…

6. **These** (devout and faithful) **souls brought Me consolation on the Way of the Cross. They were that drop of consolation in the midst of an ocean of bitterness.** Diary ¶1214 Hail Mary…

7. **The loss of each soul plunges Me into mortal sadness. You always console Me when you pray for sinners.** Diary ¶1397 Hail Mary…

8. **The flames of compassion burn Me. I desire greatly to pour them out upon souls.** Diary ¶1190 Hail Mary…

9. **Draw all the indulgences from the treasury (64) of My Church and offer them on their behalf** (who are in the prison of purgatory). **Oh, if you only knew the torments they suffer, you would continually offer for them the alms of the spirit and pay off their debt to My justice.** Diary ¶1226 Hail Mary…

10. **The cause of your falls is that you rely too much upon yourself and too little on Me. But let this not sadden you so much. You are dealing with the God of mercy, which your misery cannot exhaust.** Diary ¶1488 Hail Mary…

FIFTH SORROWFUL MYSTERY – THE CRUCIFIXION
"God so loved the world that He gave His only Son." (John 3:16) NASB

-- Our Father –

1. **From all My wounds, like from streams, mercy flows for souls, but the wound in My Heart is the fountain of unfathomable mercy. From this fountain spring forth all graces for souls.** Diary ¶1190 (Brief pause) Hail Mary…

2. **At three o'clock, implore My mercy, especially for sinners; and if only for a brief moment, immerse yourself in My passion, particularly in My abandonment at the moment of agony.** Diary ¶1320 Hail Mary…

3. **This is the hour of great mercy for the whole world. I will allow you to enter into My mortal sorrow.** Diary ¶1320 Hail Mary…

4. **In this hour, I will refuse nothing to the soul that makes a request of Me in virtue of My Passion…** Diary ¶1320 Hail Mary…

5. **Distrust on the part of souls is tearing at My insides.** Diary ¶ 50 Hail Mary…

6. **The distrust of a chosen soul causes Me even greater pain; despite My inexhaustible love for them they do not trust Me."** Diary ¶ 50 Hail Mary…

7. **Even My death is not enough for them, Woe to the soul that abuses these** (gifts)." Diary ¶ 50 Hail Mary…

8. **Today, bring to Me all mankind, especially all sinners, and immerse them in the ocean of My mercy. In this way you will console Me in the bitter grief into which the loss of souls plunges Me.** Diary ¶1210 Hail Mary…

9. **My Secretary, write that I am more generous toward sinners than toward the just. It was for their sake that I came down from heaven; it was for their sake that My Blood was spilled.** Diary ¶1275 Hail Mary…

10. **On the cross the fountain of My mercy was opened wide by the lance for all souls. – no one have I excluded!** Diary ¶1182 Hail Mary...

FIRST GLORIOUS MYSTERY – THE RESURRECTION
"I am the resurrection and the life; whoever believes in me, though he should die will come to life." (John 11:25-26) NABRE

-- Our Father –

1. **Today bring to Me the meek and humble souls and the souls of the children, and immerse them in My mercy. These souls most closely resemble My Heart.** Diary ¶1220 (Brief pause) Hail Mary...

2. **They** (meek and humble souls) **strengthened Me during My bitter agony. I saw them as earthly angels, who would keep vigil My alters. I pour out upon them whole torrents of grace.** Diary ¶1220 Hail Mary...

3. **Only the humble soul is able to receive My grace. I favor humble souls with confidence.** Diary ¶1220 Hail Mary...

4. **Today bring to Me the souls who especially venerate and glorify My mercy, and immerse them in My mercy. These souls sorrowed most over My Passion and entered most deeply into My spirit.** Diary ¶1224 Hail Mary...

5. **They** (souls who especially venerate and glorify My mercy) **are living images of My Compassionate Heart. These souls will shine with a special brightness in the next life.** Diary ¶1224 Hail Mary...

6. **Not one of them** (souls who especially venerate and glorify My mercy) **will go into the fire of hell. I shall particularly defend each one of them at the hour of death.** Diary ¶1224 Hail Mary...

7. **I Myself will defend as My own glory, during their lifetime, and especially at the hour of their death, those souls who will venerate My fathomless mercy.** Diary ¶1225 Hail Mary...

8. **Were a soul like a decaying corpse so that from a human standpoint, there would be no (hope of) restoration and everything would already be lost, it is not so with God. The miracle of Divine Mercy restores that soul in full.** Diary ¶1448 Hail Mary…

9. **Look at the splendors of My mercy and do not fear the enemies of your salvation. Glorify My mercy.** Diary ¶1487 Hail Mary…

10. **Have confidence, My child. Do not lose heart in coming for pardon, for I am always ready to forgive you. As often as you beg for it, you glorify My mercy.** Diary ¶1488 Hail Mary…

SECOND GLORIOUS MYSTERY – THE ASCENSION
"I am indeed going to prepare a place for you." (Jn 14:3)

-- Our Father –

1. **Your humility draws Me down from My lofty throne, and I unite myself closely with you.** Diary ¶1109 Hail Mary…

2. **My daughter, secretary of My mercy, your duty is not only to write about and proclaim My mercy, but also to beg for this grace for them, so that they too may glorify My mercy.** Diary ¶1160 Hail Mary…

3. **In one moment I can give you more than you are able to desire.** Diary ¶1169 Hail Mary…

4. **My child, do you fear the God of mercy? My holiness does not prevent Me from being merciful.** Diary ¶1485 Hail Mary…

5. **Tell sinful souls not to be afraid to approach Me; speak to them of My great mercy.** Diary ¶1396 Hail Mary…

6. **But for Me to be able to act upon a soul, the soul must have faith. O how pleasing to me is living faith!** Diary ¶1420 Hail Mary…

7. **Tell souls not to place within their own hearts obstacles to My mercy, which so greatly wants to act within them My mercy works in all those hearts which open their doors to it.** Diary ¶1577 Hail Mary…

8. **Let the weak, sinful soul have no fear to approach Me, for even if it had more sins than there are grains of sand in the world, all would be drowned in the immeasurable depths of My mercy.** Diary ¶1059 Hail Mary…

9. **Oh, if sinners knew My mercy, they would not perish in such great numbers.** Diary ¶1396 Hail Mary…

10. **I am Love and Mercy itself. There is no misery that could be a match for My mercy, neither will misery exhaust it, because as it is being granted – it increases.** Diary ¶1273 Hail Mary…

THIRD GLORIOUS MYSTERY – THE DESCENT OF THE HOLY SPIRIT

"Receive the Holy Spirit, Whose sins you forgive, they are forgiven them." (Jn 20:22) CPDV

-- Our Father –

1. **Every time you can go to confession, immerse yourself entirely in My mercy, with great trust, so that I may pour the bounty of my grace upon your soul.** Diary ¶1602 (Brief pause) Hail Mary…

2. **When you approach the confessional, know this, that I Myself am waiting there for you. I am only hidden by the priest, but I Myself act in your soul. Here the misery of the soul meets the God of mercy.** Diary ¶1602 Hail Mary…

3. **My daughter, be always like a little child towards those who represent Me, otherwise you will not benefit from the graces I bestow on you through them.** Diary ¶1260 Hail Mary…

4. **Write, speak of My mercy. Tell souls where they are to look for solace: that is in the Tribunal of Mercy** (the Sacrament of Reconciliation). **There the greatest miracles take place** (and) **are incessantly repeated.** Diary ¶1448 Hail Mary…

5. **To avail oneself of this miracle, it is not necessary to go on a pilgrimage or to carry out some external ceremony; it suffices to come with faith to the feet of My representative and to reveal to Him one's misery, and the miracle of Divine Mercy will be fully demonstrated.** Diary ¶1448 Hail Mary…

6. **My daughter, just as you prepare in My presence, so also you make your confession before Me. The person of the priest is, for Me, only a screen.** Diary ¶1725 Hail Mary…

7. **Never analyze what sort of a (89) priest it is that I am making use of; open your soul in confession as you would to Me, and I will fill it with My light.** Diary ¶1725 Hail Mary…

8. **Tell My priests that hardened sinners will repent on hearing their words when they speak about My unfathomable mercy, about the compassion I have for them in My Heart.** Diary ¶1521 Hail Mary…

9. **To priests who proclaim and extol My mercy, I will give wondrous power; I will anoint their words and touch the hearts of those to whom they will speak.** Diary ¶1521 Hail Mary…

10. **Daughter, when you go to confession, to this fountain of My mercy, the Blood and Water which came forth from My Heart always flows down upon your soul and ennobles it.** Diary ¶1602 Hail Mary…

FOURTH GLORIOUS MYSTERY – THE ASSUMPTION
"Rejoice, O highly favored daughter! The LORD is with you." (Luke 1:28) NKJV

-- Our Father –

1. "When a soul approaches me with trust, I fill it with such an abundance of grace that it cannot be contained within itself, but radiates to other souls," Diary ¶1074 (Brief pause) Hail Mary…

2. "My daughter, write that the greater the misery of a soul the greater its right to My mercy; (urge) all souls to trust in the unfathomable abyss of My mercy, because I want to save them all." Diary ¶1182 Hail Mary…

3. [Let] the greatest sinners place their trust in My mercy. They have the right before others to trust in the abyss of My mercy." Diary ¶1146 Hail Mary…

4. I delight particularly in a soul which has placed its trust in My mercy. Diary ¶1541 Hail Mary…

5. I desire trust from My creatures. Encourage souls to place trust in My fathomless mercy. Diary ¶1059 Hail Mary…

6. The greatest sinners would achieve great sanctity, if only they would trust My mercy. The very inner depths of My being are filled to overflowing with mercy, and it is being poured out upon all I have created. Diary ¶1784 Hail Mary…

7. Mankind will not have peace until it turns with trust to my mercy." Diary ¶300 Hail Mary…

8. Tell souls that from this fount of mercy (7) souls draw graces solely with the vessel of trust. If their trust is great there is no limit to My generosity. Diary ¶1602 Hail Mary…

9. The soul that trust in My mercy is most fortunate, because I myself take care of it. Diary ¶1273 Hail Mary…

10. Souls that trust boundlessly are a great comfort to Me, because I pour all the treasure of My grace into them. Diary ¶1578 Hail Mary…

FIFTH GLORIOUS MYSTERY – THE CORONATION

"God who is mighty has done great things for me, Holy is His Name; His Mercy is from age to age on those who fear Him." (Luke 1:49-50) KJV

-- Our Father –

1. **"Now you shall consider My love in the Blessed Sacrament. Here I am entirely yours, soul, body and divinity, as your bridegroom. You know what love demands: one thing only, reciprocity...** Diary ¶1770 (Brief pause) Hail Mary...

2. **Entrust yourself completely to My will saying, "Not as I want, but according to your will, O God, let it be done unto me." These words, spoken from the depths of one's heart, can raise a soul to the summit of sanctity in a short time. In such a soul I delight. Such a soul gives Me glory.** Diary ¶1487 Hail Mary...

3. **My daughter, know that My Heart is mercy itself. From this sea of mercy, graces flow out upon the whole world.** Diary ¶1777 Hail Mary...

4. **No soul that has approached Me has ever gone away unconsoled. All misery gets buried in the depths of My mercy, and every saving and sanctifying grace flows from this fountain.** Diary ¶1777 Hail Mary...

5. **How very much I desire the salvation of souls! My dearest secretary, write that I want to pour out My divine life into human souls and sanctify them. If only they are willing to accept My grace.** Diary ¶1784 Hail Mary...

6. **Proclaim that mercy is the greatest attribute of God. All the works of My hands are crowned with mercy.** Diary ¶ 301 Hail Mary...

7. **The prayer most pleasing to Me is prayer for the conversion of sinners. Know, My daughter, that this prayer is always heard and answered.** Diary ¶1397 Hail Mary...

8. **My child, life on earth is a struggle indeed; a great struggle for my kingdom. But fear not, because you are not alone. I am always supporting you, (92) so lean on Me as your struggle, fearing nothing.** Diary ¶1488 Hail Mary…

9. **Tell,** [all people] **My daughter, that I am Love and Mercy itself.** Diary ¶1074 Hail Mary…

10. **My daughter, write down these words: All those souls who will glorify My mercy and spread its worship, encouraging others to trust in My mercy, will not experience terror at the hour of death. My mercy will shield them in that final battle…** Diary ¶1540 Hail Mary…

†

THE GREAT GIFT OF THE NEW ERA GIVEN TO US IN MODERN TIMES - THE PROMISE OF DIVINE MERCY

> *Jas 2:13 NASB95* - For judgment will be merciless to one who has shown no mercy;
> **MERCY TRIUMPHS OVER JUDGMENT.**

In His great Mercy, Jesus promises a great deal to those who venerate this image (image at beginning of Twenty decade rosary)

"I promise that the soul that will venerate this image will not perish. I also promise victory over [its] enemies already here on earth, especially at the hour of death. I Myself will defend it as My own glory." (Diary, 48) **"By means of this image I shall grant many graces to souls. It is to be a reminder of the demands of My mercy..."** (Diary, 742)

"These rays shield souls from the wrath of My Father. Happy is the one who will dwell in their shelter, for the just hand of God shall not lay hold of him. I desire that the first Sunday after Easter be the Feast of Mercy." (Diary, 299)

Through the Chaplet you will obtain everything, if what you ask for is compatible with My will (Diary, 1731, see also 1541).

Even if there were a sinner most hardened, if he were to recite this chaplet only once, he would receive grace from My infinite mercy (Diary, 687). **When they say this chaplet in the presence of the dying, I will stand between My Father and the dying person, not as the just Judge but as the Merciful Savior** (Diary, 1541). **Whoever will recite it will receive great mercy at the hour of death** (Diary, 687). **"At three o' clock implore My mercy, especially for sinners; and if only for a brief moment, immerse yourself in My Passion, particularly in My abandonment at the moment of agony: This is the hour of great mercy for the whole world. I will allow you to enter into My mortal sorrow. In this hour, I will refuse nothing to the soul that makes a request of Me in virtue of My Passion."** (Diary 1320)

It may be said at any time, but our Lord specifically told Saint Faustina to recite it during the nine days before the Feast of Mercy (the first Sunday after Easter). **"On that day are open all the divine flood gates through which graces flow. Let no soul fear to draw near to Me, even though its sins be as scarlet."** (Diary, 796).

Whoever will go to confession and Holy Communion on that day will receive complete forgiveness of sin and punishment. Mankind will not enjoy peace until it returns to My Mercy.

Litany of Divine Mercy
(From the Diary of St. Faustina Kowalska) 949

"The Love of God is the flower- Mercy the fruit.
Let the doubting soul read these considerations
and become trusting." 949

Eternal God, in whom mercy is endless and the treasury of compassion -- inexhaustible, look kindly upon us and increase Your mercy in us, that in difficult moments we might not despair nor become despondent, but with great confidence submit ourselves to Your holy will, which is Love and Mercy itself. 950

Divine Mercy: gushing forth from the bosom of the Father,
I trust in You.
Divine Mercy, greatest attribute of GOD, I trust in You.
Divine Mercy, incomprehensible mystery, I trust in You.
Divine Mercy, fountain gushing forth from the mystery of the Most Blessed Trinity, I trust in You.
Divine Mercy, unfathomed by any intellect, human or angelic,
I trust in You
Divine Mercy, from which wells forth all life and happiness,
I trust in You.
Divine Mercy, better than the heavens, I trust in You.
Divine Mercy, source of miracles and wonders,
I trust in You.
Divine Mercy, encompassing the whole universe,
I trust in You.

Divine Mercy, descending to earth in the Person of the Incarnate Word, I trust in You.
Divine Mercy, which flowed out from the open wounded of the Heart of JESUS, I trust in You.
Divine Mercy, enclosed in the Heart of JESUS for us, and especially for sinners, I trust in You.
Divine Mercy, unfathomed in the institution of the Sacred Host, I trust in You.
Divine Mercy, in the founding of Holy Church, I trust in You.
Divine Mercy, in the Sacrament of Holy Baptism, I trust in You.
Divine Mercy, in our justification through JESUS CHRIST, I trust in You.
Divine Mercy, accompanying us through our whole life, I trust in You.
Divine Mercy, embracing us especially at the hour of death, I trust in You.
Divine Mercy, endowing us with immortal life, I trust in You.
Divine Mercy, accompanying us every moment of our life, I trust in You.
Divine Mercy, shielding us from the fire of hell, I trust in You.
Divine Mercy, in the conversion of hardened sinners, I trust in You.
Divine Mercy, astonishment for Angels, incomprehensible to Saints, I trust in You.
Divine Mercy, unfathomed in all the mysteries of GOD, I trust in You.
Divine Mercy, lifting us out of every misery, I trust in You.
Divine Mercy, source of our happiness and joy, I trust in You.
Divine Mercy, in calling us forth from nothingness to existence, I trust in You.
Divine Mercy, embracing all the works of His hands, I trust in You.
Divine Mercy, crown of all God's handiwork, I trust in You.
Divine Mercy, in which we are all immersed, I trust in You.
Divine Mercy, sweet relief for anguished hearts, I trust in You.

Divine Mercy, only hope of despairing souls, I trust in You.
Divine Mercy, repose of hearts, peace amidst fear,
I trust in You.
Divine Mercy, delight and ecstasy of holy souls,
I trust in You.
Divine Mercy, inspiring hope against all hope,
I trust in a You.

SACRAMENT OF CONFESSION - Divine Mercy Fount

When you go to confession, to this fountain of mercy, the Blood and Water which came forth from My Heart always flow down upon your soul (1602) ...In the Tribunal of Mercy [the sacrament of Reconciliation] **...the greatest miracles take place and are incessantly repeated (1448) ...Here the misery of the soul meets the God of Mercy. (1602)**

Come with faith to the feet of My representative... (1448) I myself am waiting there for you. I am only hidden by the priest... I Myself act in your soul... (1602) Make your confession before Me. The person of the priest is, for Me, only a screen. Never analyse what sort of a priest it is that I am making use of; open your soul in confession as you would to Me, and I will fill it with My light... (1725)

Were a soul like a decaying corpse, so that from a human standpoint, there would be no hope of restoration and everything would already be lost, it is not so with God. The miracle of Divine Mercy restores that soul in full... From this fount of mercy souls draw graces solely with the vessel of trust. If their trust is great, there is no limit to My generosity. (1448)

Our Lord has emphasized the need for us to go to confession and to receive Him in the Holy Eucharist in order to obtain the greatest gifts of His Mercy.

We as Catholics have the source of Mercy in the confessional and in the Precious Blood of the Eucharist. Let us proclaim this message.

A NEW CHAPLET OF MERCY
(as inspired in the prayer life of Fr. Einer R. Ochoa (1997)
(meditations by Gloria)

Contemplate the Cross
Beloved Lord, as I contemplate your passionate sacrificial love I embrace in your great love, mercy and compassion all the sorrows of this world, in the nations, in the churches, in our homes, in our lives and in our hearts. Make us to return to you all that you desire. Fill us Lord with your perfect love that we may love you perfectly. Make our thoughts and desires fervent toward you according to all that is holy and pleasing to Our Father in Heaven.

Start with the Creed on the first bead
2. **The Nicene Creed (381 AD in Nicea)**
I believe in one God, the Father, the Almighty, Creator of heaven and earth, of all that is visible and invisible; I believe in one Lord, Jesus Christ, the only-begotten Son of God, eternally begotten of the Father, before all ages. Light from Light, true God from true God, of one essence with the Father, through whom all things were made, Who for us and for our salvation He came down from heaven and was incarnate by the Holy Spirit and the Virgin Mary, and was made man. For our sake He was crucified under Pontius Pilate; He suffered death and was buried. Rising on the third day according to the Scriptures and ascending into the heavens is seated at the right hand of the Father. He will come again in glory to judge the living and the dead, and His kingdom will have no end. We believe in the Holy Spirit, the Lord, the Giver of life, who proceeds from the Father. Who together with the Father and the Son He is worshiped and glorified. Who spoke through the Prophets. I believe in one holy catholic and apostolic Church. I acknowledge one baptism for the remission of sins. **I expect the resurrection of the dead**, and the life of the age to come. AMEN.

Pray the Our Father
Our Father
Our Father, who art in heaven; hallowed be Thy name; Thy kingdom come; Thy will be done on earth as it is in heaven. Give us this day our daily bread; and Forgive us our trespasses and make us forgive those who trespass against us. Lead us not into temptation but deliver us from evil. Amen..

Three Hail Mary's on the next three beads
1. For Perfect Love, that we may be One with Our Lord.
2. For Perfect Faith, that Jesus the finisher of Our Faith, will indeed finish us in His faith and make us whole and pleasing to Our Lord in His great love
3. For Perfect Charity, that the treasure of our hearts be pleasing to Our Lord, fit for Him alone, Our King

Hail Mary
Hail Mary, full of grace, the Lord is with you; blessed are you among women, and blessed is the fruit of your womb, Jesus. Holy Mary, Mother of God, pray for us sinners, now and at the hour of our death. Amen.

Glory be to the Father
Glory be to the Father, and to the Son, and to the Holy Ghost. As it was in the beginning, is now, and ever shall be, world without end. Amen.

FIRST DECADE
On the Our Father bead of the Rosary say,
"Sacred hearts of Jesus and Mary, I Offer you my mind, my body, my heart, and my soul that the will of God be done in me"

Mediation on the Life of Christ go to Meditations of the Rosary

On the ten beads of the rosary say: (JITIU) "Jesus I trust in You" "Jesus I trust in You" "Jesus I trust in You" "Jesus I trust in You" "Jesus I trust in You" " Jesus I trust in You" "Jesus I trust in You" "Jesus I trust in You" "Jesus I trust in You" "Jesus I trust in You"
Glory be to the Father
Glory be to the Father, and to the Son, and to the Holy Ghost. As it was in the beginning, is now, and ever shall be, world without end. Amen.

Finish with the "Salve Regina"
HAIL, HOLY QUEEN

Hail, Holy Queen, Mother of Mercy! our life, our sweetness and our hope! To thee do we cry, poor banished children of Eve; to thee do we send up our sighs, mourning and weeping in this valley of tears. Turn then, most gracious advocate, thine eyes of mercy toward us, and after this our exile, show unto us the blessed fruit of thy womb, Jesus. O clement, O loving, O sweet Virgin Mary!
V. Pray for us, O Holy Mother of God.
R. That we may be made worthy of the promises of Christ.
Let us pray. O GOD, whose only begotten Son, by His life, death, and resurrection, has purchased for us the rewards of eternal life, grant, we beseech Thee, that meditating upon these mysteries of the Most Holy Rosary of the Blessed Virgin Mary, we may imitate what they contain and obtain what they promise, through the same Christ Our Lord. Amen.

Meditations of the Rosary (these may be said with the chaplet or with the rosary)

First Joyful Mystery: The Annunciation of the Coming King
I return to you Oh Lord, these magnificent words, announcing You to all your creation, Come to us Lord Jesus:
Hail full of grace, You are the Loving Lord, Almighty and all Powerful, Blessed are you who comes in the Name of the Lord, and Blessed is Mary Most Holy your first chosen among all flesh. "Hail Mary full of grace, the Lord is with you, blessed are you among women and blessed is the fruit of your womb, Jesus!" Maranatha! (10 JITIY, 1 Glory Be, 1 Sacred Hearts)

Second Joyful Mystery: The Visitation – Mary visits Elizabeth
Beloved King of Glory, you sent Mary, the Mother of My Lord when she was filled with the Holy Spirit to visit Elizabeth. I ask that you also allow her to come into my heart that my heart may be immaculate and pure like hers, filled with a love so favorable to You that you cannot refuse returning to me and to us on earth, that your longsuffering may cease and that you would greatly desire to deliver us from evil so that we may once again be united to you in eternal love. Please awaken all who are asleep in Your Love in the Lord Jesus! (10 JITIY, 1 Glory Be, 1 Sacred Hearts)

Third Joyful Mystery: The Birth of Jesus
-who were born, not of blood nor of the will of the flesh nor of the will of man, but **(the will) of God.** *John 1:13 NASB95*

According to John 1:13 the children of God are born of the will of God.

Beloved Father, I give to you my free will. Remove from my heart all treasures of the earth and allow me to obey your commands, statues, precepts and ordinances without reservation or hesitation so that Your Will is born in me and that Your Holy Spirit possess me.

Beloved Lord come into the stable of my heart, make room in the deepest depth of my inner-most being. May the Inn of my heart be perfected to be the chambers in which My Lord is loved perfectly as He has desired from the beginning of time. (10 JITIY, 1 Glory Be, 1 Sacred Hearts)

Fourth Joyful Mystery: The Presentation
A PRAYER OF CONSECRATION

Oh Gracious Father of Everlasting Love, before the Holy Trinity, Our Heavenly Mother and the whole Heavenly Court, I present myself to You, resisting, rebuking and renouncing Satan and all of his works. United with Jesus, in Jesus, through Jesus, and in His Armor of Light, I approach Your throne, united with His sacrifice on Calvary and His most precious Blood and Water that gushed forth filled with Your loving mercy, I offer and consecrate my whole life and total existence to the Sacred Heart of Jesus and the Immaculate Heart of Mary. In You I want to live, move and have my being.

I consecrate myself to the Holy Ghost you have given to me, I consecrate myself to Your Divine Will
I consecrate myself to Your Way, Your Truth, and Your Life,
I consecrate myself to My Heavenly Father and all that He desires for the Glory of God, In the Name of Jesus. Blessed be God, Blessed Be His Holy Name. Jesus I Trust in You!

My Lord, as Our Blessed Mother responded to Your call, I also respond: Behold, I am the handmaid of the Lord, Be it done to me according to Your Word. And as Jesus responded to Your call, I also respond: Not my will Heavenly Father, but thine, take this cup from me. My Jesus, I await the fulfillment of Your promise to deliver us from evil, My Savior, My Redeemer, Blessed is He who comes in the Name of the Lord. Blessed Mother pray for us that we may be made worthy of the promises of Jesus Christ. I pray in the Name, in THE Holy Name of my Beloved Jesus. Thank You, Father for hearing my prayer. It is granted, it is done. (10 JITIY, 1 Glory Be, 1 Sacred Hearts)

Fifth Joyful Mystery: The Finding of the Child Jesus In the Temple
- So Jesus said to them, "Truly, truly, I say to you, Unless you EAT the flesh of the Son of Man and drink His blood, **you have no life in yourselves**. *John 6:53* NASB95

Oh Lord, Remember me and Receive me. Dear Lord You are the Way, make me to find you. Please make the intent and desire of my heart, holy and pleasing to you. Make me to make your joy complete, Help me to help my brothers that we may be of the same mind, maintaining the same love, united in the same spirit, intent on one purpose in your unconditional love.

Consummate this union Lord with your intense and unfathomable love. My soul magnifies you and my spirit rejoices in you. Beloved Want of my all, there is no other! Allow me to enter into the New Covenant and partake. Transform me and let me be One with You. Give to me Life in your Eternal Love. Thank you for the Living Bread you have given this body to eat that has given me eternal life in Your love everlasting. **Jesus**, you are My Holy Communion, My Wedding, My Bridegroom in this Bread of Life, in this Holy Temple. Thank You Lord! (10 JITIY, 1 Glory Be, 1 Sacred Hearts)

Sorrowful Mysteries of the Rosary
First Sorrowful Mystery: The Agony in the Garden
Dearest Lord, with great love in the garden you took upon yourself all of my burdens and made them Light. You washed them with the blood of your sweat. I offer to you all my burdens and sufferings. Allow me Lord to be all that you have desired, I ask for the grace to live in your light pleasing you in all that I am.

Allow me to take Your yoke upon me and teach me and give me rest Release and free me from all evil and let me find relief in you.

Give to me the loving grace and confidence of trusting in Your Divine Providence as I have never before understood or acted upon.

Holy and Beloved Lord, stand with me and strengthen me! Write Your law upon my heart and allow Your Word and the Holy Spirit to guide, govern and possess me. (10 JITIY, 1 Glory Be, 1 Sacred Hearts)

Meditation based on these scriptures:
- "Take my yoke upon you and learn from Me, for I am gentle and humble in heart and you will find rest for your souls. For My yoke is easy and My burden is light." *Mat 11:29-30 NASB95*
- But the Lord stood with me and strengthened me, so that through me **the proclamation** might be fully accomplished, and that all the Gentiles might hear; and I was rescued out of the lion's mouth. *2Ti 4:17 NASB95*
- For, "the one who desires life, to love and see good days, must keep his tongue from evil and his lips from speaking deceit. *1Peter 3:10 NASB95*
- But He answered and said, "It is written, `Man Shall Not Live On Bread Alone, **BUT ON EVERY WORD THAT PROCEEDS OUT OF THE MOUTH** of GOD.' *Mat 4:4 NASB95*

Second Sorrowful Mystery – The Scourging at the Pillar
Beloved King of Longsuffering, I offer to you my life past, present and future. Please fill me with your grace. I ask you to bless my enemies; may you be glorified in all that I say and do. Make me to return to you my very breath and my Spirit. Make me Lord to be consumed by your perfect love that conquers all of our enemies, bears all things and casts out fear. You are my God of Love Blessed and Holy, Glorified above all of heaven and earth.
(10 JITIY, 1 Glory Be, 1 Sacred Hearts)

Meditation based on these scriptures:
- Bless those who persecute you; bless and do not curse. *Romans 12:14 NASB95*

-and if children, heirs also, heirs of God and fellow heirs with Christ, if indeed **we suffer with Him** so that we may also be glorified with Him. *Romans 8:17 NASB95*

Third Sorrowful Mystery: The Crowning With Thorns

Oh Beloved Lord, how little the agony of the worries and stress I experience here on earth. As big as they may seem to me, they are like a grain of sand compared to your suffering. I embrace your strength and your Godly thoughts and great love and compassion towards those who hated you during the time you were crowned with thorns and wore it passionately for the sake of my salvation. Take my thoughts and make my mind obedient to you, give to me a mind of Christ as you have repeatedly requested of us in your Glorious Word. Allow me to Honor you and to Return to You with great love. Glory and Praise to you dear Lord in all that you do to me, with me and for me. Thank You! (10 JITIY, 1 Glory Be, 1 Sacred Hearts)

Meditation based on these scriptures:

-"Do not judge, and you will not be judged; and do not condemn, and you will not be condemned; pardon, and you will be pardoned. *Luke 6:37 NASB95*

-For judgment will be merciless to one who has shown no mercy;

MERCY TRIUMPHS OVER JUDGMENT. *Jas 2:13 NASB95*

Fourth Sorrowful Mystery: Jesus carries the Cross

Dearest Lord, how many times in my humiliation have I cried or complained, forgive me my inequities, surely I have been deserving of these humiliations. Be my strength, give to me the grace to bear all things in your unfathomable love. Allow me Lord to rejoice in my trials and tribulations for your glory and from them teach me to be like you. Allow me Lord to live where love is rather than where I live. Make me Lord to please you, be my stronghold and allow me, your bond slave to obey You without hesitation or resistance with unconditional love and mercy.

(10 JITIY, 1 Glory Be, 1 Sacred Hearts)

Meditation based on these scriptures:

- **"IN HUMILIATION HIS JUDGMENT WAS TAKEN AWAY;** WHO WILL RELATE TO HIS GENERATION? *Ac 8:33 NASB95*

-Therefore I urge you, brethren, by the mercies of God, to present your bodies a living and holy sacrifice,acceptable to God, **which is your spiritual service of worship**. *Romans 12:1 NASB95*

Fifth Sorrowful Mystery: The Crucifixion
Majestic King of Unconditional Love, great is your longsuffering, mercy, compassion and love. Make me Lord to repent fully that I may detach myself from all things on earth; and unite myself to you. As I unite my suffering to Your crucifixion teach me all things and help me to realize the loving hope in your perfect plan. Use me Lord as you will not as I will, for your glory and for the salvation of mankind. Jesus I Trust in You! (10 JITIY, 1 Glory Be, 1 Sacred Hearts)
Meditation based on these scriptures:
- "For there is hope for a tree, When it is cut down, that it will sprout again, And its shoots will not fail. *Job 14:7 NASB95*

- For it was fitting for Him, for whom are all things, and through whom are all things, **in bringing many** sons to glory, **to perfect the author of their salvation through sufferings.** *Heb 2:10 NASB95*

First Luminous Mystery: The Baptism of Jesus
God of Light, God of Truth, God Redeemer of the World, Teacher, Leader, Father of all I beg you to lead everyone to do what is required to please you that all will be saved. Make me to be merciful to the merciless that you may be pleased. Make me Lord to obey You. Make me Lord to be of one accord with The Holy Spirit, the water and the blood. Help me Lord to accept and to respond to you as you have perfectly planned for our salvation. Let thy will be done in my life for your glory. (10 JITIY, 1 Glory Be, 1 Sacred Hearts)
Meditation based on these scriptures:
- and they were being baptized by him in the Jordan River, **as they confessed their sins.** *Matthew 3:6 NASB95*
"And we are witnesses of these things; and so is the Holy Spirit, **whom God HAS GIVEN TO THOSE WHO OBEY HIM.**" *Acts 5:32 NASB95*

- "He who has believed **and has been baptized shall be saved;** but he who has disbelieved shall be condemned. *Mark 16:16 NASB95*
- This is the One who came by water and blood, Jesus Christ; not with the water only, but with the water and with the blood. It is the Spirit who testifies, because the Spirit is the truth. For there are three that testify: *1 John 5:6-7 NABRE*
- the Spirit and the water and the blood;
and **the three are of one accord.** *1 John 5:8 NABRE*

Second Luminous Mystery: The Wedding At Cana

Beloved Lord, I desire greatly to obey God rather than Man. I desire greatly to not lean on human understanding because your ways are higher and you are my teacher. Help me Lord to accept your Truth and to live in it. Make me strong to defend your Word, do not let doubt enter in. Lord although the apostles were obedient to man, they knew when to oppose them. Father in Heaven accept me as your own, show me your ways and guide me to perfect obedience in your loving light that you may be pleased in all I say and do. (10 JITIY, 1 Glory Be, 1 Sacred Hearts)

– "His mother said to the servants, "**Whatever He says to you, do it.**" *John 2:5 BBE*
- "He who believes in the Son has eternal life; but **he who does not obey the Son will not see life**, but the wrath of God abides on him." *John 3:36 NASB95*
- "If you keep My commandments, you will abide in My love; just as I have kept My Father's commandments and abide in His love. *John 15:10 NASB95*
- But Peter and the apostles answered,
"We must obey God rather than men. *Acts 5:29 NASB95*

Third Luminous Mystery: The Proclamation of the Kingdom

Beloved Lord of Hosts, You are God of all kingdoms, come and reign in our hearts, in our lives and receive us into Your kingdom that we may be made one. I knock, I seek and ask that my Father be made known to me, that I may know my holy family and dwell in the house of the Lord. I desire righteousness, Remember me, receive me Oh majesty of life's glory complete me. (10 JITIY, 1 Glory Be, 1 Sacred Hearts)

- He who has the Son has the life; he who does not have the Son of God does not have the life. *1John 5:12 NASB95*
-But seek first His kingdom and His righteousness, and all these things will be added to you. *Mat 6:33 NASB95*
- "O LORD of hosts, the God of Israel, who is enthroned above the cherubim, You are the God, You alone,
of all the kingdoms of the earth.
You have made heaven and earth. *Isa 37:16 NASB95*

Fourth Luminous Mystery: The Transfiguration

Beloved Jesus, I renounce corruption and all evil works and manifestations. Make my heart to be a refection of You that I may be like You. Renew my mind and let me enter into the New Covenant for the Glory of God according to His will which is good and acceptable and perfect. (10 JITIY, 1 Glory Be, 1 Sacred Hearts)

-Corruption must put on incorruption *1Cor 15:53 KJV*
-As in water face reflects face,
So the heart of man reflects man. *Pr 27:19 NASB95*
-And do not be conformed to this world,
but be transformed by the renewing of your mind,
so that you may prove what the will of God is, that which is good and acceptable and perfect.
Romans 12:2 NASB95
- Beyond all these things put on love,
which is the **perfect bond of unity.** *Col 3:14 NASB95*

Fifth Luminous Mystery: The Institution of the Eucharist

Beloved King of All Authority, I beg you to lead all to receive of the bread of life without bringing condemnation or judgment upon themselves. Make us Lord of a right spirit, right mind, right heart and a right love in You, be Our One and Only Stronghold bonded to Your Perfect Love.. (10 JITIY, 1 Glory Be, 1 Sacred Hearts)

- I am the living bread which came down from heaven: if any man **Eat of this bread, he shall live for ever**: and **the bread that I will give is my flesh,**
which I will give for the life of the world. *John 6:51 KJV*

-In the same way He took the cup also after
supper, saying, "**This cup is the new covenant in My blood;** do this, as often as you
drink it, in remembrance of Me." *1Cor 11:25* NASB95
- Day by day continuing with **one mind** in the temple, and
breaking bread from house to house,
they were taking their meals **together with gladness
and sincerity of heart**, praising God and having favor with
all the people. And **the Lord was adding to their number
day by day those who were being saved.** *Acts 2:46-47* NASB95
- by abolishing in His flesh the enmity,
**which is the Law of commandments contained in
ordinances,** so that in Himself He might make
**the two into one new man,
thus establishing peace,** *Eph 2:15* NASB95

First Glorious Mystery: The Resurrection

Lord as there is hope for a tree when it is cut down that it will sprout again, I proclaim my confidence in Your great mercy and unfanthomable love in the salvation for all and of all. Make me Lord to obey you without hesitation with a heart mind and soul that is right in your sight. Grant to me that incorruptible love so that I may love without corruption in Your Holy love. Amen (10 JITIY, 1 Glory Be, 1 Sacred Hearts)

And having been made perfect, **He became
to all those WHO OBEY HIM the source of eternal
salvation,** *Heb 5:9* NASB95
- "For there is hope for a tree, When it is cut down, that it will sprout again, And its shoots will not fail. *Job 14:7* NASB95
- Grace be with all those who love our Lord Jesus Christ
with incorruptible love. *Eph 6:24* NASB95

Second Glorious Mystery: The Ascension of Jesus into Heaven

Glorious Lord of impossibilities, who desires that I be perfect as my Father is perfect, I thank you for your Great Love and all that you have done to assure me that your Word will be accomplished in me, in You, with You, through You, and for You.

My Hope is the hope of Mary, that you will come sooner, so that we may live in unity with you in your everlasting love from age to age without end. (10 JITIY, 1 Glory Be, 1 Sacred Hearts)

> -"Therefore **you ARE TO BE perfect**,
> as your heavenly Father is perfect. *Matthew 5:48* NASB95
> -For **in hope we have been saved**, but hope that is seen is not hope; for who hopes for what he already sees? But if we hope for what we do not see, with perseverance we wait eagerly for it. *Romans 8:24-25* NASB95

Third Glorious Mystery: The Descent of the Holy Spirit
Beloved Lord, I repent for all the times I have grieved the Holy Spirit you have granted to me. I beg for a right spirit and strength and grace to obey so that I may please you and be possessed by You. (10 JITIY, 1 Glory Be, 1 Sacred Hearts)

> "And we are witnesses of these things; and so is the Holy Spirit, **whom God HAS GIVEN TO THOSE WHO OBEY HIM.**" *Acts 5:32* NASB95
> -"When the Helper comes, whom I will send to you from the Father, that is the Spirit of truth who proceeds from the Father, He will testify about Me, *John 15:26* NASB95
> - We know that **no one who is born of God sins; **
> but He who was born of God keeps him, and **the evil one does not touch him.**
> We know that we are of God, and that
> **the whole world lies in the power of the evil one.**
> And we know that the Son of God has come,
> and has given us understanding so that we may know Him who is true; **and we are "in Him" who is true,
> in His Son Jesus Christ.**
> This is the true God and eternal life. *1 John 5:18-20* NASB95

Fourth Glorious Mystery: The Assumption of Mary into Heaven
Beloved Lord, thank you for allowing Mary to say Yes to your great plan of redemption. Make me to please you as she did, that I may also be full of grace and arise on that last day into Your loving glory. (10 JITIY, 1 Glory Be, 1 Sacred Hearts)

- "For **He has had regard for the humble state of His bondslave;** For behold, **from this time on all generations will call me blessed.** "For the Mighty One has done great things for me; and holy is His name. "AND HIS MERCY IS UPON GENERATION AFTER GENERATION TOWARD THOSE WHO FEAR HIM. *Luke 1:48-50 NASB95*
- "He has brought down rulers from their thrones, And has <u>exalted</u> those who were <u>humble</u>. *Luke 1:52 NASB95*

Fifth Glorious Mystery: The Coronation

"Remain faithful until death, and I will give you the crown of life" *Rev 2:10 NASB95*

Dearest Holy Trinity, Father, Jesus and Holy Ghost, I submit myself to You; I resist, rebuke, and renounce Satan and all his works.
I repent, and with a contrite heart, mind and soul and with the greatest love that is within me, I lay down my crown.
Help me Lord, to do Your will and to please You in all Your ways, in Your truth and in Your loving light. Make me Lord, to do what I must to become the lowest, be my everlasting loving King.
I embrace all my brothers and sisters in Christ, with Your love and as ONE with all of our hearts mind and soul I ask You to claim our souls as Yours alone and accept the crowns we lay before You. I return to God, His throne, all my love and all that I am.
I confess by my Holy Temple and by the Holy Spirit within me, By Heaven, by the Throne of God, By Him who sits on it, Our Father That Jesus is King and He is My Lord, My Master Jesus is one with the Father, one with My Holy Spirit to Him I submit and in Him, I desire to live move and have my being. I surrender to His Divine Will. In the Name of Jesus I stand firm to the Profession of My Faith.
(10 JITIY, 1 Glory Be, 1 Sacred Hearts, Hail Holy Queen)

BLESSED IS HE WHO COMES IN THE NAME OF THE LORD!
HOLY! HOLY! HOLY! YOU ARE LORD GOD,
KING OF ALL CREATION! I LOVE YOU! I LOVE YOU!
I LOVE YOU LOVE EVERLASTING WITH EVERLASTING LOVE!

ESCALATING STEPS TO THE NARROW ROAD

(Know that it is difficult to do these things, but the Lord sent us a Helper, the Holy Spirit who is in us, acknowledge Him, Desire to please and love the Lord above all and pursue God's will): Don't stress out over not being able to do these... You are right! There is NO WAY we can do this without Our Helper the Holy Spirit. We must diligently and persistently ask God for Help!

TRUST, ACKNOWLEDGE AND HONOR the Lord In all thy ways
TRUST IN THE LORD & LEAN NOT ON HUMAN UNDERSTANDING!
DESIRE THE LORD! WANT HIM AS HE WANTS YOU!
DESIRE to LOVE GOD FIRST ABOVE EVERYONE & EVERYTHING,
DESIRE TO OBEY THE COMMANDMENTS
CHOOSE TO BE BORN OF THE WILL OF GOD
CHOOSE YOUR FATHER
RECEIVE THE BAPTISM OF REPENTANCE (*Mr1:4; Lk3:3*)
ACKNOWLEDGE YOUR SINS!
GIVE to the Lord your first fruits and first male born
BE BORN OF WATER In the Name of the Father, Son and Holy Spirit
DESIRE TO BE PERFECT AS OUR FATHER IS PERFECT
BE BORN OF SPIRIT/BE POSSESSED BY THE LORD
DESIRE TO BE "IN HIM" – SIN NO MORE – BE POSSESSED BY HIM
BE BORN INTO EVERLASTING LIFE - EAT LIVING BREAD
ENTER INTO THE NEW COVENANT – DRINK HIS BLOOD
CHOOSE YOUR MOTHER
PRAY WITH YOUR WHOLE HEART, MIND & SOUL!
DESIRE TO PRAY WITHOUT CEASING! Call to Heaven!
HUMBLE YOURSELF IN THE SIGHT OF THE LORD
PUT OTHERS FIRST
DO NOT LIMIT THE POWER OF GOD. HE CAN DO ANYTHING!
GIVE THANKS TO GOD FOR ALL THINGS & IN EVERYTHING
GIVE GOD THE GLORY HE SO HIGHLY DESERVES!
DO NOT JUDGE For You Will Be Judged As You Judge.
BRIDLE YOUR TONGUE – BLESS! DO NOT CURSE
DESIRE TO SOW AS HE SOWS, LOVE AS HE LOVES, BE AS HE IS, OFFER YOURSELF AS A LIVING SACRIFICE
DESIRE TO WALK AND LIVE IN THE SPIRIT
HOPE FOR THE SALVATION OF ALL
DESIRE TO BE OF CHASTE HEART, MIND, BODY & SOUL

- **TRUST, ACKNOWLEDGE AND HONOR the Lord In all Thy Ways And He Shall Direct Thy Paths.**
  Proverbs 3:5-10 Ref Honor Our Lord and Honor Him again by Honoring & Loving Our Blessed Mother whom Our Lord chose to bear His Son. **Are you so vain to deny the Mother of God as your own?** She is Blessed indeed! She bore Our Holy & Beloved Savior, Jesus Christ. Their blood mingled and was made ONE. Jesus can call her Mother, will you?

- **TRUST IN THE LORD & LEAN NOT ON HUMAN UNDERSTANDING!**

In heartfelt submission and persistent pursuit, If you ask Him to teach you, He will. He desires it and so should we.

> - Trust in the LORD with all your heart And do not lean on your own understanding. *Proverbs 3:5 NASB95*

- **DESIRE THE LORD! WANT HIM AS HE WANTS YOU!**
  "ONE" IS YOURS WITHOUT COST! FREE!!!
  DESIRE HIM!
  Desire to be all that He wants you to be... Perfect in Him! The Living Waters in our being are given by Our Lord. They are not of this world.

> -let the one who DESIRES
> take the water of life
> without cost *Rev 22:17 NASB*

- **DESIRE to LOVE GOD FIRST ABOVE EVERYONE & EVERYTHING, Tell Him you desire it, ask to be taught**
  > -Master, which is the great commandment in the law? Jesus said unto him,
  > **Thou shall love the Lord thy God with all thy heart, and with all thy soul, and with all thy mind.** This is the first and great commandment. And the second is like unto it, Thou shall love thy neighbor as thyself.
  > **On these two commandments hang all the law and the prophets.** *Matthew 22:36-40 KJV*

Love God desperately. Love Him above all things and above everyone else. Allow His Holy Spirit to work in you. He waits for your permission to come into your life and into your heart, it is when you say "yes" that He can help you to resist the evil one and help you to remove the darkness in your life.

• Return yourself to God. Give to Him all that He came to redeem "your love, your hate, your suffering, your joy, the sacrifice of your Life."
• Love one another even unto death
• Abide in Him and Read His Word
• If you Love Him, Keep His commandments *(see Tabel of Contents)*

- **DESIRE TO OBEY THE COMMANDMENTS**
    If today the Lord would tell you to move, would you move? You must desire to obey His every command!
    -"If you love Me, you will keep My commandments. *John 14:15 NASB95*
    -"He who believes in the Son has eternal life; but **he who does not obey the Son will not see life,** but the wrath of God abides on him." *John 3:36 NASB95*
    - But Peter and the apostles answered, "We must obey God rather than men. *Acts 5:29 NASB95*
    - "And we are witnesses of these things; and so is the Holy Spirit, whom God has given to those who obey Him." *Acts 5:32 NASB95*
    - Do you not know that when you present yourselves to someone as slaves for obedience, you are slaves of the one whom you obey, either of sin resulting in death, or of obedience resulting in righteousness? *Romans 6:16 NASB95*
    - By lovingkindness and truth iniquity is atoned for, And by the fear of the LORD one keeps away from evil. *Pr 16:6 NASB95*

- **CHOOSE TO BE BORN OF THE WILL OF GOD**
    John 1:13 NASB95
    Give your free will to the Lord! He loves you unconditionally, how can you give to him anything less. The Word of God was born of the Will of God, Jesus.

Exalted Love, be Forever Praised and in my life continuously increase.

    -who were born, not of blood nor of the will of the flesh nor of the will of man, but **(*the will*) of God.** *John 1:13 NASB95*
-This is the One who came by water and blood, Jesus Christ; not with the water only, but with the water and with the blood. It is the Spirit who testifies,
because the Spirit is the truth.
For there are three that testify: *1 John 5:6-7 NASB95*
-the Spirit and the water and the blood;
and **the three are of one accord.** *1 John 5:8 NASB95*

- **CHOOSE YOUR FATHER**
Believe and desire with all your heart, mind, and soul to Claim Him as Your Father and yourself as His child through His son Jesus Christ and Mary the Mother of God, our Mother too. Love HIM first. Submit to God. Resist, Rebuke, and Renounce the devil in all things, We live by faith and not be sight! A difficult concept, only God can teach.
    -"No servant can serve two masters; for either he will hate the one and love the other, or else he will be devoted to one and despise the other. You cannot serve God and wealth." *Luke 16:13 NASB95*
    - "Do not call anyone on earth your father; for One is your Father, He who is in heaven. *Matthew 23:9 NASB95*

- **RECEIVE THE BAPTISM OF REPENTANCE**
Mark1:4; Luke3:3 NASB95
    - Acknowledge your sins *Mark1:5; 1John2:8 NASB95*
    -Therefore bear fruit in keeping with repentance *Matthew 3:8 NASB95*
    - Therefore, confess your sins to one another, and pray for one another so that you may be healed. The effective prayer of a righteous man can accomplish much. *James 5:16 NASB95*

Reconciliation to God, to ourselves and to one another
We must forgive! Leave your gifts at the altar & be reconciled.
Experience the healing!
The Sign of Jonah is repentance in sackcloth & ashes
"Repent for the Reign of God is at hand"

-Corruption must put on incorruption *1Cor 15:43 KJV*

- **GIVE TO THE LORD YOUR FIRST FRUITS AND FIRST MALE BORN**

"**The first offspring from every womb belongs to Me**, and all your male livestock, the first offspring from cattle and sheep. 20"You shall redeem with a lamb the first offspring from a donkey; and if you do not redeem it, then you shall break its neck **You shall redeem all the firstborn of your sons None shall appear before Me empty-handed.** *Ex 34:19-20 NASB95*

"You shall celebrate the Feast of Weeks, that is**, the first fruits of the** wheat harvest, and the Feast of Ingathering at the turn of the year. 23"**Three times a year all your males are to appear before the Lord GOD, the God of Israel. 24"For I will drive out nations before you and enlarge your borders, and no man shall covet your land when you go up three times a year to appear before the LORD your God.** *Ex 34:22-24 NASB95*

- (As it is written in the law of the Lord, Every male that openeth the womb shall be called holy to the Lord;) *Luke 2:23 KJV*

- **BE BORN OF WATER** - Holy Baptism of water; John the Baptist set the example, after people acknowledged their sins
    - and they were being baptized by him in the Jordan River, **as they confessed their sins**. *Matthew 3:6 NASB95*
    - "He who has believed **and has been baptized shall be saved;** but he who has disbelieved shall be condemned. *Mark 16:16 NASB95*

- **DESIRE TO BE PERFECT AS OUR FATHER IS PERFECT**
    - "Therefore **you ARE TO BE perfect**, as your heavenly Father is perfect. *Matthew 5:48 NASB95*
    Contemplate Mary... *HOPE TO BE ONE WITH THE LORD!* SHE WAS MADE ONE WITH THE LORD

Overshadowing of the Spirit *A Moment Of One;
The Word became Flesh in her womb, *Mary the Tabernacle; Mary the Temple; *Christ the Lord adored in the Temple Jesus, the man- God in HER womb, ,*Mary the Mother of God; The Word the Sword of the Spirit, *Mary the Sheath of the Sword; Union with Our Lord, *† Flesh, Unfathomable Divine Mercy and Unfathomable Divine Love Unite; MADE ONE DESIRE for your soul to magnify the Lord and for your Spirit rejoice in God Our Savior! It is by grace that this will be accomplished.

- **BE BORN OF SPIRIT/BE POSSESSED BY THE LORD**
    - "And we are witnesses of these things; and so is the Holy Spirit, **whom God has given to those who obey Him.**" *Acts 5:32 NASB95*
    - "And I remembered the word of the Lord, how He used to say, 'John baptized with water, but you will be baptized with the Holy Spirit.' *Ac 11:16 NASB95*
    - "When the Helper comes, whom I will send to you from the Father, that is the Spirit of truth who proceeds from the Father, He will testify about Me, *John 15:26 NASB95*
    - He who has the Son has the life; he who does not have the Son of God does not have the life. *1John 5:12 NABRE*

Know that if you lie, the Spirit of Truth is not in you. Repent quickly! Submit to the Holy Ghost. Receive the Holy Spirit by faith. Hope to be possessed by Jesus. Pray to obtain the gifts of the Holy Spirit. Pray to obtain the fruits of the Holy Spirit. Desire the Holy Spirit in you. Desire to be completely obedient to the Lord. In the Book of Acts, after praying for nine days, the Apostles received the Holy Ghost. We must pray! There is a Novena among Catholic prayers that is prayed for nine days which is said to be the one that the apostles prayed before Pentecost when they received the Holy Spirit. Start the novena today.

- **SIN NO MORE – DESIRE TO BE "IN HIM" BE POSSESSED BY HIM**
BELIEVE! Make Him Your WANT!
    - We know that **no one who is born of God sins;**

but He who was born of God keeps him, and
the evil one does not touch him. We know that we are of
God, and that **the whole world lies in the power of the evil
one.** And we know that the Son of God has come, and has
given us understanding so that we may know Him who is true;
and we are "in Him" who is true, in His Son Jesus Christ.
This is the true God and eternal life. *1 John 5:18-20 NASB*
-**Whoever possess the Son has life;** whoever
does not possess the Son of God does not have life.
1 John 5:12 NABRE

• BE BORN INTO EVERLASTING LIFE - EAT LIVING BREAD

- I am the living bread
which came down from heaven:
if any man **Eat of this bread, he shall live for ever**: and
the bread that I will give is my flesh,
which I will give for the life of the world. *John 6:51 KJV*
- "Verily, verily, I say unto you, **except ye Eat
of the flesh of the Son of man, and drink his blood, YE
HAVE NO LIFE IN YOU**. *John 6:53 KJV*

You must love the Lord in whatever form He manifests Himself. Love and Exalt the Bread of Live. Take of the Bread and Wine in which He is manifested; receive **Holy Communion** with great love and admiration, adoration and submission to the Great ONE. Believe and desire to become ONE. Beg for it! Receive daily if possible. If unable, ask the Lord to allow you to receive spiritually. Ask the Lord to remember You, Receive YOU as He wants us to Remember Him and Receive Him. Desperately as He has been for us!

• ENTER INTO THE NEW COVENANT – DRINK HIS BLOOD

-In the same way He took the cup also after
supper, saying, "**This cup is the new covenant in My
blood;** do this, as often as you **drink it,
in remembrance of Me.**" *1Cor 11:25 NASB95*

- **CHOOSE YOUR MOTHER**
  Are you so vain to think you are better than Mary, whom Our Father himself chose to exalt. Consecrate yourself to Her Immaculate Heart that you may be transformed with a heart that is immaculate.
  - "For **He has had regard for the humble state of His bondslave; For behold, from this time on all generations will call me blessed.** "For the Mighty One has done great things for me; and holy is His name. "AND HIS MERCY IS UPON GENERATION AFTER GENERATION TOWARD THOSE WHO FEAR HIM. *Luke 1:48-50* NASB95
  - "He has brought down rulers from their thrones, **And has exalted those who were humble**. *Luke 1:52* NASB

Do not call anyone on earth your mother; for One is your Mother, She who is in heaven, Mother of God.

The Fifth Commandment:
  - "Honor your father and your mother, that your days may be prolonged in the land which the LORD your God gives you. *Exodus 20:12* NASB95

• **PRAY WITH YOUR WHOLE HEART, MIND & SOUL!**
Cry and Beg, mean it! Repetitive prayers are prayers said **heartlessly** – Do NOT pray that way!
Ask the Lord to teach you to pray.
  -We do not know how to pray as we should..."
  Romans 8:26 NASB95

Jesus Repeated Prayer: Jesus repeats his prayers in the Garden of Gethsemane three times Mat 26:39,42, 44;
He does not condemn repeated prayers.
Psalms are often very repetitive. For example, Psalm 136 repeats the same phrase 26 times: "God's love endures forever;"

• **DESIRE TO PRAY WITHOUT CEASING! The Call to Heaven**
  - pray without ceasing; *1Th 5:17* NASB95

Obtain The Grace To Pray without ceasing By Praying The Rosary with Your Whole Heart, Mind, Soul and Strength! DESIRE IT! It is not how you feel when you pray, it is a great desire and

great want to please the Lord. The Rosary is Grace Bearing and Blooming in Love! <u>SATAN vs WEAPON = The Rosary IT IS NOT JUST FOR CATHOLICS!</u> Always pray! *The ROSARY IS THE WORD RETURNING TO GOD:*
The Hail Mary is THE CALL TO HEAVEN!

- **HUMBLE YOURSELF IN THE SIGHT OF THE LORD**

Fast with good will and good intent. If it is difficult for you to fast begin by giving up your favorite drink, ice cream or meal. Some people go without eating all day. You can also fast by helping someone in need. Ask the Lord to give you the grace to have an open hand in your giving and in service to others.

- **PUT OTHERS FIRST,** for the last will be first.

This world is so engrossed in "self" and inequity. We live in an adulterous generation! In all you do and say, do it and say it, as if unto the Lord. Jesus. He was Servant and Submissive to Our Father. Yes He put Himself last, We must follow His example! I pray that the Lord will help us to follow such a difficult walk, never letting us stray.

> -Sitting down, He called the twelve and said to them, "If anyone wants to be first, he shall be last of all and servant of all." *Mark 9:35 NASB*

- **DO NOT LIMIT THE POWER OF GOD. HE CAN DO ANYTHING!**

and even more beyond our imagination. Understand this –
Manifestations And The Power Of God: How many products do you buy at the store that has many functions? One product but it can do many things, and those are made by man. What can God do? Why do we limit the power of God? He can bring to Life anything He desires! He can transform all He desires! He is all powerful, almighty, omnipotent and loving!

> -"For nothing will be impossible with God." *Luke 1:37 NASB*
> - "Again I say to you, it is easier for a camel to go through the eye of a needle, than for a rich man to enter the kingdom of God." *Matthew 19:24 KJV*

- **GIVE THANKS TO GOD FOR ALL THINGS & IN EVERYTHING GIVE GOD THE GLORY HE SO HIGHLY DESERVES!**
    - Every knee shall bow to me, and every tongue shall give praise to God." *Romans 14:11* NASB95
    - Through Him then, let us continually offer up a sacrifice of praise to God, that is, the **fruit of lips that give thanks to His name**. *Hebrews 13:15* NASB95

- **DO NOT JUDGE For You Will Be Judged As You Judge.**
    -"Do not judge, and you will not be judged; and do not condemn, and you will not be condemned; pardon, and you will be pardoned. *Luke 6:37* NASB95
    God is the Judge and the Bible is His rule book. These pretty much say the same thing (Grasp it!):
    1. You reap what you sow,
    2. you are what you think, how could you yourself know bad traits in another if you are not familiar with that trait in yourself. Let the person without sin cast the first stone.
    3. You are forgiven as you forgive
    4. You are condemned if you condemn;
    Resented if you resent;
    "for the measure you use is the measure
    in which you yourself will be measured."

- **BRIDLE YOUR TONGUE – BLESS! DO NOT CURSE**
    Resolve to think and speak only positive, loving thoughts and words.
    - Bless those who persecute you; bless and do not curse. *Romans 12:14* NASB95
    - And the tongue is a fire, **the very world of iniquity**; the tongue is set among our members as that which defiles the entire body, and sets on fire the course of our life, and is set on fire by hell. *James 3:6* NASB95
    -But no one can tame the tongue; it is a restless evil and full of deadly poison. *James 3:8* NASB95
    - "But the things that proceed out of the mouth **come from the heart,** and those defile the man. *Mat 15:18* NASB95

- But He answered and said, "It is written, 'Man Shall Not Live On Bread Alone, **BUT ON EVERY WORD THAT PROCEEDS OUT OF THE MOUTH** of GOD.' *Mat 4:4 NASB95*

-As in water face reflects face, So the heart of man reflects man. *Pr 27:19 NASB95*

- For, "THE ONE WHO DESIRES LIFE, TO LOVE AND SEE GOOD DAYS, MUST KEEP HIS TONGUE FROM EVIL AND HIS LIPS FROM SPEAKING DECEIT. *1Peter 3:10 NASB95*

-But above all, my brethren, **do not swear**, either by heaven or by earth or with any other oath; but your yes is to be yes, and your no, no, so that you may not fall under judgment. *James 5:12 NASB95*

- But the Lord stood with me and strengthened me, so that through me **the proclamation** might be fully accomplished, and that all the Gentiles might hear; and I was rescued out of the lion's mouth. *2Ti 4:17 NASB95*

- **DESIRE TO SOW AS HE SOWS, LOVE AS HE LOVES, BE AS HE IS**
    - "When he puts forth all his own,
    he goes ahead of them,
    and the sheep follow him
    because they know his voice. *John 10:4 NASB95*
    - "I am the good shepherd, and
    I know My own and My own know Me, *John 10:14 NASB95*

Jesus, who laid his crown down before his Father,
to become the lowest. we, NOW, must follow Jesus, Our Shepherd
With the greatest of love - We must
LAY DOWN OUR CROWN AT THE FEET OF JESUS!

- **OFFER YOURSELF AS A LIVING SACRIFICE**
    -and if children, heirs also, heirs of God and fellow heirs with Christ, if indeed **we suffer with Him** so that we may also be glorified with Him. *Romans 8:17 NASB95*
    -Therefore I urge you, brethren, by the mercies of God, to present your bodies a living and holy sacrifice, acceptable to God, **which is your spiritual service of worship**. *Romans 12:1 NASB95*

-And do not be conformed to this world, but be transformed by the renewing of your mind, **so that you may prove what the will of God is, that which is good and acceptable and perfect.** *Romans 12:2* NASB95

- For it was fitting for Him, for whom are all things, and through whom are all things, **in bringing many** sons to glory, **to perfect the author of their salvation through sufferings.** *Heb 2:10* NASB95

• **DESIRE TO WALK AND LIVE IN THE SPIRIT**
Put on the new man. Put on incorruption. Put on immortality. Desire it! Do all that you can to obtain it. Be desperate! I believe the Lord desires it and so should we. I also believe He will grant it if you want it and let Him. Glory and Praise to Him who loves us.

-We know that **no one who is born of God sins;** but He who was born of God keeps him, and **the evil one does not touch him.**
We know that we are of God, and
that **the whole world lies in the power of the evil one.**
And we know that the Son of God has come, and has given us understanding so that we may know Him who is true; **and we are "in Him" who is true, in His Son Jesus Christ.**
This is the true God and eternal life. *1 John 5:18-20* NASB95

- Therefore there is now no condemnation for those who are in Christ Jesus. For the law of the Spirit of life in Christ Jesus has set you free from the law of sin and of death. *Romans 8:1-2* NASB95
-so that the requirement of the Law might be fulfilled in us, who do not walk according to the flesh but according to the Spirit. *Romans 8:4* NASB95

• **HOPE FOR THE SALVATION OF ALL**
-For **in hope we have been saved**, but hope that is seen is not hope; for who hopes for what he already sees? But if we hope for what we do not see, with perseverance we wait eagerly for it. *Romans 8:24-25* NASB95

- Who will separate us from the love of Christ? Will tribulation, or distress, or persecution, or famine, or nakedness, or peril, or sword? *Romans 8:35* NASB95

Mary Hoped for the savior to come and offered herself chaste for His coming. Sara also had great hope and Abraham was made father of many nations. We must hope for the Return of Jesus!

Can we posses the Lord? Will the Lord Possess us? Oh Lord, Our Hope is in you! Please possess us.
- "Is not your fear of God your confidence, And the integrity of your ways your hope? *Job 4:6* NASB95
-"So the helpless has hope, And unrighteousness must shut its mouth. *Job 5:16* NASB95
- "Though He slay me, I will hope in Him. Nevertheless I will argue my ways before Him. *Job 13:15* NASB95
- "For there is hope for a tree, When it is cut down, that it will sprout again, And its shoots will not fail. *Job 14:7* NASB95

- **DESIRE TO BE OF CHASTE HEART, MIND, BODY & SOUL**

Pray that the Lord will prepare us to be acceptable to Him when He comes. Pray that He will receive us and teach us all things to be pleasing to Him. Desire it! Hope in it! Hope that we may be of a chaste heart, mind and soul and the intentions of our heart pure. Chaste, pure, sacred and immaculate…
- These are the ones who have not been defiled with women, for they have kept themselves chaste. These are the ones who follow the Lamb wherever He goes. These have been purchased from among men as first fruits to God and to the Lamb. *Rev 14:4* NASB95
-Blessed are they who wash their robes so as to have the right to the tree of life and enter the city through its gates. Outside are the dogs, the sorcerers, **the unchaste**, the murderers, the idol-worshipers, and all who love and practice deceit *Rev 22:14* NABRE

If you have any doubt about what I have written, then diligently seek with all your heart, mind and soul; ask the Lord. Submit to Him and I am sure He will guide you too. May we all become of one mind in Christ!

THE MERCY OF OUR LORD IS YOURS
IF YOU WANT IT
DESIRE TO AMEND YOUR WAYS
DESIRE HIS LOVE
AND LOVE HIM BACK!

WARNING!!!

Jesus Came To SAVE – Not To Condemn!!!

Neither do I condemn you...
I too am a sinner
My Hope is that you may
Contemplate...
Desire to Obey the Lord...
And consider...

Who Is Who and What Is What?

These are strong words and thoughts...
Discern for yourselves ask the
Help of the Holy Spirit

All things are imperfect until perfection comes!

My hope is that you will be led to rcpcnt
and be led to become Christ like

Corruption shall put on incorruption
Mortality shall put on immortality

Trust in Jesus no matter what!

ABOVE ALL THINGS WRITTEN
IN THIS BOOK

CONTEMPLATE and DESIRE

**THE UNCONDITIONAL
LOVE OF GOD
MERCY
AND REPENTANCE**

**DESIRE
TO LOVE HIM and OTHERS
AS HE LOVES YOU
RECIPOCATE EVERYTHING TO THE
LORD
(RETURN TO GOD)**

DESIRE TO PLEASE HIM

AND LOVE HIM FIRST

ABOVE EVERYONE

AND EVERYTHING

WHEN HE SAYS "REMEMBER ME" YOU SAY TO HIM "
LORD REMEMBER ME, RECEIVE ME AS YOUR OWN"

MAY YOU BE BLESSED!

MESSAGE FROM THE LORD – SEPTEMBER 1, 2004:

TO THE CHURCHES

Do you love me, says the Lord?
Then forgive your brother
Walk with your brother
Do not be afraid of your brother
Lean not on human understanding
for my ways are higher than yours
All things have been perfectly planned
All things shall pass away
but my word will not pass away

To all, you must repent
To all, you must forgive or you will not be forgiven
To all, you must not resent or you will be resented
To all, you must not condemn
or you will be condemned
To all, if you think they are wrong,
then surely it is you that is wrong
For all things are exactly as I have prescribed,
the measure you use,
is the measure you will be measured with

All things are all for My Glory
Acknowledge, Honor and Trust Me
through Jesus my Son

To all, love me desperately as I love you desperately
To all, you must walk as I walk

I am the master of longsuffering,
it began in Genesis with the first sin
and has multi-multiplied fold after fold,
I have suffered for the love of you

I suffered with my Son in whose person I also walked,
for we are ONE

I still suffer, I love you beyond love,
I desperately and deeply want to be
with you and in you
in love and in peace as you have never known,
together in My Kingdom

I say to you again, Repent!!
The kingdom of God is at hand!
There is no greater love,
than to lay down one's life for his brethren

Do you love me?

Would you lay down your life for your brother?
Do not be afraid, love him and bless him?
Unite with him.

Reflect upon my passion
Think of yourself as myself,
for I am in you and you are in me and we in the Father
Think of my passion, re-live my passion, be in my passion, with my
passion and through my passion where there is victory

Did I rebel against the enemy?
Was my example clear to you?
It is through being humiliated that you gain the virtue of humility
Reflect upon my humiliation, my suffering;
I have suffered all that you have suffered and more, much more

Do not be afraid to walk as I walk
I in my stillness, meek and lowly,
prayed and asked my Father to Bless Them, and so should you.

Submit to me, give to me your mind, body and soul
Obtain a mind of Christ,
desire to be perfect as my Father is perfect

Be filled with the fruits of the Holy Ghost
Love, joy, peace, longsuffering, gentleness,
goodness, faith, meekness, temperance
For I am made of all these things
and greater than understanding

Trust in Jesus, He will lead you, let Him possess you

My Exalted Bread of Life
Is the source of Your Life with me and in me eternally
You must be living in the fruits of the Holy Ghost
Your mouth must be Reverent, Pure and Immaculate
Wanting me desperately,
As I have been desperate for you unto death
Pleading for your repentance

The churches must unite
Who will demonstrate the fruits of the Holy Ghost
Who will be so humble and demonstrate humility
And say "Please forgive me, I am sorry, it is my fault"

For surely, even ONE word spoken in condemnation
Has rolled over many times, making many others to sin
Who will be so humble and demonstrate humility
And join with his brother church?

I love you immeasurably, do you love me?
I will teach you all things, if you ask me
Can you give to me your free will?
This is the door in which the enemy enters.
Can you love my mother as I love my mother?
Can I teach you about her,
that you may love her as I love her?
She is the Mother of Mercy suffering as I did,
humiliated as I was;
she is loving as I am; Full of grace as I am,
Perfect as my Father is Perfect
as I am; we are ONE.

The true church is The Mother Church loving my Mother
Who has believed her, has loved her,
has believed the hope in her messages;
The Roman Catholic Church.

I will make all things good for those who love me
For though we walk in the flesh
We do not war after the flesh
Lean not on human understanding

Submit to Me; Repent!

Trust in Jesus, the victory is His!
Be As Daniel And Darius
Enter The Lions Den In Love Exalting The Lord!
Do Not Let The Right Hand Know What The Left Hand Is Doing
May the Lord Guide you and Bless you indeed -- Gloria 9/1/04

Love one another as I have loved you!

MESSAGE FROM THE LORD – DECEMBER 4, 2004:

UNITY OF THE CHURCHES

The following was sent to a pastor on December 6, 2004. The pastor's name, church names and who he helped has been changed. The message has been slightly modified to be universal. My hope is that all who read this will whole heartedly seek the Lord, and be open to all the Lord desires, discerning and acting on His love and in complete obedience to Him alone. Allow the Lord to lead you in His Way to His Truth in His Light. This seems to be a simple solution from Jesus, Our Lord of Simplicity. Consider the letter as sent to you:

Beloved PASTOR †,

I want you to know that what you have done for the Jewish people is so wonderful.
I do believe we are all anxious for the Lord to deliver us from evil. You most certainly have been a wonderful instrument of the Lord, Our Great God of Everlasting Love and Immeasurable Divine Mercy.

If you remember I had a message on September 1, 2004 that the Lord gave to me, "To all Churches". I am resending it, in case you have misplaced it. I am also thinking that you have put aside the book that the Lord used my hands to type SEALED BY THE SPIRIT OF GOD. I can only wonder, who will believe, for even Noah was not believed.

I have another message for you. In this world, in the flesh, man creates such complexities, we live in Babylon, even the churches are in Babylon. I believe the Lord has shown to me the unity of the churches.

On First Saturday, December 4th, 2004 the Lord put the following thoughts into my mind:

1. And Jesus knew their thoughts, and said unto them, Every kingdom divided against itself is brought to desolation; and **every city or house divided against itself shall not stand;** *Mathew 12:25 KJV*

And if a house be divided against itself, that house cannot stand. *Mark 3:25 KJV*

But he, knowing their thoughts, said unto them, Every kingdom divided against itself is brought to desolation; and a **house divided against a house falleth.**
Luke 11:17 KJV

2. He brought back to mind that On September 1, 2004 the Lord ended the Message with **"Do not let the left hand know what the right hand is doing"** this to me, indicated that the differences would not be settled in the flesh

3 With that message in mind, the Lord drilled the following into my thoughts:
BLESSED IS HE
    WHO COMES IN THE NAME OF THE LORD
BLESSED IS HE
    WHO COMES IN THE NAME OF THE LORD
BLESSED IS HE WHO COMES IN THE NAME
BLESSED IS HE WHO COMES IN THE NAME
IN THE NAME
IN THE NAME
IN THE NAME
IN THE NAME

4. I Believe the Lord was telling me how the unity of the churches would occur
IN THE NAME
IN THE NAME
Examples:
THE STONE THE BUILDERS REJECTED **Catholic Church**

(All churches to unite in the name "CATHOLIC" which means universal)

5. United in Christ the difference lies among men. We wrestle not against flesh and blood, but against the principalities, against the powers, against the rulers of darkness of this world, against spiritual wickedness in high places. Let us stand firm, and let the Lord be Our Capstone. Let the Lord rule one Catholic Church, all believers of Our Beloved Jesus whose sacrificial love is beyond understanding.

We must each ask Him to teach us all things,
we have been born in a wicked world,
we must ask Him to teach us to love,
teach us to repent,
teach us about His Mother,
teach us to be all that He wants us to be,
so that in Him we can Truly Live Move and Have our Being…

May the Lord Bless You Indeed!!
May He Shine His Light upon you
And Lead us all to Everlasting Life.…

In Christ
I give to you my love for Jesus with the Heart of Mary
And my Love for Mary with the Heart of Jesus,
With these two perfect hearts, I unite mine To yours,
my beloved brother and pastor
Love unto death!!
Gloria (December 4, 2004)

MESSAGE FROM THE LORD ON THE FEAST OF OUR LADY OF THE ROSARY – OCTOBER 7, 2005
(Amos, a minor prophet in the Old Testament)

Why this feast to receive this message? After having gone to non catholic churches for years, being told that we should not pray the rosary, I was afraid to pray it. One day, I touched the rosary hanging on my bed post and I felt the power of the Lord all over me. I had to repent. Perhaps, this also is a confirmation to me for the need to repent in this message. Ever since then, I have come to love praying it with my whole heart mind and soul. Satan hates it, it is a weapon against all evil, **it is grace bearing and love awakening.** Thank you Lord! Thank you to the Mother of My Lord!

When I first received this message, I was fearful. However, now I believe it is to honor My Father in Heaven that this is necessary.

This also, is a confirmation of what is written on the back cover of the book *WE LAY DOWN OUR CROWN Sealed by the Spirit of God*, asking for your approval. Again, I ask you to please say "yes" to the Lord.
Fear of the Lord is a beautiful gift from the Lord; a fear so profound of being separated from Him; a fear of offending Him, a fear and sorrow of being the reason for His many tears.
I pray that the Lord will give me/us the grace to endure whatever He has in store for me/us, I trust that He will. Beyond fear of the Lord, is Trust in the Lord. Trust in the Lord, allowing Him to do to me whatever He wants for His glory, as He did to Jesus, who was glorified so that we might be saved. I know I can never of my own accord do anything, for I, by myself am nothing but dust, I am food for worms, and even less than that, I am wretched and unworthy scum. I am dumber than dumb.
But, He who loves me, He who is good beyond compare,
He who is love beyond love,
He who wants everyone to be saved,
He knows all things and He knows what must be done
and so I pray that His will be done in my life,

hoping that he will be kind and gentle to me,
but whatever the Lord chooses, I also chose.
The following are the scriptures to which the Lord led me.
In the following lines, "you" is to be understood as plural. The following was the first scripture that caught my eye, taken from the Holy Bible, the New International Version:

> **Amos 3:2** *NASB95* - "You only have I chosen among all the families of the earth; Therefore I will punish you for all your iniquities."

I believe the resolve is to repent in sackcloth and ashes and to become little and the lowest, really small. The Lord is all forgiving, and all merciful. My hope is that I may repent fully and completely pleasing to the Lord. Pray for me/us that He will teach and lead me/us and keep me/us in His Armor of Light. The Lord then scrolled my eyes to the next verse.

> **Amos 3:3 -5** *NASB95* - Do two men walk together unless they have made an appointment? Does a lion roar in the forest when he has no prey? Does a young lion growl from his den unless he has captured something? Does a bird fall into a trap on the ground when there is no bait in it? Does a trap spring up from the earth when it captures nothing at all?

This message is pointing out that I have agreed to walk with the Lord. In giving Him my free will and offering myself to Him, I have agreed to His terms "Thy will be done", "Let it be done to me according to thy word, I am a handmaid of the Lord" and "Jesus I Trust in You".

> **Amos 3:7** *NASB95* - Surely the Lord GOD does nothing
> Unless He reveals His secret counsel
> To His servants the prophets.

The above verse confirms that the Lord is kind and gentle and waits for us to ask Him to come into our lives and the degree of our submission to Him. The Lord asked the Apostles: are you willing to drink from my cup - you do not know what you are asking. The Lord is gentle and kind beyond measure, we must be willing to be used as His instruments for the glory of God and for the salvation of all mankind. We must give our all to Him, we must deny ourselves and return everything to Him.

> **Amos 4:6, 8, 9, 10, 11** _NASB95_
> "You have not returned to me" declares the Lord.

The Lord repeats five times (once in each verse) that we have not returned to Him. Our Blessed Mother Mary in her many apparitions has continued to ask us to return to God, she asks us to repent, fast and to pray.

> **Amos 5:6** _NASB95_ - "Seek the LORD that you may live,
> Or He will break forth like a fire, O house of Joseph,
> And it will consume with none to quench it for Bethel,

> **Amos 5:15** _GNT_ Hate evil, love Good
> Perhaps the Lord will have mercy

I hope for the greatest love, wisdom, knowledge, understanding, reason and intelligence and a greater faith to stand firm on that evil day. I hope to seek Him fully, and I hope to be "In Him" where He will fight the battle for me, in this shell made of dust. Pray and fast that the Lord will have mercy on me, on us.
I have been longing for the day of the Lord...
Oh how I have hoped that He would already be here. I was stunned at reading the next verse.

> **Amos 5:18-20** _NIV_ - Woe to you who are longing for the day of the LORD! Why do you long for the day of the LORD? That day will be darkness and not light. It will be as though a man fled from a lion only to meet a bear, as though he entered his house and rested his hand on the wall only to have a snake bite him. Will not the day of the LORD be darkness not light - pitch-dark, without a ray of brightness?

I hope that when darkness comes, I (we) will stand firm in His Love and in His Armor and Light with the Shield of Faith and the

Sword which is the Word of God piercing the enemy; where there will be no fear in the presence of the Lord when confronted by a lion, a bear and even a snake. The Lord has already given us word of the three days of darkness. I do not know if this is the darkness to which He refers. We must pray, fast and repent. We must humble ourselves in the sight of the Lord. Jesus I Trust in You!

Amos confirms the Babylon in the churches (in Ch 5:21-26, verses are not written here).

Chapter 7, also confirms the message in who is the King... we must become the lowest, we must become the littlest
according to Amos Chapter 7, Jacob is so small and the Lord relents.

So we must also desire to be so small. We must relent of our treasures on earth, deny ourselves all, pick up our cross and follow Our Good Shepherd, Jesus.

> **Amos 7:2** *NASB95* - And it came about, when it had finished eating the vegetation of the land, that I said, "Lord GOD, please pardon!
> **How can Jacob stand, For he is small?"**
>
> 7:3 The LORD changed His mind about this.
> **"It shall not be," said the LORD.**
>
> 7:4 - Thus the Lord GOD showed me, and behold, the Lord GOD was calling to contend with them by fire, and it consumed the great deep and began to consume the farm land.
>
> 7:5 - Then I said, "Lord GOD, please stop!
> **How can Jacob stand, for he is small?"**
>
> **7:6 -The LORD changed His mind about this. "This too shall not be," said the Lord GOD.**

How small can we be? How small do we desire to be?
We must be so small there is no room for our self,

but only for the Lord
in this shell made of dust
our hearts must be empty of this world
We must be the lowest, the littlest, so small;
Lord, help me to relent that you may relent.
Lord, help me to be the smallest.
"God's mercy endures forever" *(Psalm 118 and 136)* NKJV

* DIVINE MERCY I TRUST IN YOU!
* Merciful Lord, Glorious Father, Jealous Love,
Help me to be so small that you will also change your mind and turn your wrath away from us. Please Pardon and have Mercy on us through Our Most Beloved Sacred Heart of Jesus and the merits of His sacred wounds, His Holy death and resurrection. Pardon and Mercy through the Sorrowful and Immaculate Heart of Our Beloved Blessed Mother and Her great love!!! Lord help me to relent that you may relent. Everlasting Loving King come and take your place in our world, and in our lives. Teach us to Love you; teach us to please you, help us, make us to be pleasing to you. Make us so small like Jacob. Savior of all mankind, Redeemer of our sinfulness, God of Divine Mercy make us to return to You, completely without conditions, without limits. Glory to Our Most Loving Immortal, Eternal, Omnipotent Father through Jesus, through Mary and through Our Holy Spirit! Pray for us Holy angels and saints that we may be made worthy of the promises of Christ. Eternal Father I offer You the Body and Blood, Soul and Divinity of Your dearly beloved Son, Our Lord Jesus Christ, in atonement for our sins, the sins of the deceased souls with stain, and those of the whole world. For the sake of His sorrowful Passion, have mercy on the poor deceased souls, on mc, on us, and on the whole world.

"Eternal God, in whom mercy is endless and the treasury of compassion — inexhaustible, look kindly upon us and increase Your mercy in us, that in difficult moments we might not despair nor become despondent, but with great confidence submit ourselves to Your holy will, which is Love and Mercy itself. (Diary of Saint Maria Faustina Kowalska)

+ + +

IN MEMORY OF DEACON ALAN
The Passing of My Beloved Friend
Father's Day June 19, 2005

Deacon Alan, a Saint in my Heart
Yes!
we must TRUST the Lord
And His Promises are True
And Our Lord does keep them
An instrument He was
An instrument returned

The Lord says you reap what you sow
And so, the Lord used many as an instrument for him
In his time of need
At the end of his days
I was amazed at the wonderful response
And the care the Lord provided
In the many novenas and prayers said
I am positive, that Deacon Alan's prayers
With promises were promises fulfilled

His fervent soul reached the heavens
And the heavens responded
Knowing that the mercy of Our Lord is as great and immeasurable
as His Unlimited and Immeasurable Love
We trust, and give our all to the Sacred Heart of Jesus
and the Sorrowful and Immaculate Heart of Mary,
we anticipate a union
beyond our understanding with Our Holy Heavenly Family

How great is the Love of Our Father
How great is the Love of the Mother of God, Blessed Mary
How great is the Love of Jesus
The love they demonstrated,
the life they lived
The example they left us
And the truth in His Wonderful Word

Is one, they desire greatly
For us to follow, to know, to love and to return to them

Deacon Alan was one who strived
To follow, to know and to love the Lord,
His Divine Will, His Word and the Holy Family
Deacon Alan taught me of the Great Divine love
between Mary and Joseph, so beautiful
And about their giving, they gave one third of their first fruits..
wow!

As Deacon Alan, became weak
I was hearing of all these people being helpful
In his time of need, And I seemed helpless,
I asked the Lord, what could I do
It was not long after that
I remember Deacon Alan called to ask me
If I could help him, I was so appreciative
Praise the Lord!

Deacon Alan asked if I knew the raindrop technique,
This is a massage technique done with high quality essential oils
Very healing!
I was so pleased to be able to participate
And help someone so beloved, so blessed
I offered it to the Lord as unto the Lord

The first time I went to his home
We decided it was okay to use his dining table with cushions
He used a blue plastic table cloth on top of them
Working with the oils caused my hands and his feet
to turn partially blue from the color on the plastic
It was quite alright, It washed off easily and
I loved having the opportunity,
To help my beloved Deacon Alan

After that,
there were a few times of great significance
I have lost track of which visit was which

But I do remember significant events and conversations
During his illness,
I emailed him a couple of times
And mentioned sackcloth, but he never responded
I guess in our ignorance, we simply do not know
What it is for, what it is, or why we should even use it
The devil keeps us away from the truth

The Lord led me to use it (sackcloth and ashes),
it took several months
To learn what it was, and He showed me how to use it
I did as the Lord led me,
I felt funny doing something so odd in this generation
But I did it in obedience to the Lord

The Lord led me to read Isaiah 58 and Nehemiah 9
So I was led to spread ashes on the ground in my backyard,
And lay on top of a landscape clothe (made of burlap)
which I laid on top of the ashes
I did as the scriptures spoke to me
When I came back into the house, the Lord instantly
Led me to psalms and as a message to me said
"That he lifted my sackcloth and
turned my mourning into dancing"
The Lord is amazing!! He is our teacher!
He is faithful! He is Love!

I believe it was the third visit that
The Lord led me to take sackcloth and ashes to Deacon Alan's home
He agreed to do as I had suggested
And he watched as I prepared it
The cloth was around 7 ft x 7 ft
I folded it in half, and put the ashes between the fold
So as to avoid such a mess
on his dining room table on which he laid
He said, "Oh, that's how you do it"
Before we started, as he laid on the sackcloth
I told him that this was a very special time to approach the Lord
With a very contrite and repentant heart, mind and soul

I also had sackcloth on me and put ashes on my head
I also approached the Lord repentant and contrite
I prayed during the massage technique
And also asked the Lord to allow Our Lord's Love to
flow through my hands
Affirming that I am nothing and only He can do such things
As I worked on Deacon Alan
I used CD's with the Rosary & Chaplet of Divine Mercy *(by Fr. Dan Papineau, MIC Rector, National Shrine of The Divine Mercy and Still Waters with Saint Faustina's Mediations on the Passion)* and
The Chaplet of Virtues *(produced by the Bread of Angels)*
Stations of the Cross *(by Dana and Fr Kevin Scallion)*
These are very powerful!
We did not converse, he meditated and so did I
At the end of the session, he sat up
And his response was
W--O--W! Loudly and boldly
I was surprised to hear him,
being the meek man that he was.
As Deacon Alan would say, so do I say: "Praise the Lord!"

Every session after that was on sackcloth and ashes
I know there were some major topics discussed
Sometimes the Lord had him sitting on his chair
Waiting for me, two different times, the words that came out of my mouth were "Let's talk"

I remember one time we spoke about
WHO IS THE THIEF? And WHO IS THE MURDERER? As mentioned in this book
But I will repeat part of that message as in this book, because of its importance in contemplation
WHO IS THE THIEF?
Is it he who took the cloak? Or is it he who denies
him? Jesus said "if he takes your cloak do not stop him
from taking your tunic. Give to everyone who asks you,
and if anyone takes what belongs to you do not demand it
back." "As you judge you are judged." In calling him a
thief is it you who is the thief? Is it you who has kept from

*those in need? Is it you who does not give your first fruits
to the Lord?... Why will you allow yourself to suffer in
selfishness, greed, and love of earthly treasures. ... Detach
yourself from the things of the earth...*
Deacon Alan then told me that he had never forgiven someone who
had stolen his bike, I believe this was brought to Light by Our Lord
for his repentance.

Another one of our conversations was the Wedding at Cana
as in the meditations in the Luminous Mystery
the Lord gave to me for end of times
This mystery pertains to separation
from all things of the earth
Including each other, loving God first above all

Another time, the discussion was
Perfect Love which casts out fear,
bears all things and conquers all of our enemies

Still another time, the Lord gave me some scriptures for
Deacon Alan
Psalm #143, #116-118, 136, 108:1-6, 108:12-13, 110:1-2,
113:1-4, 134, 135
I only read some of them, but when I read them, we both
had on sackcloth and ashes, he then asked me to invite
Nadine also at which time I put ashes and sackcloth on her
I do not know about them or how this affected them
But for myself, I had a sense of being cleaned out inward,
this helped me too

I do remember another conversation, but this one was for me.
I share it hoping that it will benefit others/you as well.
It was in regard to the Spirit of Gluttony.
I had been told long ago,
That I was not overweight because of what I ate
I mentioned to Deacon Alan, that I have been trying to fast more
than I had ever done in my life, and that I had researched and
learned that the Spirit of Gluttony was the father of many spirits
The father of the spirit of unsatisfiable desires, fornication,

passions, the big "I want and I get", etc.
Deacon Alan told me that
we have to deny ourselves all things to
get rid of it, not just food.

There was another incident, I am sad to recall
because I felt as if I was correcting Deacon Alan
who was elder than I, and I love him so much
I apologized to him and had tears as I said it
However, today, as I was reflecting upon it
The Lord gave me peace
it was the Lord who was directing the words spoken
and this message is for all of us
I am not going into the details, although they were minor
We all are guilty of this:
Many of us, who take our loved ones for granted
Do not treat them as we do others
Sometimes we speak freely in a rough manner
maybe because we see each other every day
and know we can get away with it
In any case, this was brought to his attention
It was told to him
That we should treat our family members as if they themselves were part of the Holy Family

"WE MUST REMEMBER,
THAT PERFECT LOVE
CONQUERS ALL OF OUR ENEMIES"

The next week when I went to Deacon Alan's home
I was amazed at the peace, the calm, the love
In their home and everyone present
I could feel it! I was truly amazed!
One of the last significant conversations was about
The Sign of Jonah
It was funny how the Lord moved both of us
I saw the sackcloth in his living room
And I asked him if he was using it
And he said yes, I asked him how

He moved his hands as a tent over his head
I told him, the Lord was leading him, as he led me
Coincidently, that same day, I took
A writing of 4 pages or so,
(it is as originally presented to him in the book WE LAY DOWN OUR CROWN, however in this book it is broken up in pieces and more is added into questions)
that the Lord had me write up that weekend
On Sackcloth and ashes also discussing
What the Lord
Revealed to me regarding **the Sign of Jonah**

How do you tell a world of people
They need to get in sackcloth and ashes?
I know this was the Lord's doing…
How do we learn to come back to the Lord
How do we convince people this or that is necessary
Bowing my head, I humbly plea and hope that the Lord
Will move us all to repent completely and totally
As pleasing to the Lord, He is Our Maker
And Only Our Lord can change us

I believe, this is one of the promises the Lord kept for
Deacon Alan, true repentance before leaving this earth.
Deacon Alan was always seeking the Lord and His Truth.
Deacon Alan was always open to the Way of the Lord.
Although other things were said, the above conversations
pertain to the Word of God which perhaps has been
lost in time and manipulated by the evil one

I will rephrase: **People do not believe the Word of God.**
They only believe what they want;
they pick and choose parts of the Word
The differences are of the flesh!
If we all unite under one house, the Lord will deliver us.
A divided house cannot stand.
We will be of one mind, one spirit, and one body, *(see the Lord's message "To the Churches" and "Unity of the Churches" in all my books).*
Even the Confusion of the Bread of Life will be resolved
and revealed to us. We must trust the Lord.
All churches are full of pride.

Many are critics and judges condemning each other,
if there are any humble and lowly,
I cannot say which one, I do not know,
I am not familiar with all churches.

The two most important conversations
Were of repenting and of The Bread of Life
Again, he was waiting for me on his chair
I do not remember all of this conversation,
I have learned that sometimes the Lord does that to us
When He speaks through us
I do remember asking him
if he had ever eaten of the leavened bread.
And that the Lord showed me that
Luke is the book for end of times
And talks about the leavened bread
The Orthodox Catholic Church uses leavened bread.
The Roman Catholic Church uses unleavened bread.
a difference of the flesh
He said he did not know.
I mentioned to him, that the churches are under so much confusion,
ALL the churches are under so much confusion
He agreed
I asked him if he would like for me to ask an Orthodox priest to administer Holy Communion to him,
this priest worked at a Roman Catholic High School.
He responded without hesitation and said "Yes",
I then asked him if he would prefer a mass said at his home, and again but this time enthusiastically responded
"that would be even better", his eyes lit up.
He asked me about the mass, if it would be in English
When I said yes,
he said he was thinking it was going to be another language
And was looking forward to that,
I did not give it a second thought
The mass did indeed occur on June 3_{rd}, 2005
It was in English, and he did receive the Leavened Bread
now he had eaten of both.
I believe this event was worth noting and am hoping that it is a

Spiritual Historic Event.

Let me explain:

I had attended a seminar on **Healing the Family Tree** given by Deacon Alan. He mentioned that within his own family there was a breach causing division among its members. This is common in many of our families. He said that when they had a family reunion, they prayed for a healing of the breach and invited those previously divided to the reunion. One of the members of the divided family accepted the invitation and went to the reunion.

Deacon Alan said, that he and a few others felt the air lift and the breach repaired.

In the same way, this mass had something, I believe no other mass has ever had. Deacon Alan had (with approval) a pix with the real presence of Our Lord in the form of unleavened bread. He had it placed on an altar in the living room where he prayed. At this mass, the Consecrated Unleavened Bread and the Consecrated Leavened Bread were in each others presence. What a magnificent event this was!! I pray that the breaking of the breach between men and its reparation have been ignited like an explosion ready to happen and happening in the hearts of the twelve present for the love of Christ for the benefit of many. Glory To God Most High! (Note: The difference being in the flesh, and now a house united, undivided is recognized, there is only ONE God, He is everywhere and in everything)

On Saturday before Fathers Day, June 18th 2005
Nadine, his wife, called and told me that he was in the hospital
Asking me if I could massage him with oils that did not smell
She said he loved it so much and it helped him so much
When I did work on him
I quickly suggested holy oil
(I offer my best to the Lord, so I use organic olive oil first cold pressed, blessed by a priest),
she said he loved the oils I applied on him but they smelled to much and that holy oil would be good

ON FATHERS DAY – JUNE 19, 2005
It was glorious to see so many continually visit
and continually pray for Deacon Alan ...
Rosaries, Chaplets of Divine Mercy, Prayers by Priests,
Other meditations, and

the songs of our hearts sung
arose to the heavens on his behalf
The Lord was very present, Praise the Lord!
when I saw him at noon with Nadine and her son Mike
He was on morphine, breathing
But he did not respond to us,

I took a small picture frame that had all these pictures in it
like a collage: Jesus and Mary holding their Hearts and offering
their hands, it was the image of the Sacred Heart of Jesus and the
Immaculate Heart of Mary, a picture of St. Michael the Archangel,
a Celtic cross, and pictures of the following medals: St. Benedict,
Our Lady of Grace – the miraculous medal, and words saying "I
hail thee, I adore thee oh Beloved Cross of Christ…; I also
took a small picture of John Paul II raising the Bread of Life in a
monstrance; and a battery operated candle.
I proceeded to use the holy oil all over his feet
As I was doing this,
I thought of his great faith
And the many times, we spoke of miracles
And the miracle of raising of the dead,
And the witnessing of unbelievable miracles that did happen
Because He was such a Blessed instrument of the Lord
At this particular moment however, I came to realize
That I had never considered the effect of "raising the dead"…
I came to understand that it robs that person from the
Glory of Heaven and drawing that person back to earth
robs that person of remaining with Our Lord
and His Great Love and Comfort,
it keeps them from dwelling in the House of Our Lord
it brings them back to this earth of trial and tribulation
I came to realize, and question myself:
Who are we to want such a selfish thing?
As I continued to put oil on his feet
I felt such a desire to kiss his feet and I did kiss one of his feet I
then, put holy oil on the crown of his head
I held his face in my hands
And asked the Lord to pour his perfect love into him
That casts out fear, bears all things and

That conquers all of our enemies
I asked Him to shine His Light upon him and
lead him out of darkness into eternal light
I believe, this was truly happening
I am thinking that some of these things are also necessary
As mentioned in the bible.
Much has been hidden from us,

And now, I do believe to a greater degree
That we do have to climb the latter of divine ascent
And there is a spiritual battle going on in this vessel of clay
When we become speechless
and are crossing over to everlasting life
Climbing the latter of Jacob
Those in the flesh do not see, do not understand
(I had a friend who also had cancer, and at the last moments of her death, repeated "I fight, I fight, I fight"; someone told me that on Saturday night Deacon Alan said "Now is the time to attack")
there was so much prayer that day, Father's day
Sensing every vibration of the Holy Spirit in my soul
as the Hail Mary flowed out of my mouth
was so profound, Her intercession is amazing and the graces
obtained are beyond understanding,
Blessed Mother pray for us!

I am sure, the Lord brought to Deacon Alan,
the persons necessary to help fulfill some of the promises
attached to prayers previously said by Alan in his life time
The Lord says "Be perfect as my father is perfect"
And although I am not yet perfect,
I know without a doubt
That He can do anything He wants
And will do a great work in us, if we let Him
I prayed perfect love for Deacon Alan
many who say they believe the word
Do not believe they can be perfect as Our Father is Perfect.
They doubt the Word of God.

I was with Nadine and Mike at the hospital until around 4pm.

I did not know if I was going to go back, I was hesitant to go
by myself and have to go through the visitor center on base and
whatever else was needed.
My insecurities were tormenting me.
Around 6pm, a friend, Helen, who rarely calls me,
called in a voice of desperation.
I knew instantly that the Lord had her to call,
so that I could go back to the hospital
He had used her once before to lead me to where I needed to be.

Back at the Hospital around 6pm
That night Deacon Alan was united to Our Lord
It was a night of wonder for me
Of the many, who saw him daily
Of the many who helped him on a regular basis
Why was I at his bedside?
He was so dear to me and to many who were presently there,
yet, I could not help but wonder
Why was I with those dearest to Him,
with those who loved him most
I felt as if I was not deserving of such a privilege
But I also knew, this was the Lord's calling
The last prayers said immediately
before his passing to a greater life
were two simultaneous and powerful prayers.
If we can only imagine, Deacon Alan meeting the Lord at this moment you will see an awesome sight:
1. At the Church he loved – a mass was being said. Now, knowing that the center of the mass is the transformation of the Bread of Life and Communion, and Union with Our Lord, this very critical moment, was one planned out for Deacon Alan by Our Lord.
2. At the hospital – the prayer being offered to Our Lord on Deacon Alan's behalf was one that promises an escort of one angel from each of the nine choirs of angels as you approach the table of the Lord, this was the Chaplet of St. Michael.
Just Beautiful!! Glory and Praise to Our God, who alone gives us light and many blessings to those who love Him.

One of the people there,

Cindy got everyone out of the room
And said to me
"You have helped Deacon Alan so much you stay in the room"
I was awed… at how the Lord was in control
Moving people, including myself
I remember my mind was not my own,
thinking swiftly and urgently
I got the bible and started looking for Psalm 23
Quit looking and gave it to Helen and
told her to look for it and read it
I went to my purse, looking for the holy oil
As she read, I put oil on his head again
Later to realize that Psalm 23, says
"You anoint my head with oil, my cup runneth over"
wow!

> *Mark 14:8 KJV* She has done what she could. She has come beforehand to anoint My body for burial.

Again, biblical happenings occurred
Perhaps the Lord had me there
To reflect and believe that perhaps Deacon Alan was made perfect
Because "I do believe that the Lord wants us to be perfect as Our Father is Perfect"
I do believe His word, His Truth as He teaches it
In a twinkling of an eye, we will be transformed
And I do ask the Lord to never let me hesitate in obedience to Him
No matter how odd it may seem
Knowing that we can not become perfect of our own accord
But Only Our Creator, can Change us as He desires

I am positive, that Deacon Alan's prayers
With promises were promises fulfilled
His fervent soul reached the heavens
And the heavens responded

Amazing!!
Beloved Deacon Alan, I love you, pray for us!

+ + +

NOTE: Deacon Alan was inspired to compile meditations entitled **Twenty Decade Scriptural Style Rosary with Divine Mercy Text**. These meditations are beautiful and are included in this book and in **WE LAY DOWN OUR CROWN** (Sealed By The Spirit Of God) by Gloria

LOVES TRUE DESIRE LYRICS ANALYSIS

The following is an analysis of what is spoken in one of the tracks in the CD entitled *Loves True Desire*. This section includes amazing explanations and what I call teachings from this unexpected unconditional love poured into my reluctant heart by My Lord.

To "THE ONE" the Lord has made me to Love

I do not write this to cause grief or guilt to "the one" the Lord led me to love. Love cannot be imposed upon anyone and I do not want to invade his ground without a reciprocate love or intent. As in the inception of all relationships, my intent has been and is friendship keeping to the commands of My Lord. I hope to always be faithful to the Lord. I desperately hope to be ready for His coming. Therefore, this is written to demonstrate another kind of love for the glory of Our Lord.

To "the one" the Lord has led me to love, with all my heart mind and soul I express my compassion and sorrow for whatever bothers you and for the discontent you have experienced by my boldness. Please keep in mind that it was not my choosing but the Lord. You are in my prayers; I hope you can forgive me for whatever imposition I have caused you. The Lord has blessed me with the love for you and of you. As I had mentioned to you from the start "You are my blessing!" May you be blessed!

About this Love

I never sought, thought nor expected to fall in love again. The Lord poured so much love into my heart for "the one" I did not even know. Having promised myself to the Lord for His return for years I have thought of no one else. Love is so beautiful and I know we all want to be loved including the Lord! No matter what the circumstances or purpose of this Love may the Lord be glorified and may love excel in all of us now and forever.

It all started when the Lord poured so much love into my heart for him. I was led to pray for him. I believed this was the purpose of this love. At first it was okay. I could accept it as that, basically because I knew He did not know me nor love me and I did not know him. Thinking I could not unite myself to anyone bearing the rejection or thought of not being mutually loved was easy. Why him? Why me? I don't understand.

Soon afterwards (a few months later), the Lord made me to sense a deeper love for "this one" embedding these words in my heart : *"I cannot live without you"*, it was a distinct message from my heart, I cannot explain it. I did not think of it, it was something *that was said to me from my heart with love poured in, as if my heart spoke.* I am certain that the Lord wants us to have a profound love towards Him as that embedded in my heart for He alone is our sustenance. And then perhaps He wants us to love each other that way too for His coming. My heart was in turmoil, the love became much greater and then I found myself grieving the love that was not returned to me. My mind would not leave him and my heart felt such sorrow.

Battling with the thought of divorce, adultery, chastity and this new love according to the laws of the Lord, I was confused as to why this was happening to me. I do not want to be separated from the Love of God nor do I want to hurt the one that I love and his salvation. Trying to understand, seeking the Lord desperately, struggling to reason it out, loving "the one" the Lord led me to love more than I could imagine, I am in awe trying to calm my troubled heart. My thought of resolve is to trust in Divine Providence knowing that the Lord is teaching me about True Love. I accept the work the Lord is doing in my life with Joy in time of sorrow.

Yet I do know the longing of my heart, the desire of love outpoured by the Lord and the absence of its reality in my life in this world. I have felt such a deep spiritual longing and love for "the one". Longing in companionship, friendship and a holy and pure love. I ask the Lord to be my stronghold and help me to respond to this love as He desires.

In my heart I know that the Lord has a purpose for the great love He has given to me for "the One" the Lord has made me to love. I think I really am okay in the flesh but my spirit longs and loves.

Yet, sometimes I am weak, when I see him it makes me happy to see him, but my heart aches that he does not talk to me. And when I don't see him, my heart aches at his absence and sometimes I cannot bear the thought of not seeing him again. And when our eyes meet, my heart wonders at the meaning of his glance as my being loves and as he scurries away. Other times, I am wondering what the Lord desires of me and whether I should look at him at all since he doesn't care, Lord Help me to be strong!

Oh Lord, what is your desire, how can I please you and still love on this earth? I return to you all that I am and all that you have made of me!

2/17/09 A thought to consider about the following script in *The Desire of Love:*

or am I to understand a deeper rejection of those whom You love that I may love You that much more

Oh Beloved King, make me right in Your sight

I have been contemplating the above verse and wondering how can a deeper rejection of those whom you love make me to love you (the Lord) more. I was trying to understand what was written. I think when I wrote this I was covering myself in the flesh in case the one the Lord has led me to love rejected me (sorry, all things are imperfect until perfection comes and we must discern). Considering truth, I do not believe the Lord rejects love and a humble and contrite heart, which is how we must be to also please the Lord. I believe He desires all of us to love each other and to reject evil.
Can love be evil? Yes, if it is out of lust, in which case it is not love at all.

On September 27, 2009 the Lord made me to realize that perhaps rejecting someone you love can be good, simply by still loving them with a chaste heart and choosing to honor the Lord by resisting the lust of the flesh.

Temptation and a Clean Heart

I trust that the Lord will keep me within all acceptable boundaries of the narrow road, since I strive to keep His Word and observe it. I hope that the Lord will be my stronghold and all temptation will be effectively resisted because the Lord is my stronghold! In the presence of the Lord the devil flees like lightening. Already I know He is strengthening me in my resistance toward sin. I strive desperately to resist, rebuke and renounce the devil. I also trust that the devil will not keep me from the love of my brothers in Christ and the love the Lord desires for each of us to have for one another. This is the Lords command, that we love each other as we love ourselves.

On Nov 12th, 2008, as I was sleeping in sackcloth I found myself as if *my body awoke and I heard my spirit* at my stomach area, begging and crying out to the Lord three times I heard *"Please don't let me sin"*. I desire to obey God. Even now, I do what I do not want to do, for it is sin that dwells in me, but I do not deny that sin dwells in me; instead I desire greatly to commit NO SIN and I repent.

I have found that as I repent and repent and strive to clean out my heart (of which everything that comes out of my mouth is what comes from my heart) the cleaner my heart becomes with repentance.

The faster I confess my sin after committing it; I have found strength in the Lord. "The Lord says rebuke renounce and resist the devil and he will flee".

I believe that my mouth will be THE SWORD OF THE SPIRIT because the Law of My Lord will be written in my purified heart. Faith comes from hearing and I do hear the Word of God, I ask the Lord to also help me to act upon it. Therefore, the Law of My Lord will be proclaimed boldly and zealously from my mouth and it will be sharper than a two edged sword and no devil will touch me. I do not fear "the one" the Lord has led me to love, the Lord is my stronghold, and I hope to love, as the Lord desires for me to love.

We must run the race the apostles ran to become purified. I am corruption putting on incorruption with repentance. Padrio Pio says that when we resist temptation we gain virtue.

True Love

It is a greater love we must seek. It is a greater love we must desire, one that will please my Lord.

We find our hearts stamped and sealed by those relations we have experienced in our life. Our hearts have been imprinted with love that will never leave us. Whether in pain, sorrow or joy, in our love we must seek to find Our Lord. Love is everlasting and so is the love in our hearts! It will always be a part of us! Will we nurture the love in our hearts with the Love Our Lord has taught us? Remembering sweet and bitter passions reflecting on Our Lord's sweet and bitter passions we come to know His love. In our sorrows He is surely there!

His Great Love is beyond our understanding! The Lord is sorrowful and desires greatly for us to desire Him greatly and to return our love to Him. His Love long-waiting and long suffering is like that of your love for someone else whose love is not returned to you but to an immeasurable magnitude.

Can we even begin to understand His pain for those who do not love Him or for those who reject him? Allowing Jesus to suffer so much for us because of our ignorance and constant rebellion is beyond our understanding. The heart of everyone created by Our Lord is imprinted in His heart with so much longing for each of us desiring to be united to us again. There is such sadness in my heart for the sacrifice Our Lord had to experience for us.

Remembering that which the Lord in His Living Word states, we are given a great hope:

"Things which eye has not seen and ear has not heard,
and which have not entered the Heart of man,
ALL THAT GOD HAS PREPARED
FOR THOSE WHO LOVE HIM." *1Co 2:9*

Strong in the Lord He teaches me that unconditional love is love that is given whether we receive it in return or not. Like St. Francis says in his peace prayer " seeking more to love than to be loved".

> **O Divine Master, grant**
> **that I may not so much seek**
> to be consoled as to console;
> to be understood as to understand;
> **to be loved as to love.**

Divine love commands us to love each other including our enemies and to bless them.
Divine mercy commands us to be merciful to each other including to the merciless.
Holy Charity commands us to give and to deny ourselves as mentioned in the Word of God and as noted in the Great Deliverance:

> *" Charity is the bond to perfection as noted in the Word, the gift of perfect charity is greater than we understand. Charity is of a greater degree according to the Lord. Yes giving without restraint, but it is also a greater giving and detachment from all things of the earth, renouncing them and not desiring them. Not allowing them to possess us."*

The **Virtue of Humility** comes through humiliation as the Lord taught me it is though humiliation that our judgment is taken away as noted in Acts 8:33. In our humiliation, although it may seem hard enduring, in reality it is joyfully rewarding when responding in a Godly manner, offering every circumstance and situation to the Lord as we acknowledge Him in everything and everyone. Contemplating His humiliation and comparing our insignificant humiliation to His, we find still a greater love. His ways are truly higher than ours. We are truly blessed in our humiliations!

It is evident to me that we must be awakened to a blind love that is unconditional so that we can be like Our loving God who came to show us how to love. True love, in a sense, is a blind love, loving no matter what we or they are like, unconditionally without reservations as Our Father in Heaven loves us. Our Lord desires that we imitate Him, loving our enemies and blessing them although not understanding their pain demonstrated by their actions.

Unconditional love is not necessarily a mutual love, however it is required that we return that Love in order to return to God. We must return love to God with all of our strength, heart, mind and soul. We must desire Our Lord greatly and also desire to love one another as God commands.

> If someone says, "I love God,"
> and hates his brother,
> he is a liar;
> for the one who does not love his brother
> whom he has seen,
> cannot love God whom he has not seen. *1John4:20* NASB95

Barriers such as resentment, bitterness, hatred, envy, vanity, and judgments etc must be brought down. They must not possess us. I refer to an unconditional love not one that requires marriage, it is a greater love like being willing to die for a friend. We must love God first with all of our strength desperately desiring to return to Him so that He will also know that we truly love Him as He loves us.

Visualizing ourselves with open arms greeting and rejoicing in the love returned to us by those, whom we love, is as I imagine Our Lord receiving us who love Him so much.

Worry and Divine Providence
I believe that the Lord was also teaching me that Divine Providence and Trust in Jesus is also a great virtue. It is by trusting Him that all worries and anxiety can be alleviated. Burdens truly become light. It is by contemplating the life of the Holy Family and comparing to the troubles in our life that we are able find the victory and a greater love toward God and each other. Therefore, entering into another state of mind, trusting that all things are of Divine Providence, perfectly planned for the glory of Our Lord. Rejoice in partaking!
Lyrics:
> "Teach me Lord to live and to trust in Your Divine Providence
> Take from my heart and mind all anxiety
> I desire to trust in you completely
> and to act upon your Word without hesitation
> make me to obey your commands, statutes and precepts
> and give to me your Holy Spirit. make me to sin no more"

Obedience to God

I want so much to be in the favor of the Lord and dwell in the house of the Lord. The following scriptures inspire me to desire to obey the Lord to receive the Holy Spirit, that is, to be possessed by the Lord. The next scripture inspires me not to want to sin because I believe when we are filled with the Holy Spirit we are possessed by the Lord and the evil one cannot touch us. My books go into more detail and prayers of surrender bring to light that which is dark.

> "And we are witnesses of these things and so is the Holy Spirit, **whom God Has given to Those Who Obey Him**" *Acts 5:32 NASB95*

> We know that **no one who is born of God sins**;
> but He who was born of God keeps him,
> and the evil one does not touch him. *1John 5:18 NASB*

Knowing Romans 3:10 " He also said there is none righteous" On Jan 8th, 2009 the following scripture caught my attention: **the Spirit is ALIVE BECAUSE of righteousness** *Romans 8:10 NASB*

(What does that mean? Not related to this script, I think it means we need to believe the Word of God, observe it and Keep it! It is alive and active and sharper than a two edged sword!)

I have desired greatly to be obedient to God, I hope to be born of God and sin no more as written in *1 John*. Reading Will the Divorce be Chaste? in The Great Deliverance will also clarify my understanding of the Word as revealed to me by My Lord. Although, I have thought that I could not have a relationship such as that in a marriage again according to the Word of God, I trust that the Lord will lead me to all truth and make me to act according to His Word not leaning on human understanding. Again, obedience to My Lord is of utmost importance and a priority in my life.

Holy Chastity, Holy Love
In Loves True Desire although "the strength of true" is briefly mentioned the teaching is awesome. This is how I believe the Lord is teaching me intimacy by comparing the love on this earth as we have known it and seeking to look beyond for a deeper, chaste, pure love much greater than anyone can understand or conceive. We must desire Him and Love Him intimately because we cannot live without Him. Also, as stated in the Word we are to love one another fervently. As mentioned in other areas of my writing or video presentations Chastity is a very great and holy virtue. Chastity with a holy love beautifully demonstrates faithfulness to our Lord and a profound love of wanting only Him physically, mentally and spiritually. I believe when we attain Perfect Chastity and desire to Love Perfectly the Lord's grace is given to us. This pleases the Lord. *2 Cor 11:2* tells us that there is only one husband and that is Christ.

> For I am jealous for you with a divine jealousy; for I betrothed you to one spouse (one husband), that I might present you as a chaste virgin to Christ. *(2 Corinthians 11:2)*

In this writing "The Desire of Love" I believe the Lord was also showing me how love conquers the devil through Holy Chastity. Loving the Lord with all of their strength Mary and Joseph were able to resist the wiles of the devil in particular in those sins mentioned in the bible : the desires of the flesh, the lust of the eyes and the pride of life.

A holy love sought is one treasured in the love of God, with the love of God and through the love of God. It is beautiful! It is one on which to cling to, unite to and of which we desire never to be separated!

The Lord has taught me the beauty of holy love. To live a life in a profound love, pure and chaste would have to be appointed, anointed and blessed by God Himself. It is in obedience to the first commandment, Loving Our Lord with all of our heart, mind, soul and strength and then loving each other as we love ourselves upon which hang all the law and the prophets. When the Lord is our Stronghold it is only with Him, in Him and though Him, loving Him with all of our strength that we are truly possessed by Him. He is our stronghold! In Him we truly live, move and have our being! He speaks through us, He moves us and we are as a boat and a sail.

Chastity must be Holy and loving the Lord with all of our strength. I believe that it is through this great love and Holy Charity that we can become perfected in Our Lord. Divine Chastity is favored by Our Lord as noted in the Book of Revelations. We must love with a pure heart. Our wayward minds on this earth when told "I love you" lead us to think of sex or to pass judgement. Chastity has been much forgotten resulting in our love lacking in purity. We must pray for a pure heart and chaste love for one another. We must desire to love divinely!

In the last couple of months the Lord has been teaching me about Chastity. Here is a definition of "Lust of the Flesh" as I believe the Lord has taught me:

> Lust of the Flesh is any form of carnal sex or sexual desire satisfying the body of self or of another, individually or jointly, in thought, word or deed other than for the purpose

of procreation (having children) with the Lord's blessing.

> But the rest of mankind,
> who were not killed by these plagues,
> did not repent of the works of their hands, ...
> And they did not repent of
> their murders or their sorceries or
> their unchastity .... *Rev 9:20-21*

I do believe all things are possible through our Great God according to His will. If the Lord would so desire for this to be in the flesh, today, in my generation, it would be for whomever the Lord desires. And if this is truly required of each of us (chastity) which I believe it is according to the Word, may the Lord be our stronghold.

We must DESIRE to please God in every way, so that He can change us. In this world - Heaven help us! Only God knows what plans He has for any of us. **I will say, that the beauty of living in the Love of Our Lord is worth all that we are, our essence and life even unto death. I cannot live without True Love, which is found only in the love of My Lord.**

~~~

Perhaps we can each make a difference one by one by deciding to love as Our Lord loves asking Him to help us to love perfectly because only He can change us. We must desire the change greatly! Perhaps we can walk together sharing the love of God and growing in the Love of God for His Glory. In all things we must acknowledge Him. Peace and Love to you!

Let us pray that the Lord will make the desire of our hearts and love pleasing to Him and that we may once again be a holy people as He is Holy.

The Desire of Love is as inspired because of the love the Lord has given to me for "the one" the Lord has led me to love, whom I will always love as I love my Lord, and I hope also to love each of you. I hope to love greatly as my Lord loves greatly.

I believe the Lord wants each of us to have a friendship of true love as we have never known before.   In this world, no one understands such beauty. We don't know how to do anything; we do not know how to love until we know true love. There is only one true love, and that is the love toward God. I ask the Lord to show each of us how to be a true friend and how to live in this world in His great love.

I pray that when someone tells you "I love you" you will not run away from it, but rather love with a chaste heart and let it grow in the love of God. Perhaps we can begin by learning to respond in a Godly way: "Yes, I love you too in the love of Jesus, may you always be blessed and in His loving care". Blessed Be God forever! Jesus I Trust in You!

Like a grain of sand in the littleness of my mind I relate as inspired in the writing "The Desire of Love".

May the Lord Bless you indeed! Saying the Name of Jesus in our every conversations ie "Jesus Be with You" will bring light to that soul.

(SINS revealed from this love can be viewed on website WWW.LOVESTRUEDESIRE.COM)

*With obedience of the greatest commandment
all others (the 10 from Old Testament) are obeyed automatically!*

NEW TESTAMENT GREATEST COMMANDMENT
<u>Mathew 22:36-46 KJV</u>

Master, which is the great commandment in the law? Jesus said unto him,
Thou shalt love the Lord thy God with all thy heart, and with all thy soul, and with all thy mind.
This is the first and great commandment.

And the second is like unto it,
Thou shalt love thy neighbour as thyself. On these two commandments **hang all the law** and the prophets.

While the Pharisees were gathered together, Jesus asked them, Saying, What think ye of Christ? Whose son is he? They say unto him, The son of David. He saith unto them, How then doth David in spirit call him Lord, saying, The LORD said unto my Lord, Sit thou on my right hand, till I make thine enemies thy footstool? If David then call him Lord, how is he his son? And no man was able to answer him a word, neither durst any man from that day forth ask him any more questions.

In the Renewal of the Ten Commandments when the Lord replaced the original stones you will find additional important commands from Our Lord. Have they been ignored?

I did not know that we were suppose to give to the Lord our first born male. I have repented, there is nothing I want to deny my Lord, all I desire is to please Him and to dwell in the House of the Lord.

They are as follows:

RENEWAL OF THE TEN COMMANDMENTS

Exodus 34 New American Standard Bible (NASB)
Copyright © 1960, 1962, 1963, 1968, 1971, 1972, 1973, 1975, 1977, 1995 by The Lockman Foundation

THE TWO TABLETS REPLACED

1Now the LORD said to Moses, **"Cut out for yourself two stone tablets like the former ones, and I will write on the tablets the words that were on the former tablets which you shattered.** 2"So be ready by morning, and come up in the morning to Mount Sinai, and present yourself there to Me on the top of the mountain. 3"No man is to come up with you, nor let any man be seen anywhere on the mountain; even the flocks and the herds may not graze in front of that mountain."

5The LORD descended in the cloud and stood there with him as **he called upon the name of the LORD.** 6Then the LORD passed by in front of him and proclaimed, "The LORD, the LORD God, compassionate and gracious, slow to anger, and abounding in lovingkindness and truth; 7who keeps lovingkindness for thousands, who forgives iniquity, transgression and sin; yet He will by no means leave the guilty unpunished, visiting the iniquity of fathers on the children and on the grandchildren to the third and fourth generations."

8Moses made haste to bow low toward the earth and worship. 9He said, **"If now I have found favor in Your sight, O Lord, I pray, let the Lord go along in our midst, even though the people are so obstinate, and pardon our iniquity and our sin, and take us as Your own possession."**

The Covenant Renewed
10Then God said, "Behold, I am going to make a covenant Before all your people I will perform miracles which have not been produced in all the earth nor among any of the nations; and all the people among whom you live will see the working of the LORD, for it is a fearful thing that I am going to perform with you. 11"**Be**

sure to observe what I am commanding you this day: behold, I am going to drive out the Amorite before you, and the Canaanite, the Hittite, the Perizzite, the Hivite and the Jebusite.

12"**Watch yourself that you make no covenant with the inhabitants of the land** into which you are going, **or it will become a snare in your midst.** 13"But rather, you are to tear down their altars and smash their sacred pillars and cut down their Asherim

14—for **you shall not worship any other god, for the LORD, whose name is Jealous, is a jealous God--**

15otherwise you might make a covenant with the inhabitants of the land and they would play the harlot with their gods and sacrifice to their gods, and someone might invite you to eat of his sacrifice, 16and you might take some of his daughters for your sons, and his daughters might play the harlot with their gods and cause your sons also to play the harlot with their gods.

17"**You shall make for yourself no molten gods.**

18"**You shall observe the Feast of Unleavened Bread** For seven days you are to eat unleavened bread, as I commanded you, at the appointed time in the month of Abib, for in the month of Abib you came out of Egypt.

19"**The first offspring from every womb belongs to Me**, and all your male livestock, the first offspring from cattle and sheep. 20"You shall redeem with a lamb the first offspring from a donkey; and if you do not redeem it, then you shall break its neck **You shall redeem all the firstborn of your sons None shall appear before Me empty-handed.**

21"**You shall work six days, but on the seventh day you shall rest**; even during plowing time and harvest you shall rest.

22**"You shall celebrate the Feast of Weeks, that is,** the first fruits of the wheat harvest**, and the Feast of Ingathering** at the turn of the year. 23"**Three times a year all your males are to appear before the Lord GOD, the God of Israel. 24**"For I will drive out nations before you and enlarge your borders, and no man shall covet your land when you go up three times a year to appear before the LORD your God.

25"**You shall not offer the blood of My sacrifice with leavened bread,**

nor is the sacrifice of the Feast of the Passover to be left over until morning.

26"**You shall bring the very best of the first fruits of your soil into the house of the LORD your God.**

"You shall not boil a young goat in its mother's milk."

27Then the LORD said to Moses, "Write down these words, for in accordance with these words I have made a covenant with you and with Israel."

28So he was there with the LORD forty days and forty nights; he did not eat bread or drink water And he wrote on the tablets the words of the covenant, the Ten Commandments.

Moses' Face Shines
29It came about when Moses was coming down from Mount Sinai (and the two tablets of the testimony were in Moses' hand as he was coming down from the mountain), that Moses did not know that the skin of his face shone because of his speaking with Him. 30So when Aaron and all the sons of Israel saw Moses, behold, the skin of his face shone, and they were afraid to come near him. 31Then Moses called to them, and Aaron and all the rulers in the congregation returned to him; and Moses spoke to them.

32Afterward all the sons of Israel came near, and he commanded them to do everything that the LORD had spoken to him on Mount Sinai. 33When Moses had finished speaking with them, he put a veil over his face.

34But whenever Moses went in before the LORD to speak with Him, he would take off the veil until he came out; and whenever he came out and spoke to the sons of Israel what he had been commanded, 35 the sons of Israel would see the face of Moses, that the skin of Moses' face shone. So Moses would replace the veil over his face until he went in to speak with Him.

OLD TESTAMENT *Exodus Ch. 20 KJV*
THE TEN COMMANDMENTS
(The American Bible at Studylight.com)

And God spake all these words, saying,
I am the LORD thy God, which have brought thee out of the land of Egypt, out of the house of bondage.
1. Thou shalt have no other gods before me.
2. Thou shalt not make unto thee any graven image, or any likeness of any thing that is in heaven above, or that is in the earth beneath, or that is in the water under the earth. Thou shalt not bow down thyself to them, nor serve them: for I the LORD thy God am a jealous God, visiting the iniquity of the fathers upon the children unto the third and fourth generation of them that hate me; And showing mercy unto thousands of them that love me, and keep my commandments.
3. Thou shalt not take the name of the LORD thy God in vain; for the LORD will not hold him guiltless that taketh his name in vain.
4. Remember the sabbath day, to keep it holy. Six days shalt thou labor, and do all thy work:
But the seventh day is the Sabbath of the LORD thy God: in it thou shalt not do any work, thou, nor thy son, nor thy daughter, thy manservant, nor thy maidservant, nor thy cattle, nor thy stranger that is within thy gates: For in six days the LORD made heaven and earth, the sea, and all that in them is, and rested the seventh day: wherefore the LORD blessed the Sabbath day, and hallowed it.
5. Honor thy father and thy mother: that thy days may be long upon the land which the LORD thy God giveth thee.
6. Thou shalt not kill.
7. Thou shalt not commit adultery.
8. Thou shalt not steal.
9. Thou shalt not bear false witness against thy neighbor.
10. Thou shalt not covet thy neighbor's house, thou shalt not covet thy neighbor's wife, nor his manservant, nor his maidservant, nor his ox, nor his ass, nor any thing that is thy neighbor's.

And all the people saw the thunderings, and the lightnings, and the noise of the trumpet, and the mountain smoking: and when the people saw it, they removed, and stood afar off. And they said unto Moses, Speak thou with us, and we will hear: but let not God speak with us, lest we die. And Moses said unto the people, Fear not: for God is come to prove you, and that his fear may be before your faces, that ye sin not. And the people stood afar off, and Moses drew near unto the thick darkness where God was. And the LORD said unto Moses, Thus thou shalt say unto the children of Israel, Ye have seen that I have talked with you from heaven. Ye shall not make with me gods of silver, neither shall ye make unto you gods of gold. An altar of earth thou shalt make unto me, and shalt sacrifice thereon thy burnt offerings, and thy peace offerings, thy sheep, and thine oxen: in all places where record my name I will come unto thee, and I will bless thee. And if thou wilt make me an altar of stone, thou shalt not build it of hewn stone: for if thou lift up thy tool upon it, thou hast polluted it. Neither shalt thou go up by steps unto mine altar, that thy nakedness be not discovered thereon.

The copyright of this book is dedicated to Our Glorious God through Jesus Christ. No enemy (devil) will come against this book, or internet, nor sell or copy this book with intent to profit, change or destroy. Upon sense, sight or nearness of this book, or copies thereof, the devil will be bound and banished; his tongue shall be shut up forever and he will be made immobile. He will not move anyone or anything ever again. The devil will not tamper with anyone or thing, used for the spread of the good news and these heartfelt prayers. Thank You Father for hearing my prayer, In the Name of Jesus.

This book is issued solely to glorify God and increase our one on one connection with Him and each other.

Praise be to Our Loving Father to whom I bow and kneel in love and adoration. May we all be His alone through Jesus Christ. I pray that this message and these prayers reach the world.

Spirits of double mindedness, dividing and separation be bound, cast out and banished forever. Readers be unveiled; Get behind me Satan, you are nothing but a stumbling block in the eyes of the Lord! Thank you Heavenly Father for hearing my prayer, all Glory, Honor and Power is Yours, In the Name of Jesus.

May I become a new creation in Christ!
Yea!!! I say again: Rise Holy Spirit Rise within me!
May He Bless Me indeed! In the name of Jesus!

REFERENCES

PUBLIC DOMAIN BIBLES QUOTED:

ASV - <u>The American Standard Version</u> (Thirty-five (35)) Scriptural verses taken from the ASV. From Wikipedia: **The American Standard Version** (ASV) is rooted in the work that was done with the Revised Version (RV) (a late 19th-century British revision of the King James Version of 1611). In 1870, an invitation was extended to American religious leaders for scholars to work on the RV project. A year later, Protestant theologian Philip Schaff chose 30 scholars representing the denominations of Baptist, Congregationalist, Dutch Reformed, Friends, Methodist, Episcopal, Presbyterian, Protestant Episcopal, and Unitarian. These scholars began work in 1872. The RV New Testament was released in 1881; the Old Testament was published in 1885. **The ASV was published in 1901** by Thomas Nelson & Sons. In 1928, the International Council of Religious Education (the body that later merged with the Federal Council of Churches to form the National Council of Churches) acquired the copyright from Nelson and renewed it the following year. The divine name of the Almighty (the Tetragrammaton) is consistently rendered Jehovah in the ASV Old Testament, rather than LORD as it appears in the King James Bible. The **ASV** was the basis of four revisions. They were the Revised Standard Version, 1971, the Amplified Bible, 1965, the New American Standard Bible, 1995, and the Recovery Version, 1999. A fifth revision, known as the World English Bible, was published in 2000 and was placed **in the public domain**. The ASV was also the basis for Kenneth N. Taylor's Bible paraphrase, The Living Bible, 1971. This Bible is in the public domain in the United States. We are making it available in the same format in which we acquired it as a public service.

BBE – <u>The Bible In Basic English</u> (Eight (8)) scripture verses taken from the BBE. **<u>The Bible In Basic English</u>** was printed in 1965 by Cambridge Press in England. Published without any copyright notice and distributed in America, this work fell immediately and irretrievably into the **Public Domain** in the United States according to the UCC convention of that time.

CPDV - Catholic Public Domain Version
(Twenty-two (22)) Scriptures were taken from **The Sacred Bible - Catholic Public Domain Version**

DRA – Douay-Rheims 1899 American Edition (DRA) (Thirty-eight (38)) Scripture verses were taken from the DRA.

The Douay-Rheims Bible is in the public domain. The Douay–Rheims Bible is a translation of the Bible from the Latin Vulgate into English made by members of the Catholic seminary English College, Douai, France. It is the foundation on which nearly all English Catholic versions are still based. It was translated principally by Gregory Martin, an Oxford-trained scholar, working in the circle of English Catholic exiles on the Continent, under the sponsorship of William (later Cardinal) Allen. The New Testament appeared at Rheims in 1582; the Old Testament at Douai in 1609. The translation, although competent, exhibited a taste for Latinisms that was not uncommon in English writing of the time but seemed excessive in the eyes of later generations. The New Testament influenced the Authorized Version.

Between 1749 and 1752, English bishop Richard Challoner substantially revised the translation with an aim to improve readability and comprehensibility. It was first published in America in 1790 by Mathew Carey of Philadelphia. Several American editions followed in the 19th and early 20th centuries; prominent among them the Douay-Rheims 1899 American Edition Version.

WEB - The World English Bible (One (1)) Scripture verse was taken from the **WEB. The World English Bible** is a 1997 revision of the American Standard Version of the Holy Bible, first published in 1901. It is in the **Public Domain**. Please feel free to copy and distribute it freely. Thank you to Michael Paul Johnson for making this work available. For the latest information, to report corrections, or for other correspondence, visit

OTHER BIBLES QUOTED –
Limitations to use were not exceeded:

GNT - <u>Good News Translation</u> (Three (3)) Scripture verses in this work were taken from the GNT.
Good News Translation® (Today's English Version, Second Edition) © 1992 American Bible Society. Used by permission. All rights reserved.

NKJV - <u>New King James Version</u> (Seventeen (17)) Scriptures were taken from NKJV. The Holy Bible, **New King James Version**, Copyright © 1982 Thomas Nelson. Used by permission. All rights reserved.

KJV - <u>King James Version</u> (One hundred ninety-three (193)) Scriptures quoted from the use of the KJV.
Scripture quotations from The Authorized (King James) Version. Rights in the Authorized Version in the United Kingdom are vested in the Crown. Reproduced by permission of the Crown's patentee, Cambridge University Press

In 1604, King James I of England authorized that a new translation of the Bible into English be started. It was finished in 1611, just 85 years after the first translation of the New Testament into English appeared (Tyndale, 1526). The Authorized Version, or **King James Version,** quickly became the standard for English-speaking Protestants. Its flowing language and prose rhythm has had a profound influence on the literature of the past 400 years. The King James Version present on the Bible Gateway matches the 1987 printing. **The KJV is public domain** in the United States.

NAB – <u>New American Bible</u> (Two (2)) Scripture texts in this work are taken from the NAB. *New American Bible, revised edition* © 2010, 1991, 1986, 1970 Confraternity of Christian Doctrine, Washington, D.C. and are used by permission of the copyright owner. All Rights Reserved. No part of the New American Bible may be reproduced in any form without permission in writing from the copyright owner.

NABRE - <u>New American Bible Revised Edition</u> (Thirty-five (35)) Scripture texts in this work are taken from the NABRE. *New American Bible, revised edition* © 2010, 1991, 1986, 1970 Confraternity of Christian Doctrine, Washington, D.C. and are used by permission of the copyright owner. All Rights Reserved. No part of the New American Bible may be reproduced in any form without permission in writing from the copyright owner.

NIV - <u>New International Version</u> (Eleven (11)) Scripture verses are taken from the NIV. The Holy Bible, New International Version®, NIV®. Copyright © 1973, 1978, 1984, 2011 by Biblica, Inc.™ Used by permission of Zondervan. All rights reserved worldwide. www.zondervan.comThe "NIV" and "New International Version" are trademarks registered in the United States Patent and Trademark Office by Biblica, Inc.™

NRSV - <u>New Revised Standard Version Catholic Edition</u> (One (1))Scripture verse is taken from the NRSV. **New Revised Standard Version Bible**: Catholic Edition, copyright © 1989, 1993 National Council of the Churches of Christ in the United States of America. Used by permission. All rights reserved worldwide.

AMP – (One (1)) scripture quotations were taken from AMP "Scripture quotations taken from the **Amplified® Bible** (AMP), Copyright © 2015 by The Lockman Foundation. Used by permission. www.lockman.org"

NASB – (Forty-seven (47)) scripture quotations were taken from NASB **New American Standard Bible** Copyright © 1960, 1971, 1977, 1995, 2020 by The Lockman Foundation, La Habra, Calif. Used by permission. All rights reserved. www.lockman.org

NASB 1977 – (Three (3)) scripture quotations were taken from NASB 1977

NASV – (Fifteen (15)) scripture quotations were taken from NASV

NASB 1995 – (Seven hundred thirty-three (733)) scripture quotations were from NASB 1995 **New American Standard Bible** Copyright © 1960, 1962, 1963, 1968, 1971, 1972, 1973, 1975, 1977, 1995 by The Lockman Foundation, La Habra, Calif. Used by permission. All rights reserved. http://www.lockman.org

OTHER BOOKS AND QUOTES REFERENCED

Marian Fathers of the Immaculate Conception of the R.V.M.. (2007). *Diary of Saint Maria Faustina Kowalska.* Marian Press, Stockbridge, MA 01263.

All Divine Mercy images and content of any kind in this book have been "Used with the permission of the Marian Fathers of the Immaculate Conception of the B.V.M."

De Sales, St. Francis. (1994). *Philothea, or An Introduction to the Devout Life.* Tan Books and Publishers, Inc. PO Box 424, Rockford, Illinois, 61105.

Sister Mary of Jesus also known as Mary of Agreda. Translated from the Original Authorized Spanish Edition by Fiscar Marison. (2006). *The Mystical City of God Vol. 1.* Tan Books and Publishers, Inc. PO Box 424, Rockford, Illinois, 61105.

Sister Mary of Jesus also known as Mary of Agreda. Translated from the Original Authorized Spanish Edition by Fiscar Marison. (2006). *The Mystical City of God Vol. III.* Tan Books and Publishers, Inc. PO Box 424, Rockford, Illinois, 61105.

Alpha House Inc. (1927). *The Lost Books of the Bible and the Forgotten Books of Eden.* World Bible Publishers Inc.

The Holy Orthodox Catholic Church in Canada and the Americas. (2003). *An Orthodox Book of Common Prayer First Edition.* The Holy Orthodox Catholic Church in Canada and the Americas, Diocese of the Southwest, Printed in Canada.

Valtorta, Maria. (1992). *The Poem of a Man-God Vol I.* Grafiche Dipro, 31056 Roncade TV, Italy for Centro Editoriale Valortiano srl

General Secretariat of the Franciscan Missions Inc. *The Prayer of St. Francis.* P O Box 130; Waterford, WI 53185

WEBSITES USED AS REFERENCE

Father Jean Baptiste Saint-Jure. *Trustful Surrender to Divine Providence.* The following is a beautiful paragraph from page 139 of the booklet: (September 2022 – I cannot find the booklet, but the following is also an internet source of same book in pdf form page 11): *TrustfulSurrenderToDivineProvidence.pdf (archive.org)*

St Bonaventure. Quote. Web: *It Is Impossible to Love Mary More Than Jesus Did| National Catholic Register (ncregister.com)*

Messages from Medjugorje Website: *Medjugorje Visionaries - Medjugorje WebSite*

St. Teresa of Calcutta Quotes "The fruit of silence is prayer, the fruit (catholic-link.org):

http://www.carmelitedcj.org/saints/scapular.asp

http://www.truecatholic.org/scapular.htm

http://www.ewtn.com/expert/answers/rosary_scripture.htm

THE GREAT DELIVERANCE
Stop a Grieving World; Raptured by the Call to Heaven

This book includes details from the original book **The Great Deliverance, Stop a Grieving World,** (this issue) however it has been updated with new revelations as of June 2022.

Know that the finale is today, in our time! God only knows when! Daniel's interpretation in Chapter 2 is trustworthy! Will you be part of it? It does not matter that we do not adhere to one another, but it is important that we combine as noted in *Daniel 2:43.* Jesus came to divide the kingdom of Satan, the world in which we are all participants. We are all one with satan as sinners, today and now. We are told in the Bible that the devil is the father of the one who sins.

Jesus came to give us a great hope for our salvation, a hope that we must believe in and allow to manifest. We must take this first step in faith, now is the time.

> ***Every kingdom divided against itself is brought to desolation*** *and every city or house divided against itself shall not stand.* Matthew 12:25 KJV

We must unite in unconditional love! The kingdom will then be truly divided, God vs Satan.

This book covers topics that will help you to realize who you are and I hope direct you to contemplate your actions for the Coming of the Lord. WARNING! These are strong words and thoughts. Discern for yourselves, ask for the Help of the Holy Spirit. Jesus came to save, not to Condemn, neither do I condemn you…. I too am running the race! I am just like you, a sinner.

I pray that we will all be one and unified in Our Lord's Unconditional Love, Unconditional Mercy, Unconditional Forgiveness, and Unconditional Repentance **for all to be saved.** Who will listen to the life saving commands of our Lord?

One thing I am sure of and that is that God is a certainty. God is not a belief. He is very real and alive! Jesus is the Son of God teaching us unconditional love and mercy. To know Him as part of your family we must repent and desire to live in His great love. May these help you to reconsider your thoughts and life to the degree of conversion to the inheritance of everlasting love and life. May you seek Him and find Him and may you be blessed!

Gotham Books
published updated version 2023

ONE
ONE LOVE, ONE HOPE, ONE GOD
by Gloria

The objectives in the book are meant to Glorify God and increase our one on one connection with Him and each other.

Salvation and Restoration for All! In Jesus' Name. All things are possible if you choose to believe! Doubt is the greatest insult to Our Divine Lord. Ignorance is the devil's strength. The devil loves tormenting you. An Orthodox priest told me that the devil cannot touch the people of God. I have found that to be true.

If you think you love God first and greater beyond compare and are willing to die for a stranger because you want to die more than anything in the world **simply to be with Our Great and Magnificent Father of Everlasting Love**, who is greater beyond compare, who is so loving, so kind, so gentle, so compassionate and so merciful as you have never known or understood; if you long to be with Him, if you crave the passion of His love and return it to Him passionately, then you probably do love Him.

If you do not know how to love God first, if you do not hope in Him, do not adore Him, do not believe, are not willing to lay down your life for a friend, then buy the book entitled **ONE**, it is a deep beginning. It is imperative that we love God first. He is very real – the devil hopes you do not believe me – I Trust in Jesus and have increased faith, I believe you do believe! Glory to Jesus who deserves more than we can ever offer to Him. I love Him so much, I now understand the expression of John of the Cross:

"I die because I do not die".

ONE, One Love, One Hope, One God
ISBN: 9781418434250

NOW AVAILABLE:
WE LAY DOWN OUR CROWN
Sealed By The Spirit Of God
by Gloria

This book has four occurrences I call miracles, I was dumbfounded by the first of them and was afraid to touch the book, a year later the Lord put it in my heart to publish it: On May 24th, 2004 I woke up early to write a prayer entitled Fruitful Harvest, that same morning (1) the Lord used my hands to type "SEALED BY THE SPIRIT OF GOD" on page 143, where copyright is dedicated to God. (2) Also on page 143, He changed the words IN GOD WE TRUST to **JESUS I TRUST IN YOU!** I did not think to do that. (3) When I was assembling the book He tore off the first page of the book, which included the worldly copyright. (4) There was also a merging of three prayers I call a miracle, entitled after the three from which it was derived. The title in itself is an awesome message!! **BE EXALTED, BREAD OF LIFE, I LOVE YOU LORD!** However, after the miracle of the three prayers, I had a different view. I found it difficult to exalt a piece of bread, much like it is difficult for people to love God because they cannot see Him. Knowing the Lord, knew me better than I know myself, I repented and asked the Lord to help me exalt the Bread of Life. He answered me and taught me a beautiful lesson, you may view it at www.LovesTrueDesire.com or in my books. Addendum I explains miracles.

ISBN: 9781420875904

***

I give to you my love for Jesus with the heart of Mary and the love of Mary with the heart of Jesus now and eternally -- **Gloria**

Books by Gloria :
Now Available...
WE LAY DOWN OUR CROWN
Sealed By The Spirit Of God

FEATURED IN THE NEW YORK TIMES

A spiritual inventory of the modern soul, a thunderous call to all those suffering from the strife and burden of the devil's twisted plots, but most of all an unparalleled celebration of those who have repented and discovered salvation.

NOW ON SALE...

WE LAY DOWN OUR CROWN
Sealed by the Spirit of God
ISBN: 9781420875904

MULTIMEDIA MUSIC CD

The following CD's ** are available at **CDBABY.COM**, it has not been determined at this point as to whether the others will be made available. Preview them on the website.

These CD's are prayers or narrations by Gloria of the books by Gloria. Songs sung without musical instruments are in italics. Please note these CD's are homemade by Gloria and have no musical instruments in them. Come to the Wedding *was put together in ten minutes.* Finding Mary *was going to be spoken and the Lord led me to sing, so this is it.*
May the Lord Bless you indeed!

Vol 1 - **Come to the Wedding - Prayers leading to perfection (approx 68 min) 1. Armor 2. Obedient Mind 3. Treasures 4. Increase in Me 5. Consecration 6. I Love You Lord 7. *Come to the Wedding* 8. Jerusalem 9. Mysteries of Illumination (scriptural style rosary) 10. Do Not Be Hid from Me

Vol 2 - **The Sign of Jonah** - Repent in Sackcloth & Ashes

Vol 3 - **Exalt the Bread of Life** - Eat of the Living Bread (Born again Bread)

Vol 4 - **Who is the King?** Vol 5 - **Break Every Yoke**

Vol 6 – This one will probably not be made available – it is the narration of the Book of Tobit or The Book of Tobis in the Old Testament, one of my favorites for couples.

Vol 7 - **Why the Hail Mary? The Call to Heaven! (approx 70 min) 1. The Hail Mary 2. Why the Hail Mary? 3. Be Not Hid from Me 4. *Ven Maria* 5. Psalm 116:15 6. *Finding Mary* 7. Circle to the Most Greatest Hope 8. *The Call to Heaven* 9. I Love You Lord 10. Honor thy Father and thy Mother 11. From Darkness into Light 12. Important Notice say "Yes" 13. Concluding Prayer from Who is the King?

*** **Loves Truc Desire** - 1. Sincere Desire 2. Be Perfect as My Father is 3. The Joy 4. The Desire of Love 5. Prayer for Everlasting Unity 6. What Great Love Does My Soul Acknowledge? 7. What More Can I Say? 8. Be Exalted Bread of Life I Love You Lord 9. Psalm 19:7-14 10. A New Chaplet of Mercy 11. Critical Moment
12. Altar of Grace 13. The Chaplet of St Michael 14. 3x The Sign of the Cross in Thanksgiving 15. Offering

*** **Website www.LovesTrueDesire.com**

www.ingramcontent.com/pod-product-compliance
Lightning Source LLC
LaVergne TN
LVHW091654070526
838199LV00050B/2171